Globalization, Trade and Foreign Direct Investment

Globalization, Trade and Foreign Direct Investment

Edited by

John H. Dunning

University of Reading (U.K.)
and
Rutgers University (U.S.A.)

1998

ELSEVIER
Amsterdam – Lausanne – New York – Oxford – Shannon – Singapore – Tokyo

ELSEVIER SCIENCE Ltd
The Boulevard, Langford Lane
Kidlington, Oxford OX5 1GB, UK

Library of Congress Cataloging in Publication Data
Globalization, trade, and foreign direct investment/edited by John
   H. Dunning. - - 1st ed.
      p. cm. - -(International business and economics)
    "Revised versions of a number of papers first presented at the 5th
   International Trade and Finance Association in San Diego in June
   1996"–Pref.
    Includes indexes.
    ISBN 0-08-043369-3
    1. Investments, Foreign. 2. International trade. I. Dunning,
John H. II. International trade and Finance Association.
Conference (5th:1996:San Diego, Calif.) III. Series.
HG4538.G555 1998
332.67′3–dc21

               98-19613
               CIP

British Library of Cataloguing in Publication Data
A catalogue record from the British Library has been applied for.

First edition 1998

ISBN: 0-08-043369-3

∞ The paper used in this publication meets the requirements of ANSI/NISO Z39.48-1992
(Permanence of Paper).

Typeset by The Midlands Book Typesetting Company, Loughborough, Leicestershire, UK.
Printed in The Netherlands.

Contents

    1965–93   175
    YINGSHING LIN AND MICHAEL SZENBERG

9. Determinants of Inter-Asian Direct Investment Flows   194
    MORDECHAI E. KREININ, THOMAS C. LOWINGER AND ANIL K. LAL

10. Trade and Production Networks of U.S. MNEs and Exports
    by their Asian Affiliates   204
    ROBERT E. LIPSEY

11. Foreign Direct Investment in Ghana's Emerging Market
    Economy   217
    KOFI AFRIYIE

12. Impact of Trade and Investment Policies on Economic
    Transformation in East Asia, the Middle East and Latin
    America   237
    M. RAQUIBUZ ZAMAN

13. Third World Multinationals Revisited: New Developments
    and Theoretical Implications   255
    JOHN H. DUNNING, ROGER VAN HOESEL AND RAJNEESH NARULA

    Author index   287

    Subject index   291

Contributors

About the Editor

John H. Dunning has been researching into the economics of international direct investment and the multinational enterprise since the 1950s. He has authored, co-authored, or edited 35 books on this subject and on industrial and regional economics. His latest volumes, both published in 1997, are *Alliance Capitalism* and *Global Business*, and two edited volumes: *Globalization, Governments and International Business, and Globalization and Developing Countries*.

Professor Dunning is Emeritus Professor of International Business at the University of Reading, U.K., and State of New Jersey Professor of International Business at Rutgers University, New Jersey, U.S.A. In addition, he has been Visiting Professor at several universities in North America, Europe and Asia. He is also Director of the Center for International Business Education and Research at Rutgers University and Chairman of the Graduate Center of International Business at the University of Reading. Professor Dunning is currently Senior Economic Adviser to the Director of the Division on Transnational Corporations and Investment of UNCTAD in Geneva, and Chairman of a London based economic consultancy Economic Advisory Group Ltd., which specializes in research on international and regional economic issues.

Professor Dunning has honorary doctorates from the University of Uppsala, the Autonomous University of Madrid and the University of Antwerp. He is also honorary Professor of International Business at the University of International Business and Economics at Beijing. He is past President of the International Trade and Finance Association, and of the Academy of International Business. Professor Dunning is Chairman of the Board of Editorial Advisors of the U.N. journal Transnational Corporations, and serves on several other editorial and advisory boards.

About the Contributors

Kofi Afriyie is Adjunct Faculty member at the Faculty of Management, Rutgers University and a staff member at the Dow Jones Markets Business Group at Dow Jones and Co.

Sergio Castello is Associate Professor at the University of Mobile, Alabama, U.S.A.

Paul Collins is a Lecturer in International Business at Kingston Business School, Kingston University, Surrey, England.

H. Peter Gray is Emeritus Professor of Economics at Rutgers University, New Jersey, U.S.A.

Erich Gundlach is Research Associate at the Kiel Institute of World Economics, Kiel, Germany.

Mordechai Kreinin is Distinguished Professor of Economics at Michigan State University, U.S.A.

Anil K. Lal is Lecturer in Economics at Pittsburgh State University, Pittsburgh, Kansas, U.S.A.

Yingshan Lin is Associate Professor of Finance at the National Institute of Technology at Kaohsiung, Taiwan.

Robert E. Lipsey is Professor Emeritus of Economics at the Graduate Center of the City University of New York, and Research Associate at the National Bureau of Economic Research, New York and Cambridge, U.S.A.

Thomas C. Lowinger is Professor of Economics at Washington State University, Pullman, Washington, USA.

Rajneesh Narula is Associate Professor of International Business at the University of Maastricht, Maastricht, The Netherlands.

Peter Nunnenkamp is Research Associate at the Kiel Institute of World Economics, Kiel, Germany.

Dominick Salvatore is Professor and Chairperson of the Department of Economics at Fordham University, New York, USA.

Michael Szenberg is Director, Center for Applied Research and Professor of Economics at the Lubin School of Economics at Pace University, New York, USA.

Virginia Ann Taylor is an Assistant Professor of Business Administration at Georgian Court College, Lakewood, New Jersey, U.S.A.

Roger van Hoesel is Research Associate at the Tinbergen Institute of the Erasmus University, Rotterdam, The Netherlands.

M. Raquibuz Zaman is Dana Professor and Chairperson of the Department of Finance and International Business, Ithaca College, Ithaca, New York, U.S.A.

Preface

The issue of globalization, and its economic impact on the economies of both developed and developing countries, continues to attract widespread attention. This volume, which contains the revised versions of a number of papers first presented at the 5th International Conference of the International Trade and Finance Association in San Diego in June 1996, and three other specially commissioned contributions (Chapters 7, 11 and 13), considers three main topics.

First, it examines the impact of globalization on the competitiveness of a variety of regions and countries, ranging from the European Union and New Zealand, to Taiwan and Ghana. Dominick Salvatore in Chapter 1 sets out the main analytical components of competitiveness, viewed from the perspective of both firms and countries.

Second, the volume describes and analyzes the interface between trade, foreign direct investment (FDI) flows, and the activities of MNEs, as each is affected by, and affects the level and pattern of globalization—and, in some cases, (e.g. Chapters 4 and 10) regionalization. In Chapter 2, Peter Gray presents a conceptual framework for evaluating this interface; and this is extended and refined by several authors—especially Eric Gundlach and Peter Nunnenkamp in Chapter 7 and John Dunning, Roger van Hoesel and Rajneesh Narula in Chapter 13.

To complement these analytical studies, a number of contributions present several new pieces of empirical research. In particular, Sergio Castello, in Chapter 6, Y. Lin and Michael Szenberg in Chapter 8 and Dunning, van Hoesel and Narula in Chapter 13 look at the determinants of outward FDI and its implication for the economic structure and competitiveness of the home country; while John Dunning, in Chapter 4, and Kofi Afriyie in Chapter 11 evaluate the impact of some of the more recent developments in the global economy—and particularly that of the liberalization of trade and investment regimes—on inbound FDI directed to one area of the developed world (the European Union), and to one of the fast emerging markets in sub-Saharan Africa, namely Ghana.

The third thrust of this volume deals with some of the consequences of globalization, and the deepening of cross-border economic relationships, on the policies of national governments. Such integration takes place mainly through trade (part of which comprises intra-firm trade (see especially Chapters 3 and 4) and the activities of MNEs. In the chapters by John Dunning, Mordechai Kreinin and his colleagues, and Robert Lipsey, the impact of regional economic integration on FDI and trade (including trade by the foreign affiliates of MNEs) is explored; while the contributions by Virginia Taylor (Chapter 5) and Raquibuz Zaman (Chapter 12) look, more specifically, at the policies pursued by national governments in response to recent economic events. Both the Dunning and the Gundlach and Nunnenkamp chapters also make reference to the implications of globalization for the macro-economic and macro-organizational policies of national administrations.

I believe that this monograph offers a rich panoply of scholarly studies which touch upon, and advance our understanding of, the changing role of trade and FDI in a globalizing economy, and how the economies of the nation state, and the economic policies of national governments, are becoming increasingly intertwined with each other. The contributors come from a wide range of intellectual and geographical backgrounds, and they are all experienced teachers and researchers. Each has applied his or her knowledge and experience to tackling a number of critical issues now emerging in the world economy, which are of interest and concern not only to academic economists, but to business practitioners, national governments and international agencies as well.

There are no easy generalizable conclusions which can be drawn from the facts and analyses presented in this book, other than globalization, in its various guises, is bringing about a restructuring of the world economy, a new international division of labor—largely fashioned by the cross-border activities of firms—and an integrated world economy. Each of these has been made possible by current generation of technological advances, and freer trade and investment regimes. Taken together, they are demanding a reappraisal of a wide range of national economic policies as the main vehicle for augmenting national economic wealth as intellectual capital is becoming more mobile across national boundaries.

Several authors hint at the tensions, particularly between MNEs and governments, and between national governments, which are now re-surfacing after a period of fairly relaxed relationships. However, these are likely to take a very different form than those which dominated the 1960s and 1970s. In particular, as Eric Gundlach and Peter Nunnenkamp emphasize, there are several attributes of the contemporary globalizing economy—and particularly its consequences for some kinds of employment and the distribution of income both between countries and within countries—which give great cause for concern. It is such issues as these which are likely to come to the fore in the next decade and will command the increasing attention, not just of national governments, but of the international community at large.

If the contents of this volume can make even a small contribution to this debate, both the Editor and, I am sure, the contributors, will be well satisfied.

Part I

Globalization and Developed Economies

1

Globalization and International Competitiveness

DOMINICK SALVATORE

The past decade has witnessed rapid globalization in tastes, in international trade and investments, and in labor markets, and this has sharply increased international competitiveness among industrial countries and between industrial countries and the newly industrializing economies (NIEs) of Asia. This chapter examines the factors that affect the international competitiveness of nations and the reasons for the United States being the most competitive economy in the world today. Rapid technological change, downsizing, and strong competition from NIEs, however, has resulted in real wages not rising very much in the United States and jobs not growing in Europe during the past decade.

Introduction

During the past decade, we have witnessed an increasingly rapid tendency toward globalization in the world economy. Rapid globalization has occurred in national tastes, in international trade and investments, and in labor markets, and this has sharply increased international competitiveness among industrial countries and between industrial countries and emerging Asian economies.

This chapter examines the rapid process of globalization that has taken place during the past decade in the world economy and the reasons for its occurrence. It then discusses the relative international competitive position of nations in 1996 and the reasons for the U.S. being in first place. The chapter then evaluates this competitiveness measure and presents an alternative measure of international competitiveness. The differential effect of globalization and international competition on labor markets in the United States and in other leading industrial countries is then outlined. Section VI examines the revolution resulting from computer-assisted design and computer-assisted manufacturing and the leadership role that the United States has in them because of its unsurpassed leadership position in software. Finally, the crucial importance of international competitiveness in the world today is discussed.

Globalization in the World Economy

We are in the midst of a globalization revolution in tastes, production, and labor markets in the world economy and this has sharply increased international competitiveness among firms and nations.

Convergence of Consumer Markets

The tremendous improvements in telecommunications and transportation have lead to a strong cross-fertilization of cultures and convergence of consumer tastes around the world. Tastes in the United States affect tastes around the world and tastes abroad strongly influence tastes in the United States. Coca-Cola has 40 percent of the U.S. market and an incredible 33 percent of the world's soft drinks market, and today you can buy a McDonald's hamburger in most major cities of the world. As tastes become global, firms are responding more and more with truly global products. For example, in 1990, Gillette introduced its new Sensor Razor at the same time in most nations of the world and used the same advertisement (except for language) in 19 countries in Europe and North America. By 1997, Gillette had sold over 200 million of its razors and more than 4 billion cartridges. In 1994, Ford spent more than $6 billion to create its "global car" conceived and produced in the United States and Europe and sold under the name of Ford Contour and Mercury Mystique in the United States and Mondeo in the rest of the world. The list of global products is likely to grow rapidly in the future as the global village moves closer and closer to a truly global supermarket.

In his 1983 article 'The Globalization of Markets' in the *Harvard Business Review,* Theodore Levitt asserted that consumers from New York to Frankfurt to Tokyo want similar products and that success for producers in the future would require more and more standardized products and pricing around the world. In fact, in country after country, we are seeing the emergence of a middle-class consumer lifestyle based on a taste for comfort, convenience, and speed. In the food business, this means packaged, fast-to-prepare, and ready-to-eat products. Market researchers have discovered that similarities in living styles among middle-class people all over the world are much greater than we once thought and are growing with rising incomes and educational levels. Many small national differences in taste do, of course, remain; for example, Nestle markets more than 200 blends of Nescafe to cater to differences in tastes in different markets. But the converging trend in consumer preferences around the world is unmistakable and is likely to lead to more and more global products. This is true not only for foods and inexpensive consumer products but also for automobiles, portable computers, phones, and many other durable products.

Globalization in Production

Globalization has also occurred in the production of goods and services with the rapid rise of global corporations (Dunning, 1994). These are companies that are run by an international team of managers, have research and production facilities in many countries, use parts and components from the cheapest source around the world, and sell their products, finance their operations, and are owned by stockholders throughout the world. In fact, more and more corporations operate today on the belief that their very survival requires that they become one of a handful of global corporations in their sector. This is true in automobiles, steel, aircraft, computers, telecommunications, consumer electronics, chemicals, drugs, and many other products. Nestle, Switzerland's largest company and the world's second largest food company, has production facilities in 59 countries, and America's Gillette in 22. Ford has component factories in 26 different industrial sites around the world, assembly plants in six countries, and employs more people abroad (201,000) than in the United States (188,000).

One important form that globalization in production often takes in today's corporation is in foreign 'sourcing' of inputs. There is practically no major product today that does not have some foreign inputs. Foreign sourcing is often not a matter of choice for corporations to earn higher profits, but simply a requirement for them to remain competitive. Firms that do not look abroad for cheaper inputs face loss of competitiveness in world markets and even in their domestic markets. This is the reason, for example, that $625 of the $860 total cost of producing an IBM PC was incurred for parts and components manufactured by IBM outside the United States or purchased from foreign producers during the mid-1980s. Such low-cost offshore purchase of inputs is likely to continue to expand rapidly in the future and is being fostered by joint ventures, licensing arrangements, and other nonequity collaborative arrangements. Indeed, this represents one of the most dynamic aspects of the global business environment of today.

Foreign sourcing can be regarded as manufacturing's new *international* economies of scale in today's global economy. Just as companies were forced to rationalize operations within each country in the 1980s, they now face the challenge of integrating their operations for their entire system of manufacturing around the world to take advantage of the new international economies of scale. What is important is for the firm to focus on those components that are indispensable to the company's competitive position over subsequent product generations and 'outsource' other components for which outside suppliers have a distinctive production advantage. Indeed, globalization in production has proceeded so far that it is now difficult to determine the nationality of many products. For example, should a Honda Accord produced in Ohio be considered American? What about a Chrysler minivan produced in Canada? Is a Kentucky Toyota or Mazda that uses nearly 50 percent of imported Japanese parts American?

It is clearly becoming more and more difficult to define what is American and opinions differ widely. One could legitimately even ask if this question is relevant in a world growing more and more interdependent and globalized. Today, the ideal corporation is strongly decentralized to allow local units to develop products that fit into local cultures, and yet at its very core is very centralized to coordinate activities around the globe.

Globalization in Labor Markets

Globalization also strongly affects labor markets around the world. Work which was previously done in the United States and other industrial countries is now often done much more cheaply in developing countries. And this is the case not only for low-skilled assembly-line jobs but also for job requiring high computer and engineering skills. Most Americans have only now come to fully realize that there is a truly competitive labor force in the world today willing and able to do their job at a much lower cost. If anything, this trend is likely to accelerate in the future.

Even service industries are not immune to global job competition. For example, more than 3,500 workers on the island of Jamaica, connected to the United States by satellite dishes, make airline reservations, process tickets, answer calls to toll-free numbers, and do data entry for U.S. airlines at a much lower cost than could be done in the United States. Nor are highly skilled and professional people spared from global competition. A few years ago, Texas Instruments set up an impressive software programming operation in Bangalore, a city of four million people in southern India. Other American multinationals soon followed. Motorola, IBM, AT&T and many other high-tech firms are now doing even a great deal of basic research abroad. American workers are beginning to raise strong objections to the transfer of skilled jobs abroad, as the fall 1995 strike against Boeing demonstrated. Of course, many European and Japanese firms are setting up production and research facilities in the United States and employing many American professionals. In the future, more and more work will simply be done in places best equipped to do the job most economically. Try to restrict the flow of work abroad to protect jobs in the United States, and the company risks loosing international competitiveness or ends up moving all of its operations abroad (Salvatore, 1996, pages 18–22).

National Competitiveness Rankings

During the 1970s and 1980s, the United States lost relative competitiveness in one industry after another with respect to Japan and, in some industries, even with respect to Europe and the newly industrializing economies (NIEs) of Asia. Since the late 1980s and early 1990s, however, the United States has recaptured most of the lost ground, and in 1994 it was ranked once again as the most competitive economy in the world, displacing Japan, which had occupied that position since 1985. During 1995 and 1996, the United States not only retained its number one position but even increased its lead over Japan and many other industrialized countries.

As Table 1.1 shows, if we assign a value of 100 to the competitiveness index of the United States in 1995, the index for Japan was 75.0; that is, Japan was about 25 percent less competitive than the United States on an overall basis in 1995. The competitiveness index for the remaining five of the G-7 (largest industrialized) countries was 71.1 for Germany, 70.0 for Canada, 60.7 for the United Kingdom, 60.7 for France, and 39.3 for Italy. Note that Singapore and Hong Kong (two of the four Asian NIEs) ranked second and third, respectively, on the competitiveness index in 1996, ahead of Japan; Chile ranked thirteenth and Taiwan eighteenth, ahead of the United Kingdom (nineteenth) and France (twentieth), and Korea ranked twenty-seventh ahead of Italy (twenty-eighth) out of a total of 46 (developed and developing) countries considered. Japan fell from first place in 1993 to third place in 1994 and to fourth place in 1995 and 1996. Between 1994 and 1996, Germany fell from fourth to tenth place, Canada remained in twelfth place, France and the

TABLE 1.1 *National Competitiveness Scores, 1996*

Rank/country	Score	Rank/country	Score
1. United States	100.0	24. Israel	57.1
2. Singapore	88.6	25. Iceland	56.4
3. Hong Kong	78.6	26. China	45.0
4. Japan	75.0	27. Korea	42.9
5. Denmark	72.9	28. Italy	39.3
6. Norway	72.1	29. Spain	38.6
7. Netherlands	71.4	30. Thailand	37.9
8. Luxembourg	71.3	31. Philippines	36.4
9. Switzerland	71.2	32. Argentina	33.6
10. Germany	71.1	33. Colombia	32.9
11. New Zealand	70.7	34. Czech Republic	32.1
12. Canada	70.0	35. Turkey	31.4
13. Chile	66.4	36. Portugal	30.7
14. Sweden	65.7	37. Brazil	27.1
15. Finland	65.0	38. India	26.4
16. Austria	64.3	39. Hungary	25.7
17. Belgium	62.9	40. Greece	25.0
18. Taiwan	61.4	41. Indonesia	24.3
19. United Kingdom	60.7	42. Mexico	22.9
20. France	60.6	43. Poland	21.4
21. Australia	60.0	44. South Africa	20.0
22. Ireland	59.3	45. Venezuela	10.7
23. Malaysia	58.6	46. Russia	5.0

Source: Elaboration on IMD (1996).

United Kingdom fell from thirteenth and fourteenth, respectively, to twentieth and nineteenth, while Italy rose from the thirty-second place to twenty-eighth place. Among the NIEs, Singapore retained its second position, Hong Kong went from fourth place to third, Taiwan remained in eighteenth place, while Korea dropped from twenty-fourth to twenty-seventh place.

Competitiveness is defined by the IMD as the ability of a country or company to generate more wealth for its people than its competitors in world markets. Eight factors were used in measuring the relative productivity of each nation. These are: (1) domestic economic strength (measured by the degree of competition in the economy); (2) internationalization (measured by the degree by which the nation participates in international trade and investments); (3) government (given by the degree by which government policies are conducive to competitiveness); (4) finance (given by the performance of capital markets and the quality of financial services); (5) infrastructure (the extent to which resources and systems are adequate to serve the basic needs of business); (6) management (the extent to which enterprises are managed in an innovative and profitable manner); (7) science and technology (scientific and technological capacity); and (8) people (availability and qualifications of human resources).

As Table 1.2 shows, the United States was ranked first among the G-7 countries on the first five and on the seventh of the above eight competitive factors, second on the sixth factor (management), after Japan, and fourth on the eighth factor (people), after Japan, Canada, and Germany (in that order). Japan was ranked first on management and people; second on domestic economic strength, finance, and science & technology; fifth on internationalization and government; and sixth on infrastructure. Canada was ranked second on government, infrastructure, and people; third on management; fifth on finance and science & technology; and sixth on domestic economic strength and internationalization. Germany was ranked third on domestic economic strength, finance, infrastructure, science & technology, and people; fourth on internationalization and government, and fifth on management. France and the United Kingdom were ranked from third to sixth place on all factors, except for the second position of France on internationalization and the seventh position of the United Kingdom on people (after Italy, which was ranked seventh on all other seven factors).

TABLE 1.2 *Ranking on Competitiveness Factors, G-7 Countries, 1996*

Country	Score*	(1)	(2)	(3)	(4)	(5)	(6)	(7)	(8)
U.S.A.	100.0	1	1	1	1	1	2	1	4
Japan	75.0	2	5	5	2	6	1	2	1
Germany	71.1	3	4	4	3	3	5	3	3
Canada	70.0	6	6	2	5	2	3	5	2
U.K.	60.7	4	3	3	4	4	6	6	7
France	60.6	5	2	6	6	5	4	4	5
Italy	39.3	7	7	7	7	7	7	7	6

* Overall competitiveness score (from Table 1.1)
Ranking on: (1) Domestic economic strength among G-7 countries (1 to 7); (2) Internationalization; (3) Government; (4) Finance; (5) Infrastructure; (6) Management; (7) Science & technology; (8) People.
Source: Elaboration on IMD (1996).

Evaluation of National Competitiveness Ranking and an Alternative Measure

Measuring international competitiveness is an ambitious and difficult undertaking and there are only a handful of such comprehensive studies. Although useful, the competitiveness study discussed above faces a number of serious shortcomings. One is the grouping and measuring of international competitiveness of developed and developing countries and of large and small countries together. It is well known, however, that developed and developing countries, on the one hand, and large and small countries, on the other, have very different industrial structures and face different competitiveness problems. Using the same method of measuring the international competitiveness for all types of countries, then, may not be appropriate and the results may not be very informative or, at least, may be difficult to interpret.

Another serious shortcoming with the above competitiveness measure is that the correlation between real per capita income and standard of living of the various nations may not be very high. For example, Thailand (with a PPP per capita income of $6,970) in 1994 has the same competitiveness index as the United Kingdom (with a PPP per capita income of $17,970) and Korea has a higher competitiveness index than Italy even though its per capita income ($10,330) is much lower than Italy's ($18,460). The question that naturally arises is: If Italy is less competitive and productive than Korea, where is its much higher per capita income and standard of living coming from? In economics, we like to think that productivity determines per capita incomes and the standard of living and it disconcerting to see such a blatant variance between expectations and reality.

Displeased by how the world competitiveness index was measured, the World Economic Forum (WEF), which until 1995 had joined the Institute for Management Development (IMD) in preparing the *World Competitiveness Yearbook*, left the partnership and set out to prepare its own separate *World Competitiveness Report*. The WEF (also based in Switzerland) defined international competitiveness as 'the ability of a country to achieve sustained high rates of growth in GDP per capita'. One of the biggest differences between the two competitiveness indices is that the WEF, unlike the IMD, now excludes such variables as GDP growth, export growth, and the inflow of foreign direct investments because it regards these as the result or consequences and not the causes of a country's competitiveness. Another difference is that the WEF, as opposed to the IMD, gives more weight to openness of the economy, the role of government, the efficiency of the financial sector, and the flexibility of labor markets than to other factors (the quality of management, infrastructures, technology, and the effectiveness of the legal and political institutions of the country).

Table 1.3 shows the WEF international competitiveness rankings. As the table shows, the United States drops from first place in the IMD ranking to fourth place in the WEF ranking, after Singapore, Hong Kong, and New Zealand. To be sure, the United States remains the most competitive of the G-7 nations. Canada rises from twelfth place in the IMD report to eighth place in the WEF report. Japan falls from fourth to thirteenth place, Britain rises from nineteenth to fifteenth place, Germany falls from tenth to twenty-second place, France from twentieth to twenty-third, and Italy from twenty-eighth to forty-first place. Thus, except for Canada and Britain, all the other five large industrialized nations have a relatively lower ranking in the WEF's report than in the IMD's report. The reason for this is that the level

TABLE 1.3 *National Competitiveness Indices, 1996*

Rank/country	Index	Rank/country	Index
1. Singapore	2.19	26. Ireland	0.13
2. Hong Kong	1.89	27. Iceland	−0.16
3. New Zealand	1.57	28. Jordan	−0.20
4. United States	1.34	29. Egypt	−0.31
5. Luxembourg	1.29	30. Indonesia	−0.36
6. Switzerland	1.27	31. Philippines	−0.51
7. Norway	1.03	32. Spain	−0.57
8. Canada	1.01	33. Mexico	−0.57
9. Taiwan	0.96	34. Portugal	−0.58
10. Malaysia	0.91	35. Czech Republic	−0.64
11. Denmark	0.75	36. China	−0.68
12. Australia	0.68	37. Argentina	−0.70
13. Japan	0.65	38. Peru	−0.74
14. Thailand	0.63	39. Greece	−0.78
15. United Kingdom	0.63	40. Colombia	−0.82
16. Finland	0.61	41. Italy	−0.91
17. Netherlands	0.50	42. Turkey	−0.97
18. Chile	0.45	43. South Africa	−1.02
19. Austria	0.40	44. Poland	−1.15
20. Korea	0.35	45. India	−1.46
21. Sweden	0.27	46. Hungary	−1.48
22. Germany	0.27	47. Venezuela	−1.69
23. France	0.24	48. Brazil	−1.73
24. Israel	0.20	49. Russia	−2.36
25. Belgium	0.16		

Source: WEF (1996).

of per capita income (which is much higher in the largest industrialized countries than in developing countries) is excluded from the measure of competitiveness in the WEF index but not from the IMD index. Germany, France, and Italy come out relatively worse in the WEF index also because of the inflexibility of their labor markets.

On the other hand, most small developing countries do much better in the WEF's competitiveness score than in the IMD's index. For example, Singapore and Hong Kong occupy first and second spot on the WEF index, but second and third, respectively, in the IMD index. Taiwan is ninth instead of eighteenth, Malaysia is tenth instead of twenty-third, Thailand is fourteenth instead of thirtieth, and Korea is twentieth instead of twenty-seventh. Chile, however, drops from eighteenth to thirteenth place. Note, however, that the WEF report does not address the two main criticisms raised against the IMD report (i.e. measuring the competitiveness index for developed and developing countries and for large and small countries and the lack of close correspondence between the ranking on the competitive index and on the nations' per capita income and standard of living). Thus, the main use of these competitiveness rankings is to compare the relative competitive positions of the various G-7 countries (and in this there is basic agreement, except for the much higher position of Britain over Germany), on the one hand, and the relative position of the small developing nations, on the other.

Relative Labor and Capital Productivity in the United States, Japan, Germany, and France

Table 1.4 shows labor productivity in terms of value added per hour worked in various industries in Japan and Germany relative to the United States in 1990. Taking the labor productivity in the United States as 100, we can see from the table that Japan's labor was more productive than U.S. labor by 47 percent in steel, 24 percent in auto parts, 19 percent in metal working, 16 percent in automobiles, and 15 percent in consumer electronics. On the other hand, U.S. labor was more productive than Japanese labor in computers, beer, soaps and detergents, and especially food. For all industries together, Japanese labor was, on the average, only 83 percent as productive as U.S. labor. Table 1.4 also shows that German labor was as productive as U.S. labor only in metal working and steel and less productive in all other industries, especially in beer production. Overall, German labor was only 79 percent as productive as U.S. labor. It should be noted that the relative overall Japanese and German labor productivity is very close to that given in Table 1, even though the two measures were obtained by very different methods.

TABLE 1.4 *Productivity of Japanese and German Labor Relative to U.S. Labor in 1990, with U.S. Index = 100*

Industry	Japanese	German
Steel	147	100
Auto parts	124	76
Metal working	119	100
Automobiles	116	66
Consumer electronics	115	76
Computer	95	89
Telecommunications	77	52
General merchandising retailing	·44	96
All industries	83	79

Source: Elaboration on McKinsey Global Institute (1993).

In a more recent study of productivity of German and French industry relative to U.S. industry, the McKinsey Global Institute (1997) found that German and French productivity increased over the past decade but at a slower rate than U.S. productivity and so it is now further behind U.S. industry today that it was a decade ago. Overall, McKinsey found that German industry is now (1997) 30 percent less efficient and French industry is 40 percent less efficient than U.S. industry. In general, the higher U.S. labor productivity is not due to bigger firms, more automation, or better managers (although these factors might be determinant in some specific industries), but is the result of greater competition and much more flexible labor practices in the United States than abroad. Specifically, the higher U.S. productivity depends on the ability of U.S. managers to introduce new and improved products much faster than abroad and the ability of U.S. engineers to invent new and more efficient ways of making products and designing products that easy to make.

Furthermore, despite the fact that the United States has, in recent years, been saving and investing less than Japan, Germany, and France (and, for that matter, less than most other nations), it seems to have secured more mileage out of its investments. In fact, the McKinsey Global Institute (1996) found that Germany and Japan use their physical capital only about two-thirds as efficiently as the United States. The Institute looked at the entire economy and in depth at five industries: telecommunications, utilities, auto manufacturing, food processing, and retailing. It found that Germany uses excessive capital for the job at hand. For example, the phone cables for Deutsche Telekom are built to withstand being run over by a tank, even though the cables are underground. Such 'gold-plating' of equipment is expensive and wasteful. Japan keeps massive electrical generating capacity idle most of the time in order to meet peek demand in hot summer days, while the United States avoids this great capital waste by creative time-of-day and summer electricity pricing schemes that discourage usage at peak times. Such higher capital productivity translates into higher financial returns for U.S. savers—9.1 percent compared with 7.4 percent in Germany and 7.1 percent in Japan. This higher U.S. capital productivity more than makes up for its lower savings rate than Germany and Japan.

Since the 1970s, the United States has moved faster than Japan, Germany, and France and other nations in deregulating (i.e. in removing government regulations and controls of economic activities on) airlines, telecommunications, trucking, banking, and many other sectors of the economy. For example, cut-throat competition makes American airlines about a third more productive than the larger regulated or government-run foreign airlines. General merchandise retailing is twice as efficient in the United States than in Japan, and so is American telecommunications in relation to German telecommunications. Most American firms today face much stiffer competition from domestic and foreign firms than their European and Japanese counterparts. Stiff competition makes most American firms lean and mean—and generally more efficient than foreign firms.

A second reason for higher productivity of U.S. than Japanese and European labor is the much higher degree of computerization in the United States than Japan or Europe. In 1997, the United States had 63 computers per 100 employed workers to Japan's 17 and even fewer in Europe. Labor flexibility is still another reason for the larger productivity of U.S. labor. While labor practices abroad are often constrained by unions, social policies and regulation, U.S. firms are much freer to hire, fire, reorganize, and use labor and other resources where they are most productive. This makes life difficult for U.S. workers who can lose their jobs when caught in a competitive squeeze, but it also enhances firms' efficiency and labor productivity. Coupled with adequate job creation, this higher labor productivity is responsible for the higher GDP per capita and standard of living in the United States than abroad.

The New Computer-Assisted Production Revolution and the International Competitiveness of U.S. Firms

Since the early 1990s, a veritable revolution in production has been taking place in the United States, based on computer-assisted design and computer-assisted manufacturing, which greatly increased the productivity and international competitiveness of U.S. firms. *Computer-assisted design (CAD)* allows research and development engineers to design a new product or component on a computer screen, quickly experiment with different alternative designs, and test their strength and reliability—all on the screen! Then, *computer-assisted manufacturing (CAM)* issues instructions to a network of integrated machine tools to produce a prototype of the new or changed product. These allow firms to avoid many possible production problems, greatly speed up the time required to develop and introduce new or improved products, and reduce the optimal lot size or the production runs to achieve maximum production efficiency. This revolution has been taking place almost exclusively in the United States, based primarily on its world leadership and superiority in computer software and computer networks.

These new developments have led to a new digital factory—an information-age marvel that is responsible for a quantum leap in the speed, flexibility, and productivity of U.S. firms resulting from the ingenious marriage of computer software and computer networks in industries as diverse as construction equipment, automobiles, PCs, and electronic pagers. This new digital factory has unheard agility that allows it to customize products down to one unit while achieving mass-production speed and efficiency. For example, as a Motorola salesperson specifies an order for a pager for a particular consumer, the digitized data flows to the assembly line where production begins immediately and is completed in a few minutes, so that the customer can have his or her customized pager the day after. This is sometimes called software-controlled continuous flow manufacturing—a process that is basically merging manufacturing and retailing. This much faster time-to-market and customizing capability is beginning to provide American firms with tremendous advantage over foreign competitors—including the Japanese, who seem bewildered by this new development. After years of losing the world competitive war, the United States is finally regaining some of the lost ground, and then some.

Computer-assisted design (CAD) is dramatically increasing the pace of innovations. For example, a designer can call up on the screen a car door she may working on, test opening and closing the door, running the window up and down, experiment with lighter materials, and direct machinery to make a prototype door. Such CAD allowed Chrysler to design and build its highly successful NEON subcompact car in 33 months instead of the usual 45 months. Even more exotically, scientists at Caterpillar, the largest earth-moving equipment builder in the world, test drive huge machinery that they are developing in virtual reality before they are even built. CAD is even used to design and simulate entire assembly lines and it can be used to send production orders to suppliers' machinery so that, in a sense, they become an extension of the firm's plant. In short, we are likely to be at the dawn of the biggest revolution in manufacturing since the perfection of the industrial lathe in the year 1800. And with the U.S. undisputed superiority in software, it is unlikely that foreign competitors can easily copy and match the new American manufacturing genius anytime soon.

The Importance of International Competitiveness

In a recent article, Paul Krugman (1994) stated that international competitiveness is an irrelevant and dangerous concept because nations simply do not compete with each other the way corporations do, and that increases in productivity rather than international competitiveness are all that matter for increasing the standard of living of a nation. In trying to prove his point, Krugman points out that U.S. trade represents only about 10–15 percent of U.S. GDP (and so international trade cannot significantly effect the standard of living, at least in the United States), international trade is not a zero-sum game (so that all nations can gain from international trade), and that concern with international competitiveness can lead governments to the wrong policies (such as trade restrictions and industrial policies).

All of these statements are true, but Krugman's conclusion that since international trade is only 10 to 15 percent of U.S. GDP, it cannot significantly affect the U.S. standard of living, simply does not follow. The reason is that if a nation's corporations innovate and increase productivity at a lower rate than foreign corporations, the nation may be relegated to exporting products which are technologically less advanced and this may compromise its future growth. For example, the U.S. superiority in software makes possible faster productivity growth in the United States both directly (because productivity growth is faster in the software industry than in many other industries) and indirectly (by increasing the productivity of many other sectors, such as automobiles, which make great use of computer software in design and production). Thus, international competitiveness is crucial to the nation's standard of living.

Pointing out, as Krugman does, that some high-tech sectors artificially protected by trade policies and/or encouraged by industrial policies have grown less rapidly that some low-tech sectors, such as cigarettes and beer production, misses the point. This only proves that wrong policies can be costly. Productivity growth and international competitiveness must be encouraged not by protectionist or industrial policies, but rather by improving the factors affecting international competitiveness discussed in Section III of this chapter. A country's future prosperity depends on its growth in productivity and this can certainly be influenced by government policies. Nations compete in the sense that they choose policies that promote productivity. As pointed out by Dunning (1995) and Porter (1990), international competitiveness does matter.

That industrial policies and protectionism only provide temporary benefits to the targeted or protected industries but slows down the growth of productivity and standards of living in the long run is clearly evidenced by the competitiveness situation in Europe vis-a-vis the United States and Japan today. Aside from banking and the space industry (and, maybe, the chemical industry), there is practically no other industry in Europe that can stand up to U.S. and Japanese competition. This is the case for the steel industry, the automobile industry, the commercial aircraft industry, the airline industry, the computer industry, and many others. Without the billions of dollars that some of these industries receive in subsidies or for repeated restructuring and trade protection, and without alliances with U.S. or Japanese firms, most European firms in these industries would be unable to compete with U.S. and Japanese firms. Seven of the top ten computer firms (including the top five) in Europe are American, one is Japanese and only two are European. In software, America has an undisputed lead. In telecommunications, online services, biotech, and aircraft also the United States has a big lead over Europe. In automobiles, Japan has an undisputed lead and even U.S. automakers are much more efficient than Europeans. To be sure, European automobiles are of high quality, but they command a much higher price than Japanese and a higher price than even American automobiles.

Although Europe has been able to keep wages and standards of living relatively high and rising during the past two decades, the rate of unemployment is now more than double the U.S. rate and three to four times higher than the unemployment rate in Japan. And while the United States, with a smaller population than Europe, has created more than 20 million jobs during the past twenty years, employment has stagnated in Europe. The United States has also been much more successful than European countries in meeting the growing competition from NIEs and other emerging economies in Asia (Rausch, 1995).

The restructuring and downsizing that rapid technological change and increasing international competition made necessary resulted in average wages and salaries not rising very much in real terms in the United States during the past decade, but millions of new jobs were created. In Europe, on the other hand, real wages and salaries grew but very few new jobs were created, and this left Europe much less able to compete on the world market than the United States and

Japan. It is true that Japan has also been very protectionistic and made extensive use of industrial policies in the past, but Japan fostered intensive competition at home, while Europe did not. The result has been that Japanese firms have become highly competitive while European firms have not. Being unable to fire workers when not needed, firms have tended to increase output by increasing capital per worker rather than by hiring more labor and this has made the return to capital lower and the wage of labor higher in Europe than in the United States.

References

BARRO, R. J. and SALA-I-MARTIN, X. (1995) *Economic Growth*, New York, McGraw-Hill.

DUNNING, J. H. (1994) Globalization, Economic Restructuring and Development, The Sixth Raul Prebisch Lecture of the United Nations Conference on Trade and Development, Geneva, April 29.

DUNNING, J. H. (1995) Think Again Professor Krugman: Competitiveness Does Matter, *The International Executive*, Vol. 37, No. 4, 315–324.

Institute for Management Development (1996) *The World Competitiveness Yearbook*, IMD, Lousanne.

KRUGMAN, P. (1994) Competitiveness: A Dangerous Obsession, *Foreign Affairs*, March-April, pp. 28–44.

LEVITT, T. (1983) The Globalization of Markets, *Harvard Business Review*, May-June, pp. 92–102.

McKinsey Global Institute (1993) *Manufacturing Productivity*, McKinsey Global Institute, Washington, DC.

McKinsey Global Institute (1996) *Capital Productivity*, McKinsey Global Institute, Washington, DC.

McKinsey Global Institute (1997) *Removing Barriers to Growth and Employment in France and Germany*, McKinsey Global Institute, Washington, DC.

PORTER, M. (1990) *The Comparative Advantage of Nations*, Free Press, New York.

RAUSCH, L. M. (1995) *Asia's New High-Tech Competitors*, National Science Foundation, Washington, DC.

SALVATORE, D. (1990) *The Japanese Trade Challenge and the U.S. Response*, Economic Policy Institute, Washington, DC.

SALVATORE, D. (1993) *Protectionism and World Welfare*, Cambridge University Press, New York.

SALVATORE, D. (1996) *Managerial Economics in a Global Economy*, 3rd edn, McGraw-Hill, New York.

World Economic Forum (1996) *The Global Competitiveness Report*, Geneva.

2

International Trade and Foreign Direct Investment: The Interface

H. PETER GRAY

The implications of multinational enterprise and foreign direct investment for the volume and pattern of international trade and for the general allocative efficiency of the global economy are complex. General static *and* dynamic models of the interaction are provided. Because of the continuous accretion of technological assets and the ability of host countries to offer complementary created factors of production, the static analysis is of interest only as a precursor to the dynamic model.

Introduction

The globalization of economic activity throughout much of the world[1] relies heavily on the abilities of modern multinational enterprises (MNEs) to transfer "created assets" (Dunning, 1993, p. 288) from industrialized to developing countries. The MNEs simultaneously integrate both their global portfolios of proprietary (ownership) and locational assets and, in the process, the economies of the home and host countries in which those assets are located. Kobrin (1995) posits that foreign direct investment (FDI) by MNEs has become the glue which constitutes the major positive thrust of globalization (given the 'passive' changes in conditions brought about by multilateral international agreements on trade and FDI).

This chapter offers an analytic framework which will identify the interactive modalities of trade and FDI as they contribute to the role of MNEs in a globalizing world economy. To distinguish the importance of the trade modality from that of the act of investment is seen as spurious since competition among MNEs relies heavily on the integration of different geographic affiliates (locational assets) by means of, *inter alia*, international trade.

Alternative Modalities of Competition Among MNEs

Modern MNEs compete in global markets with other MNEs in the production of Schumpeter (S-) goods and services[2] which rely heavily on the possession of proprietary technology, product differentiation and other activities in which there exist economies of scale, scope and common governance.[3] Analysis of the interrelationship between the twin activities of foreign direct investment and international trade requires a two-stage, static/dynamic model. The emphases on managerial efficiency and on S-goods makes the Heckscher-Ohlin-Samuelson model of international trade inadequate. The model to be used in this chapter is an extension of Dunning's eclectic paradigm (Gray, 1996). In it, MNEs are seen as maximizing the return on their existing portfolios of ownership and locational assets and concurrently examining how best they can maintain or increase their market shares (competitiveness) by investing in new ownership and locational assets. International trade is the most important of the linkages which allow the MNEs efficiently to exploit their twin asset portfolios.[4] Because the integration of spatially-located assets is a complex operation, it is necessary that the level of managerial efficiency (broadly defined to include the realization of potential internalization economies; Gray, 1996) of an individual firm be as high as (or higher than) that of its competitors.

Every MNE competes on the basis of its own historic or path-dependent record since its current viability is determined by the relative strengths of its portfolios of ownership and locational assets and the relative efficiency with which it exploits them. In many product lines, competition can be 'explosive' so that a firm (or a division in a particular product line) which falls behind is likely to fall further behind as declining market share, low profits and a cash squeeze limit the degree to which it can generate or acquire the new assets needed to maintain or re-establish its competitive position. Maintaining competitiveness and an adequate internally-generated free cash flow is therefore crucial for continued viability (Milberg and Gray, 1992).[5]

An Analytic Framework

We now offer a general analytic framework of the relationship between international trade and foreign direct investment (FDI) under the aegis of globally-competitive MNEs when impediments to both kinds of transaction are declining steadily or are low (i.e. in a globalized world). The developments which generate greater globalization can either be exogenous to the international economy (i.e. through the availability of new technologies or spontaneous changes in national policies regarding foreign involvement) or endogenous as supra-national institutions successfully encourage independent nations to facilitate global integration through mutually agreed-upon reduced impediments to trade and investment. Major mutually-reinforcing changes in global conditions governing both trade and FDI as well as in the technological capacity for managing complex portfolios of inter-linked locational assets have contributed starkly to the growth of internationally-integrated production systems (IIPSs) in recent years (UNCTAD, 1993).

Static Conditions

For a given set of economic attributes in countries and given levels of impediments to international trade and investment, an MNE will have acquired a portfolio of locational assets (foreign affiliates and other modalities serving to access foreign economies) and it will possess a portfolio of ownership assets (including proprietary product and process technologies) which will be made available to foreign affiliates according to the perceived best interests of the parent MNE.[6] The spatial or international distribution of the twin asset portfolios will, given the regnant economic conditions in each of the countries in which the MNE has affiliates, determine the degree of international trade undertaken by the MNE. If the assumption of full employment is dropped, it becomes possible for MNEs to equalize rates of capacity utilization in different subsidiaries through the global reallocation of production (and trade).

John Cantwell (1994, pp. 315–16) emphasizes the interaction between location characteristics and the ownership assets so that, for example, proprietary technology may have a greater effect and undergo greater refinement in one location than in another. This location-specific development of a basic technology can contribute to intra-industry trade among industrialized countries.[7] Some international transactions will be intra-firm between affiliates and home-country production units, some will be intra-firm between affiliates and some will be arm's-length with unrelated firms (Hipple, 1995). Under stationary conditions, all firms will be in equilibrium so that there is no need to conduct further FDI[8] and the international transfer of assets will have been determined by the varying degrees of asset mobility and the difficulties of integrating the activities of all of the MNE units. Similarly, demand characteristics in one country can provide an affiliate with a distinctive competitive edge in one differentiated good within the MNE. For example, a plant will design, develop, and produce those products or product variants that are in the greatest demand in the country where it is situated and export them even to the home country of the MNE (Womack, *et al.*, 1990: Ch. 8). This opens up the possibility for a complex interaction among the economics of product design, economies of scale, and intra-firm international trade.

These conditions require recognition of the existence of firm-level product-specific attributes in the production and sale of S-goods (Gray, 1980). In each Schumpeterian industry, MNEs will have augmented the resource bases of the host countries and will use the foreign assets to supply the home corporation or other foreign affiliates with both intermediate and final products which can, by virtue of the transfer of created assets and the economies of internalization, now be made more cheaply in the host country. A model of trade with given transfers of resources at the firm level is given in Gray (1992): in this model, the macroeconomic constraints of the host country and its attractiveness for inward investment are identified by the rate of exchange of its currency.[9] There is, therefore, competition among industries to take advantage of favorable conditions in a host country as Schumpeterian firms compete for those limited local resources which provide the source of attraction for having an affiliate located there.

Under the usual assumptions of balanced international payments and full employment of resources, FDI will have brought about an improvement in global productive efficiency along lines similar to the generation of gains from trade through the exchange of goods with different input mixes or opportunity costs.[10] Since market-seeking production affiliates can displace international trade and efficiency-seeking trade will increase the volume of trade, there is no way of knowing whether the volume of trade will be larger or smaller.[11] However, the introduction of FDI and MNEs allows the benefits from the exchange of goods to be increased by adding the possibilities of the movement of resources internationally and the transfer of technological assets to countries in which they are lacking (the factor-proportions theory does not encompass differences in either the availability of or the skill in exploiting such technologies in different countries). The increased global gain will also be enhanced by any economies of internalization in hierarchies or quasi-hierarchies reaped by MNEs, their affiliates and longstanding suppliers (Gray and Lundan, 1993, p. 646).

Dynamic Conditions

The dynamic solution is less well defined. To maintain or increase their existing market share, MNEs must enhance their three attributes (ownership assets, locational assets and managerial efficiency), at a rate at least equal to that of their competitors. The task throws a great responsibility on the skills of the entrepreneurial executives because it requires allocating (internally- and externally-generated) funds to increasing the relative value of the twin asset portfolios and to being able to integrate those ownership and locational assets. Increases in assets located abroad, particularly if the investment is efficiency-seeking and generates an IIP (and distribution) system, will be meshed primarily through international trade so that the investment decision must countenance the ability of management to mesh assets located in different countries largely through international, and possibly, intra-firm trade.[12] Investment decisions of this kind are clearly more complex than simple closed-economy investment decisions and become increasingly difficult with the dimensionality of the IIPS.[13]

As political risk factors in different countries and other attributes of macro-organizational policies change, the optimal mixes of both portfolios will change. More important than changes in policies and conditions in individual nations are the changes in technologies and global arrangements which facilitate (or impede) international trade, direct investment and the management of complex organizations. Thus, greater liberalization of international trade régimes (greater integration of the international economy either globally or region-ally),[14] greater ease of establishment and greater assurance of national treatment are all likely to result in changes in firms' portfolios of locational assets.[15] Asset portfolios will now require meshing in new ways.

The interlinking of international trade and FDI suggests that it would be efficient policy for the two sets of regulations (governing trade and FDI) to move in unison and possibly to be conceived as subcomponents of a single régime. When changes in conditions governing both trade and ease of establishment have the same direction and are simultaneous, managers of MNEs will be able to avoid two sets of sequential adjustment to new conditions. Greater liberalization will increase the proportion of assets located abroad and global integration. In general, both policy- and technologically-created reductions of impediments to international trade and investment are likely to promote efficiency-seeking investments and to lead to more trade-creating activities than to increases in market-seeking FDI which will supplant trade.[16]

The Pattern of FDI-Affected Trade

The pattern of trade in standardized goods (using only generic factors of production and not substantively reliant on proprietary assets) can be expected to take place in greater volume between countries with substantially different resource endowments. Of course, this inference must be qualified by the influence of the set of demand and supply elasticities which prevail. In this, the factor-proportions theory is underspecified since allowance must be made, *inter alia*, for the efficiency of institutions in the labor-intensive (less-sophisticated) country and the amenability of its population to working under factory conditions.

There is no reason to expect that the poorer countries will enjoy a competitive advantage in hosting FDI and in the production of S-goods. To be able to compete for the supply of outward FDI emanating from industrialized and newly-industrialized economies, a would-be host country must be able to provide co-operating inputs to modern production systems.[17] Efficiency-seeking FDI will, therefore, tend to be located in those countries which are able to supply a skilled and disciplined workforce and good technological and physical infrastructure. MNE-instigated international trade in S-goods will tend, therefore, to take place largely between countries with different income levels but the host country's income level cannot be too different from that of the parent country.[18] In East Asia, where international trade among MNEs has grown spectacularly, outward FDI from middle-income countries such as Malaysia and Thailand, has created integrated international production systems with countries at a lower level of economic development such as Vietnam, Laos and the People's Republic of China.

Conclusions

The analytic framework sketched in above is necessarily general. Proprietary technologies and other sources of MNE competitiveness are industry- or product-specific, so that the effects of a general reduction of impediments to trade and FDI would need to be applied individually to both industries and countries. Similarly, no change in the level of global impediments to trade and investment can possibly be neutral with respect to all industries and all countries: their impacts must be uneven.

Appendix A: Schumpeter Goods

Schumpeter (S-) goods comprise those products in which privately-owned (proprietary) technology is used with other inputs in the course of production and sale. The goods comprise tangible products and services which use 'created' factors of production (as distinct from generally-available factors) such as proprietary technology, sector- or even product-specific skills, firm-level managerial efficiencies and what can be called 'marketing-and-distribution (m&d) assets and technology'. They are differentiated by the producing firm and require firm-specific proprietary technology which can be either protected by patent or kept internal to the firm as well related product- or industry-specific skills.

S-goods are traded in markets in which the new products and new versions of old products, the degree of differentiation, scale economies and costs of production evolve through time as competing firms in the same or different countries try to expand their global market share at the expense of their competitors. These firms are termed 'Schumpeterian' by Aharoni (1993, p. 26) because they compete by continuous innovation and by inter-temporal heterogeneity and because they face a constant need to adapt to changing conditions as well as to create changes. It seems reasonable to suppose that, in such industries, the quality of executive decisions and managerial efficiency in general are likely to be vital in affecting the success of the firm. Schumpeterian firms correspond much more closely with the modern concept of the role of the executive as a dynamic shaper of strategy than firms producing standardized goods. The *creation and exploitation* of proprietary factors are predominantly undertaken at the level of the individual firm although in recent years alliances among competing firms have become important as they attempt to economize on the costs of product development and to marry complementary areas of expertise in partner firms.

References

AHARONI, Y. (1993) From Adam Smith to Schumpeterian Global Firms. In RUGMAN, A. M. and VERBEKE, A. (eds) *Global Competition: Beyond the Three Generics*, JAI Press, Greenwich, Conn., pp. 17–39.

AMENDOLA, G., DOSI, G. and PAPAGNI, E. (1993) The Dynamics of International Competitiveness, *Weltwirtschaftliches Archiv*, Vol. 129, (Heft 3), pp. 452–471.

CANTWELL, J. (1994) The Relationship between International Trade and International Production. In GREENAWAY, D. and WINTERS, L. A. (eds) *Survey in International Trade*, Basil Blackwell, Oxford, pp. 303–328.

DUNNING, J. H. (1981) Explaining the International Direct Investment Position of Countries: Towards a Dynamic or Develop-mental Approach, *Weltwirtschaftliches Archiv*, Vol. 119, pp. 30–64.

DUNNING, J. H. (1992) The Global Economy, Domestic Governance, Strategies and Transnational Corporations: Interactions and Policy Implications, *Transnational Corporations*, Vol. 1, pp. 7–45.

DUNNING, J. H. (1993) *Multinational Enterprises and the Global Economy*, Addison Wesley, Wokingham.

DUNNING, J. H. and NARULA, R. (eds) (1996) *Foreign Direct Investments and Governments*, Routledge, London.

GRAY, H. P. (1980) The Theory of International Trade Among Manufacturing Nations, *Weltwirtschaftliches Archiv,* Vol. 116, pp. 447–470.
GRAY, H. P. (1992) The Interface between the Theories of International Trade and Production. In BUCKLEY, P. J. and CASSON, M. C. (eds) *Multinational Enterprise and International Direct Investment: Essays in Honour of John H. Dunning,* Edward Elgar, Cheltenham, pp. 41–53.
GRAY, H. P. (1993) Introduction: The Role of Transnational Corporations in International Trade. In GRAY, H. P. (ed.) *Transnational Corporations and International Trade and Payments,* Routledge for the United Nations Library on Transnational Corporations, London, pp. 1–18.
GRAY, H. P. (1996) The eclectic paradigm: the next generation, *Transnational Corporations,* Vol. 5, pp. 51–65.
GRAY, H. P. (1998) Free International Trade in a World of Schumpeter Goods, *The International Trade Journal,* Vol. XII, (forthcoming).
GRAY, H. P. and LUNDAN, S. (1993) Japanese Multinationals and the Stability of the GATT System, *The International Trade Journal,* Vol. VII, pp. 635–653.
GUNDLACH, E. and NUNNENKAMP, P. (1998) Some Consequences of Globalization for Developing Countries, Chapter 7 in this volume.
HIPPLE, F. S. (1995) *Multinational Corporations in United States International Trade,* Quorum Books, Westport, CT.
KOBRIN, S. J. (1995) Regional Integration in a Globally Networked Economy, *Transnational Corporations,* Vol. 4, 15–33.
MILBERG, W. S. and GRAY, H. P. (1992) International Competitiveness and Policy in Dynamic Industries, *Banca Nazionale del Lavoro Quarterly Review,* 59–80.
United Nations Conference on Trade and Development (UNCTAD) (1993) *World Investment Report, 1993: Transnational Corporations and Integrated International Production,* United Nations, New York.
WOMACK, J. P., JONES, D. T. and ROOS, D. (1990) *The Machine that Changed the World,* Rawson Associates/MacMillan, New York.

Notes

1. Gundlach and Nunnenkamp (1997) show that many countries run the risk of becoming delinked from the global economy as a result of the new developments and their inability to absorb the technologies and trading and investment conditions which are the foundation of globalization.
2. This category of goods is described in Appendix A.
3. MNEs whose foreign assets are resource-seeking derive their competitiveness largely from the economies of internalization and from the oligopolistic benefits of having assured sources of raw materials. These activities are likely to generate intra-firm trade as extraction is conducted in one country and downstream processing in another (Cantwell, 1994). The efficiency with which the internalization advantages are exploited could crucially affect the competitiveness within natural-resource goods industries.
4. Clearly, the intra-firm transfer of created assets and perceived internalization advantages are crucial in the determination of whether or not to add to the portfolio of locational assets.
5. Multiproduct and multi-locational firms can reallocate funds internally if a unit

(product or site) is in danger of failure if the operation is deemed to be potentially viable. Similarly, large established firms can have access to external sources of funds to permit a temporary shortfall in internal cash flow. These features dampen the tendency for competition to be explosive.

One must also recognize that a loss of market share and reduced profits can be the catalyst that generates increases in managerial (or X-) efficiency within a firm (see Amendola *et al.*, 1993).

6. The ultimate reliance of this model on Dunning's eclectic paradigm (Dunning, 1993, pp. 79–86) is evident. Ownership assets will not necessarily be available in all affiliates because of concerns with local political risk and problems of appropriability.

7. The question of the role of international production on the recent growth of intra-industry trade is a complex one and Cantwell (1994, p. 321) rejects the idea of a strong relationship between intra-industry and intra-firm trade.

8. The optimality of locational assets is a very severe restriction of the static general equilibrium model, particularly so when the focus of analysis is world welfare (i.e. global allocative efficiency).

9. The real rate of exchange (an index number) identifies what would be the terms of trade that exist between two economies in a non-monetary model.

10. The actual distribution of MNE-controlled resources will be sensitive to the distribution of macro-organizational policies in the world (Dunning, 1992). In a static model, these policies must also be assumed to be unchanging.

11. Gray (1993) addresses the twin effects of trade-creating and trade-supplanting FDI.

12. In Dunning's terminology, an IIPS is merely a multidimensional system of efficiency-seeking investments in several countries.

13. The current pattern of trade involving MNEs depends upon the portfolio of existing productive units and not upon future planned increases (or changes) in the portfolio of locational assets.

14. Any simplification of international shipment of goods *and* any reduction in transport costs will tend to generate more trade, even with an unchanging mix of portfolios on the part of MNEs.

15. Note that the deeper integration that follows from the establishment of regional blocs may be expected to delineate the conditions governing freedom of establishment and national treatment and to ensure the existence of a minimal independence of foreign affiliates from hostile action by the host government. Regional integration may exert its major effect through FDI as MNEs reduce perceived political risk in nations which are members of the same regional bloc.

16. For a discussion of this issue see Gray (1998).

17. See Dunning (1981) and Dunning and Narula (1996) on the development of the investment development path.

18. The People's Republic of China is an exception and this exception can be attributed to the capacity of the Chinese people to acquire knowledge and to the creation of export processing zones by the Beijing government.

3

Regional Trading Blocks and Foreign Direct Investment

PAUL COLLINS

Most foreign direct investment (FDI) flows from a few developed economies into other developed economies. Flows to developing economies have recently increased but are still smaller and the world stock of FDI is very unevenly spread. The emergence of regional trading blocks and new areas for FDI has somewhat changed these flows. The chapter aims to examine the data and speculates on the impact these changes will have on future flows of FDI and on trade.

Introduction

In today's global economy, foreign direct investment (FDI) has superseded trade with global sales by multinational enterprise (MNE) affiliates worth $5.2 trillion in 1992 compared with world-wide exports of goods and services of $5.0 trillion in 1992 (UNCTAD, 1995). In 1993 global trade had increased from $3.7 trillion to $4.2 trillion in 1994, and by 1995 had accelerated to $5.0 trillion (UNCTAD, 1995). Moreover an estimated one-third of world trade is intra-firm trade within MNEs. In 1995, FDI outflows increased by 38 percent over 1994 values, and this was a substantially greater increase than that of exports of goods and services, which increased by 18 percent in 1994, whilst world output increased by 2.4 percent and gross domestic capital formation (GDFCF) by 5.3 percent over 1994 (UNCTAD, 1996). Thus in 1995, FDI outflows again exceeded the increases in trade and world output. In consequence, the role and importance of MNEs in the global business environment has continued to increase.

With such growth continuing, it is therefore interesting to see which countries are sources of FDI outflows and which are recipients, and to see how the three main trading blocks in the world economy have so far influenced these flows, and also to speculate on future changes.

Outflows of FDI

Over the past decade, there has been an underlying upward trend in FDI outflows, although they have been affected by cyclical downturns in the international economy. FDI outflows in 1990 and 1991 declined but recovered in 1993 and 1994, and by 1995 FDI outflows had reached record heights of $318 billion, which was an increase of 38 percent over 1994.

Of total outflows of FDI over the period 1982–91, 94 percent came from developed countries. This percentage was to decline marginally over the 1990s, falling to 85.3 percent by 1993, and 83.0 percent in 1994; however in 1995 it recovered to 85.1 percent (UNCTAD, 1996).

Over the period 1982–91, the developing economies were responsible for only just over 6 percent of total FDI outflows (a total of $16 billion compared with $188 billion from developed economies). However this absolute amount increased, as did their share, so that by 1992 they were responsible for 10.6 percent, increasing to 14.6 percent in 1993, and to 16.8 percent in 1994, although this was to decline to 14.8 percent in 1995. But the amount of FDI outflows by developing countries in 1995, at $47 billion, was also their highest ever. This indicates that developing countries are accelerating their integration into the world economy (UNCTAD, 1996), although the proviso needs to be made that these outflows come from a limited number of countries, as does FDI from developed economies.

With the globalization of the international economy has come a greater interdependence between countries. This is clearly illustrated by the fact that five OECD countries—France, Germany, Japan, the U.K. and the U.S.A.—had, during the 1980s (and before), been responsible for nearly 70 percent of all FDI outflows that came from

TABLE 3.1 *Total FDI Outflows 1984–95 (US$ millions)*

Total outflow	1984–89 annual average	1990	1991	1992	1993	1994	1995
	121,630	240,253	210,821	203,115	225,544	230,014	317,849

Source: UNCTAD (1996).

TABLE 3.2 *FDI Inflows and Outflows of Developed and Developing Countries (percent of total)*

	Developed countries		Developing countries	
	Inflows	Outflows	Inflows	Outflows
1982–86	69.4	93.0	30.6	7.0
1987–91	81.6	93.8	17.8	6.2
1992	67.8	89.3	30.0	10.6
1993	62.2	85.3	35.2	14.6
1994	58.8	83.0	38.5	16.8
1995	64.5	85.1	31.6	14.8

Note: The balance represents flows into and out of Central and Eastern European economies
Source: UNCTAD (1995, 1996).

developed countries (see Table 3.3), while in 1995 it was to exceed this former total. The importance of these FDI outflows on the economy and prosperity of both home and host countries is well documented by Dunning (1993) and other writers.

The U.S.A. had been the largest source of global outward investment and over the 1980s and '90s seldom lost that position. The dominance of the U.S.A. is illustrated by the fact that it has been the largest single source of FDI for four out of the last six years.

The U.K.—a country which historically had been a major source of FDI—still continues to export substantial amounts of FDI. Over the period 1982–86 the U.K.'s capital outflows amounted to $10 billion compared with the U.S.A.'s $11 billion, but over the 1980s and '90s, as world outflows of FDI grew rapidly, the U.K.'s volume remained relatively stable. Thus as world FDI volumes grew, the U.K.'s share fell, although in 1993, 1994 and 1995 it was to re-emerge into second position.

TABLE 3.3 *FDI Outflows of Selected Countries: Shares in Total (percent)*

Year	France	Germany	Japan	U.K.	U.S.A.	Total
1982–86	5.3	11.5	12.3	17.5	19.3	64.9
1987–91	10.3	9.2	17.9	14.3	12.8	64.6
1992	16.2	8.4	8.9	9.9	20.4	63.9
1993	9.5	7.7	6.3	11.7	31.1	66.2
1994	10.4	9.5	8.1	11.2	20.7	59.4
1995	5.5	11.1	6.7	11.9	30.0	65.2

Source: UNCTAD (1995, 1996).

TABLE 3.4 *Top Three Countries Engaging in Outward FDI*

	1990	1991	1992	1993	1994	1995
First	Japan	Japan	U.S.A.	U.S.A.	U.S.A.	U.S.A.
$ million	48,024	42,619	38,978	68,978	45,648	95,509
Second	France	U.S.A.	France	U.K.	U.K.	U.K.
$ million	34,823	33,456	31,269	25,671	25,334	37,839
Third	U.S.A.	France	Germany	France	France	Germany
$ million	27,175	23,932	21,916	20,403	22,802	35,302

Source: UNCTAD (1996).

The emergence of Japan as a major source of FDI in the late 1980s was a most striking phenomenon of the period. In 1980, Japan's FDI outflow was less than 5 percent of the total of the 12 OECD countries. In the late 1980s, massive Japanese outflows increased her share to nearly 20 percent of yearly outflows from the major OECD countries, although the scale of these outflows was to decline after 1991 although she was still responsible for the largest FDI outflows in 1990 and 1991. In 1980, the U.K. undertook more outward FDI than Japan but by 1988 Japan had equalled the U.K., and in 1989, the peak in Japanese FDI outflows, she was to overtake even the U.S.A. in her FDI outflows. Japanese FDI was directed to Europe and the U.S.A. for the following reasons: (1) to avoid the protectionist pressures emerging in both areas; (2) to overcome the problem of the strong yen; (3) to overcome the very high Japanese production costs; and (4) as a progression to servicing those markets by host country assembly or manufacturing in place of exports.

However the most noticeable feature of the 1995 figures is the emergence of Germany as one of the leading outward investors overtaking both Japan and France and virtually equalling the U.K. Indeed, Germany was the largest investor in the U.S.A. in 1995 with $11 billion followed by the U.K. with $10 billion (UNCTAD, 1996). High costs at home were a factor, as with Japan, that contributed to more German foreign production as opposed to trade.

Destinations of FDI Outflows

Global interdependence is again highlighted by the destinations for FDI. FDI outflows by MNEs have flowed from developed economies into other developed economies and have been a factor that has helped sustain and improve the continued economic development of the host country. In the early and mid 1980s, developed economies received 69.4 percent of inflows, but after increasing to 81.6 percent in the late 1980s, the percentage that they received fell on an annual basis to between 58.8 percent and 67.8 percent in the 1992–95 period. Inflows of FDI into Central and Eastern Europe rose from virtually nothing in the 1980s to 3.8 percent in 1995. The corresponding figure for outflows in 1995 was 0.9 percent.

Regional Destinations of FDI Inflows

FDI Inflows into Developed Countries

In the early and mid 1980s, FDI inflows into developed countries divided roughly equally between two major regions—North America and Europe. Over this period, the U.S.A. received over half of total FDI inflows, although Western Europe was not far behind with 43 percent. This left only 6 percent available for all other developed economies. In 1991 70.7 percent of total FDI inflows into developed countries went into Western Europe, and in 1992 this figure rose even higher to 71.8 percent. The relatively large flows into Western Europe were probably sparked off by the introduction of the Single Market of the EU as non-European firms established a European presence by take-over of existing European firms or greenfield investment, in order to avoid the common external tariffs that this block was to introduce (see also Chapter 4 of this volume). Over the period 1990–95, the share of the U.S.A. has fluctuated from a low of 15.4 percent in 1992, the year in which the impact of the completion of the European Market was probably at its peak, to a high of 37.5 percent in 1994.

Developing Countries' Share of FDI

In the 1990s, developing countries claimed a larger share of annual FDI flows (see Table 3.3). In 1992 they had 30.0 percent of these inflows, but by 1994, as FDI in the industrialized world continued to

TABLE 3.5 *FDI Inflows into Developed Countries by Regions (percent of Total Inflows)*

	1980–85	1984–90	1991	1992	1993	1994	1995
Europe	43	47.6	70.7	71.8	59.8	51.5	56.9
U.S.A.	51	42.1	19.3	15.4	31.8	37.5	29.6
Others	6	10.3	10.0	12.8	8.3	11.0	13.5

Source: Derived from UNCTAD (1996).

fall, their share rose to 38.5 percent. However one developing country, China, is the second largest recipient of FDI after U.S.A. with inflows of $34 billion in 1994 compared with $49 billion into the U.S.A. Thus China received 40 percent of all FDI attracted by developing countries, so all the other developing countries had to share the remainder between them. But the figure for FDI into China needs to be treated with some caution as there is a significant difference between the proposed inflows into China and the actual inflows of money for actual start-up of projects. Additionally FDI inflows into developing countries are very unevenly distributed, with the Asia-Pacific region absorbing 70 percent of all inflows, whilst the ten most popular countries account for about two-thirds of total FDI stock in developing countries. Thus the distribution of FDI between developing countries is similar to that of developed countries in that a few receive the bulk of inbound MNE activity. While this is not surprising, as FDI is privately-owned funds looking for profit, it is still nevertheless a problem for those developing countries looking for FDI inflows as a means of assisting their economic development.

Recent Inflows of FDI

Recent Data on FDI Flows

Recent figures (UNCTAD, 1996) show that there has been a cyclical pattern in the volume of inward FDI flows into regions, with troughs in 1991 and 1992, and recovery coming in 1993 onwards. The EU, as already mentioned, had a greater share of these total inflows in 1990, 1991 and 1992, largely at the expense of NAFTA, and still attracts a larger proportion than either NAFTA or Asia. Flows into the newly industrializing countries of South and South East Asia remained at a relatively stable level throughout the period—at around 7 percent of total flows. China, however, dramatically increased her share in the 1990s. From an annual average figure over the period 1984–89 of 2.0 percent, which was to fall in 1990 to 1.7 percent, China was to rapidly increase her share between 1991 and 1994, so that by that latter year she was absorbing nearly 15 percent of the total world inflows of FDI—a truly remarkable achievement. Moreover aggregating the totals for the Asian Seven, Japan and China shows that in 1994 22.5 percent of total FDI inflows went into South and South East Asia—a total that virtually rivalled the inflows into the EU and NAFTA.

FDI Destinations within Europe

For many years, the European Union has received roughly 90 percent of all FDI coming into Europe. In the 1980s within Europe, the U.K.

TABLE 3.6 *Distribution of Flows of Inward FDI (percent)*

	1984–89 annual average	1990	1991	1992	1993	1994	1995
World $ million	115,370	203,812	157,773	168,122	207,937	225,660	314,933
EU	32.7	47.8	49.2	47.5	35.8	28.4	35.5
NAFTA	44.3	28.6	18.7	15.8	24.3	28.3	24.9
Asian 7*	5.0	6.9	9.7	7.9	7.8	7.2	7.1
Japan	0.1	0.9	1.1	2.1	0.1	0.4	0.0
China	2.0	1.7	2.8	6.6	13.2	14.9	11.9
Latin America and Caribbean	6.7	4.4	9.7	10.5	9.4	11.2	8.4

*Korea, Singapore, Taiwan, Malaysia, Indonesia, Philippines, Thailand.
Source: UNCTAD (1996).

has been consistently the largest recipient of FDI inflows, with shares ranging from nearly 40 to 25 percent. France has also been popular, but has attracted less than half of the amount that came into the U.K., with Spain attracting nearly as much as France. These three locations attracted, on average, 64 percent in the 1980s (see Table 3.7) and 62 percent in the 1990s (see Table 3.8). Thus a very uneven spread of inward FDI occurred within Europe.

Reasons for the Popularity of U.K. for FDI in 1980s

The U.K. has a language and business culture similar to that of the U.S.A., which is well-researched by both Japanese as well as American firms. Unlike the position in some other EU countries (particularly France), regional, financial and other incentives have not, for much of the time, been tied to the number of jobs created. The U.K.

TABLE 3.7 *National Shares of Western European FDI Inflows 1980–90 (percent)*

	1980–85	1986	1987	1988	1989	1990
France	15.9	16.3	14.1	15.6	13.7	14.3
Spain	11.7	17.2	12.6	12.9	11.2	15.6
U.K.	35.1	36.5	38.7	33.6	37.3	37.6
Total	62.7	70.0	65.4	62.1	62.2	67.5

Source: Derived from UNCTAD (1995).

TABLE 3.8 *National Shares of Western European FDI Inflows 1991–95 (percent)*

	1990	1992	1993	1994	1995
France	19.5	27.4	27.7	26.8	18.0
Spain	16.1	16.6	10.9	14.6	7.4
U.K.	20.9	18.7	19.4	15.7	26.7
Germany	5.2	3.0	0.4	4.7	8.3
Total	61.8	65.7	58.6	61.8	60.4

Source: UNCTAD (1996).

government has, moreover, imposed no restrictions on the size or scale of foreign ownership of U.K. companies. Labor costs have become virtually the lowest in Europe for an industrialized economy and, whilst labor costs are but a small part of total costs, their relatively low level in the U.K., together with a ready supply of a skilled and now, largely non-militant labor force, over the last decade or so, have been factors that have made the U.K. attractive to foreign MNEs. Indeed the U.K.'s good labor relations have been highlighted by some foreign MNEs as an important factor in influencing their locational choice in favor of the U.K. Thus the U.K. has been very successful in attracting much Japanese FDI as well as American and other European, and latterly, Asian FDI. Japanese firms aim to increase their global output from their U.K. based plants very considerably so as to service EU markets by production in Europe rather than by exports. Indeed, at times, U.K.-made auto components have been exported back to Japan. Japanese quality control methods, introduced into the U.K., ensured quality standards were maintained, whilst the strength of the yen against sterling ensured that the price of these U.K. components was lower than that of identical ones made in Japan. In the auto sector, for example, two companies (Toyota and Honda) are raising their combined total investment in the U.K. to more than £2 billion with the U.K. set to be the fastest growing car producer in Western Europe in the second half of the 1990s.

In the 1990s, the U.K. seems to have lost much of its attractiveness to inward FDI, for by 1990 France had virtually equalled the U.K.'s share, and, in 1991, 1993 and 1994, was to overtake the U.K. and attract into France a significantly larger share of FDI coming into the EU than did the U.K. The anti-European statements and views of the U.K. government, and many of its supporters, may well have diverted FDI into countries of the EU more firmly committed to the principles and practices of the Single Market and the single currency.

Regional Distribution of Inward FDI

The world stock figures of inward FDI show the effect on the total stock of the continuing inflows of FDI into different geographical areas. In 1980 Western Europe was the host region to 41.6 percent of world stock of inward FDI, North America had 28.5 percent and the other developed countries together had only 7.5 percent. This clearly demonstrates that, in the 1970s, MNEs had been investing heavily in Western Europe rather than North America and had thus built up a large stock of assets in Europe. FDI inflows into North America, from both Europe (especially from the U.K. but in 1995 also from Germany) and also from Japan have significantly increased. However, the North American share of the total world stock of inward FDI has remained relatively stable and has followed a relatively similar pattern and level to that of the whole of the group of developing countries. At the same time, the bulk of the North American stock is in one country, the U.S.A., whilst amongst developing countries this total has to be shared out amongst many countries. By contrast, the total share in developing countries is slowly increasing, although only very slowly.

Central and Eastern Europe have got a very long way to go before they have a significant share in this world stock. Indeed, over time, while changes in the annual flows do influence the stock levels within regions, it will take several years and a significant change in attitude by MNEs before the current imbalance is significantly changed. But recent figures show that FDI flows into Central and Eastern Europe accelerated in 1995 so that its stock of FDI rose by 60 percent to $45.7 billion at the end of 1995, compared with $28.7 billion at the end of 1994. Whilst some of these recent inflows are for servicing local markets, some is FDI that is going into Central instead of into Western Europe, especially the EU. If such flows continue, they will have a

TABLE 3.9 *World Stock of Inward FDI by Regions (percent of total)*

	1980	1985	1990	1994	1995
Western Europe	41.6	33.3	44.2	41.5	40.9
North America	28.5	33.9	29.6	26.0	25.6
Other developed countries	7.5	6.0	6.2	6.3	6.2
Total	77.5	73.2	80.0	73.8	72.7
Developing countries	22.5	26.8	19.9	25.3	26.1
Central and Eastern Europe	0.0	0.0	0.1	0.8	1.2
Total	100.0	100.0	100.0	100.0	100.0
Total ($ millions)	481,907	734,928	1,716,850	2,342,182	2,657,859

Source: UNCTAD (1996).

greater effect in that the east's share will increase and the west's share will decrease, thus narrowing the gap. But there is still a very large gap and a long way to go.

FDI Inflows into Europe

FDI Inflows from Asia

For companies from Asia looking to internationalize their operations, Europe is one of the preferred locations. Japan has done so for some time but now companies from South Korea, Taiwan and Malaysia are also coming to Europe, especially as European governments play an active role in attracting foreign investors. So FDI inflows into the EU from Asia seem set to increase as firms such as Daewoo and Samsung of South Korea and Chang Hwa of Taiwan undertake FDI within the EU in order to service the Single Market from within rather than by exports. North America, however, remains the largest contributor of FDI into Europe.

FDI Inflows into Central and Eastern Europe

Central and Eastern Europe are not yet major players for inflows and outflows of FDI. In 1995 total inflows into this region ($12.1 billion) accounted for only 3 percent of world-wide inflows and was lower than the inflow into Singapore, whilst the region's stock of FDI ($31.8 billion) was similar to that of Sweden. However the situation is changing since FDI inflows into the 15 former communist states doubled in 1995 compared with an increase of 57.0 percent over the preceeding two years. Moreover recent announcements by firms of their expansion plans suggest that this picture is changing. Until recently, despite promises of opportunities and growth in Central and Eastern Europe, American and European firms have advanced with caution and Japanese firms even more so—hence the low figures for FDI inflows and stocks. Yet now the world's leading firms, especially in the motor car industry, are increasingly confident about this region's future. There are, at present, very large expansion programs taking place within this one industry which will very significantly increase the output of cars for both export to western Europe, but also for local markets. To finance such expansion, very large amounts of FDI has started to go into Central and Eastern Europe, and will increase significantly in the next few years as MNEs (such as General Motors, Fiat and Volkswagen) implement their expansion plans. However Daewoo of South Korea—a recent new entrant into the European market—has very ambitious plans and aims to use Central and Eastern

Europe as a base from which to service all of Europe in which it is one of the most dynamic and growing companies in the whole of the industry. Initially this may involve using the region as an export platform to service Western European markets from a low-cost production base, although some output will be for local sale, and, as local income gradually increases, so too will local sales.

Ownership of the World's Stock of FDI

In 1980, five countries (France, Germany, Japan, the U.K. and the U.S.A.) owned 75.3 percent of the total stock of outward direct investment. This is hardly surprising as these countries are the parents of the majority of MNEs operating in the world economy and undertaking FDI in foreign locations. In 1985 the U.S.A.'s share was 36.6 percent with the U.K. owning 14.6 percent. By 1994 the U.S.A.'s share had declined to 25.3 percent and the U.K.'s share was now at 11.7 percent while Japan had emerged with 11.2 percent. This was only a relative decline for the U.S.A. and the U.K. for, as other countries increased their total outward FDI, it is difficult for any one country to maintain its share of the ever expanding total. Inward FDI stock figures reveal that, in 1995, 43 percent was located in Europe, 27 percent in North America and 6 percent in other developed countries, making a total world inward stock figure in developed countries of 76 percent. Moreover, within these developed countries FDI stocks were concentrated in the Triad of the U.S.A., the EU and Japan, with 39 percent of inward stock and 44 percent of outward FDI stocks.

Regional Trading Blocks and FDI

Types of Regional Trading Blocks

Economic integration within members of regional trading blocks (RTBs) can take a variety of forms. Of the three RTBs that have

TABLE 3.10 *World Outward FDI Stock by Home Country (percent)*

Home country	1980	1985	1990	1994	1995
France	4.6	5.4	6.5	7.6	7.4
Germany	8.4	8.7	8.0	8.2	8.6
Japan	3.7	6.5	12.2	11.8	11.2
U.K.	15.7	14.6	13.7	11.7	11.7
U.S.A.	42.9	36.6	25.8	25.3	25.8
As a percentage of total	75.3	71.8	67.2	64.6	64.7

Source: UNCTAD (1996).

emerged so far, the EU has developed furthest along the continuum since the creation of the Single Market. Since 1992 all trade and non-trade barriers to trade have been abolished, thus allowing the free movement of goods, people and money within this single market. The degree of intra-European trade, and economic integration, will be further assisted by monetary union that will occur if, and when, the single currency is introduced within Europe at, or soon after, 1999. Thus Europe will move further along the continuum.

NAFTA does allow the free movement of goods between member countries but this does not extend to people and thus is a very different extent of economic integration. However, NAFTA does allow firms to profit from different factor endowments between countries within this RTB, and so prompt a more efficient use of most but not all factors of production (not labor) within this RTB.

The Asia Pacific Economic Co-operation (APEC) block is a much looser form of economic co-operation and is more, at present, 'a consensus to achieve certain goals', although there is a binding commitment to achieve those goals. APEC has agreed to become operational for developed countries within the region by the year 2010, and by 2020 for developing countries, although much co-operation does already take place. There is an agreement to establish free trade within the region by 2020 at the latest, whilst much FDI has and will continue within the region as MNEs of members undertake FDI within the regional block.

That a country may be a member of more than one RTB is illustrated by the U.S.A. and Canada which are members of both NAFTA and APEC. Within an RTB, governments of member countries agree to harmonize their macro-economic policies in the cause of regional economic stability. Thus having these two RTBs as 'overlapping sets' will mean that, as they are responsible for such a large percentage of world trade and world FDI, such regional economic stabilization between such a large number of countries will greatly assist global economic stabilization.

Effects and Features of RTBs

Economic theory suggests that the creation of an RTB will have an effect on both trade and FDI decisions within the RTB by member as well as non-member countries' firms.

A feature of RTBs is that they are intended to promote cross or inter-country trade and mobility of factor services from and within member countries by fostering a more market-orientated pattern of intra-regional resource allocation. As Chapter 4 will show, the abolition of the trade and non-trade barriers within the Single Market of the

EU has helped to stimulate intra-European trade and has led to cross-border rationalization of production as European firms react to these changes. Trade is influenced by the fact that firms that have some competitive advantage will now find that, as a result of the creation of free trade within the RTB, they are able to export to other member countries' markets, access to which was previously restricted by tariffs, quotas and administrative controls. Exports and trade within the RTB are thus likely to increase. Indeed, the Cecchini Report (1988) emphasized that the abolition of tariff and non-tariff barriers to trade within the (then) European Community were an important element that would create increased prosperity and employment within the RTB of the Single Market. Firms which have the ability to compete in European markets will thus find their opportunities for capturing new outlets within the RTB have increased. Thus there will be a 'trade creation' effect within the RTB as these more efficient firms now trade with other markets within the RTB formerly closed off by tariffs and non-tariff barriers.

The internal market may also require additional cross-border investment by these more successful MNEs in order to capture scale, size and specialization economies. In order to reap the full benefits of scale compatible with the technological advances, there will be an incentive to expand as fully as possible the plants in those countries which have the largest markets which need not be in the home country of the firm. Thus the 'trade creation' effect of the RTB will have an effect, not only on the size of investment by firms operating within the RTB, but also on the actual location of both investment and thus production. This will, of course, impact on trade flows. Existing firms within the RTB will rationalize their European value-added activity so as to source the RTBs market from optimal locations when previously a number of locations were used to overcome the now abolished internal tariffs and quotas.

The creation of the RTB will also affect the decision and timing of FDI decisions by MNEs whose countries are not members of the RTB. Such an FDI decision may well be brought forward now that the size of the unified market within the RTB has increased. Moreover the actual location decision of the non-member country MNE may also be influenced as the FDI can now be allocated in a more optimal manner. The common external tariff of the RTB against firms of non-member countries' imports will then induce some import-substitution FDI as non-member firms either acquire local firms or start-up a 'greenfield' operation in order to keep their former export markets within the RTB. Chang Hwa of Taiwan—the world's largest producer of monitors for personal computers—formerly sourced the various member countries of the EU from its manufacturing bases in

South East Asia. With the massive expansion in the demand for personal computers both now and in the near future, and with the tariff now imposed on imports into the EU, together with the possible additional anti-dumping duties that were being talked about for this product, this firm announced that it was going to service the growing EU market for PC monitors from within the EU and establish a plant in the U.K.

Mergers and acquisitions will often be an attractive means of doing this since these capture local brands, protect existing market shares and acquire new fixed assets and human resources for the acquiring firm. Thus a takeover is a speedy and therefore attractive method by a MNE that wishes to enter quickly into the RTB so as to protect its position and market share which previously came from exports.

So prior to, and continuing after the creation of an RTB, there will be an 'initial surge' of FDI into the region as MNEs from non-member countries enter in order now to be classified as local. Thus the location decisions of the MNEs have been affected by the creation of the RTBs. However it may merely have brought forward an FDI decision that would otherwise have occurred due to the size of the separate member countries' markets. In the EU, for example, the creation of the Single Market led to the appearance of one unified market in place of the 12 (and now 15) separate ones that existed before. Thus it would be entirely logical for MNEs to switch to FDI and away from exporting in the new enlarged market that now exists within Europe. So, in summary, RTBs will have an impact on the amount and direction of trade that takes place between member countries, the scale and location of their investment decisions, and also on the timing and location of the FDI decisions made by foreign MNEs now producing within the RTBs.

FDI between and within RTBs

Much of the existing flows of FDI take place between and within the three pivotal RTBs in the world. The U.S.A. is the dominant force in NAFTA whilst Japan seems to hold sway in APEC and the Franco-German alliance is the dominant force within the EU.

FDI within RTBs. Much intra-RTB FDI has and is still taking place as member countries undertake FDI in other countries of the RTB. For example, over the period 1980–84, 44.1 percent of EU FDI outflows went to non-member countries, with only 5.2 percent being intra-EU FDI. But over the period 1985–89 intra-EU FDI increased to 12.4 percent of total EU outflows. Whilst this indicates that intra-EU FDI had more than doubled in this short time, nevertheless, the EU was not an area in which European firms invested very much. However, by the early 1990s intra-EU FDI annual outflows were to total 24 percent of the total outflows undertaken by EU firms. This illustrates the large amount of FDI undertaken within Europe by European firms as they rationalize production in the run-up to the creation of the Single Market in 1992. Within APEC also much intra-RTB FDI is occurring as firms from Japan and Taiwan relocate away from their high-cost home countries into other lower-cost locations within APEC, such as China, Vietnam and Thailand. FDI in APEC in 1994 totaled $145.7 billion of which over half (55.9 percent) came from other APEC nations (JETRO, 1996) which clearly shows the size and importance to this RTB of the flows of FDI that are occurring within the block. It is also worth noting that these FDI flows within APEC are occurring before there has been a firm agreement to allow the free movement of capital within the RTB, which is an essential characteristic of any RTB.

FDI between RTBs. FDI between RTBs is still occurring and seems likely to remain and even increase as MNEs in North America view Europe as the most important location for expansion in the future, especially in consumer goods industries while European MNEs view the U.S.A. with similar favor (UNCTAD, 1996).

The developing countries in Asia—the core of the APEC block—form the most significant developing region in terms of FDI (UNCTAD and EC, 1996).

FDI inflows into developing Asia reached $59 billion in 1994, an increase of 84 percent on the 1992 figure. The result of these recent large FDI inflows into the region is shown in that between 1988 and 1993, developing Asia almost doubled its total stock of inward FDI—an increase that no other developing region achieved. Now almost half

TABLE 3.11 *FDI Inflows by the Triad into Developing Asia ($ million and percent)*

	1985–87		1990–93	
	Value	Share of total FDI	Value	Share of total FDI
EU	697	11.9	3,501	10.5
Japan	1,558	27.2	5,316	15.9
U.S.A.	1,299	22.7	3,686	11.0
Triad total	3,536	61.7	12,502	37.4
All countries	5,731	100.0	33,473	100.0

Source: UNCTAD and EC (1996).

of the total stock of FDI in developing countries is located within this region. Japan, the U.S.A. and the EU are the predominant sources of these FDI inflows. However the EU has the smallest stock amongst the Triad of FDI in developing Asia. In 1993 this was 12.9 percent of the total stock, lower than that of the U.S.A. and half of Japan's share of the region's FDI stock. Japan's share of inward FDI into developing Asian countries amounted to 21.0 percent of the region's total stock as Japan relocated some of its industries to lower-cost locations within Asia (UNCTAD and EC, 1996).

One might conclude that the three trading blocks that have emerged have not significantly altered the existing FDI scenario but have supported and strengthened it. With the common external tariffs that now face exporters to NAFTA and the EU, firms that previously exported to these markets may well now undertake export-substituting FDI in order to preserve their former export markets there. The figures for FDI inflows into both areas before their creation do support this argument. This would also support the contention that the creation of these blocks will further increase the importance of FDI compared with trade, as those firms that wish to sell within these emerging blocks will find it easier to retain and also gain market share by producing there rather than by exporting.

Annual average FDI inflow figures into the U.S.A., Canada and Mexico—the countries that were to become founder members of NAFTA—in the late 1980s averaged 44.3 percent of total world FDI inflows (see Table 3.6). But of this total inflow into the region the U.S.A. took 86.0 percent. Over the 1990s this proportion was to fall steadily, reaching its lowest level in 1993 when only 66.4 percent of the FDI inflows went into the U.S.A., but the U.S.A.'s share recovered in 1994 to 77.9 percent and in 1995 was 76.8 percent. Inflows into

TABLE 3.12 *FDI Stocks by the Triad in Developing Asia ($ millions and percent)*

	1980		1985		1993	
	Value	Share of total FDI	Value	Share of total FDI	Value	Share of total FDI
EU	4,779	16.4	9,058	17.2	29,846	12.9
Japan	7,313	25.1	13,090	24.9	48,607	21.0
U.S.A.	4,657	16.0	11,099	21.1	32,617	14.1
Triad total	16,748	57.5	33,248	63.2	111,070	48.1
All countries	29,115	100.0	52,645	100.0	230,933	100.0

Source: UNCTAD and EC (1996).

TABLE 3.13 *FDI Inflows into Countries in NAFTA ($ millions and percent)*

	1984–89 annual average	1990	1991	1992	1993	1994	1995
U.S.A.	86.0	82.2	76.4	66.4	81.4	77.9	76.8
$ million	43,938	47,918	22,020	17,580	41,125	49,760	60,236
Mexico	4.8	4.4	16.1	16.6	8.7	12.5	8.9
$ million	2,436	2,549	4,742	4,393	4,389	7,978	6,984
Canada	9.2	13.4	7.5	17.0	9.9	9.6	14.3
$ million	4,718	7,855	2,740	4,517	4,997	6,043	11,182

Source: UNCTAD (1996).

Mexico started from a low base point in the late 1980s being only 4.8 percent of the total. But in 1991 its share dramatically increased to 16.1 percent, and increased still further in 1992 to 16.6 percent. Indeed, from 1991 onwards, FDI inflows into Mexico were to become double the amounts that flowed in during the late 1980s, whilst by 1994 the value of Mexican FDI inflows was to double again. This indicates that, whilst the U.S.A. always attracts the vast majority of FDI going into this region, Mexico has become a more attractive location and is now rivalling Canada as a host for FDI inflows. Thus there has been some slight diversion effect on FDI inflows, although not strong. Moreover some of the inflows may well have gone in irrespective of NAFTA membership. FDI inflows into Mexico, however, are likely to increase still further in the future due to its lower-cost advantages compared with the other existing members of NAFTA, although any enlargement will again influence the choice of host country location within this RTB.

A recent change in FDI flows has been the growing importance of South, East and South East Asia. Very significant amounts of FDI are now flowing into this region—the ASEAN group have attracted some inflows.

The emergence of China as a major recipient of FDI since the late 1970s has been the major change within the region that has already been highlighted. By 1995 China was estimated to have attracted a stock of foreign investment of $129.0 billion and is currently attracting more than one-third of all FDI annual inflows into developing economies. This trend is likely to continue as China continues to industrialize and prosper with the assistance of FDI and foreign technology.

The emergence of India as a major force on the industrial stage in

Asia, especially in selected sectors of industry (e.g. the information technology industry and soon the auto industry) is also a feature of note in the region. Indian inward investment has risen from around $150 million in the late 1980s and early 1990s to $1,750 million in 1995. Many of the inflows of FDI at present going into India are, in fact, coming from other parts of APEC, particularly Asia. South Korean companies are planning to invest more than $3 billion over the next five years and India is likely to join China, Vietnam and Mexico as a prime destination for South Korean companies. Firms in the electronics, petrochemical, and construction industries all have ambitious expansion programs in India, while both Hyundai and Daewoo are to build auto plants there at a cost of $6 billion. Such Asian FDI inflows are already due to occur in India—and they will almost certainly be followed by many others as India continues on its rapid path of industrialization. At present, India is not a member of APEC but, as its industrialization continues to quicken, it will surely apply for membership and be welcomed into this regional trading block. FDI in India is now occurring as MNEs start to undertake additional local production in order to service this vast domestic market for goods, such as personal computers and motor cars, both products which are estimated to be due for massive growth there.

The growth in importance of the ASEAN group of countries into which FDI is now flowing is also worthy of comment. Whilst some of this is export-generating FDI intended to benefit from lower wage costs (e.g. Texas Instruments going to Thailand to make semi-conductors for its own world-wide use), much is also to service local markets by local assembly and manufacturing.

So FDI within APEC is occurring on quite a significant scale as the latest White Paper by JETRO emphasizes (JETRO, 1996).

The Asia-Pacific Economic Co-operation (APEC) trading block is planning to become operational for developed countries as a regional block by 2010, and by 2020 for developing countries. However, considerable trade liberalization has, and is, taking place there. Within this region, the U.S.A. and Japan are currently the economically dominant countries. The recent growth in importance of this region to American trade is easily overlooked. But the future economic strength and power of China is also a force to be reckoned with. As we have seen, FDI is still flooding into China in considerable quantities, while China's foreign trade is estimated to grow by 12 percent annually over the next five years and to exceed $400 billion by year 2000. So China is set to emerge very quickly as a major economic force within APEC and the world economy, especially in certain industries. China, under the Car Industry Policy announced in late 1994, signalled her intention to become a major player in the auto industry by the year

2010. By that year China plans to be producing between 3.5–4.0 million autos, of which a significant proportion will be for export. China plans to use foreign MNEs to assist in this expansion—via joint ventures—so FDI inflows into China seem set to increase even more in the future as this policy is implemented. However, the very strength, power and economic rivalry of the U.S.A., Japan and China may stop APEC achieving the level of integration that has been achieved in the EU. So one major change that is already occurring that will increase in size is the re-direction of FDI on an increasing size to the Asian part of APEC, as this part of the regional trading block continues to expand partly through intra-block FDI.

Non-Asian FDI inflows into Asia to service the regional market are still increasing and will continue to do so. Indeed the main reason quoted by managers for investing abroad in the Arthur Anderson report 'International Investment towards year 2000' (1995) was to improve access to foreign markets and not to cut production costs by using Asia as a low-cost production center. The enormous potential and growth of the region is a most compelling factor that will continue to attract larger shares of the world flows of FDI into this region. Over time, this will affect the overall global distribution of the world's stock of FDI. Intra-Asian FDI flows are also likely to increase significantly. In 1993, outflows from Japan into South, East and South East Asia were $30 billion, while the reverse flow was $4 billion. The emerging ASEAN countries are now attracting more Asian FDI. Toyota and Mitsubishi have both announced plans to establish plants in Vietnam, while Nissan started assembly operations in Indonesia in mid-1996.

FDI outflows from Asia have so far originated mostly from Japan, as protectionist pressures in her markets in the U.S.A. and Europe, the strength of the yen and the sheer size of these markets made foreign assembly and production the rational decision. However now this same path, following the 'flying geese' pattern identified by Ozawa (1992), is being taken by firms from other more recently industrialized countries of South East Asia, especially South Korea and Malaysia. Thus, as more Asian countries look to internationalize their operations, Europe is one of their prefered locations. Just as Japan undertook FDI in Europe to avoid anti-dumping dumping duties on its electronic and other exports to Europe, Asian firms are now following the same path. The Bank for International Settlements estimated Asian FDI into Europe to be $73.6 billion in 1991; $72.2 billion in 1992; $67.0 billion in 1993; and $62.4 billion in 1994. The annual average between 1976 and 1980 was $14.3 billion, which grew to $60.5 billion between 1986 and 1990.

The Arthur Anderson report (1995) highlights that, along with Asia, Latin America and Eastern and Central Europe were named as priority areas for FDI. The U.S.A., Western Europe and Japan were rated as less important than in the first half of the 1990s. This report surveyed the views of 260 business managers in the U.S.A., Europe and Asia while the Ernst & Young survey of investment patterns found that 20 percent of U.S.A. FDI going into Europe was now going into Eastern Europe. Firms in the motor car industry are investing heavily there. In Poland, which has the largest car industry in Central Europe, many of the major world players are already established and have ambitious plans for expansion. Privatizations have brought in two major players (Fiat and Volkswagen) and, with the expansions planned by Daewoo, it is estimated that FDI will flow into Europe from South East Asia in considerable quantities.

The planned enlargement of the EU by the incorporation of new members (e.g. Poland and the Czech Republic) is also likely to affect FDI flows. Whilst current flows of FDI into Central and Eastern Europe are small, they are also concentrated into a few countries, some of which are the most developed and stable, and are due to join the EU shortly. So the surges going into Poland can be viewed in part as a strategy to establish a local market share and a cheaper EU location from which to service other parts of the EU. This is particularly true for Volkswagen which is faced at home by the highest European labor costs in Europe, while Fiat have decided to use Poland, rather than Italy, as a location to implement their new strategy of achieving a greater degree of globalization of their business activities.

The planned expansion of NAFTA is to include Chile. In 1994, out of a total FDI inflow into Chile of $2,533 million, 59 percent ($1,502 million) came from NAFTA, with the remainder coming from APEC.

Future enlargement of both blocks is also likely. The EU will soon probably include most of Central and Eastern Europe and Turkey, and perhaps some of the North African countries bordering on the Mediterranean (e.g. Egypt which is an emerging industrial country in certain industrial sectors). FDI is already flowing into several of these countries, especially Turkey, which is the fastest growing economy in the region. Moreover Turkey, from 1st January 1996, has a Customs Union with the EU and has adopted its common external tariffs from this date, so has effectively become part of the Single Market. Further inflows of FDI into Turkey and other Mediterranean countries are likely to lead to a diversion effect of FDI from Western Europe and the U.K. to these areas. Further expansion of the EU may occur if the discussions between the EU and the representatives of the Mediterranean and Middle Eastern countries, held in November 1995, led to the successful introduction of a free trade block by the year 2000. The Middle Eastern countries are not at present members of the current regional trading blocks and, while geography might dictate a link with

Europe, history and religion would push them more towards APEC.

NAFTA may well also expand to incorporate much of Central and South America over a longer time horizon, whilst APEC will surely quickly aim to accept India as a member. Enlargement of all three regional trading blocks will inevitably increase the FDI flows within blocks as each becomes bigger, whilst FDI flows between blocks will also increase—again at the expense of trade.

Conclusions

FDI flows are likely to continue to flow between the regional trading blocks, although the countries which provide this investment and the countries to which it goes are likely to change over time. FDI outflows from South East Asia are starting now. Very soon this area will become a major source of FDI, and the ascendancy of those mature OECD countries which in the past provided most of the FDI will soon be over. MNEs are likely to continue to undertake FDI within the regional blocks in order to continue to benefit from regional comparative advantage and also to overcome the external tariffs that are imposed on imports into the trading block.

References

Arthur Anderson Report (1995) International Investment towards year 2000. For French Government, Paris.

Business Monitor (1994) Overseas Direct Investment. HMSO, U.K.

CECCHINI, P. (1988) *The European Challenge 1992—the benefits of a Single Market*. European Commission, Brussels.

DUNNING, J. H. (1993) *Multinational Enterprises and the Global Economy*. Addison Wesley, Wokingham, Berkshire.

DUNNING, J. H. (1996) *European Market Programme and Inbound FDI*, Reading Mimeo (see also Chapter 4 of this volume).

EDEN, L. (ed.) (1994) *Multinational Enterprises in North America*, Calgary University Press, Calgary.

Japanese Trade and Research Organisation (JETRO) (1996) *White Paper on FDI*. Tokyo. Internet address: http://www.jetro.go.jp

OZAWA, T. (1992) Foreign Investment and Economic Development, *Transnational Corporations*, Vol. 1, 27–54.

United Nations Conference on Trade and Development (UNCTAD) and European Commission (1996) *Investing in Asia's Dynamism*, European Commission, Brussels.

United Nations Conference on Trade and Development (UNCTAD) (1995) *World Investment Report 1995, TNCs as Engines for Growth*, UN, Geneva and New York.

United Nations Conference on Trade and Development (UNCTAD) (1996) *World Investment Report 1996, Investment, Trade and International Policy Arrangements*, UN, Geneva and New York.

4

The European Internal Market Program and Inbound Foreign Direct Investment[1]

JOHN H. DUNNING

This chapter reviews the changing inward FDI position of the European Community (now the European Union) over the past twenty years. After describing the growth of intra-ED FDI since 1985, the chapter considers the empirical validity of four hypotheses, drawn from FDI theory, which examine the likely affect of the completion of the internal market on intra-EC and exra-EC trade and FDI flows and the relationship between the two.

Introduction: European Integration Prior to 1985

During the late 1960s and 1970s, there were several scholarly attempts to assess the impact of the European Common Market (ECM)—the first phase of economic integration within the European Community (EC)[2]—on foreign direct investment (FDI), both between member states and from countries outside the EC to countries within it.[3] Most of these studies were longitudinal and used time series, rather than cross-sectional, statistics. Although their results were sensitive to the data and the econometric models chosen,[4] all supported the proposition that, while the removal of intra-EC tariffs, and the establishment of a common external tariff, increased both intra- and extra-EC FDI—and sometimes significantly so—,[5] other determinants of FDI (e.g. market size, market growth, relative factor costs, agglomeration economies, etc.) were at least as important, if not more so, particularly once the initial (and sometimes once-for-all) effects of the ECM had worn off.[6]

Furthermore, the studies showed that the impact of European integration (hereafter called Mark 1 integration) on FDI was strongly conditional on the type of investment being considered; and also on the time frame of the analysis. Thus, while the direct, or first order, impact of the removal of tariffs was to reduce *defensive import substituting* FDI, and to replace it by exports from the investing country, it also led to the restructuring of existing intra-EC FDI, wherever its trade creating consequences stimulated a geographical concentration of production in those activities in which foreign-owned firms had a competitive advantage. The indirect, or second order, effects of integration (e.g. increased competitiveness of local firms, augmented income levels and market growth), were shown to lead to more *rationalized* (or efficiency seeking) and *offensive* (or market seeking) FDI—particularly by non-EC multinational enterprises (MNEs) in the EC. While the former was also associated with an increase in trade (particularly intra-EC trade), the effects of the latter were more ambiguous.[6]

An examination of the FDI data for the period 1957–85[7] reveals the following main points:

(1) Although, as a proportion of their total outbound FDI, that of both EC countries and of non-EC countries—particularly the U.S.—rose quite substantially,[8] non-EC MNEs continued to account for the majority of FDI in the EC.[9]

(2) Around 90 percent of inbound extra- and intra-EC FDI prior to 1985 was concentrated in the 'core' countries of the EC;[10] and, much of this (a rough estimate would be about three-fifths) was within a 500 mile radius of Frankfurt. This geographical pattern of economic activity was broadly similar for both extra- and intra-EC FDI; although the latter tended to favor the U.K. and Germany relatively less, and Belgium and France relatively more.

(3) In the early 1980s, about one-third of all FDI from EC countries was directed to other EC countries; this compared with 35 percent of US FDI and 15 percent of Japanese FDI[11] to all EC countries. The total share of the inbound FDI stock in the EC originating from other EC countries (i.e. the EC's FDI-intensity ratio) was generally higher than its share of worldwide FDI (excluding the FDI stock of the investor country).[12] Corresponding trade-intensity ratios for intra- and extra-EC transactions for the same year were very similar, although a little higher for intra-EC transactions[13] (UNCTAD, 1994; EAG, 1996).

(4) There are few reliable data on the impact of Mark 1 integration on the sectoral distribution of FDI in the EC. The best we have relate to the sales of U.S. manufacturing subsidiaries in the EC. Here, there is some suggestion that the growth of such sales between 1972 (the year before the U.K. acceded to the Community) and 1985 was most

marked in those manufacturing and service sectors subject to plant economies of scale; where the U.S. firms had the most marked competitive (or ownership specific) advantages; where the pre-EC, intra-EC tariffs were highest; and where the post-EC barriers to U.S.–EC trade were the most severe.[14] More generally, Eurostat (1995) data show that, by the mid-1980s, nearly 80 percent of all extra-FDI in manufacturing was accounted for by the metal based fabricating sectors (notably transport equipment, electrical and electronic equipment and machinery); although, already by that time, the most pronounced sectoral concentration of such investment was directed to infra-structural services, notably finance, banking, insurance, and trade supporting activities.[15]

Throughout the 1970s and early 1980s, the sectoral composition of intra-EC FDI was rather different.[16] Although, by the mid-1980s, as with extra EC-FDI, the tertiary sector (including real estate) accounted for the bulk of new FDI flows,[17] within the manufacturing sector, the metal based sectors[18] accounted for only 42 percent. The fact that some 30 percent of intra-EC MNE activity was directed to the chemical industry alone suggests that the reorganization and rationalization of production associated with Mark 1 integration was more evident in the processing than in the fabricating sectors.[19]

(5) There is some casual evidence that, apart from some extra-EC defensive import substituting FDI, most kinds of intra- and extra-EC FDI were either trade neutral or trade enhancing. Molle and Morsink (1991) found that, over the period 1973–83, there was a direct correlation between the intensity of intra-EC trade and FDI flows, once the trade intensity index had reached a certain level. U.S. data suggest that the ratio between the sales of U.S. manufacturing affiliates in the EC and exports from the U.S. to the EC increased markedly in the 1960s—and much more so than in the U.K., which did not join the EC until 1973. Thereafter, this ratio fell from a peak of 5.8 to 4.9 in 1977 and to 4.0 in 1985[20] (UN, 1993a).

However, perhaps the most dramatic affect of Mark 1 integration was on intra-EC trade between the affiliates of U.S. firms. In 1957, 85 percent of all sales by such affiliates were to domestic purchasers, and 1 percent were exported to the U.S.; almost all of the rest, *viz.*, 14 percent, were to other EC countries or the U.K. By 1966, the exports to countries other than the U.S. had risen to 26.7 percent, by 1977 to 38.3 percent, and by 1982 to 45.7 percent (UN, 1993a); and in both 1977 and 1982, 69 percent of these exports were between U.S. affiliates (i.e. intra-firm exports). Other data suggest that intra-EC trade was most pronounced between the core European countries,[21] and was particularly concentrated in sectors characterized by plant economies of scale and (relatively) low or declining transport costs. By the mid-1980s, the rationalization and integration of U.S. MNEs in the EC was well advanced—and considerably more so than that of their EC counterparts.

In short, the first phase of European integration was accompanied by a substantial net increase in both EC related intra- and extra-FDI and trade flows. However, the largest increases in FDI were from countries outside the EC; and the evidence strongly suggests U.S. (and later Japanese) MNEs were able to take advantage of the removal of tariff barriers, and surmount the transaction costs of the remaining non-tariff barriers better than their EC equivalents.[22] Although, during the period 1958 to 1985, there was a sizeable increase in intra-EC FDI,[23] intra-EC trade grew much faster—and the great majority of this was between, rather than within firms. By contrast, U.S. FDI in the EC increased more rapidly than U.S. exports for the first twenty years of the ECM, after which (until 1985 at least) exports rose more rapidly. But, during this period, the most impressive trading performance was recorded by the EC affiliates of U.S. MNEs. The fact that between 1957 and 1982 the *share* of exports to non-U.S. countries (mainly European) of their total sales rose three-fold and over two-thirds of this trade was *intra*-firm, points strongly to the complementary interplay between *extra*-EC FDI and *intra*-EC trade.[24]

European Integration: 1985 to Date

Some Theoretical Insights

In 1985, the Internal Market Program (IMP) was initiated by the European Commission in Brussels. The intention of the program was to eliminate all remaining non-tariff barriers to trade in goods, services and assets between the member countries of the EC by the mid-1990s. These barriers were classified into four main groups, *viz.*, discriminatory purchasing procedures, border controls, differences in technical standards and differences in fiscal duties.[25] Between 1985 and the late 1990s, it is anticipated that some 319 directives, intended to remove or drastically reduce these barriers, will be put into effect by the (then) twelve Member States.

Like the eradication of tariff barriers, that of the non-tariff barriers is expected to have different consequences for individual countries, industrial sectors and firms; and also, indeed, for the modalities of production and servicing markets. These differences essentially are to do with the production and transaction costs of doing business. For example, the principal consequence of Mark 1 integration was to allow member countries to better exploit their dynamic trading advantages, based both on their natural and created resource endowments and economies of scale. It also helped promote the common ownership of cross-border activities in FDI intensive sectors (Markusen, 1995). Insofar as the transaction costs of non-tariff barriers are different from those of tariff barriers[26] and differentially affect countries, sectors and firms, it may be expected that their impact on the modalities of production and servicing markets may also be different.

However, before proceeding to consider how EC-1992 has affected, and is affecting, FDI in the EC, it might be helpful to rehearse the kind of expectations suggested by received economic analysis. Economists normally draw upon two sets of analytical tools to analyze the consequences of economic integration,[27] *viz.*, the theory of trade, and the theory of FDI, or more particularly the theory of international production.[28] These should be regarded as complementary, rather than competing, theories. The theory of trade is essentially concerned with the effects of economic integration on the *location* of economic activity, and the extent to which particular markets in the integrated area are serviced by exports or by local production. However for the most part, received trade theory pays only scant attention either to the nationality of ownership of economic activity, or to the possibility that such activity might be of part a diversified or multinational firm.[29] In other words, the particular characteristics of *foreign* owned (as opposed to *domestically* owned) production are not (and have never been) of much interest to trade theorists.

By contrast, the theory of FDI is primarily interested in the consequences of regional integration for FDI, either into or out of the Member States; and whether this takes the form of extra- or intra-regional FDI. While, in so doing, it draws upon the theory of trade and location, it is also concerned with identifying the consequences of the *foreign* ownership of economic activity within the integrated region on the structure and location of that activity. In other words, FDI theory examines the impact of integration on the competitive advantages of firms of different nationalities, the location of activities associated with these advantages, and the way in which these advantages are organized jointly with the resource capabilities of the host countries.[30]

There is, of course, much in common between these two analytical approaches, if for no other reason than many of the factors which influence the location of economic activity are likely to be independent of the nationality of ownership. Take, for example, the removal of a substantial *ad valorem* tariff on a product traded between (say) France and Denmark. Assume the product (say a pharmaceutical preparation) is subject to substantial plant economies of scale, but neither the inputs nor the final product cost much to transport. Assume, too, that the product is considerably cheaper to produce in France. Then, one might expect that, as a result of the removal of a tariff between France and Denmark, not only might Danish owned firms in Denmark be out-competed by French owned firms in France, but that French MNEs currently supplying the Danish market from a Danish subsidiary might decide to close down their Danish plants and export the product from their French plants. Whether there is, in fact, any difference in response by these two groups of firms to integration depends on how it affects their respective abilities to compete, and, in particular, whether the advantages arising from the common ownership of the Danish and French plants influence their locational preferences.[31]

However, in most cases, the consequences of economic integration for trade and FDI are less straightforward. For example, the increased competitive pressures arising from the removal of trade barriers, together with the improved opportunities to exploit plant economies of scale, might lead to *strategic asset augmenting FDI*. In this case, there may be a change in the *ownership* of economic activity (e.g. an investment *diversion* affect) but not its location; and, as a result, the consequences of trade flows—initially at least—may be quite trivial. Similarly, where integration leads MNEs to rationalize the existing value-added activities of foreign subsidiaries, this may lead both to a geographical concentration of scale-related production, and to an increase in intra-EC trade, over and above that which might be expected to occur between independently owned EC firms.[32] Integration, in this case, will be FDI diverting and, in all probability— due to efficiency gains—investment and trade creating.

To keep this chapter to manageable proportions, while attempting to address the more important economic consequences of the IMP, we shall concentrate on four generic hypotheses suggested by the trade and FDI literature.

Hypothesis 1. The first hypothesis is that the IMP will have a positive effect on intra-EC trade, and an ambivalent effect on intra-EC FDI. Depending on the form and height of existing non-tariff barriers, it is likely to have an ambivalent effect on extra-EC trade, but a positive affect on extra-FDI and on the intra-EC trade by the foreign affiliates of non-EC MNEs. The precise nature of these effects is likely to vary according to: (1) country; (2) sector; and (3) type of FDI considerations.[33] Both trade and FDI theory[34] suggest that intra-EC trade creation will arise as a result of more efficient resource allocation within the EC; and will be most pronounced in those sectors which supply products subject to plant economies of scale, and which cost little to transport. While, depending on the level of the external tariff, extra-EC defensive FDI will be relatively unaffected or increased, depending on the competitive enhancing affects of integration, efficiency seeking FDI may increase,[35] although there is likely to be some FDI diversion towards countries most suitable as export platforms for the rest of the EC. The IMP is also likely to affect the significance of at least some of the variables determining FDI. It might, for example, be hypothesized that country specific demand related variables (e.g. market size and growth), will become less important for integrated (cf. stand alone) EC affiliates; while country specific supply related variables (e.g. infrastructure and agglomerative economies) may become relatively more important.

Hypothesis 2. The IMP will have an ambivalent effect on the geographical distribution of FDI within the EC, both by EC and non-EC MNEs. However, while the literature[36] suggests that the locational response of foreign investors will vary according to the country of origin of the parent companies, there is no obvious reason why the site specific factors affecting the allocation of activity between an MNE's home country and an EC country (or, in the case of intra-EC FDI, another EC country) will be very different from that as between two separately owned firms in the two countries. At the same time, Markusen and Venables (1995) have demonstrated that, as countries become similar in size, relative factor endowments and technical efficiency (the last two determining per capita income), cross-border activity will become increasingly dominated by MNEs, which will displace trade, provided that transport costs are not insignificant. More generally, they, and other trade economists (e.g. Helpman and Krugman, 1985; Krugman, 1990) suggest that economic integration will lead to a more concentrated geographical distribution of economic activity in the EC in intensive technology sectors in which plant economies of scale relative to transport costs are important, but a less concentrated pattern where products are more dependent on classical resource endowments for their competitiveness.

Hypothesis 3. Depending on both country and sector specific factors, the IMP will have an ambivalent effect on the ownership of production in the EC. Both the trade and FDI literature suggest that perhaps the most critical components explaining the presence of FDI between and among industrialized countries is the juxtaposition between firm level economies of scale and scope, e.g. such as those that arise from the spreading of various headquarters activities and research and development; plant level economies of scale; the costs of coordinating cross-border activities and spatially related costs. MNEs are likely to dominate those sectors where the first and last ingredients are significant, relative to intra-firm coordination costs and plant-level scale economies (Markusen, 1995; Caves, 1996). If it could be shown that those sectors which have been identified by the European

Commission (Buiges, Ilzkovitz and Lebrun, 1990) as being likely to be the most sensitive to the IMP, were more FDI intensive than the non-sensitive sectors, *and* that integration enhances the kind of ownership advantages specific to MNEs, then it may be reasonably hypothesized that the IMP will lead to an increased share of the foreign ownership of activities in the EC in those sectors.

Hypothesis 4. This hypothesis naturally follows from Hypothesis 3. Since, as the European Commission has suggested, some sectors are likely to be affected more by the IMP than others, it follows that its consequences for trade and FDI will, at least to some extent, be sector specific. Moreover, both the extant literature and empirical data on FDI clearly demonstrate that MNEs—at least from advanced industrial countries—tend to concentrate in sectors which demonstrate one or more of the following characteristics: (1) a high level of R&D relative to sales, and/or an above average share of professional and technical workers in the total work force; (2) supply intermediate products that are technically advanced and complex, and offer opportunities for scale economies in their production; (3) supply final products which are highly differentiated and income-elastic in demand; (4) are trade and/or FDI supporting and information intensive; and (5) where the cross-border intra-firm costs of coordinating inter-related activities are low, relative to cross-border transport of goods and services from the investing countries (Hirsch, 1976). As it happens, most of the sensitive goods and services sectors identified by the European Commission possess one or other of these attributes. *Therefore, it is reasonable to hypothesize that FDI in these sectors, or in countries in which these sectors tend to concentrate,[37] will be more affected by EC-1992 than the less sensitive sectors and countries in which the FDI is less well concentrated.* Of particular note in this connection is the likely impact of the IMP on FDI intensive services—and particularly those which were relatively unaffected by Mark 1 integration. At the same time, because services tend to be less tradeable than goods, it may be hypothesized that the IMP will increase the FDI/trade ratio of the latter, although, due to advances in information technology and telecommunications, trade in some kinds of services, e.g. banking and insurance, is also likely to increase.

Some Stylized Facts

Before proceeding to analyze the evidence for and against these hypotheses, let us first outline the main trends in intra- and extra-FDI in the EC since 1985, and its distribution between member states. The experience of Mark 1 integration (the completion of which took longer to accomplish than is intended for Mark 2 integration),[38] and our knowledge about FDI trends prior to the prescribed date for market unification (*viz.*, 1st January 1993),[39] suggests that the first five to eight years after the start of the implementation of economic integration are (for most sectors at least) the most critical.[40]

(a) The geography of FDI. Table 4.1 gives details of the changing share of the EC as a host region to foreign direct investors (including those originating from other EU countries) between 1980 and 1995. It shows that in 1980, the stock of FDI directed to the EC[41] was 36.7 percent of that of all recipient economies, and 47.4 percent of that of developed economies. Over the five years immediately prior to the announcement of the IMP, these shares declined to 29.4 percent and 40.0 percent respectively. However, by the end of five years after its announcement, the EC's shares had risen to 40.0 percent of all economies and 49.8 percent of all developed economies. Thereafter, the EC's share of FDI directed to developed economies stabilized, and by 1995 it was 50.4 percent (a slight *decrease* over 1993 of 51.3 percent). At the same time, because of the increasing attractiveness of developing economies, and particularly China, to foreign investors, the EC's share of the worldwide FDI stock in that year was identical to that in 1980, *viz.*, 36.7 percent (UNCTAD, 1996)

Whatever else these data show,[42] they reveal a substantial increase in the activity of foreign investors in the EC in the latter part of the 1980s. Normalizing for differences in the growth of GNP between the EC and the rest of the world does not affect this conclusion.[43] However, at least part of this increase in inbound FDI has been at the expense of the capital formation of indigenous firms (i.e. those of individual EC countries). For example, while gross fixed capital formation (GFCF) in the EC hovered around one-fifth of gross domestic product between 1981 and 1994, the contribution of FDI flows to that capital formation rose from 2.6 percent in the 1981–85 period to 5.9 percent in the 1986–90 period.[44] Between 1991 and 1993 it ranged from 5.5 percent to 5.7 percent, but in 1994 it dipped to 4.8 percent.[45]

Table 4.2 gives some details on changes in the distribution of the FDI stock[46] within the EC over the last decade. We have chosen to divide such countries into two groups, *viz.*, the six core countries of the EC, which are also the high income countries, and the non-core or largely medium income countries.[47] The table shows that, between 1980 and 1985, the core countries accounted for 78.4 percent of the increase in FDI stock. In the following five years (1986–90), this ratio increased marginally to 84.5 percent; but, in the following five years (1991–95), mainly due to a substantial increase in Spanish inbound

TABLE 4.1 *Changing Share of Foreign Direct Investment Inward Stock by Host Region and Economy, 1980–95 (%)*

Host region/economy	1980	1985	1990	1993	1995
Developed economies	77.5	73.5	80.3	75.2	72.7
Western Europe	41.4	33.3	44.4	42.5	40.9
European Community (12)	36.7	29.3	40.0	38.6	36.7*
Core countries	32.8	25.7	34.2	31.5	29.8
Non-core countries	3.9	3.6	5.8	7.1	6.9
Other Western Europe	4.7	4.0	4.4	3.9	4.2
North America	28.6	34.3	29.7	26.5	25.6
Canada	11.3	8.9	6.6	5.1	4.4
United States	17.3	25.4	23.1	21.4	21.2
Other developed economies	7.5	5.9	6.2	6.2	6.2
Australia and New Zealand	3.4	3.7	4.9	4.8	4.9
Japan	0.7	0.7	0.6	0.8	0.7
South Africa	3.4	1.5	0.7	0.6	0.4
Israel	–	–	–	–	0.2
Developing economies	22.5	26.5	19.6	24.1	26.1
Africa	4.3	3.7	2.4	2.4	2.2
Latin America and the Caribbean	10.0	10.0	6.8	8.1	8.5
Asia	7.9	12.6	10.2	13.4	15.2
Other developing economies	0.3	0.2	0.2	0.2	0.2
Central and Eastern Europe	0.0	0.0	0.1	0.7	1.2
Total inward stock	100.0	100.0	100.0	100.0	100.0
Total inward stock value (USm$)	480,611	727,902	1,709,299	2,079,538	2,657,859

*Excludes Austria, Finland and Sweden which joined the European Union (previously called the European Community) in 1995.
Source: UNCTAD (1996). All figures obtained directly from official sources by UNCTAD have been converted into US dollars at the average exchange rate for the year in question.

FDI and a fall in the dollar value of U.K. inbound FDI stocks,[48] it dropped back again to 71.5 percent.

We now turn to consider similarities and differences between the extra- and intra-EC FDI in the EC over the past decade or so.

Table 4.3 presents data on the distribution of inbound FDI in the

TABLE 4.2   *The Geographical Distribution of Changes in the Inward Foreign Direct Investment Stock Within the EC, 1980–85 to 1991–95**

		1980–85 (%)	1986–90 (%)	1991–95 (%)
(1)	Core countries			
	Belgium and Luxembourg	4.1	5.9	16.4
	France	28.6	11.3	26.1
	Germany	0.8	15.8	7.8
	Italy	26.8	8.3	2.3
	Netherlands	15.4	10.4	10.0
	U.K.	**2.7**	**32.8**	**8.9**
	Total			
(2)	Non-core countries			
	Denmark	−1.5	1.2	4.3
	Greece	10.1	1.2	1.8
	Ireland	2.4	0.1	0.2
	Portugal	0.6	0.8	0.6
	Spain	**10.1**	**12.2**	**21.5**
	Total	21.7	15.5	28.4
All EC countries		100.0	100.0	100.0

*Excluding Austria, Finland and Sweden, which joined the European Union (previously the European Community) in 1995.
Source: As for Table 4.1.

EC by the leading source regions and countries since the mid-1980s, and Table 4.4 looks at the significance of the EC as a host region from the perspective of the three largest source countries or regions. The main conclusion to be drawn from Table 4.3 is that the EC countries[49] have attracted a rising share of FDI since the mid-1980s, although part of the reason for this increase share was the retrenchment of MNE activity in the U.S. in the late 1980s and early 1990s.[50] Within the EC, the *stock* of FDI directed to the core countries decreased slightly from around 90 percent in 1995 to nearer 85 percent in 1993.[51]

By contrast, Table 4.4 shows that the intra-EC share of FDI by EC countries (excluding Ireland and Greece) more than doubled between the mid-1980s and the early 1990s. These data immediately suggest that EC specific factors—such as the IMP—may have had a considerably greater impact on intra-EC FDI than on extra-EC FDI, a conclusion which is quite the opposite from that drawn about the effects of Mark

TABLE 4.3 *Source of FDI Flows and FDI Stocks in European Community 1984–87 to 1990–93*

	Flows, % of total*			Stocks, % of total†		
	1984–87	1988–90	1991–93	1985	1990	1993
1. North America	**21.7**	**13.8**	**18.7**	**34.6**	**32.2**	**29.7**
of which US	19.6	12.6	15.7	33.4	30.3	28.0
2. Western Europe	**58.5**	**68.3**	**69.2**	**53.3**	**55.4**	**57.4**
of which EC	45.0	52.9	59.4	40.4	39.2	43.5
3. Other OECD	**7.3**	**10.2**	**5.7**	**3.0**	**7.6**	**7.3**
of which Japan	5.3	7.3	2.8	2.7	4.7	4.6
4. Other countries	**12.5**	**7.7**	**6.4**	**9.1**	**4.8**	**5.6**
Total:	100.0	100.0	100.0	100.0	100.0	100.0
Total amount in US$ million:	72,325	214,025	180,145	173,832	498,561	586,012

*Annual average
†Included countries: France, Germany, Italy, Netherlands and U.K.
Source: OECD (1995).

1 economic integration. It should, however, be observed that the dramatic deceleration of new investment in EC FDI in the U.S. helped focus more attention on the EC.[52]

Throughout 1985–1993, a somewhat higher proportion of intra-EC FDI was attracted to the non-core countries than in the case of Japanese and U.S. FDI, and, over the period as a whole, there is some suggestion of a decentralization of intra-EC FDI, particularly to Southern Europe.[53] However, within the core countries, a noticeable difference between extra- and intra-EC FDI is the considerably lower attraction of the U.K. as an investment outlet in the former, than in the latter, case.[54]

To what extent does FDI tend to cluster in particular regions or countries, and how far has such clustering (e.g. to take advantage of agglomerative economies) increased in recent years? Table 4.5 compares the FDI intensity ratios[55] of EC countries in selected host regions in the late 1980s or early 1990s, compared (where the data are available) with the respective ratios in the early 1980s. Looking, first, at intra-EC FDI intensities, the table reveals that, in all countries except the U.K., these intensities were greater than 1.00 in the latter period, although, again, apart from the U.K., they were even more pronounced for the 'other' Western Europe region. Second, in the five EC countries for which we have data, the intra-EC intensity ratios increased in the 1980s. Third, the FDI intensity ratios of EC countries in non-European countries were generally less than 1.00 in 1990 (an exception is the above average U.K./U.S. ratio), and that, except in

TABLE 4.4 Japanese, U.S. and EC Foreign Direct Investment by Regions and Countries, 1985–93 (% of World Total)

Host region/economy	Japan (annual average)			United States (annual average)			European Community (annual average)		
	1985–87	1988–90	1991–93	1985–87†	1988–90†	1991–93	1985–87	1988–90	1991–93
Developed economies	68.2	77.3	71.3	64.3	68.7	61.7	88.1	89.3	82.0
European Community (12)	17.0	20.9	20.3	38.8	44.6	44.2	30.6	50.8	57.7
Core countries	15.9	20.1	18.8	33.5	38.9	40.1	26.4	42.9	45.1
Belgium and Luxembourg	5.0	1.4	1.0	1.2	3.0	2.9	2.7	8.3	8.6
France	0.8	1.7	1.6	4.0	5.7	4.7	3.7	6.8	6.7
Germany	1.2	1.6	2.4	3.2	2.9	8.9	1.4	6.4	8.8
Italy	0.2	0.4	0.7	1.9	4.4	3.2	2.4	3.0	3.6
Netherlands	3.1	5.7	5.0	9.9	3.1	0.7	8.1	9.4	9.7
U.K.	5.7	9.4	8.2	13.4	19.8	19.7	8.2	9.1	7.7
Non-core countries	1.0	0.8	1.5	5.3	5.7	4.1	4.2	7.8	12.5
Denmark	0.0	0.0	0.0	-0.7	0.2	0.3	0.1	0.3	0.5
Ireland	0.3	0.1	0.6	3.6	3.0	2.8	0.7	1.8	4.0
Southern periphery*	0.7	0.7	0.9	2.4	2.5	1.0	3.4	5.7	8.0
Other western Europe†	0.7	1.3	1.1	5.5	6.7	7.8	2.8	4.0	5.4
United States	44.8	47.0	41.9	0.0	0.0	0.0	48.1	27.9	15.9
Canada	1.5	1.8	1.9	14.6	9.8	4.8	3.2	2.7	0.9
Japan	0.0	0.0	0.0	3.1	2.9	1.8	0.6	0.9	-0.1
Australia and New Zealand	4.2	6.3	6.2	2.4	4.8	3.3	2.8	2.9	2.2
Developing economies	31.8	22.7	28.3	35.8	31.3	37.0	11.8	10.5	15.3
Africa	1.1	1.1	1.4	-0.1	-2.0	0.7	0.7	1.1	1.1
Latin America	17.5	8.8	8.2	33.0	26.4	23.1	5.3	4.9	3.8
Middle East	0.2	0.2	0.9	0.4	-0.3	1.7	0.7	0.6	0.6
Asia	12.8	12.2	17.1	3.6	6.9	11.1	2.3	1.8	3.5
Other developing economies‡	0.2	0.4	0.7	-1.1	0.4	0.4	2.9	2.2	6.3
Central and Eastern Europe	0.0	0.1	0.4	0.0	0.0	1.3	0.1	0.2	2.6
Total	100.0	100.0	100.0	100.0	100.0	100.0	100.0	100.0	100.0
World total (US$m)	67,497	170,922	111,212	59,405	79,771	124,910	125,876	268,431	268,352

*Greece, Spain, Portugal.
†Austria, Finland, Norway, Sweden, Switzerland.
‡Includes Malta and Cyprus and other countries not reporting separately.
Source: Japanese Ministry of Finance, US Department of Commerce, OECD (1995).

TABLE 4.5 *Intensity Ratios of Selected Foreign Investing Countries by Host Region, Early 1980s–92*

Investor country	Year	European Community	Other Western Europe	North America	United States	Canada	Japan	Rest of the world
European Community								
Belgium and Luxembourg	1980	1.65	2.18	-0.14	-0.31	0.09	0.29	1.26
	1988	n.a.	n.a.	n.a.	n.a.	n.a.	n.a.	n.a.
Denmark	1982	1.31	3.68	0.86	0.86	n.a.	0.01	0.62
	1991	1.42	5.45	0.38	0.36	0.45	0.77	0.40
France	1982	1.00	1.88	1.15	1.99	-0.21	0.11	0.79
	1991	1.37	1.63	0.62	0.72	0.30	0.16	0.49
Germany	1980	1.02	2.44	0.84	1.21	0.25	0.17	0.84
	1992	1.19	2.60	0.79	0.91	0.27	0.84	0.38
Italy	1989	n.a.	n.a.	n.a.	n.a.	n.a.	n.a.	n.a.
	1992	1.52	2.84	0.31	0.37	0.12	0.41	0.59
Netherlands	1984	0.89	1.65	1.19	1.44	0.43	0.15	0.44
	1992	1.03	2.27	0.99	n.a.	n.a.	0.48	0.52
United Kingdom	1981	0.50	0.52	1.09	1.43	0.55	0.09	1.25
	1992	0.58	0.80	1.32	1.52	0.65	0.61	0.89
Portugal	1985	1.23	0.04	0.49	0.65	0.01	–	1.27
	1988	n.a.	n.a.	n.a.	n.a.	n.a.	n.a.	n.a.
Spain	1984	n.a.	n.a.	n.a.	n.a.	n.a.	n.a.	n.a.
	1989	1.39	1.02	0.31	0.39	0.06	0.18	1.13
Other countries								
United States	1980	0.60	1.05	0.47	–	1.14	0.26	0.63
	1990	0.73	1.34	0.41	–	1.80	1.74	0.73
Canada	1980	0.45	0.45	2.24	3.63	–	0.06	0.66
	1990	0.45	0.38	1.91	2.44	–	0.40	0.62
Japan	1980	0.30	0.26	0.98	1.44	0.24	–	2.13
	1990	0.38	0.24	1.26	1.54	0.24	–	1.28

Ratios are derived from data on stock of foreign direct investment using formula set out in Note 55.
Source: Based on UN (1993a) and a variety of national statistical sources.

the case of FDI in Japan, these ratios generally fell in the previous decade. Fourth, the FDI intensity ratios of both the U.S. and Japan in the EC rose in the 1980s, in spite of the attractions of other parts of the world (notably East Asia) for U.S. investors and the U.S. for Japanese investors. Part of the reason for this increase of the EC ratios of the two major non-EC investing countries is most surely the concern over future external barriers to trade between themselves and the European Community.

(b) The sectoral distribution of FDI. Data on the changing sectoral distribution of extra- and intra-EC FDI are only available for a few countries. Perhaps the best statistics are those compiled by the U.S. Department of Commerce. Unfortunately, such data are only published for selected years.[56] In Table 4.6, we set out the increases in the sales of US affiliates in Europe[57] between 1982 and 1989 (which embrace the years before and immediately after the announcement of the IMP), and between 1989 and 1993. The sectors are classified into three groups according to their likely sensitivity (as perceived by the European Commission) to the IMP.[58] We also present similar data for the rest of the world (ROW). The difference between the Europe and the ROW indices might be interpreted as reflecting, in part at least, the 'European' (including the IMP) effect.

The data clearly reveal two things. First, the sales of U.S. affiliates in the highly and moderately sensitive sectors rose distinctly faster than those in other sectors between 1982 and 1989 but only marginally so between 1989 and 1993.[59] Second, the average rate of growth in sales for all sectors—but particularly for some of the most sensitive sectors between 1982 and 1989 in Europe—have consistently outstripped that of the ROW.

Other data published by Eurostat (1994) demonstrate an increasing concentration of FDI by both EC and non-EC investors in the tertiary sector, and particularly in finance, banking and insurance, telecommunications and business services.[60] How much this is due to the IMP *per se*, and how much to the deregulation and liberalization of service-related markets in general, it is difficult to say. But, it is, perhaps, worth noting that the sectoral composition of intra-EC foreign direct investment flows and that of non-EC countries in the EC between 1984 and 1992 is broadly similar.

This conclusion is also supported by a study by Agarwal *et al.* (1995), which shows that the industrial composition of post-1985 French, German, Dutch and U.K. FDI in the EC has been very similar to that in other industrialized countries.[61] Their work also reveals that only very modest changes have occurred in the sectoral composition of intra- and extra-EC FDI by these same countries between the mid-1980s

TABLE 4.6 *Growth of Sales by US Affiliates in Europe and the Rest of the World by Sectors, 1982–93*

Sector	1982–89 (1982 = 100)			1989–93 (1989 = 100)			1982–93 (1982 = 100)		
	All Countries	Europe	Rest of World	All Countries	Europe	Rest of World	All Countries	Europe	Rest of World
High impact									
Beverages	173.9	162.2	183.3	170.1	204.3	147.2	295.8	331.4	269.9
Drugs	182.0	214.8	141.3	167.3	168.6	164.7	304.5	362.2	232.7
Office/computing	324.3	296.4	400.2	116.1	101.7	145.0	376.6	301.5	581.4
Radio, TV communications	80.5	98.2	84.7	132.4	96.9	143.2	106.6	95.2	121.3
Electronic components	229.5	203.5	244.6	147.5	154.9	143.9	338.5	315.2	352.2
Instruments	195.6	181.2	247.6	125.3	125.1	125.6	245.1	226.7	311.1
Finance, except banking	247.8	555.8	164.6	159.5	206.2	98.8	372.7	1146.1	162.6
Insurance	182.4	183.0	182.1	143.7	138.8	153.0	262.1	254.0	278.6
Total high impact	219.9	255.0	187.4	138.2	145.3	131.8	289.6	370.5	247.0
Moderate impact									
Other food products	164.5	218.0	112.8	154.1	155.1	152.4	253.5	338.1	175.0
Other chemical products	145.6	193.6	100.4	115.1	114.3	116.4	167.6	221.3	114.8
Other machinery	127.9	124.2	132.3	92.5	99.8	78.6	118.3	124.0	104.0
Household appliances	321.1	311.5	328.8	119.0	151.5	94.4	382.1	472.0	310.4
Transportation equipment	200.0	218.8	185.1	115.2	186.5	114.2	230.3	253.4	211.4
Textile products and apparel	148.9	140.6	158.7	142.4	160.6	123.8	212.1	225.8	196.5
Rubber products	144.5	237.8	101.9	110.4	102.5	118.8	159.5	243.7	121.1
Glass products	187.0	180.0	200.2	95.4	115.7	61.6	178.4	208.2	123.3
Wholesale trade	179.8	174.5	192.4	120.7	112.4	138.4	217.0	196.1	266.3
Business services	158.1	152.9	171.4	194.4	201.5	178.2	307.4	308.1	305.4
Total moderate impact	177.2	185.6	165.5	120.7	119.0	123.4	213.9	220.9	204.2
Total low impact	161.9	168.0	155.8	122.8	135.1	112.7	198.8	227.0	175.6
All industries (less petroleum)	181.1	193.0	167.3	126.0	125.5	126.7	228.3	242.2	212.0

Source: U.S. Department of Commerce Department Benchmark Surveys (various) since 1989.

and the early 1990s;[62] while there is no real evidence that the growth of extra-EC FDI in the sectors in which intra-EC trade has expanded the most rapidly has been at the expense of extra-EC FDI in other developed countries.[63] The only exception may be in some service sectors—notably in finance, insurance, telecommunications and data processing services, where the gains from IMP have been higher simply because the earlier barriers to intra-EC trade or investment were so high.

Two other features about the sectoral distribution of FDI by EC countries since the early or mid-1980s are worthy of note. The first is that the sectors in which the increase in intra-EC (as opposed to extra-EC) FDI was most marked differs between the core countries. Although for the EC as a whole, we have seen that the sectoral pattern of growth of FDI has broadly corresponded to that of its U.S. and Japanese counterpart, this relationship breaks down for particular EC countries. Thus, while French intra-EC FDI in chemicals has largely outpaced FDI in other countries, this has not been so in the case for U.K. investors. Similarly, there has been a distinctive geographical re-orientation towards the EC of German FDI in transport equipment, and of Dutch FDI in the services sectors. Outside the sensitive sectors, there is little reason to suppose that the IMP has slowed down the redirection of FDI in textiles and clothing from the EC to Asia, nor (more latterly) to North African countries and Central and Eastern Europe (UNCTAD, 1995).

The second feature refers to the intra-EC distribution of FDI in the leading manufacturing and service sectors. Here, U.S. data (at a two-digit sectoral level) show very clearly that, measured in terms of the proportion of the gross product (sales) of U.S. affiliates in Europe accounted for by the three leading recipient countries, there was a slight *decline* in geographical concentration between 1982 and 1991 in all sectors except services. This decline is in contrast to an *increase* in geographical concentration which occurred between 1972 and 1982 (Matoloni and Goldberg, 1994; U.S. Department of Commerce, 1981, 1985, 1992; U.S. Tariff Commission, 1973). It is, however, consistent with the increase in the share of the gross product of U.S. affiliates in the EC accounted for by the medium income EC countries (*viz.*, Greece, Ireland, Portugal and Spain) from 6.7 percent in 1982 to 10.0 percent in 1991. It is also supportive of the hypothesis of trade economists (e.g. Hirsch, 1974; Hufbauer and Chilas, 1974; Helpman and Krugman, 1985; Markusen and Venables, 1995) that economic integration is more likely to disperse the production of Ricardo and Heckscher-Ohlin goods[64] away from high income countries, while concentrating the production of Schumpeterian goods within high income countries. Thus, for example, the share of the total EC output of the former two types of goods,[65] accounted for by the medium income countries rose, from 4.3 percent to 9.3 percent between 1982 and 1991, compared with that of the more dynamic goods which rose only from 9.5 percent to 11.1 percent.

(c) The trade and FDI relationship. In an earlier part of this chapter, we asserted that both trade and FDI theory posited that the relationship between intra- and extra-EC trade and FDI was conditional on the kind of trade and FDI being considered, and the conditions under which each took place. However, it is reasonable to hypothesize that the greater the similarity between the industrial and/or geographical patterns of trade and FDI, the more likely it is that they will be complementary with, rather than substitutable for, each other. Modern trade theory, a useful summary of which is contained in UNCTAD (1996),[66] in contrast to its neo-classical predecessor, allows for the specificity of factors of production, and suggests that, as impediments to trade in goods are relaxed, so factor mobility, including FDI, will normally increase.[67]

We offer three pieces of evidence in support of these propositions. The first relates to the pattern of regional clustering of the two forms of servicing markets. Drawing upon data compiled by Petri (1994) for 1990, part of which is reproduced in Table 4.7, it can be seen that there is a close correspondence between the FDI and trade intensities.[68] Both the trade and FDI of the major EC countries, Sweden and Western Europe as a whole,[69] is clustered elsewhere in Europe—except (as earlier tables have shown) in the case of the UK which has a major FDI stake in the U.S. At the same time, the intra-EC trade intensity ratios tend to be marginally higher (and much so for the U.K.) than the FDI intensity ratios. This is in marked contrast to the pattern of the transactions between non-European countries and Europe where the FDI ratios are considerably higher. These data are consistent with the fact that extra-EC trade barriers, and the notion of 'Fortress Europe' perceived by some non-EC foreign investors, has led to more defensive (and possibly trade-replacing) FDI than in the case of intra-EC transactions.

In an econometric analysis of the trade and FDI relationships for the four major outward investors—namely the U.S., Japan, the U.K. and Germany—Petri finds a positive and significant correlation between each set of relationships, with both trade and FDI being clustered in the same regions. Although his analysis, which is based only on 1990 data, does not investigate the causal link between trade and FDI, he is able to conclude that 'the regional concentration of FDI is either directly associated with the regional concentration of trade, or are both driven by common factors' (Petri, 1994, p. 19). This

TABLE 4.7 Intensity Ratios for Foreign Direct Investment and Trade of Ten Major Investor Countries by Selected Host Region 1990

	FDI (stock)				Trade			
	North America	Latin America	Europe	East Asia	North America	Latin America	Europe	East Asia
North America	**1.97**	**1.12**	**0.84**	**0.80**	**5.52**	**3.08**	**0.38**	**1.22**
Canada	2.23	0.80	0.49	0.13	4.90	0.78	0.23	0.54
United States	1.99	1.15	0.88	0.84	4.43	3.64	0.41	1.38
Europe	**0.98**	**0.53**	**1.32**	**0.56**	**0.46**	**0.63**	**1.49**	**0.37**
France	1.00	0.23	1.56	0.14	0.42	0.76	1.46	0.33
Germany	0.82	0.52	1.55	0.38	0.39	0.64	1.60	0.40
Italy	0.33	1.04	1.76	0.26	0.40	0.71	1.52	0.30
Netherlands	0.86	0.54	1.42	0.54	0.33	0.52	1.51	0.24
Sweden	0.61	0.31	1.90	0.00	0.54	0.59	1.48	0.40
United Kingdom	1.32	0.53	1.32	0.56	0.73	0.51	1.31	0.49
Australia	**0.70**	**0.68**	**0.93**	**3.06**	**1.15**	**0.37**	**0.42**	**2.36**
Japan	**1.34**	**1.13**	**0.46**	**1.85**	**1.60**	**1.08**	**0.38**	**2.25**
East Asia	**1.28**	**1.09**	**0.50**	**1.94**	**1.55**	**0.99**	**0.38**	**2.26**

Note: Intensity ratio: The share of the partner region in the total of a given country divided by the share of the partner region in worldwide FDI stock or trade in goods and services excluding the FDI stock or trade with the given country.

Source: Adapted from Petri (1994) and UN (1993a).

finding is confirmed by Nunnenkamp *et al.* (1994), who, in a study of
bilateral trade and FDI flows for Germany, Japan and the U.S. over
the period 1989 to 1992, discovered not only that such flows were
positively correlated—and significantly so in the case of Japan—but
that this complementarity was a natural outcome of the regionalization
or globalization strategies of the leading MNEs.[70]

The second piece of evidence is that which relates to changes in the
FDI[71] of U.S. MNEs in Europe,[72] to exports of goods and services from
these MNEs to their European affiliates and to the intra-EC trade of
their affiliates. Table 4.8 presents such data as we have been able to
assemble. It shows that on average, between 1982 and 1993, the three
sets of data reveal similar trends; which points not only to a complementarity between the sales of affiliates and exports from the investing
countries, but also between both of these variables and intra-EC trade.
With a few exceptions—noticeably in sectors the least likely to produce
Schumpeterian type goods—this complementarity also holds at a sectoral
level, and particularly between affiliate sales and intra-EC trade. The
data also suggest that the two FDI/trade ratios for most sectors fell slightly
in the second period, *viz.*, between 1989 and 1993, and that the largest
increases in both affiliate sales and intra-European trade were recorded
in the finance, insurance and business services sectors, which have been
among those most affected by the IMP.

The third piece of evidence relates to the response of EC-based
firms to two particular aspects of the IMP, namely public procurement
liberalization and the deregulation of markets. Prior to the IMP, only
2–3 percent of the public procurement of goods—which in the early
1990s, accounted for 15–20 percent of total GNP of the EC—was
directed to suppliers from other member states (Davies and Lyons,
1996), while the dispersion of prices across the community of regulated
product markets and services ranged upwards of 16 percent (Buigues
et al., 1990). Both trade and FDI theory suggest that the IMP should
lead to a major increase in intra-EC trade, but a reduction in intra-EC
FDI in such sectors. In fact, as we have already seen, while intra-EC
trade has increased in these sectors, so has intra-EU FDI—at least in
the FDI intensive sectors.[73] However, other data on the pharmaceutical
and telecommunications sectors suggest that there was only a weak
positive relationship between intra-EC trade to intra-EC mergers
(M&As) over the period 1989 to 1994[74] (EAG, 1996).

(d) The share of FDI in EC capital formation. While much of our
previous discussion has been concerned with the *locational* competitiveness of EC, and that of its Member States, it is possible that
part of any increase in FDI (or sales by foreign firms) might represent
an increased *share* of the total investment (or sales) of all EC located

TABLE 4.8 Changes in Sales of US Affiliates in Europe, U.S.-Europe Trade and Intra-Europe Trade 1982–93

| | 1982–89 Sales | 1982 = 100 Trade | | 1989–93 Sales | 1989 = 100 Trade | | 1992–93 Sales | 1982 = 100 Trade | |
	U.S. affiliates	U.S.-Europe	Intra-Europe	U.S.-affiliates	U.S.-Europe	Intra-Europe	U.S. affiliates	U.S.-Europe	Intra-Europe
Manufacturing	**201.6**	**184.7**	**184.6**	**122.0**	**122.7**	**132.2**	**246.0**	**226.7**	**244.2**
Food, drink and tobacco	176.6	111.4	207.3	161.7	79.1	168.6	285.6	85.9	349.5
Chemicals and allied products	195.7	180.4	184.5	127.8	114.2	132.9	250.1	206.0	245.2
Primary and fabricated metals	132.7	144.5	160.8	115.4	109.2	115.0	153.1	154.5	184.9
Machinery (except electrical)	245.1	270.0	180.3	101.1	107.1	136.3	334.1	288.9	245.7
Electrical and electronic equipment	142.6	187.1	150.9	127.7	136.1	132.7	182.1	254.6	200.2
Transport equipment	218.3	202.8	214.9	116.1	233.8	118.6	253.4	474.1	254.9
Other manufactured products	213.1	143.0	168.8	125.4	134.0	129.5	267.2	191.6	218.6
Wholesale trade	**174.5**	**166.7**	**121.7**	**112.4**	**120.3**	**117.5**	**196.1**	**200.5**	**143.0**
Finance & insurance	**330.3**	**neg.**	**337.6**	**179.1**	**neg.**	**359.8**	**591.6**	**neg.**	**1214.7**
Business services	**152.9**	**186.4**	**187.1***	**201.6**	**823.2**	**183.4***	**308.2**	**1543.8**	**343.1***
All industries	**157.3**	**173.5**	**140.8**	**124.8**	**124.9**	**134.5**	**196.3**	**216.7**	**189.4**

*All services

Source: U.S. Department of Commerce, various publications. The sales of European affiliates of U.S. firms are given in Tables III.D4 of 1982 Benchmark Survey and Tables III.E4 of 1989 Benchmark Survey and Preliminary estimates of 1993 Survey of Overseas Assets (US Department of Commerce 1995). The U.S. exports to Europe are those of U.S. MNEs shipped to their European affiliates, as set out in Tables III.G4, III.H6 and II.H6 of the above publications. Intra EC exports of U.S. affiliates are taken from Tables III.E5, Table III.F8 and Table III.F of above publications. Although data on exports to Europe are not given separately, it is known that, overall, these account for between 85 and 90 percent of all exports of affiliates, other than those to the U.S.

firms. Such an increase in the foreign ownership of production might occur either as a result of the improved competitiveness of established foreign affiliates, or through foreign firms acquiring or merging with domestic firms in individual European countries.[75] As an earlier section has shown, the received literature would regard such M&As as a means of sustaining or increasing the ownership (O) advantages of the acquiring firms. However, while in some cases, the location of the acquired company may be relevant, in others it may have no significance at all.

Table 4.9 reveals that the share of foreign direct inflows to GFCF in the world economy increased in the second half of the 1980s, but that this increase was mainly confined to the EC and North America. By contrast, in the 1990s, the rise in the foreign share of GFCF was confined to the developing economies. The increased participation of foreign owned firms in the EC (which is confirmed by other data)[76] is entirely consistent with our knowledge about M&As. Both intra-EC and M&As, and cross-border acquisitions of EC firms by non-EC purchasers[77] corporations, increased over ten-fold between 1985–1986 and 1989–1990, before dropping back in the early 1990s to nearer their 1986–1987 levels (Walter, 1993).[78]

So much for some stylized facts about recent FDI into the EC, which lend some support to the four hypotheses set out earlier in this article, we now turn to examine more rigorously, the empirical evidence for these hypotheses, and also some related work of other scholars on the effect of the IMP on both extra- and intra-EC FDI and trade.

Isolating the Affects of the IMP

We now come to the more difficult part of our analysis—and the one which (almost inevitably, because of data limitations) produces the least satisfactory results. The question of interest is straight forward enough: 'What has been the (specific) impact of the IMP on the level and pattern of extra- and intra-FDI in the EC?' The answer is much more complex and, even if all the data were available (which they are not), it would be conditional on: (1) the kind of FDI being discussed; (2) particular country and industry specific factors; (3) how one measures the IMP effect; and (4) what assumptions one makes about what would have happened in the absence of the IMP, *viz.*, the *anti-monde* or *alternative* position.

Basically, there are two main ways of proceeding. One is to construct a model in which an IMP variable is added to the usual determinants of FDI, hypothesized by received FDI, and/or trade theory; and then, attempt to estimate the significance of that variable. In principle, such an exercise could be conducted for extra- and intra-EC FDI, and for

TABLE 4.9 The Ratio of Foreign Direct Investment Inflows to Gross Fixed Domestic Capital Formation 1981–94 (%)

Host region/economy	1981–85 (Annual average)	1986–90	1991	1992	1993	1994
All economies	2.3	4.1	3.5	3.6	4.3	3.9
Developed economies	2.2	4.6	3.3	3.0	3.5	3.3
Western Europe	2.6	5.8	5.4	5.4	5.7	4.8
European Community (12)	2.7	6.0	5.7	5.5	5.7	4.8
Belgium and Luxembourg	7.6	16.1	22.8	25.0	26.7	17.5
Denmark	0.4	2.5	7.3	4.7	8.4	23.0
France	2.0	4.1	5.9	8.2	8.9	7.1
Germany	1.2	2.0	1.2	0.6	0.1	-0.9
Greece	6.0	7.9	8.7	8.1	7.7	7.5
Ireland	4.0	1.1	1.3	1.3	1.3	1.1
Italy	1.1	2.2	1.0	1.3	1.6	0.9
Netherlands	6.1	13.3	10.7	11.9	10.8	6.8
Portugal	3.0	10.0	13.7	8.5	8.1	6.5
Spain	5.3	9.4	10.0	10.6	8.6	9.9
United Kingdom	17.9	19.9	9.5	11.6	10.2	0.6
Other Western Europe	1.7	4.6	4.0	12.3	3.3	4.8
North America	2.8	6.8	2.9	2.5	4.7	4.9
Canada	1.0	5.8	2.4	4.2	5.1	5.9
United States	2.9	6.9	3.0	2.2	4.7	4.8
Other developed economies	0.7	0.9	0.7	0.8	0.4	0.6
Developing economies	3.3	3.2	4.0	4.8	6.3	7.5
Africa	2.3	3.5	4.2	4.4	4.9	7.5
Latin America and the Caribbean	4.1	4.2	5.2	7.4	6.6	7.4
Asia	3.1	2.8	3.4	4.1	6.5	7.2
Central and eastern Europe	neg.	0.1	0.4	0.6	0.9	0.9

Source: UNCTAD (1995, 1996).

different kinds of FDI (e.g. defensive market seeking, efficiency seeking, strategic asset seeking, etc.). In practice, the data on FDI only allow us to travel this path to a limited extent. We shall, however, review the research which has recently been conducted on this issue.

The second approach is more deductive and predictive, in that it seeks to test a number of specific hypotheses about the likely effects of economic integration on FDI which directly emerge from the trade and FDI literature.

In practice, the two approaches are quite similar, and use virtually identical testing procedures. Moreover, they confront the same analytical and measurement problems. Both, for example, need to construct a quantifiable proxy for what is essentially a non-quantifiable phenomenon, *viz.*, the removal of non-tariff barriers to intra-EC trade in goods and services. Both, too, in the design and specification of their chosen models, face the difficulty that many of the other variables hypothesized to influence FDI are, themselves, likely to be affected by the IMP. Foremost among these are income levels, agglomeration economies, exports and structural convergence and/or divergence. Introducing leads and lags may help resolve this latter problem, but only to a very limited extent.

Since, up to now, most attempts to explain recent movements in FDI into the EC have followed the first approach, we will give most of our attention to these.

Incorporating IMP into Traditional FDI Models

We are aware of only two attempts to do this, *viz.* Clegg (1995) and Pain and Lansbury (1996), although other models have identified the significance of non-IMP variables influencing FDI in the EC (or Western Europe[79]). In such cases, it *could* be argued that the value of the residual (i.e. unexplained) variables might be taken as a proxy for the IMP,[80] or, at least, a reflection of its importance, *apart* from its effects on the value of the other variables. An alternative procedure is to estimate the impact of the IMP on the non-IMP variables (following the deductive approach outlined earlier) and then to credit the IMP with that impact in any explanation of FDI. Thus, for example, if it could be shown that, over the five year period 1987–92, the IMP had raised GNP by 6 percent (the most optimistic forecast of the Cecchini report (Cecchini, *et al.* 1988), then, using the estimates of Julius (1990) and the UNCTAD (1993a), of the elasticities of FDI with respect to changes in the GNP—at between 3.5 and 4.5 percent[81]—one could then infer that 21–27 percent of any increase in FDI over those years was due to the IMP. And, in principle, the same kind of exercise could be conducted for other FDI related variables, e.g. changes in the exchange rate, domestic capital formation, information costs and agglomeration economies.

The European Commission, which is currently assessing the consequences of the IMP, has not published the results of any of its impact studies. Of the more recent scholarly research which have sought to evaluate the determinants of FDI in the EC, those of UNCTAD (1993a), Buigues and Jacquemin (1994), Srinivasan and Mody (1996), Clegg (1995) and Pain and Lansbury (1996) are worthy of special attention. The specifications and formal results of the models designed by these scholars are set out in the Appendix. We will now briefly summarize the results in the following paragraphs.

UNCTAD (1993)

The UNCTAD study regressed the annual flows (t) of FDI, (both intra- and extra-EC) into the EC and other developed countries, over the period 1972–88, against five explanatory variables, *viz.*, the level of GNP in year t-1, the change in GNP between t-1 and t, the ratio of domestic investment to GNP in year t-1, the exchange rate at year t (defined as the ratio of the domestic currency to the US dollar) and the squared deviation of the exchange rate from its mean over the period 1972–88. The authors found that, apart from the exchange rate variable, which was insignificant, the remaining four factors explained about 90 percent of the fluctuations in FDI in both the EC and other developed countries; and that the coefficients of the explanatory variables always had the correct size. Of these variables, GNP was consistently the most significant, with its coefficient being much larger for the EC than for the other developed countries. The share of domestic investment in GNP was also positively and significantly associated with FDI for both the EC and other developed countries, which suggests that, for the period in question at least, changes in domestic and inbound foreign investment were complementary to each other.[82] The variance in the exchange rate was seen to have a significant negative effect on FDI inflows.

The UNCTAD study also estimated the elasticity of the response of FDI to changes in the value of the independent variables. It found that an increase in both the level of GNP and the ratio of domestic investment to GNP in the EC in one year coincided with an increase in the inflow of FDI of 4 percent in the following year; while, a 1 percent change in the variance of the exchange rate would have a relatively small negative (but statistically significant) impact on FDI inflows of $37 million.

Unfortunately, the data in this study do not go up beyond 1988; nor do the authors split their analysis into a pre- and post-IMP time-frame. But, some projections for the period 1989–95, made from a variety of sources, including the IMF and World Bank—and which implicitly take account of the IMP—suggested that the annual rate of growth of FDI flows in the EC would outpace that of other developed nations, except Japan. Primarily, this was because the projected growth of GNP and the ratio of domestic investment to GNP was higher in the EC[83] than in other regions of the world. Although the UNCTAD study did not specifically incorporate an IMP variable into their model, the results do suggest that the *indirect* approach to evaluating its significance, *viz.* by its effects on GNP, domestic investment and the exchange rate, might offer a promising line for further research.

Srinivasan and Mody (1996)

This study was confined to U.S. and Japanese FDI for the period 1977–92. It embraced 35 countries, including 10 EC countries. One of its main purposes was to evaluate the significance of four rather different groups of factors which the literature have suggested influence FDI. These are:

1. *Classical factors*—which the authors proxied by host country market size, and local labor and capital costs;
2. *Agglomeration factors*—proxied by the previous level of FDI and the quality of supportive infrastructure to FDI;
3. *Trade restricting factors*—proxied (in reverse) by the degree of openness of an economy, and a dummy for the IMP variable;
4. *Risk factors*—proxied by information provided by various corporate data banks on country risk assessment.

The authors compiled a number of multi-regression equations, using mainly log linear estimates of the FDI function for all developed countries, and for the EC separately.[84] They found that, for each group of countries, both the size of market and cost of labor were significant explanatory variables[85]—but not the cost of capital in the case of the EC. Agglomeration factors, measured in this instance by the production of electricity per capita, and the number of telephone lines *per capita*, were significantly related to FDI in the case of the EC, but not for developed countries as a whole. However, for the level of previous FDI, the relationship was the other way around.[86] As might be expected, and in contrast to the situation in developing countries, country risk was of only trivial importance in influencing the FDI flows directed to any developed country, but openness (or negative trade restrictions) was positively and significantly signed in both groups, but particularly so in the EC. Eliminating country risk, these three groups of factors explained about 70 percent of the variation in FDI in the EC (and rather less in the case of FDI in all developed countries).

In some later calculations undertaken by the authors, Srinivasan and Mody found that, when they split their data into three time periods, *viz.* 1977–81, 1982–86 and 1987–92, there was no evidence that the formation of the IM significantly improved the EC's share of either U.S. or Japanese FDI. Indeed, the case of Japanese FDI, assuming last Asia to be the benchmark group of countries, the share of FDI directed to the EC fell in the period 1987–92.[87]

Clegg (1995)

In a long range longitudinal study, Clegg attempted to model the determinants of U.S. FDI in the original six member countries of the EC between 1951 (seven years before the European Common Market (ECM) came into effect) and 1990. The unique characteristics of his model were: first, he attempted to incorporate both real and financial variables into three multiple regression equations (one embracing the whole and one each for two sub-periods, 1951–72 and 1973–90); and second, in the latter sub-period, he introduced a dummy variable for the IMP.[88]

Clegg found that of the ten or eleven explanatory variables included in his equations, market size (proxied by GNP or GDP deflated to constant prices) market growth, a trade discrimination variable, the exchange rate (of the dollar against the six EC currencies) and relative interest rates were all significantly and correctly signed explanatory variables for one or other of the sub-periods, or for the forty year period as a whole. However, contrary to expectations, for the forty-year period, market size was shown to be negatively associated with FDI—and significantly so—although, for the first two decades, the two variables were positively correlated. Clegg suggests the reasons for this was that, whereas in the 1950s and early 1960s, most U.S. FDI was defensive and was directed to the larger local markets in Europe, in the later years, particularly after the U.K. joined the EC, it was more of an efficiency or strategic asset seeking kind, and geared to exploiting the EC market as a whole.[89]

Clegg's insertion of a dummy variable for the IMP (set to unity for the period 1987–90) gave inconclusive results. For the period 1951–90, the variable was positively but insignificantly associated with FDI; but for the sub-period 1973–90, it was negatively associated. Part of the reason for the apparent conflict in these findings may be that the significance of the other variables in the equation (e.g. market size) quite dramatically changed in the 1980s. At the same time, as Clegg himself recognized, the use of an aggregate dummy for the IMP inevitably fails to capture the industry-specific effects of the program.

Buigues and Jacquemin (1994)

One of the distinctive features of this study is that attempts both to evaluate the relationship between extra-EC FDI in the EC and exports to the EC and to estimate the significance of trade barriers as a determinant of FDI. Taking the share of global FDI directed to 7 or 9 manufacturing sectors in the EC by U.S. and Japanese MNEs as the dependent variable, the authors regressed its value against that of four independent variables, *viz.* the share of total U.S. and Japanese exports directed to the EC, intra-EC non-tariff barriers, the sectoral growth in demand in the EC divided by the growth in demand in the U.S. and Japan, and the Community's sectoral specialization, which they defined as the EC's exports for sectors in the total EC exports of manufactured goods divided by the same index for all OECD countries.[90]

The relevant linear regressions are set out in the Appendix to this chapter. The estimates of the coefficients are generally consistent with our expectations. In particular, extra-EC FDI and trade are seen to be significantly complementary to each other (see Hypothesis 1, earlier in this chapter). Second, while non-tariff barriers to trade appear to be a significant determinant of Japanese FDI, they play only a minor role in influencing U.S. FDI.[91] For U.S. sectoral demand growth and EC sectoral specialization—the latter is taken to be an index of the comparative locational advantages of the EC—the results are different for U.S. and Japanese investors. In the Japanese case, both variables are shown to have a significant positive association with FDI, while, for the U.S., only the sectoral specialization variables are significantly related. Although the authors did not include an industrial agglomeration variable in their analysis, they found that both U.S. and Japanese firms tended to strengthen their FDI and exports in those sectors in which they already had a comparative advantage in 1980, while there was a relative contraction in the presence of both groups of firms in the sectors in which they had an initial comparative disadvantage.

Pain and Lansbury (1996)[92]

Since, as we have seen, the effects of the IMP are unlikely to be evenly distributed between industries, it is only by incorporating sector specific variables that one can properly evaluate the impact of the IMP. Moreover, apart from our own estimates presented later in this chapter, the Pain and Lansbury study is the only one we know which has made a formal attempt to incorporate *discriminate* dummy variables to proxy the IMP.

The Pain and Lansbury study is unique in another respect, in that it examines the impact of the IMP on the outward intra-EC FDI[93] of two of the core EC countries—the U.K. and Germany.[94] In doing so, it uses received FDI theory[95] to test three hypotheses. These are:

1. that intra-EC FDI by U.K. and German firms has risen more rapidly than it would have done in the absence of the IMP;
2. that intra-EC by U.K. and German firms has risen either more rapidly than that outside the EC or at the expense of such investment;[96]
3. that the IMP has had a more marked effect on the growth of FDI by U.K. and German firms in the less trade intensive sectors—notably financial services, since, in the past, non-tariff barriers have constrained both FDI and trade in these sectors relative to that in the more trade intensive sectors.

The econometric model devised by Pain and Lansbury consisted of both location and internalization[97] specific explanatory variables. Of the former, they included the size of the sectoral output in the host country, relative factor costs, currency variability, the extent of trade barriers and the corporate financial conditions in the home country.[98] Of the latter, they used data on the U.S. registered patents of U.K. and German firms as proxy for their preference for the FDI, rather than cross-border licensing; the idea being that firms would be more likely to internalize the markets for their technology and organizational expertise in high value added sectors than in low value added sectors.[99] Estimates of the non-tariff barriers—ranging along an ordinal scale of 1 to 3—as they were perceived to effect particular sectors—were obtained from the Buigues, Ilzkovitz and Lebrun (1990) and Sapir (1993).[100]

The sample period taken for the dependent and explanatory variables apart from the IMP was 1981–92 in the U.K. case, and 1980–92 in the German case. The main results for the two studies are presented in the Appendix. For each country, the authors first calculated a (log linear) multi-regression equation *excluding* the IMP variable. In each case, the results were similar and broadly consistent with those of other studies. Host country output was shown to be positively and significantly correlated with U.K. and German FDI in the EC, although the (sectoral) output elasticities (1.54 and 0.84) were considerably lower than that recorded for GNP by the UNCTAD study (4.34).

Both the U.K. and German equations recorded a positive, but not significant, relationship between relative unit labor costs and FDI. This finding is consistent with the notion that high labor costs may reflect the availability and productivity of highly skilled labor, and associated agglomeration economies, rather than low (real) labor productivity. Both the corporate gearing ratios and the proxy variable used to capture the currency variability were correctly signed, but insignificant. Of particular interest was the effect of including a firm specific variable in the equation. Taking a three year cumulative measure of patents registered by the two groups of firms in the U.S., they found that in equations the coefficients were correctly signed and significant.[101] Overall, Pain and Lansbury estimated that the coefficient between the dependent and the five explanatory variables was very high at 0.972, although, almost certainly, there was some auto correlation between the explanatory variables.

The authors then produced two equations embodying the IMP indicator ordinally ranked according to perceived sensitivity (3 = high, 1 = low). This variable was shown to be positively and significantly related to FDI in the case of both the U.K. and Germany, i.e. it led directly to an increased level of FDI in the EC, although the coefficient was somewhat higher for the U.K. The effect of the inclusion of this variable was to reduce the elasticities on output (in the U.K. case) and patents (in the U.K. and German cases), which confirms an earlier point made in this chapter that, in the absence of a specific IMP variable, some of its affects are captured by other variables. Otherwise, apart from a marginal improvement in the overall explanatory power of the model, the coefficients and standard errors were little changed.

The next part of the Pain and Lansbury exercise was to estimate the difference made to the *value* of FDI in the EC as a result of the IMP. Using the estimates in the equations set out in the Appendix, Pain and Lansbury calculated that, by the end of 1992 the IMP may have raised the constant price stock of U.K. FDI by $15 billion (or 31 percent of the capital stake at that date) and the stock of German FDI by $5 billion (or 6 percent of the aggregate stock level). In both instances, the prime gainers were shown to be the financial and other service sectors and the electronics sector (which includes telecommunications equipment). For the U.K., major gains were also recorded in the distribution and food, drink and tobacco sectors, in both of which the U.K. has a comparative advantage.

Because of the differences in the industrial structure of individual EC countries,[102] the impact of the IMP on U.K. and German intra-EC FDI investment is likely to be country specific—at least to some extent. Thus, according to Pain and Lansbury, the primary beneficiary of the IMP, insofar as it has affected German outward FDI, has been in the U.K., in which it is estimated that the German stake in 1992 was $4.3 billion, or a third higher than it might otherwise have been. Other gainers appear to be Italy, the Netherlands and Portugal, but France and Belgium are both shown to have lost German investment as a result of the IMP, mainly, it would seem, because of the size of

German chemicals and distribution investment there. All in all, the study offers little support for the proposition that the IMP has led to a more pronounced intra-EC concentration of economic activity.

A final hypothesis examined by Pain and Lansbury was that the IMP may have diverted FDI away from other countries—and particularly other developed countries. To calculate whether or not this was so for the 1980s, the authors compared the impact of the IMP on intra- and extra EC FDI by the U.K. and Germany, by introducing a sectorally weighted internal market indicator for the U.S., and, in the case of German FDI, for Austria as well.[103] In both cases, the variable had the same sectoral pattern as the equivalent EC indicator, except that it was set to zero for all EC sectors. The results indicated that, while intra-EC U.K. FDI rose faster than extra-EC FDI, it was not, on average, at the expense of FDI in the U.S.[104] By contrast, the hypothesis was upheld in the case of extra-EC and German FDI, as this was shown to have been lower than might otherwise have been expected in Austria and the U.S.[105,106]

Formulating Specific Hypotheses about the Efficiency of the IMP

So much for an examination of a selection of recent studies which have sought to add an IMP dimension to the explanation of extra- or intra-FDI in the EC; or which help shed light on that dimension if its impact on other explanatory variables could be assessed. At the same time, without formally specifying the predictions of trade and FDI theory, they have frequently produced results which either confirm or deny these predictions. The following paragraphs return to consider more specifically the hypotheses set out earlier in the chapter, and to examine first how far the studies so far described throw light on these, and, second, to present some new findings of our own.

Hypothesis 1

The first hypothesis is that the IMP will have a positive effect on intra-EC trade, and an ambivalent effect on intra-EC FDI. Depending on the form and height of existing non-tariff barriers, it is likely to have an ambivalent effect on extra-EC trade, but a positive affect on extra-FDI and on the intra-EC trade by the foreign affiliates of non-EC MNEs.

While the Barrell and Pain study shows that Japanese FDI in the EC is significantly and positively related to non-tariff barriers, the Buigues and Jacquemin, and Clegg studies support the proposition that the IMP is leading to an increase in extra-EC FDI, as U.S. and Japanese seek to be 'insiders' in a market favoring the production of firms located in that market.[107] At the same time, research by both Agarwal *et al.* (1995) and Pain and Lansbury (1996) would appear to refute the hypothesis that intra-EC FDI will fall as a result of deeper economic integration (see Hypothesis 1). On the relationship between FDI and trade, the Buigues and Jacquemin research confirms that U.S. and Japanese exports to the EC are complementary to, rather than a substitute for, U.S. and Japanese FDI in the EC. Another study conducted by ourselves (to be considered in more detail a little later in the chapter) shows a positive relationship exists between these variables and intra-EC transactions, although, consistent with trade theory, the ratio between exports and FDI flows is higher in intra-, than in extra-, EC transactions.

Other evidence on the relationship between intra- and extra trade and FDI is more casual, although none the less instructive. Data on both extra- and intra- FDI in the EC suggest that the growth in downstream services (notably wholesale trade and business services) is closely correlated with exports from the investing country. For example, the gross product (= value added) of EC based wholesale trading affiliates of U.S. firms rose by 102.9 percent between 1982 and 1989, and by 9.6 percent in the following three years; while over the same time periods, the exports of the U.S. MNEs shipped to their European affiliates rose by 73.7 and 28.2 percent. Over the period 1982–89, the rank correlation coefficient between changes in the stock of U.S. assets in EC wholesaling affiliates and U.S. exports to EC countries about which data are available was +0.53, but for that of 1989–93 it was –0.08.[108]

How far do the above conclusions hold for intra-EC trade and FDI, and to what extent are they country and industry specific? Certainly, as shown by both Eurostat and national data, there appears to be a significantly positive correlation between the recent growth in intra-EC FDI in trade related activities and exports from the investing countries,[109] although the former has tended to outpace the latter.[110] As, in their more general model, Pain and Lansbury calculated that the IMP program raised intra-EC U.K. and German FDI in distribution by 27 percent and 2 percent of the 1992 stock of FDI, so it may be concluded that, in part at least, the rise in intra-EC trade is also the result of the IMP.[111]

Earlier in this chapter, we made reference to Peter Petri's work on the regional clustering of trade and FDI. The data lent casual support to the proposition that trade and FDI intensity were closely related to each other. Petri, however, subjected this idea to more formal testing by relating the intensity of FDI in a 'partner' region or country[112] to the latter's population and GNP, and to its trade intensity (defined in a similar way) with that region or country. This he did for two EC countries (Germany and the U.K.) and two extra-EC foreign investors (the U.S.A. and Japan). The results are set out in Table 6 in the Appendix. Although the formulation cannot be used to establish the direction of the relationship between trade and FDI intensities, the results very clearly show that the two forms of cross-border transaction are strongly and positively associated in all the equations. Indeed, in these equations, unlike those which do not incorporate this additional measure, the significance of the regional dummy variables disappears. It will also be noted that, while in the Japanese and U.S. equations, a given difference in trade intensity is associated with a smaller difference in FDI intensity, in the case of the two EC countries the coefficient is close to one. This is just another piece of evidence suggesting an even closer link between intra-EC trade and FDI than between FDI and trade of the leading extra-EC investors in the EC.

Next, we would offer a brief observation about the interface between trade and FDI in particular industrial sectors. In their analysis of the changing share of U.S. and Japanese FDI in exports to the EC, for the period 1984–90, by 2-digit manufacturing sectors, Buigues and Jacquemin (1994) found a Pearson coefficient of +0.10 for the former and +0.64 for the latter. (The respective coefficients which related the share of exports and of FDI for 1990 were +0.75 and +0.28.) However, a more detailed industrial breakdown between changes in the sales of U.S. affiliates in Europe and exports shipped by parent companies to their European affiliates between 1982 and 1989 reveals less impressive correlation coefficients of +0.15 in the case of 22 'sensitive sectors' and a +0.08 in the case of 12 'non-sensitive sectors.'

There is one other trade related FDI issue which we touched upon earlier. While, as hypothesized, the IMP has almost certainly led to an increase in extra-EC FDI in the EC, relative to exports to the EC from the leading foreign investors, it may, at the same time, facilitate intra-EC trade between the affiliates of foreign MNEs.

This scenario is most likely to occur in sectors where: (1) foreign firms possess substantial competitive advantages—including the economies of common governance—over indigenous firms in the EC; (2) transport costs and other trade barriers between the investing and recipient countries are relatively high; (3) there are substantial plant economies of scale; and (4) where intra-EC distance related costs are relatively small. An examination of the sectoral structure of both U.S. and Japanese FDI in the EC suggests the sectors in which the percentage of exports by their EC subsidiaries to other EC countries were around or above the average (43 percent in the case of U.S. subsidiaries in 1989, and 38 percent in the case of Japanese affiliates in 1990) were, indeed, those which possessed one or more of these characteristics; and, most noticeably, the motor vehicles, domestic electrical, electronic components, appliances, computers, drugs, office equipment and industrial instruments sectors. In correlating the increase in sales of U.S. affiliates in Europe in 34 sectors with those of the increase in (our proxy of) intra-EC exports by these subsidiaries, between 1982 and 1989, we came up with a R2 of +0.34. The corresponding coefficient for sectors sensitive to the IMP was considerably higher at +0.57, while for the non-sensitive sectors it was –0.42.

At the same time, there are other sensitive products identified by the European Commission in which intra-EC trade did not markedly increase in the 1980s, e.g. beverages and textiles. This could explain why, between 1982 and 1989, there was little change in the percentage of goods exported by EC-based U.S. subsidiaries,[113] while the high export propensity of Japanese subsidiaries primarily reflected the replacement of imports into the EC from a single or limited production outlet in the EC.

Details on the relationship between the sectoral distribution of intra-EC FDI and trade are hardly better! We have drawn on two sources of data. The first are that contained in a study by Davies and Lyons (1996),[114] which examined changes in intra- and extra-EC FDI penetration ratios[115] and the export shares of German, French and Spanish industries, between 1987 and 1992. The authors showed there was little systematic relationship between either the level of foreign ownership, or changes in that ownership, and the level and change in either intra- or extra-EC trade. While, for example, trade and FDI appeared to closely parallel each other in computers, this was not so in the aerospace and the more traditional sectors, while in the Spanish telecommunications sectors and German electrical machinery sectors, a decrease in foreign ownership was associated with an increase in the significance of both intra- and extra-EC trade flows.[116]

The second source of data is that of intra-EC FDI and intra-EC trade, published by Eurostat (or related agencies) for the years 1984–92; these data are only available for some two digit industrial groups. In Table 4.10a we set out a comparison between the changing share of intra-EC FDI flows and intra-EC trade; and, in Table 4.10b, the changing trade/FDI ratios over this period.

Three particularly interesting features emerge from these tables. The first is the increasing share of intra-EC FDI flows directed to the less technology intensive sectors particularly in the 1980s; this is in marked contrast to the industrial pattern of U.S. and Japanese direct investment in the EC. However—and secondly—as shown by the changing share of trade flows, it would seem that the intra-EC exports of EC countries is also becoming less technology intensive. Since the more technology intensive sectors are also those which tend to be more integrated across national boundaries, these data suggest that, even by the early 1990s, the European MNEs had still not geared their

TABLE 4.10a *Comparisons Between Share of Intra-EC FDI and Trade by Broad Industrial Sector 1984–92 (%)*

	1984–86*		1987–89		1990–92	
	FDI	Trade	FDI	Trade	FDI	Trade
More technology intensive	73.0	59.9	47.0	61.3	50.6	62.1
Chemicals	30.8	18.4	28.4	16.6	9.9	15.9
Non-electrical machinery	15.7	10.6	3.2	11.4	10.1	11.1
Electrical and electronic equipment	18.4	14.8	13.3	15.4	15.3	15.6
Transport equipment	8.1	16.1	2.1	18.0	15.3	19.5
Less technology intensive	26.9	40.1	43.0	38.7	49.5	37.9
Primary and processed food products	9.6	12.5	22.7	11.3	27.2	10.8
Metal and metal products	0.7	3.6	6.4	3.8	3.5	4.1
Other industries	16.5	23.9	23.9	23.7	18.8	23.1
All industries	100.0	100.0	100.0	100.0	100.0	100.0
[ECUs (billion)	1.33	319.9	6.67	424.2	9.02	547.2]

TABLE 4.10b *Intra-EC Trade/FDI Ratios, 1984–92*

	1984–86	1987–89	1990–92
More technology intensive	196.4	82.9	74.4
Chemicals	142.7	37.1	97.2
Non-electrical machinery	160.8	325.5	66.5
Electrical and electronic equipment	192.9	73.8	61.9
Transport equipment	478.1	540.3	77.5
Less technology intensive	355.6	46.4	46.6
Primary and processed food products	312.2	31.5	24.1
Metal and metal products	1047.2	37.7	69.7
Other industries	346.5	62.9	74.6
All industries	239.5	63.5	60.7

*Annual average. Intra-EC FDI is defined as inward investment flows into all Member States of the EC from other Member States of the EC; and intra-EC trade as value of exports between members of the community.
Source: Eurostat (1994).

European operations to meet the needs of the internal market. However, until a more detailed sectoral breakdown is available for intra-EC FDI flows, this is as much as a hypothesis as an established fact. Thirdly, as revealed by Table 4.10b, the trade/FDI ratios have fallen substantially over the last decade, although there is no distinct sectoral pattern which emerges.[117]

Hypothesis 2

> Economic integration will lead to a more concentrated geographical distribution
> of economic activity in the EC in intensive technology sectors in which plant
> economies of scale relative to transport costs are important, but a less concentrated
> pattern where products are more dependent on classical resource endowments
> for their competitiveness.

We set out some of the changes in the geographical distribution of
both extra- and intra-FDI in the EC over the past decade or so. Overall,
as revealed by Agarwal *et al.* (1995), the share of all FDI by the major
EC countries directed to the EC has increased in almost all manufacturing and service sectors between the mid-1980s and early 1990s.
However, there seems little to suggest that there has been any general
increase in the geographical concentration or agglomeration of FDI
within the EC, except in a few technology or information intensive
sectors thought likely to be the most responsive to the IMP program.
For example, the U.K., which already had a revealed comparative FDI
advantage in financial services, has continued to maintain that
advantage, although this is almost entirely due to the continued
preference of U.S. and Japanese MNEs to invest, and/or acquire
businesses in London, rather than in Frankfurt, Rome or Paris.[118] In
the pharmaceutical sector, there has been further concentration of
both intra- and extra-EC FDI in the U.K. and France. The six core
countries accounted for 91.3 percent of the cross-border M&A transactions between 1989 and 1994. However, if anything, the data—
fragmentary as they are—suggest that there has been a modest decrease
in concentration of FDI in the electronic components, office and
computing machines, industrial instruments and business services in
the four largest EC countries, *viz.* France, Germany, Italy and the
U.K.[119]

Outside the high technology and information intensive sectors, we
observe that, while the core EC countries have continued to attract
the bulk of new FDI and cross-border M&A activity, in auto components
and in auto assembling, Spain has become a major new production
outlet and has attracted both Japanese auto companies and joint
ventures of EC and U.S. MNEs (Agarwal *et al.*, 1995). In chemicals,
too, there has been some geographical restructuring of new FDI,
particularly from Germany and the U.K. towards the Netherlands and
Spain. At the same time, all the major EC chemical MNEs have
increased their share of production both elsewhere in the EC (and,
outside the EC, in the U.S.) since the IMP program was first announced.
This pattern of regionalization and globalization going hand-in-hand
is also repeated in the textile and clothing industry. However, in spite
of the increased Europeanization of this sector, imports from outside

the EC continued to rise at the expense of the output of indigenous firms (Agarwal *et al.*, 1995).

A related hypothesis to the one stated at the beginning of this section is that the lowering or removal of non-tariff barriers will reduce the growth of *extra*-EC FDI in those sectors in which *intra*-EC FDI expands the most rapidly. According to Agarwal *et al.* (1995), this has not happened. By considering up to nine sectors for each of five countries (France, Germany, the Netherlands and the U.K.), the authors secured bi-variate correlation coefficients between changes in the intra- and extra-FDI between 1985 and 1992, which were generally positive, rather than negative, as might be predicted. This, in the words of the authors, suggests that the 'globalization strategies of the major EC investors were largely independent of integration in Europe' (Agarwal *et al.*, 1995, p. 12).

Hypothesis 3

> By enabling firms to better spread their extra-plant fixed costs and to exploit the common governance of related cross-border activities, the IMP will increase the foreign ownership of activities in the EC, especially in those sectors where such advantages are associated with the privileged possession of firm specific intangible assets.

Earlier in this chapter, we presented some data which show that the share of FDI inflows to the GFCF of all EC countries, except Ireland, increased markedly in the five years immediately following the announcement of the IMP, since when it has stabilized between 5.5 and 5.7 percent.[120] As might be expected, the share of FDI in GFCF of particular countries in any one year fluctuates considerably more, not least because of the lumpiness of M&As, whenever these involve a capital export from the acquiring country. It may be further noted that, although the share of inbound FDI to GFCF varies between Member States (in 1993 it varied from 0.5 percent in Germany to 10.3 percent in the U.K.), the same or similar rate of increase between the first and second half of the 1980s was experienced by most countries, apart from Greece, where it only rose from 6.0 to 7.9 percent, and Portugal where the foreign owned component rose more than three-fold.[121] Taking the period 1981–93 as a whole, there is little suggestion that the competitive or ownership advantages of foreign firms have become more pronounced relative to those of one nationality of EC firms, rather than to those of another.

When the foreign participation ratio of the EC is compared with that of other developed countries, including the rest of Europe, it can be seen that, in the early 1990s, there was some retrenchment of FDI as compared with indigenous investment in North America, although, in 1994, the ratios for both Canada and the U.S. were nearer their late 1980s' level. The buoyancy of the foreign participation ratio in the EC in the 1990s is entirely consistent with the increased share of intra-EC cross-border M&As in all cross-border M&As.

Although we only have piecemeal evidence about the changing share of the foreign ownership of particular sectors in EC countries, we do know that, during the 1980s, the share of foreign enterprises in the manufacturing production of five EC countries (France, Germany, Ireland, Italy and the U.K.), increased in all cases except for Germany where it remained the same.[122] We also know the sectors in which MNEs or their affiliates tend to concentrate, *viz.* computers, motor vehicles, pharmaceuticals, electronic equipment and industrial instruments (OECD, 1993;[123] Dunning, 1993a). If one, then, examines the industrial composition of the sales of U.S. affiliates in the EC manufacturing in 1993, one sees that 70–75 percent were one or the other sensitive sectors identified by the Commission; and that this percentage has hardly changed since 1982.[124] This percentage compares with a figure between 50 percent and 55 percent of the value added in all manufacturing by both indigenous and foreign owned firms in the Community (Buigues *et al.,* 1990). Since the pattern of FDI by the other major foreign investors in the EC is broadly similar to that of the U.S., it may be reasonably concluded that, relative to locally owned firms, the affiliates of foreign MNEs are more concentrated in IMP sensitive sectors; and, excepting for medical instruments, that their share of the output of the most sensitive sectors has increased—at least marginally—since the early or mid-1980s.[125]

To some extent, then, these data are further corroboration that, since the mid-1980s, quite a substantial part of FDI[126] in both North America and Europe has been undertaken as part of a deliberate strategy of MNEs designed to maintain or advance their global competitive positions. Insofar, too, as economic integration increases inter-firm rivalry, and reduces the transaction costs of engaging in cross-border M&As, it may lead to a change in the ownership of firms, without there being any change in the location of production or trading patterns.[127]

Again, such fragmentary evidence as we have points to M&As being concentrated in the sectors which have been most affected by the IMP. Using data on M&As involving U.S. and European companies[128] between 1985 and 1991 and classified by 19 industrial sectors, it can be shown that 69 percent of the value of the transactions, in which U.S. firms were the buyers and 75 percent of those in which European firms were the buyers, were in the sensitive sectors. For this chapter, we conducted an additional econometric exercise which attempted to test the proposition that changes in the sectoral distribution of U.S.

FDI in the leading EC countries would be related to the sensitivity of the sectors to the IMP program. The proposition here, derived from the trade and FDI literature, is that the FDI directed to the EC, both absolutely and relative to trade, will be positively correlated to the removal of the trade barriers as U.S. firms seek to become 'insiders' in a more liberalized EC market.

In testing this hypothesis, we related (by use of pooled data for two time periods, *viz.* 1982–89 and 1989–93), the change in the sales of U.S. affiliates in Europe, in 31 industrial sectors between 1982 and 1993 to five explanatory variables: (1) the sales of established U.S. affiliates in 1982 and 1989 (this we took to be a proxy for agglomeration economies and a 'familiarity' index for new investors);[129] (2) changes in market size of the EC; (3) changes in the value added per person employed in the EC (as a measure of labor productivity); (4) changes in exports of U.S. MNEs to their European affiliates; and (5) a dummy variable for the IMP, which we relate to the perceived sensitivity of the sectors on a scale of 1 (little sensitivity) to 3 (high sensitivity).[130]

We calculated two equations: one with and one without an IMP variable. The results of the former are set out in Table 7 in the Appendix. Only the market size variable was statistically significant at the 5 percent level for a one-tailed test. The perceived impact of the IMP was shown to be negatively (although not significantly) related to the sectoral increases in the sales of U.S. subsidiaries.

Inadequate sectoral statistics preclude us from conducting such a detailed exercise for intra-EC FDI. The best we can do is to use the Eurostat data on the sectoral composition of intra-EC FDI flows for the period 1985–92, and see how far these are related to the kind of variables identified in the earlier exercise. However, we did not, in this instance, calculate an agglomeration variable, partly because there are no data on the stock of intra-EC FDI in the early 1980s, and partly because the sectoral breakdown is too broad to calculate a meaningful index. Also, in place of variable 4 in the previous exercise, we computed an index of intra-EC trade published by DEBA (vd). However, because Eurostat FDI data are only available for seven industrial sectors—and there are no sectoral breakdowns by countries—we have divided the period into six three-year intervals[131] to obtain an acceptable number of observations. All FDI data are then expressed as a ratio of the three-year average flow to the average FDI flow for 1984 and 1985. For the first three explanatory variables, *viz.* change in market size, labor productivity and intra-EC trade, we adopt a similar procedure. However, instead of introducing of a dummy variable for the IMP of 1–3, we ranked each of the seven sectors according to their perceived sensitivity of that to the removal of non-tariff barriers (1 = high and 7 = low).[132]

We again formulated two regression equations; one with and one without the IMP variable. The results of the former are set out in Table 8 in the Appendix (Dunning ii). Although these should be treated with even greater caution than the previous exercise, they suggest that the negative effect of IMP on defensive market seeking FDI was outweighed by its positive effect on other forms of FDI—including strategic asset seeking FDI; productivity was also significant at the 1 percent level and correctly signed.

Hypothesis 4

> The impact of the IMP is likely to have the greatest response by foreign investors in sectors in which they have the most pronounced competitive advantages, *vis-à-vis* indigenous firms. These will be in sectors wherever the fixed costs of the core ownership specific advantages of firms are high, and where the intra-firm costs of coordination and transaction are low and where cross-border transport and costs are low.

Previous sections of this chapter have, in fact, touched upon this hypothesis indirectly in as much as we have shown that many of the effects of the IMP have been sector specific. Moreover, we have indicated the types of sectors in which the foreignness or multi-nationality of enterprises is perceived to confer a competitive advantage. However, it is worth recalling that the main indigenous competitors to foreign firms investing in the EC are significant MNEs in their own right. Moreover, for the most part, the MNEs for Europe are from the same industrial sectors in which inbound FDI is concentrated.[133]

To test Hypothesis 4, we propose to sidestep the issue of the distinctive characteristics of MNEs—and, indeed, that of the intra-firm coordination and transaction costs—by estimating the revealed employment advantage (REA) of foreign—in this case the U.S.—affiliates in the EC. This we do by calculating the share of total EC employment in the EC accounted for by US affiliates in each of some 30 industrial sectors in 1993 and then dividing that share by the share of all EC industrial employment accounted for by all U.S. affiliates. A ratio above 1 would indicate U.S. firms had a comparative REA in that sector; and a ratio below 1 that they had a comparative disadvantage.

The REA is the first of the explanatory variables we relate to the dependent variable, which, again, is the increase in the sales of U.S. affiliates in Europe between 1982 and 1993. The other independent variables are export/local sales (FDI) ratios of U.S. MNEs, which we use as a proxy for the preference of U.S. firms to satisfy their European markets from a U.S. compared to a European location, and a dummy variable (on a scale of 1 to 3) which measures the perceived sensitivity of the sector to the IMP.

The results, which are also set out in the Appendix, explain almost 30 percent of the sales growth of U.S. affiliates. Both the REA and export/local sales ratios are significant at the 5 percent level; however, the IMP variable adds little explanatory value. The REA variable is positively related and the export/FDI ratio is negatively related to the increase in the sales of U.S. subsidiaries in Europe.

Conclusions

The preparation of this chapter has been like doing a difficult jigsaw puzzle with many pieces missing! Only very faintly and imperfectly is one able to see the full picture.

We have used most of the statistical evidence at our disposal to examine changes in the extent and pattern of extra- and intra-FDI in the EC (or Europe) since the early 1980s. That part of the jigsaw is reasonably clear. FDI in the EC has risen faster than in most other parts of the world (save for Japanese FDI in parts of East Asia), but there is little reason to suppose that this has been at the expense of non-EC FDI.

Within the EC, there have been some discernible changes, both in industrial structure and in the geographical distribution of economic activity. Of the former, the relative growth of FDI in technology and information intensive (and especially in service related activities) is, perhaps, the most significant trend—although this is by no means confined to Europe. Of the latter, the access of Greece, Portugal and Spain—and particularly Spain—has led to a modest decentralization of other than the most technology and information intensive activities from the six core EC countries.

Our chapter also confirms that the growth of intra-EC and Japanese FDI has outpaced that of the U.S. over the last decade or more. However, whereas the proportion of goods exported from U.S. subsidiaries in the EC has remained about the same since 1982, other forms of intra-EC trade—including that of European MNEs, have risen quite rapidly.[134]

When trying to isolate the significance of the possible explanation for these events, one is faced with almost intractable conceptual and data problems; and our conclusions must be extremely tentative. We would, however, make five observations:

1. While regionalization and globalization are distinct spatial concepts, it is difficult to perceive how globalization could have had the consequences it has in Europe if the IMP program (or something

like it) had not come about. This is particularly the case in sectors which are most integrated in their international operations; although, it is worth recalling that even the most globally oriented MNEs tend to practice regional, rather than global, production strategies (UNCTAD, 1993b).

2. Almost all the studies examined in this chapter point to the fact that the main dynamic impact of the IMP on FDI flows is through its effects on other variables affecting FDI—and noticeably market-size, income levels, the structure of economic activity and agglomeration economies. *Inter alia*, this makes it very difficult—and indeed of questionable value—to consider IMP (or a proxy for same) as an independent variable—except, perhaps, in the years immediately following 1985, when FDI was influenced more by the expectations of the program's outcome, i.e. prior to dynamic effects coming on stream. But, even considering the IMP as an independent variable, and the difficulties associated with its measurement, the few studies—including some new ones presented in this paper—all generally agree that it has stimulated both extra and intra EC FDI, but the former more than the latter—but not as significantly so as have other variables.

3. It seems clear that the effects of IMP are industry specific, and there is some evidence that, as hypothesized by trade and FDI theory, extra-EC FDI has increased more in sensitive than in non-sensitive sectors since the early 1980s—and equally important—more in these sectors than elsewhere in the developed world. The Pain and Lansbury study also reveals that, within the IMP, both U.K. and German FDI elsewhere in the EC would have been less—and particularly so in some of the more sensitive sectors, e.g. finance and insurance.

4. Our chapter has examined the validity of several propositions which emerge from trade and FDI theory. First, we have suggested that there is only limited evidence that the geographical con-centration of economic activity has increased, even in the sectors which benefit from the substantial plant economies of scale. At the same time, the fact that higher value activities have remained so highly embedded in the core countries, while the markets for the products has increased substantially, is testimony to the continuing drawing power of the economies of agglomeration in these sectors. Again, consistent with the predictions of neo-classical trade theory, the IMP may well have helped disperse resource based and/or lower value activities; and, in part at least, this is confirmed by the changing structure of intra-EC FDI and trade. Second, we have found that there is a complementarity between FDI and trade in most of (but not all) industrial sectors, and that

the IMP has done nothing to lessen this complementarity. However, this relationship is less strong for intra-EC than for extra-EC FDI. Third, as predicted by FDI theory, the most significant growth in the *share* of sales of foreign affiliates, has occurred in those sectors and countries in which the competitive advantages of the former firms are the most marked. Such fragmentary evidence as we have gives no support to the proposition that non-MNEs have improved their competitive positions *vis-à-vis* MNEs; though, in some sensitive sectors, but not generally in the most advanced technological sectors,[135] EC based MNEs have improved their competitive position *vis-à-vis* U.S. and Japanese MNEs; and it is highly likely the IMP has contributed towards this improvement.

5. A substantial proportion of the extra- and intra-EC FDI in the EC over recent years has taken the form of M&As; and part of the rationale for this has been to acquire strategic assets to advance the regional and/or global competitiveness of the acquiring firm. Although such M&As are essentially a global phenomenon (Walter, 1993), those involving EC firms as sellers have undoubtedly been facilitated by the IMP.[136] The result of these M&As on the intra-EC location (c.f. the ownership) of economic activity is ambiguous; but, in the majority of cases, there has been some restructuring of activity of the acquired firm; and this, as well as the distinctive sourcing and exporting policies of the acquiring firms may well effect both intra- and extra-EC trade.[137]

Our final observation is that, while for some sectors and for some foreign investors the dynamic effects of the IMP program have already largely materialized, for others—and especially for the service sectors and for Japanese (and possibly some European) investors—these consequences have yet to work themselves out. Hopefully, the next three or four years will help us fit some new pieces into the jigsaw portraying the effects of an integrated EC.

Appendix

1. UNCTAD (1993)

APPENDIX TABLE 1 *Regression results for the determinants of FDI in developed countries, the European Community and other developed countries, 1972–88 (t-statistics in parenthesis)*

Variable	Developed countries	European Community	Other developed countries
Constant	−304.37	−113.39	−139.41
	(6.29)	(5.63)	(3.33)
GNP_{t-1}	0.022	0.029	0.017
	(11.35)	(7.23)	(8.92)
ΔGNP_t	0.37	0.74	0.22
	(3.19)	(4.49)	(1.45)
$(I/GNP)_{t-1}$	834.96	278.87	329.87
	(4.92)	(5.26)	(2.01)
$V(XR)_t$	−414.41	−64.11	−448.04
	(4.35)	(2.64)	(2.52)
r^2	0.92	0.87	0.88
D/W	1.51	2.05	1.78

The basic model for each region or country (indicated by j, which has been omitted here for simplicity) takes the form:

$$FDI_t = \alpha_0 + \alpha_1 GNP_{t-1} + \alpha_2 \Delta GNP_t + \alpha_3 (I/GNP)_{t-1} + \alpha_3 XR_t = \alpha_4 V(XR)_t + [\text{other variables}]$$

where

FDI_t	=	inflow of FDI to a particular region or country in year t,
GNP_{t-1}	=	the level of GNP in year t–1 (which signifies the size of the market),
ΔGNP_t	=	the change in GNP between years t–1 and t,
$(I/GNP)_{t-1}$	=	the ratio of domestic investment to GNP in year t–1,
XR_t	=	the exchange rate, defined as a ratio of the domestic currency to the dollar, at year t, and
$V(XR)_t$	=	the squared deviation of the exchange rate from its mean over the period 1972–88.

The model is estimated using regression analysis with annual data for the period 1972–88.

2. Srinivasan and Mody (1996)

APPENDIX TABLE 2 *Log-Linear Estimates of U.S. Foreign Investment Determinants in Foreign Manufacturing Industry: Countries by Geographic Location and Size of Income: 1977–88*

	EEC	Latin America	East Asia	Low Income	Middle Income	High Income
Constant	−7.047	−8.841	−6.261	−5.946	−7.392	−8.222
Market size	1.399*	1.200*	1.969*	1.172*	0.394*	0.605*
	(3.3)	(15.7)	(3.4)	(5.7)	(2.3)	(2.3)
Cost of labor	−0.991*	−0.074*	−1.492*	−0.037	−0.208†	−0.521
	(2.4)	(3.3)	(2.5)	(0.8)	(1.8)	(1.3)
Cost of capital	1.637	−0.144	−1.560*	−2.299*	0.251	0.170
	(1.5)	(1.1)	(2.9)	(8.6)	(0.9)	(0.5)
Previous FDI	0.449	0.150*	0.772*	0.364*	0.822*	0.727*
	(1.4)	(2.2)	(2.7)	(6.1)	(4.6)	(3.8)
Infrastructure	1.931*	0.820*	0.474	0.764*	0.052	0.161
	(3.5)	(6.4)	(1.1)	(4.9)	(0.3)	(0.4)
Country risk	2.389	0.817*	0.827*	0.763*	0.566*	1.011
	(1.3)	(7.4)	(3.0)	(2.8)	(3.3)	(1.1)
Openness	1.481*	−0.200	−0.927*	0.312	−0.063	0.441
	(3.5)	(1.2)	(2.2)	(0.8)	(0.3)	(1.1)
	N=82	N=103	N=56	N=68	N=129	N=163
	R^2=0.76	R^2=0.92	R^2=0.72	R^2=0.76	R^2=0.76	R^2=0.68

*Significance at the 5% level
†Significance at the 10% level

3. Clegg (1995)

APPENDIX TABLE 3 Multiple Regression Results for the Determinants of U.S. FDI in the EC-6, 1951–90

	M*	ΔM	ΔTD	EC92	ΔXR	Exp.XR	ΔRI	Exp.RI	DCAP	Constant	R^2	F Stat	Durbin Watson
Full period 1951–90	-2.212 (-2.795)[a]	0.463 (0.843)	2.355 (2.021)[b]	19.371 (1.004)	-0.382 (-1.447)[c]	8.982 (0.587)	-29.778 (-0.508)	31.737 (0.718)	-10.009 (0.811)	36.784 (0.600)	0.589	3.665[a]	1.986
Sub-period 1 1951–72	5.588 (1.636)[c]	-1.048 (-2.166)[b]	-0.468 (-0.477)	n.a.	-0.077 (-0.279)	-29.672 (-1.966)[b]	-118.330 (-2.034)[b]	-76.782 (-1.861)[b]	-48.698 (-2.697)[a]	151.757 (2.496)[b]	0.622	2.670[b]	1.973
Sub-period 2 1973–90	1.650 (0.562)	4.790 (1.531)[c]	n.a.	-7.882 (-0.224)	1.498 (1.097)	7.462 (0.198)	-188.037 (-1.492)[c]	-137.139 (-1.064)	n.a.	85.816 (0.653)	0.672	1.824	3.140

Notes:

Figures in parentheses are t statistics.

Significance levels are denoted by [a](1%), [b](5%) and [c](10%)

n.a. denotes not applicable.

* The coefficients for the market size variable are multiplied by a factor of 100,000 to improve intelligibility.

Key to variables:

M   Market size of the EC-6, proxied by GNP or GDP, deflated to constant prices.

ΔM   Annual percentage change in market size of the EC-6.

ΔTD   Relative trade discrimination against U.S. exports to the EC-6. The first differences are taken, as tariff dismantlement is naturally highly trended.

EC92   A dummy variable of 1 from 1987 onwards and 0 before that date.

ΔXR   The annual effective (weighted bilateral) exchange rate of the U.S. dollar against the currencies of the EC-6. Because the raw data are highly trended, the variable is entered in the form of first differences.

EXP.XR A variable to capture expectations about the likely direction of changes in the exchange rate, based on whether the current value is above or below long term trend. This variable is greater than unity if the dollar exchange rate is expected to fall, and vice versa.

ΔRI   The ratio of the U.S. nominal domestic interest rate to the EC-6 host interest rate ($i^{U.S.}/i^{EC}$), weighted by the GNP of each member. This variable is expressed as first differences in order to eliminate the strong time trend.

EXP.RI A variable to capture expectations about the likely direction of changes in the U.S. nominal domestic interest rate relative to EC-6 host interest rates. It is based on whether the current value is above or below long term trend. This variable is greater than unity if the U.S. interest rate is expected to fall, and vice versa.

DCAP   A dummy variable scheme to reflect the policy of U.S. government-imposed capital controls on outward U.S. FDI, i.e. the voluntary (1965–67) and mandatory (1968–72) capital controls programs.

4. Buiges and Jacquemin (1994)

APPENDIX TABLE 4 *The Determinants of U.S. and Japanese Foreign Direct Investment in Seven or Nine Manufacturing* Sectors 1980–90 (Linear Regression Equations)*

	1 Constant term	2 EC's share of exports	3 NTB	4 ΔM	5 SS	R^2	F
U.S.	11.00 (–1.04)†	0.72 (3.29)	0.03 (1.21)	0.50 (0.36)	0.20 (1.80)	0.37	10.18
Japan	–14.19 (6.18)	0.26 (5.68)	0.05 (2.84)	1.41 (3.02)	0.10 (8.04)	0.73	60.70

*Sectors are: Food products, chemicals, non-electrical machinery, electrical and electronic equipment, transport equipment, textiles, paper and other manufactured products in the Japanese case; and these sectors excluding textiles and paper in the U.S. case.
†Figures in parentheses are values of t statistics.

Dependent variable = EC's share of total U.S. or Japanese exports
2 = EC's share of total U.S. or Japanese exports in the seven sectors examined.
3 = Intra EC non-tariff barriers as identified by Buiges *et al.* (1990).
4 = Growth of EC demand = production + (imports – exports) of sectors examined divided by growth of U.S. or Japanese demand in the seven sectors example.
5 = EC's exports for each of the seven sectors in total EC exports of manufactured products divided by the same index for all OECD countries.

5. Pain and Lansbury (1996)

APPENDIX TABLE 5   *The Determinants of U.K. and German Outward FDI (Log Linear Regressions)*

Dependent variable: ln $(FDI)_t$ Sample period: 1981–92
(a) **U.K.**

	1	2	3	4	5
ln$(FDI)_{t-1}$	0.5501 (7.7)	0.5594 (8.1)	0.5318 (7.3)	0.5481 (7.9)	0.5509 (7.9)
ln$(Y)_t$	0.6934 (2.6)	0.5148 (2.0)	0.5157 (1.9)	0.3061 (1.5)	0.4654 (1.8)
ln$(REL)_t$	0.2965 (0.8)	0.4711 (1.3)	0.5009 (1.3)	0.2516 (0.6)	0.5066 (1.3)
ln$(PAT)_t$	0.9140 (5.1)	0.7386 (4.1)	0.8253 (4.2)	0.5994 (3.2)	0.8061 (4.3)
$CASH_{t-1}$	–0.7488 (1.9)	–0.7750 (2.0)	–0.8049 (2.0)	–0.8042 (2.1)	–0.7950 (2.0)
$USME_t$	–0.9665 (4.3)	–0.9375 (4.3)	–0.9059 (4.1)	–0.9034 (4.2)	–0.9140 (4.2)
IM_t		0.0699 (3.2)		0.0951 (3.7)	
$IMCH_t$			0.1483 (1.2)		
$IMME_t$			0.0319 (0.3)		
$IMEE_t$			0.1550 (1.2)		
$IMFD_t$			0.0291 (0.2)		
$IMOM_t$			0.2948 (2.4)		
$IMDS_t$			0.2601 (2.1)		
$IMFS_t$			0.2811 (2.2)		
$IMUS_t$				0.0583 (1.9)	
$IMIND_t$					0.0539 (2.1)
$IMSER_t$					0.1032 (2.9)
R^2	0.943	0.946	0.946	0.954	0.953
Standard Error	0.2054	0.1989	0.1999	0.1971	0.1988

APPENDIX TABLE 5 (continued)   *The Determinants of U.K. and German Outward FDI (Log Linear Regressions)*

Dependent variable: ln (FDI)$_t$ (b) **German**				Sample period: 1980–92	
	1	2	3	4	5
ln(FDI)$_{t-1}$	0.4513 (8.4)	0.4430 (8.2)	0.4511 (8.6)	0.4426 (8.2)	0.4436 (8.2)
ln(Y)$_t$	0.4630 (3.8)	0.4755 (3.9)	0.3700 (2.9)	0.5022 (4.1)	0.3854 (3.1)
ln(REL)$_t$	0.1999 (1.9)	0.1973 (1.9)	0.2464 (2.3)	0.2565 (2.2)	0.2059 (1.9)
ln(PAT)$_t$	0.7162 (5.9)	0.6271 (5.1)	0.6358 (4.8)	0.6762 (5.4)	0.7419 (5.9)
ln(REC)$_{t-1}$	−0.1861 (3.2)	−0.1051 (1.5)	−0.1680 (2.3)	−0.1332 (1.9)	−0.1400 (2.0)
EXCH$_t$	0.1140 (2.5)	0.1317 (2.8)	0.1205 (2.7)	0.1327 (2.9)	0.1192 (2.6)
IM$_t$		0.0393 (2.9)		0.0248 (1.6)	
IMCH$_t$			−0.0625 (1.1)		
IMME$_t$			−0.0642 (1.1)		
IMEE$_t$			0.0181 (0.3)		
IMTR$_t$			0.1451 (2.2)		
IMOM$_t$			0.0748 (1.3)		
IMDS$_t$			0.0069 (0.1)		
IMFS$_t$			0.2391 (3.7)		
IMUS$_t$				−0.0315 (1.2)	
IMOE$_t$				−0.0311 (1.3)	
IMIND$_t$					0.0154 (0.4)
IMSER$_t$					0.1229 (2.5)
R^2	0.972	0.973	0.973	0.973	0.973
Standard error	0.2274	0.2267	0.2236	0.2266	0.2272

Definition of variables:

FDI	+	Stock of U.K. or German FDI ($ million, 1990 prices)
Y	=	Sectoral output ($ million, 1990 prices)
REL	=	Relative U.K. (or German) foreign unit labor costs
PAT	=	Stock of U.K. (or German) sectoral patents (3-year cumulation)
CASH	=	Ratio of debt interest payments to U.K. corporate cash flow
USME	=	Dummy variable for outlier in investment in U.S. mechanical engineering sector
IM	=	Sectoral internal market indicator for EU (zero before 1987)
IMUS	=	Sectoral internal market indicator for U.S. (zero before 1987)
IMCH	=	Dummy variable for EU chemicals (1 from 1987–92)
IMME	=	Dummy variable for EU mechanical engineering (1 from 1987–92)
IMEE	=	Dummy variable for EU electronics (1 from 1987–92)
IMFD	=	Dummy variable for EU food, drink and tobacco (1 from 1987–92)
IMOM	=	Dummy variable for EU other manufacturing (1 from 1987–92)
IMDS	=	Dummy variable for EU distribution (1 from 1987–92)
IMFS	=	Dummy variable for EU financial services (1 from 1987–92)
IMIND	=	IMCH + IMME + IMME + IMFD = IMOM
IMSER	=	IMDS + IMFS

6. Petri (1994)

APPENDIX TABLE 6 *Trade and foreign direct investment intensity regressions: Germany, U.K., U.S. and Japan*

		Dependent variable	
	Trade	Outward FDI stock intensity	Outward FDI stock intensity
(i) Germany			
Constant	−0.354	−1.211	−0.751
	(−0.783)	(−1.201)	(−0.902)
America's dummy	−0.776‡	−1.651‡	0.359
	(−5.396)	(−2.027)	(1.074)
Asia dummy	−1.093‡	−1.593‡	−0.172
	(−7.292)	(−4.764)	(−0.431)
Log population	0.001	0.012	0.01
	(0.029)	(0.102)	(0.104)
Log gross domestic product	0.055	0.125	0.054
	(1.247)	(1.276)	(0.659)
Trade intensity			1.301*
			(−4.917)
Adjusted R^2 F-statistic	0.596	0.356	0.575
	8.438	42.04	27.759
(ii) U.K.			
Constant	0.093	−0.481	−0.568
	(0.128)	(−0.393)	(−0.550)
America's dummy	−0.949‡	−0.854*	0.031
	(−3.781)	(−2.018)	(0.074)
Asia dummy	−0.635‡	−0.244	0.348
	(−2.748)	(−0.626)	(0.971)
Log population	−0.076	0.027	0.098
	(−0.913)	(0.190)	(0.815)
Log gross domestic product	0.035	0.019	−0.013
	(0.507)	(0.165)	(−0.136)
Trade intensity			0.932*
			(−4.146)
Adjusted R^2 F-statistic	0.284	0.003	0.29
	5.365	1.036	4.602

APPENDIX TABLE 6 (continued)

	Dependent variable		
	Trade	Outward FDI stock intensity	Outward FDI stock intensity
(iii) U.S.			
Constant	1.504*	0.489	−0.099
	(2.261)	(0.753)	(−0.157)
Europe dummy	−1.459‡	−0.622‡	−0.05
	(−6.408)	(−2.792)	(−0.182)
Asia dummy	−0.823‡	−0.663‡	−0.341
	(−2.988)	(−2.462)	(−1.262)
Log population	0.136*	−0.111	−0.164*
	(−1.691)	(−1.409)	(−2.193)
Log gross domestic product	−0.085	0.041	0.074
	(−1.251)	(0.621)	(1.193)
Trade intensity			0.391*
			(−3.089)
Adjusted R^2 F-statistic	0.466	0.125	0.319
	13.009	2.966	18.25
(iv) Japan			
Constant	−0.543	−1.31	−0.928
	(−0.845)	(−1.244)	(−0.958)
America's dummy	−1.084‡	−1.020‡	−0.257
	(−4.562)	(−2.619)	(−0.604)
Europe dummy	−1.746‡	−1.910‡	−0.681
	(−8.039)	(−5.364)	(−1.368)
Log population	0.013	0.132	0.123
	(0.174)	(1.117)	(1.142)
Log gross domestic product	0.113*	0.109	0.03
	(1.791)	(1.058)	(0.307)
Trade intensity			0.704*
			(−3.26)
Adjusted R^2 F-statistic	0.619	0.422	0.565
	19.474	10.503	36.768

*Significance level = 10 percent
†Significance level = 5 percent
‡Significance level = 1 percent
Source: UNCTAD (1993).

7. Dunning (i)

APPENDIX TABLE 7 *The Determinants of Changes in Sales of U.S. Industrial Affiliates in Europe Classified by Industrial Sector 1982–93*

	Δ Sales*
Constant	0.5317
	(0.7407)
Actual sales†	–0.0171
	(1.0563)
Change in market size‡	0.6500††
	(0.3694)
Change in productivity§	0.4444
	(0.7065)
Change in exports¶	–0.0298
	(0.0688)
Dummy**	–0.1175
	(0.1360)
Adjusted R²	0.1020
F statistic	1.976

*   Change in sales of U.S. affiliates in Europe 1982–83 and 1989–93. These are treated as pooled data.

†   Actual sales of U.S. affiliates in Europe 1982, 1989.

‡   Change in EC market size 1982–89 and 1989–93.

§   Change in EC labor productivity 1982–89 and 1989–93.

¶   Change in exports of U.S. MNEs to Europe 1982–89 and 1989–93.

** Dummy variable on a scale of 1–3 to reflect perceived sensitivity of the sector to IMP.

†† Significance level 5% (one-tailed test).

Source: U.S. Department of Commerce (1985, 1992 and 1995), Eurostat (1994), Buiges *et al.* (1990).

8. Dunning (ii)

APPENDIX TABLE 8 *The Determinants of Changes in Intra-EC FDI Flows*

	Δ Intra-EC FDI*
Constant	−28.4742
	(8.9720)
Change in market size†	−2.0322
	(19.5751)
Changes in productivity‡	36.0070**
	(9.4544)
Change in intra-EC trade§	−0.3782
	(14.8770)
Dummy¶	1.3865**
	(0.2225)
Adjusted R^2	0.6521
F statistic	15.244

* Intra-EC FDI flows, expressed as 3-year moving averages from 1985 to 1992, as a percentage of an average of the base years 1984 and 1985.

† Change in EC market size by industrial sector; 3 year moving averages (apparent consumption).

‡ Change in EC labor productivity by industrial sector; 3-year moving averages.

§ Change in intra-EC trade by industrial sector; 3-year moving averages.

¶ Dummy variable on a scale of 1–7 to reflect perceived sensitivity of the sector to IMP.

** Significance level 1%.

Source: U.S. Department of Commerce (1985, 1992 and 1995), Eurostat (1994), Buiges *et al.* (1990).

9. Dunning (iii)

APPENDIX TABLE 9 *Some determinants of Change in Sales of U.S. Affiliates in the EU Classified by Industrial Sector*

	Δ Sales*
Constant	0.9814**
	(0.3258)
REA†	0.7227¶
	(0.2776)
Log export/FDI intensity‡	–0.3891**
	(0.1389)
DUM§	–0.0309
	(0.1182))
Adjusted R^2	0.2827
F statistic	7.174

[a] Change in the sales of U.S. affiliates in Europe, 1989/1982 and 1993/1989. These are treated as pooled data.

† Revealed Employment Advantage (REA) of U.S. affiliates in Europe (EU). The first step was to calculate individual year values for 1982, 1989 and 1993. The numerator here is the ratio of the percentage of employment in U.S. affiliates of all employment in the EC for each industrial sector, and the denominator is the percentage of the employment in U.S. affiliates of all employment in the EC for all industrial sectors. The second step was to use these values to calculate changes in the REA ratio between 1982 and 1989, 1989 and 1993.

‡ Export/FDI intensity is the ratio of the growth of exports of U.S. MNEs to their European affiliates (1989/1982 to 1993/1989), the growth of sales of the EC affiliates of U.S. firms (1989/1982 and 1993/1989).

§ Dummy variables (on a scale of 1 to 3) perceived sensitivity of the sector to the IMP.

¶ Significance level 5%.

** Significance level 1%.

Source: U.S. Department of Commerce (1985, 1992 and 1995), Eurostat (1994), Buiges *et al.* (1990).

References

AGARWAL, J. P., HIEMENZ, U. and NUNNENKAMP, P. (1995) *European integration: a threat to foreign investment in developing countries,* Kiel Institut für Weltwirtschaft an der Universitat Kiel, Discussion Paper No. 246.

AGMON, T. and HIRSCH, S. (1995) Outsiders and insiders: competitive responses to the Internal market, *Journal of International Business Studies,* Vol. 26, No. 2, 1–18.

BARRELL, R. and PAIN, N. (1993) Trade Restraints and Japanese Direct Investment Flows, NIESR, London (mimeo).

BENSEL, T. and ELMSLIE, B. T. (1992) Rethinking international trade theory: a methodological approach, *Weltwirtschaftliches Archiv,* Vol. 128, Heft 2, 249–265.

BRAINARD, S. L. (1993) *An Empirical Assessment of the Proximity-concentration Ratio between Multinational Sales and Trade,* NBER Working Paper No. 4583, December, Cambridge, Mass.

BRAUNERHJELM, P. and SVENSSON, R. (1995) Host Country Characteristics and Agglomeration in Foreign Direct Investment, Stockholm: Industrial Institute for EC and Social Research (mimeo) October.

BUIGUES, P., ILZKOVITZ, F. and LEBRUN, J. (1990) The impact of the internal market by industrial sector; the challenge of member states, *European Economy,* Special Edition, 1–114.

BUIGUES, P. and JACQUEMIN, A. (1994) Foreign investment and exports to the European Community. In MASON, M. and ENCARNATION, D. (eds) *Does Ownership Matter?* Clarendon Press, Oxford.

CANTWELL, J. and HODSON, C. (1991) Global R&D and UK competitiveness. In CASSON, M. C. (ed) *Global Research Strategy and International Competitiveness,* Basil Blackwell, Oxford, pp. 133–82.

CAVES, R. (1980) Investment and location policies of multinational corporations, *Zeitschrift fuer Volkswirtschaft und Statistik,* Vol. 3, 321–7.

CAVES, R. (1996) *Multinational Firms and Economic Analysis,* Cambridge University Press, Cambridge.

CECCHINI, P., CATINAT, M. and JACQUEMIN, A. (1988) *The European Challenge 1992. The Benefits of a Single Market,* Wildwood House, Aldershot, Hants.

CLEGG, J. (1995) The determinants of United States foreign direct investment in the European Community: a critical appraisal, University of Bath (mimeo), Bath.

DAVIES, S. and LYONS, B. (1996) *Industrial Organization in the EC,* Oxford University Press, Oxford.

DEBA (Data for European Business Analysis) (various dates) Various statistics on EC trade, production and employment issues, Brussels: European Commission.

DELONG, G., SMITH, R. C. and WALTER, I. (1996) *Global Merger and Acquisition Tables 1995,* Salomon Center (mimeo), New York.

DUNNING, J. H. (1993a) *Multinational Enterprises and the Global Economy,* Addison Wesley, Wokingham, England and Reading, Mass.

DUNNING, J. H. (1993b) *The Globalization of Business,* Routledge, London and New York.

DUNNING, J. H. and CANTWELL, J. (1991) Japanese direct investment in Europe. In BURGENMEIER, B. and MUCCHIELLI, J. L. (eds) *Multinationals and Europe 1992,* Routledge, London and New York, pp. 155–184.

EAG (1996) *The Development of Foreign Direct Investment Flows Inside the EU Due to the*

Internal Market Program. Report submitted to DG XV/01 Commission of the European Communities, June.

European Commission (1998) *The Single Market Review Subseries IV Impact on Trade and Investment. Volume 1: Foreign Direct Investment,* Kogan Page, London.

Eurostat (1994) *EU Direct Investment 1984–1992,* The European Commission, Luxembourg.

Eurostat (1995) *Panorama of EU Industry,* The European Commission, Brussels.

FRANKO, L. (1976) *The European Multinationals,* Harper and Row, New York.

GRAY, H. P. (1994) *A Firm Level Theory of International Trade in Dynamic Goods,* Rutgers University (mimeo), Newark.

HELPMAN, E. and KRUGMAN, P. R. (1985) *Market Structure and Foreign Trade,* MIT Press, Cambridge, MA.

HIRSCH, S. (1974) Capital and technology confronting the neo-factor proportions and new-technology accounts of international trace, *Weltwirtschaftliches Archiv,* Vol. 110, No. 4.

HIRSCH, S. (1976) An international trade and investment theory of the firm, *Oxford Economic Papers,* Vol. 28, 258–70.

HUFBAUER, G. C. and CHILAS, J. G. (1974) Specialization by Industrial Countries, extent and consequences. In GIERSCH, H. (ed.) *The International Division of Labor: Problems and Perspectives,* J. C. Mohr, Tubingen.

HUGHES, K. (1993) Foreign multinationals and economic competitiveness: the UK experience. In HUMBERT, M. (ed.) *The Impact of Globalization in Europe's Firms and Industries,* Pinter, London and New York.

JULIUS, D. A. (1990) *Global Companies and Public Policy,* Royal Institute of International Affairs, London.

KRUGMAN, P. (ed.) (1986) *Strategic Trade Policy and the New International Economics,* MIT Press, Cambridge, MA.

KRUGMAN, P. (1990) *Rethinking International Trade,* MIT Press, Cambridge, MA.

MARIOTTI, S. and PISCITELLO, L. (1995) Information costs and location of FDIs within the host country: empirical evidence from Italy, *Journal of International Business Studies,* Vol. 26, No. 4, 815–41.

MARKUSEN, J. R. (1995) The boundaries of multinational enterprises and the theory of international trade, *Journal of Economic Perspectives,* Vol. 9, No. 2, 169–89.

MARKUSEN, J. R. and VENABLES, A. (1995) *Multinational Firms and the New Trade Theory,* NBER Working Paper No. 5036, February, Cambridge.

MATALONI, R. J. and GOLDBERG, L. (1994) Gross product of US multinational companies 1977–1991, *Survey of Current Business,* February, 42: 63.

MOLLE, W. T. M. and MORSINK, R. L. A. (1991) Intra-European direct investment. In BÜRGENMEIER, B. and MUCCHIELLI, J. L. (eds) *Multinationals and Europe 1992,* Routledge, London.

MUNDELL, R. (1957) International trade and factor mobility, *American Economic Review,* Vol. 47, 321–35.

NUNNENKAMP, P. GUNDLACH, E. and AGARWAL, J. (1994) *Globalization of Production and Markets,* J. C. B. Mohr, Tübingen.

OECD (1993) *The contribution of FDI to the productivity of OECD Nations,* OECD, Paris.

OECD (1995) *International Direct Investment Statistics Yearbook 1995,* OECD, Paris.

OMAN, C. (1994) *Globalization and Regionalization: The Challenge for Developing Countries,* OECD Development Center, Paris.

PAIN, N. and LANSBURG, M. (1996) The impact of the internal market on the evolution of European direct investment, NIESR, (mimeo), London.

PELKMANS, J. (1984) *Market Integration in the European Community*, Martinus Nijhoff, The Hague.

PETRI, P. A. (1994) The regional clustering of foreign direct investment and trade, *Transnational Corporations*, Vol. 3, No. 3, 1–24.

RUIGROK, W. and VAN TULDER, R. (1995) *The Logic of International Restructuring*, Routledge, London and New York.

SAPIR, A. (1993) Sectoral dimension in market services and European integration, *European Economy*, Vol. 3, 23–40.

SRINIVASAN, K. and MODY, A. (1996) Location determinants of foreign direct investment: an empirical analysis of US and Japanese investment, *Canadian Journal of Economics* (forthcoming).

SWEDENBORG, B. (1990) The EC and the locational choice of Swedish multinational companies, Stockholm: Industrial Institute for Economic Social Research, Working Paper No. 284.

THIRAN, J. M. and YAMAWAKI, H. (1995) Regional and country determinants of locational decisions: Japanese multinationals in European manufacturing, Louvain-la-Neuve Université Catholique de Louvain Département des Sciences Economiques Discussion Paper No. 9517.

UN (1993a) *From the Common Market to EC*, UN Transnational Corporations and Management Division, Department of Economic and Social Development, New York.

UN (1993b) *World Investment Directory, 1992 Vol. III Developed Countries*, UN Transnational Corporations and Management Division, Department of Economic and Social Development, New York.

United Nations Conference on Trade and Development (UNCTAD) (1993a) *World Investment Report 1993, Transnational Corporations and Integrated International Production*, UN, New York and Geneva.

United Nations Conference on Trade and Development (UNCTAD) (1993b) *World Investment Report 1993, Transnational Corporations and Integrated International Production*, UN, New York and Geneva.

United Nations Conference on Trade and Development (UNCTAD) (1993c) *Explaining and Forecasting Regional Flows of Foreign Direct Investment*, United Nations, New York.

United Nations Conference on Trade and Development (UNCTAD) (1994a) *World Investment Report 1994: Transnational Corporations, Employment and the Workplace*, UN, New York and Geneva.

United Nations Conference on Trade and Development (UNCTAD) (1994b) *World Investment Report 1994: Transnational Corporations, Employment and the Workplace*, United Nations, New York and Geneva.

United Nations Conference on Trade and Development (UNCTAD) (1995) *World Investment Report 1995: Transnational Corporations and Competitiveness*, UN, New York and Geneva.

United Nations Conference on Trade and Development (UNCTAD) (1996) *World Investment Report 1996: Investment Trade and International Policy Arrangements*, UN, New York and Geneva.

United States Department of Commerce (1981) *US Direct Investment Abroad 1977*, Bureau of Economic Analysis International Investment Division, Washington, DC.

United States Department of Commerce (1985) *US Direct Investment Abroad 1982*, US Government Printing Office, Washington, DC.

United States Department of Commerce (1992) *US Direct Investment Abroad, 1989 Benchmark Survey*, Provisional Results, Bureau of Economic Analysis, Washington, DC.

United States Department of Commerce (1995) *US Direct Investments Abroad, Provisional Results 1993*, US Government Printing Office, Washington, DC.

United States Tariff Commission (1973) *Implications of Multinational Firms for World Trade and Investment and for US Trade and Labor*, US Government Printing Office, Washington, DC.

WALTER, I. (1993) The role of mergers and acquisitions on foreign direct investment. In OXELHEIM, L. (ed.) *The Global Race for Foreign Direct Investment*, Springer-Verlag, Berlin and New York.

YAMAWAKI, H. (1993) Location Decisions of Japanese Multinational firms in European Manufacturing Industries. In HUGHES, K. (ed.) *European Competitiveness*, Cambridge University Press, Cambridge, pp. 11–28.

YANNOPOULOS, G. N. (1992) Multinational corporations and the single European market. In CANTWELL, J. C. (ed.) *Multinational Investment in Modern Europe: Strategic Interaction in the Integrated Community*, Edward Elgar, Aldershot, Hants and Brookfield, Vermont.

Notes

1. A more extensive version of this chapter was published as a two-part article in the *Journal of Common Market Studies*, Vol. 35, No. 1, March 1997, pp. 42–86 and Vol. 35, No. 2, June 1997, pp. 189–220. See also EAG 1996 and European Commission (1998).

2. Now called the European Union (EU). However, as most of the analysis contained in this chapter predates the formation of the European Union, we shall use the expression European Community (EC) throughout.

3. For a review of these studies, see UN (1993a).

4. Some, for example, compared FDI in the EC versus that in non-EC countries in Western Europe; others compared FDI flows in the pre-EC period with those in the post-EC period, and attempted to explain the differences with respect to a number of explanatory variables, including a proxy for the ECM.

5. Particularly in the Irish case, where intra- and extra-EC inward investment increased dramatically in the decade after Ireland joined the EC in 1973.

6. A good example is provided by Spain and Portugal. In the five years after their accession to the EC, the average annual increase in the stock of extra- and intra-EC FDI into Portugal was 56.7 percent and into Spain 128.3 percent. In the period 1990–93, the corresponding increases were 1.7 percent and 17.8 percent. Moreover, a serious deficiency of multi-variate studies is that they rarely consider the second-order affects of FDI on the other variables—notably market size and GNP per head—which are usually included in the regression equations.

7. The year prior to the announcement of the Internal Market Program (IMP).

8. Data are extremely patchy. In the early years of the EC, the *number* of subsidiaries set up, or acquired, by EC MNEs in the rest of the EC rose more rapidly than elsewhere in Europe or in the rest of the world (Franko, 1976). In the UK, the

stock of outward investment to the rest of the EC, as a percentage of all outbound investment, rose from 8.0 percent in 1962 to 21.9 percent in 1974 and 21.1 percent in 1984. The corresponding percentages for German outward investment for 1976 and 1986 were 36.4 percent and 39.8 percent, and for the Netherlands 50.6 percent in 1973, 46.5 percent in 1979 and 38.4 percent in 1984. The stock of US FDI directed to the ten member states of the EC (as of 1973), as a percentage of all U.S. FDI, was 15.0 percent in 1957, 28.5 percent in 1972 and 35.0 percent in 1984. Between 1955 and 1984, the percentage share of Japanese FDI stock directed to the same ten member states fluctuated between 11 percent and 17 percent; indeed, it was lower in 1984 (12.7 percent) than ten years earlier (16.6 percent) (UN, 1993a).

9. Estimates by scholars again vary. Yannopoulos (1992) calculated that, for the period 1980–84, extra-EC FDI *flows* were two-thirds of all inbound FDI; this compared with an estimate made by Molle and Morsink (1991) for the years 1975–83 of 75 percent; and that by Pelkmans of the percentage of extra-FDI stocks for 1978 of total FDI in the EC of 57 percent (Pelkmans, 1984).

10. Defined both in terms of their GNP per head, and the proximity of their industrial and commercial heartlands to Central Western Europe, *viz.*, Belgium, Luxembourg, France, Germany, Italy, Netherlands and United Kingdom. We accept, of course, that *parts* of industrial France, the U.K. and Italy are as far removed from the Ruhr Valley as is Southern Denmark!

11. Once again, the data are neither comprehensive nor directly comparable. The figure of one-third was derived from FDI stock data for the leading EC countries in 1980 and from flow data for all the EC countries in 1984–86.

12. The ratio is a kind of revealed comparative advantage of the EC in attracting FDI from other EC countries. In 1980 the ratio for German/EC FDI was 1.06; for France 1.00; for Belgium/Luxembourg 1.65; for Denmark 1.31; for the Netherlands 0.89; and for the U.K. 0.50. The below average figures for the Netherlands and the U.K. reflected the above average share of North American FDI attracted to these countries. By contrast, the U.S./EC intensity ratio was 0.60 and the Japanese/U.S. ratio was 0.30.

13. Which, *inter alia*, points to a complementary, rather than a substitutable, relationship between the geographical pattern of trade and FDI at the end of the first phase of European integration.

14. Dunning (1993b), Chapter 7. The main source of statistical data is the U.S. data on outward FDI published regularly in the *Survey of Current Business*.

15. These sectors alone accounted for two-fifths of all extra-FDI in the years 1984–86. It is, however, likely that part of the $2,600 million involved was in direct response to the announcement of EC 1992. See Eurostat (1994).

16. As shown especially by U.K. and German intra-EC FDI, as published by their national authorities. See also Dunning and Cantwell (1991).

17. 74.6 percent, as compared with 61.1 percent for extra-FDI.

18. *Viz.*, machinery, transport equipment and electrical and electronic products.

19. Possibly because extra-EC (and particularly U.S. and Japanese) MNEs' products have shown a greater ability to overcome intra-EC non-tariff barriers than their EC counterparts.

20. The fall was most marked in the case of the U.K. Although in the first five years of the U.K.'s membership in the EC, the U.S. sales/export ratio rose from 7.5

to 7.7, by 1985 it had dropped back to 4.4, the lowest figure of the (post-1957) period (UN, 1993a).

21. In 1977, the U.K. and German subsidiaries alone accounted for 50 percent of intra-EC exports of all EC subsidiaries and 42 percent of the imports (UN, 1993a, pp. 67 and 69).

22. Obviously there were exceptions to this rule. Philips of Eindhoven is one example of an EC MNE which totally restructured its European activities in the first 20 years of the ECM.

23. The most noticeable increase was, perhaps, recorded by the U.K. where the share of its outward stock directed to the EC rose from 7 percent in 1960 to 15 percent in 1971 and 21 percent in 1985. However, it is worth recalling that a sizeable proportion of that investment (15 percent in 1960 and 19 percent in 1985) was directed to distribution (i.e. *trade* enhancing activities).

24. The relationship between FDI and trade is explored in more detail in later sections of this chapter.

25. It is worth observing that although, at the time of the formation of the ECM, it was intended that non-tariff, as well as tariff, barriers should be lowered, if not entirely eliminated, most of the thrust of liberalization, at least until the early 1970s, took the form of the removal of tariff barriers.

26. The transaction costs of tariff barriers primarily represent an addition to the transport costs of exporting or importing goods and services. Those of non-tariff barriers represent a whole range of cost-enhancing measures which affect not only the *plant*-specific costs for production of goods and services, but *firm* specific costs of transacting and coordinating the various extra-plant activities, including the procurement of inputs and the marketing and distribution of outputs. It is only very recently that economists have paid serious attention to the effects of economic integration on these latter costs—and on how integration may help upgrade the competitive advantages of multi-product firms whose activities spread across national boundaries.

27. The theory of integration *per se* identifies various static and dynamic economic consequences which may result from various forms of integration, such as customs unions, free trade areas or preferential trading agreements. In the context of this chapter, the analytical techniques used are based either on trade theory or FDI theory.

28. The theory of international production attempts to explain the extent and pattern of the foreign owned value activities of firms (i.e. production financed by FDI). Like trade, the unit of account is the output of firms and countries, as distinct to FDI, which is an input measure. At the same time, FDI is often taken to be a proxy for foreign production.

29. But, see the work of some modern trade theorists, especially Helpman and Krugman (1985) and Markusen and Venables (1995).

30. For a survey of the current state of FDI theory, see Dunning (1993a) and Caves (1996).

31. The theoretical case for suggesting there are advantages of the common (as opposed to the separate) ownership of at least some activities has been nicely set out by Richard Caves in a somewhat neglected article (Caves, 1980).

32. Because of the efficiency enhancing advantages of the common ownership of activities earlier described.

33. According to Brainard (1993), the *share* of the sales of the foreign affiliates in the sum of exports and affiliate sales is positively related to trade barriers and transport costs. Thus, the removal of trade barriers would lead to a substitution towards trade, although they may also increase the *levels* of both trade and FDI.
34. And, by implication, integration theory.
35. This it may do for two reasons. First, the IMP is likely to improve the efficiency of 'insider' relative to 'outsider' firms (this, after all, is one of its main intentions). Second, it will encourage the restructuring of activities by foreign firms insomuch as the unified market enables a more efficient disposition of resources.
36. As summarized in Dunning (1993a).
37. As set out in Buigues *et al.* (1990, p. 27).
38. Although the Common Market came into being on 1st January 1958, it was not until the late 1960s that a tariff-free zone in the EC was finally accomplished.
39. Although between 1985 and 31 December 1992, the majority of directives designed to remove non-tariff barriers had already been put into effect.
40. Two exceptions appear in business services and telecommunications. Between 1982 and 1989 (which included) the first four years after the announcement of the IMP, the sales in business services of the EC subsidiaries of U.S. MNEs rose by 52.9 percent. In the following four years, *viz.* 1989–93, they increased by 101.6 percent (U.S. Department of Commerce, 1985, 1992, 1995). In the case of telecommunications, restructuring is taking a good deal longer, partly because in the past this sector has been so heavily regulated; and second, the costs of restructuring are considerable. It is also worth observing that until recently the vast majority of telecommunications were intra-country, rather than cross-border, and much more noticeable in the U.S. than in Europe.
41. Throughout, we consider the 12 countries. These include Spain, Portugal and Greece which joined the EC in the early 1980s, but exclude Austria, Finland and Sweden, which acceded to the EU in 1995.
42. An alternative way of analyzing the data in Table 4.1 is to compare rates of growth of FDI stock in the EC with that of the rest of Western Europe, all developed countries and the world. Between 1980 and 1985, the *average annual* rate of growth for the EC and the other regions were respectively 4.3 percent, 4.8 percent, 8.8 percent and 10.3 percent. In the following five years, the corresponding percentages were 43.9 percent, 32.4 percent, 31.3 percent and 27.0 percent, and in the five year period ending in 1995 they were 8.5 percent, 10.5 percent, 8.2 percent and 11.0 percent. One of the reasons for the high figure for the rest of Western Europe was the spectacular increase of inbound FDI into Sweden (it averaged 32.7 percent per annum between 1990 and 1995) (UNCTAD, 1996).
43. There are, of course, other normalizing factors which one should consider, e.g. changes in exchange rates. Most data in this paper are expressed in U.S. dollars and there have been some noticeable fluctuations in the value of that currency relative to European countries over the past 15 years—and particularly in the £/$ rate.
44. Of course, for individual sectors of the EC, the share of FDI was considerably higher. For further details see UN (1993b).
45. Mainly as a result of a sharp fall in the contribution of FDI to GFCF in the U.K., the Netherlands and Belgium.

46. Broadly equivalent to flows, except that changes in stock are more likely to incorporate reinvested profits than the flow data.
47. For the purposes of this exercise, we have included Denmark in the non-core countries.
48. At the end of 1990, the £ was worth $2.32; by 1994 this had dropped to $1.50.
49. Greece joined the nine EC countries in 1981 and Portugal and Spain in 1985.
50. For further details, see the various annual surveys on foreign direct investment in the U.S., published in the Survey of Current Business (U.S. Department of Commerce).
51. Estimated from OECD and individual country data, but not shown in Table 4.3. The proportion for the manufacturing industry is rather lower. In 1993, for example, Spain was the second biggest recipient of Japanese FDI in the auto industry in the EC; and accounted for a larger proportion of the work-force in Japanese affiliates than any other EC country apart from the U.K., Germany and France. This is also some evidence of a regional clustering of Japanese owned firms in the EC notably around the Bayeon area of Germany, the South East of England and Wales, the Ile de France of France and the Este area of Spain. For further details, see Thiran and Yamawaki (1995).
52. Omitting North America from the calculation, then the share of intra-EC increased from 60.4 percent in 1985–87 to 72.3 percent in 1991–92.
53. These two countries alone increased their share of intra-EC FDI from 3.3 percent in 1985–87 to 8.6 percent in 1992–93.
54. Particularly—and rather surprisingly—in the financial services sector. While, for example, in the period 1989–94, 56.9 percent of all extra EC mergers and acquisitions (M&As) involved U.K. target firms, the corresponding U.K. proportion for intra-EC M&As was 15.4 percent.
55. Defined as the ratio of the share of a recipient (host) country (or region) (b) of the total FDI from another (= home) country (or region) (a) to the share of the former country (or region) of the total FDI from all countries, excluding that of the investor country. Expressed algebraically, $qab = Iab/Ia*/[I* b/I*-I*a]$, where qab = intensity of a's investment in b, Iab = investment by a (home country) in b (host country) and $*$ = summation of FDI across all countries (world). See Petri (1994).
56. In 1990, the European Commission identified 40 industrial (e.g. goods producing) sectors which, prior to the announcement of the IMP, were subject to high or moderate non-tariff barriers. To this list may be added some service sectors, notably finance, insurance, business services and wholesale trade in the service sector. See Buigues et al. (1990), and Sapir (1993).
57. Namely the years of the benchmark surveys of U.S. foreign direct investment (1977, 1982 and 1989) and for each year from 1991 onwards.
58. Unfortunately, there are no recent separate data for the EC itself, but, since the sales of FDI in the EC in 1992 were 90 percent of those in all Western Europe, these data serve as a good proxy for those of the EC.
59. One exception is the business services sector. Particularly impressive was an increase in sales of computer and data processing services of U.S. affiliates in Europe of 399.6 percent between 1989 and 1993.
60. Which includes business services.
61. The Pearson correlation coefficients calculated by Agarwal et al.(1995, p. 10),

in respect of the changes in sectoral structure of French FDI in the EC, compared with that in the industrialized countries, worked out 0.42* between 1985 and 1987 and 0.39* between 1990 and 1992. Corresponding coefficients (* = significance at 10 percent level and ** = significance at 1 percent level) for Germany, Netherlands and the U.K. were 0.84** and 0.94**, 0.80** and 0.84** and 0.73** and 0.29 respectively.

62. The authors note some exceptions to the rule, e.g. German FDI in all developing countries and in Asia, and UK FDI in Asia.

63. Contrary to the investment diversion hypothesis, the correlation coefficients (again for France, Germany, Netherlands and the U.K.) between trade and investment were shown to be positive and significant (Agarwal *et al.*, 1995).

64. In the literature, Ricardo goods are largely the output of natural resources (including relatively unskilled labor). Heckscher-Ohlin goods are those produced with a standard technology and manufactured under constant returns to scale (although it is possible to modify to incorporate standard goods subject to increasing returns in this category). Schumpeterian goods are those in high technology sectors, and the competitiveness of which rests more on innovatory and other firm specific advantages than purely country specific advantages. The role of firm specific advantages in influencing trade patterns is explored by Gray (1994).

65. The relative high share of medium income countries of more technology intensive sectors in 1982 largely reflected the attractions of Spain and Ireland as recipients of FDI in the chemical industry.

66. See also Bensel and Elmslie (1992), Helpman and Krugman (1985), Krugman (1986) and Krugman (1990).

67. For example, in his analysis, Robert Mundell (1957) assumed that production functions were identical in all countries and regions. This led him to the inevitable conclusion that trade and capital movements were substitutes, rather than compliments, for each other.

68. Trade intensities are calculated in exactly the same way as FDI intensities (see Note 57), except that trade replaces FDI as the unit of investment.

69. Petri does not identify the EC separately.

70. For an examination of these strategies see Oman (1994), Ruigrok and Van Tulder (1995) and UNCTAD (1993b and 1995).

71. Or more particularly, the sales of their European affiliates.

72. In 1993, the 12 EC countries accounted for 92 percent of all European gross product of U.S. subsidiaries.

73. In some sectors, e.g. aerospace, shipbuilding and railway equipment, between 1987 and 1992, intra-EC trade increased very much more than the degree of intra-EC specialization of production. However, these are also sectors in which there is very little FDI (Davies and Lyons, 1996).

74. Throughout the 1980s, M&As accounted for an increasing proportion of cross-border FDI. More particularly, in the period 1987–93, they were responsible for about two-thirds of FDI flows between developed countries (UNCTAD, 1994). Such M&As were also concentrated in sectors identified by the European Commission as being sensitive to the IMP.

75. Notably where agglomerative economies are present, e.g. in some high technology sectors.

76. When expressed as a proportion of the GNP of EC countries, the stock of inbound FDI increased from 4.8 percent in 1980 to 10.6 percent in 1990 and 12.2 percent in 1993.

77. Mainly U.S. According to Walter (1993), the value of cross-border M&As involving EC firms (but excluding extra-EC M&As, where EC were the buyers) rose from $11,526 million in 1985 to $139,033 million in 1989–90.

78. For more recent data, see De Long *et al.* (1996), who suggest there was a marked acceleration of intra-EC mergers in 1994 and 1995.

79. Often taken as a proxy for EC when separate data on the EC are not available.

80. And, of course, of other determinants not identified by the other variables.

81. Julius for 1963–88 and the UNCTAD for 1972–88. It is interesting to note the UNCTAD estimates of FDI elasticities were very similar for the EC and other developed countries (4.36 and 4.26 respectively).

82. This relationship would hold even, though, as we have seen, the *share* of FDI in total investment has increased.

83. A prediction which seems unlikely to be borne out by the facts!

84. For U.S. FDI only. The study also included an analysis of FDI in developing countries, but we are not concerned with these results here.

85. The latter being negatively correlated with FDI.

86. A recent study on Swedish FDI, covering the period 1975–90, confirmed the significance of agglomerative effects, particularly in high technology sectors, but finds that market size and the availability of skilled labor are generally more important locational determinants (Braunerhjelm and Svensson, 1995).

87. Information provided by Krisha Srinivasan in a letter to the author in December 1996.

88. A dummy variable of 1 was included for each year from 1986 onwards and 0 for 1985 and previous years.

89. The size of which was, itself, increasing as a result of more intra-EC trade and FDI. This idea is confirmed in a study by Yanawaki (1993) on the intra-EC distribution of employment in 236 Japanese manufacturing subsidiaries in 1988. Yanawaki found that the most significant explanatory variables were relative labor costs, market size and the quality of indigenous technological capacity. His regression analysis supports the predictions of trade theory that inbound FDI will be attracted by the advantaged factor endowments of host countries. However, it would appear that Japanese investors—at least in the 1980s—were still cautious about the integrating effects of the IMP, as they preferred to locate their activities where labor costs were low and *local* markets were sizeable. In a fully operating common market among Member States of similar economic structure and income levels, these cross-national differences should be minimal.

90. As set out by Buigues *et al.,* (1990).

91. This is also the conclusion of Barrell and Pain (1993), in a study of trade barriers (proxied by anti-dumping measures) to Japanese FDI in Europe. The authors find that, after controlling for market size and relative labor costs, Japanese investment flows to individual EC countries between 1980 and 1991 were strongly influenced by anti-dumping actions taken by the EC. Excluding the anti-dumping variable, relative labor costs and the level of export market penetration were both shown to be primary determinants of the geography of Japanese FDI in the EC.

92. The following paragraphs set out some of the results of a study by the authors, commissioned by the Economists Advisory Group (EAG). Fuller results appear in EAG (1996), and were published by the European Commission as part of their *Single Market Review Studies* in 1997. We are grateful to EAG and the Commission for allowing us to use some of the material contained in the above reports.

93. Apart from that in Ireland.

94. These two countries accounted for 45 percent of the outward FDI stock of EC countries in 1994.

95. The study also looked at other hypotheses, but these are more properly considered later in this chapter.

96. Although not formally derived from the predictions of integration and modern trade theory, each is consistent with these. See also the next section of this chapter.

97. As defined in the FDI literature. See Dunning (1993a).

98. These were predicated to affect the availability of finance for foreign investment.

99. Perhaps an even more telling statistic might have been the share of U.S. registered patents by firms of particular countries attributable to research undertaken by their foreign affiliates. See, for example, Cantwell and Hodson (1991).

100. Current work is proceeding which ranks the sectors (on a scale of 1 to 7) in order of their perceived sensitivity to the IMP.

101. The respective patent elasticities for the U.K. and German firms were 1.3 and 2.3 respectively. This variable was also found to be significant in the case of Japanese FDI in the EC by Yanawaki (1993).

102. Buigues *et al.* (1990, p 30), for example, have estimated the share of total industrial value added accounted for the sensitive sectors in 11 EC countries, excluding Luxembourg. The proportions range from 60.9 percent in the case of Ireland to 42.1 percent in the case of Denmark around an (unweighted) average of 52.7 percent. The average for the six core EC countries was 52.1 percent and for the remainder 53.7 percent.

103. See Equation 5a and 5b in the Appendix.

104. When separate dummies are introduced for each of the main sectors, the same conclusion holds good, with the notable exception of investment in distribution and, to a much lesser extent, in the chemical sector.

105. The authors accept there may be other reasons than those identified in the analysis of why a rise in the intra-EC FDI may have nothing to do with the IMP. These include exchange rate fluctuations and the vintage effect of investments made at different times in different countries.

106. There is also a time dimension, the significance of which Pain and Lansbury have tested. Their results (which are not reproduced here) suggest that the effects of the IMP on intra-EC FDI—particularly in the more sensitive sectors—have built up over time, even though there has been some slowing down of intra-EC FDI, apart from in certain service sectors, since 1990.

107. Swedenborg, and Agmon and Hirsch came to a similar conclusion in respect of Swedish and Israeli FDI in the EC (Swedenborg, 1990; Agmon and Hirsch, 1995).

108. *Viz.* share of total U.S. exports directed to EC growth of demand in EC divided by growth of demand in the U.S./European market and non-tariff barriers.

109. See especially Eurostat data on intra EC FDI and trade since 1984, and U.K. and German data on FDI, and exports to the other EC countries since the mid-1970s.
110. Between 1984–86 and 1990–92 intra-EC FDI in manufacturing industry rose by 239.4 percent, and inter-EC exports of manufactured goods by 70.9 percent (Eurostat, 1994).
111. Presumably it would be possible to test this hypothesis directly by replacing the FDI related dependent variable by a trade related variable.
112. As defined on page 67.
113. For all sectors, the proportion of the sales of EC affiliates of U.S. firms exported to the rest of Europe fell slightly from 42.1 percent in 1982 to 37.4 percent in 1989 and 40.6 percent in 1993.
114. For the pharmaceuticals, computers, electrical machinery, telecommunications, aerospace, medical instruments, boilers and containers, shipbuilding and rail stock sectors.
115. Equals imports as a percent of demand.
116. Exports divided by total production.
117. Since we have no data on the sales of EC affiliates in other EC countries, the ratios themselves tell us little about the significance of FDI, relative to exports, as a modality of penetrating EC markets. However, the changes in the ratios do tell a reasonably consistent story.
118. Even here, the U.K. appears to be losing some of its competitive edge. For example, while in 1989–90, the U.K. accounted for 48.9 percent of cross-border M&A activity in financial services; by 1993–94, this had fallen to 29 percent.
119. This tentative conclusion is based on data on cross-border M&As from that on U.S. FDI in Europe, as published in the benchmark surveys of the U.S. Department of Commerce and from various JETRO surveys on Japanese manufacturing activities in Europe.
120. See Table 4.9.
121. See Table 4.9.
122. The relevant percentages for 1980 and 1990 (or nearest year) were from France 26.6 percent and 28.4 percent, for Germany 23.2 percent and 22.8 percent, for Ireland 46.1 percent and 55.1 percent, for Italy 19.2 percent and 22.3 percent, and for the U.K. 19.3 percent and 25.3 percent.
123. In the case of the U.K., the share of foreign affiliates of total U.K. gross output between 1981 and 1989 rose in the auto, office, machinery and computers, chemicals and electrical and electronic equipment sectors, and declined in instrument, engineering, machinery (other than office machinery), rubber and plastics and man-made fiber sectors (Hughes, 1993).
124. These and other data are derived from the periodic benchmark surveys of U.S. foreign direct investment published by the U.S. Department of Commerce. More exact estimates are not possible due to differences in the industrial classification used by the Department of Commerce and the European Commission.
125. In their estimates of the changing foreign ownership ratios of nine sensitive sectors in three countries, *viz.* France, Germany and Spain (27 observations), Davies and Lyons (1996) found that in 18 of these the ratio had increased or remained the same.

126. How much, it is difficult to say as acquisitions do not always show themselves in the FDI. At the same time, we know that M&A and FDI inflows in Western Europe do very closely parallel each other (UNCTAD, 1994, p. 23).

127. At the same time, there is a good deal of evidence which suggests foreign affiliates—at least when they pursue regional or global production strategies—both export and import more than their indigenous competitors (Dunning, 1993a).

128. As derived by the Securities Data Corporation Merger and Corporate Transactions Data base.

129. For a discussion on the relationship between information costs and FDI, see Mariotti and Piscitello (1995).

130. Again, as derived from the European Commission.

131. These are (i) 1985, 1986, 1987, (ii) 1986, 1987, 1988, (iii) 1987, 1988, 1989, (iv) 1988, 1989, 1990, (v) 1989, 1990, 1991, (vi) 1990, 1991, 1992.

132. We did this by expressing employment in the 3-digit sensitive sectors—as identified by the Commission as a proportion of the employment in the seven 2-digit sectors—and ranked these latter sectors by the size of the percentages we obtained.

133. In other words, the EC is involved in a good deal of intra-industry FDI (as well as intra-industry trade).

134. An examination of the annual reports and press releases of the largest EC industrial MNEs, e.g. ICI, Siemens, Philips Electronics, Unilever, Volkswagen, etc., reveals an increasing proportion of their sales being directed to other parts of the EC.

135. With the possible exceptions of chemicals.

136. Particularly in service related sectors such as financial services and telecommunications.

137. The effect of M&As on the trading structure of the acquired firms—and the implications this has for the economic welfare of the host country is an unresearched topic in the literature.

5

Economic Policy, MNE Competitiveness and Local Content: An Application of the Lecraw-Morrison Framework

VIRGINIA A. TAYLOR

This chapter identifies factors grounded in economic and management theory that are posited to affect local content value. It provides an application of the holistic approach to value creation set forth by Lecraw and Morrison (1991). The lack of common understanding about just what constitutes local content value is addressed by an examination of the underlying reasons for perceptual differences in the valuation of localizing MNE value-added activity. A model using constructs derived from the Lecraw-Morrison framework (1991) is developed.

Introduction

Today industrial rivalry crosses country borders. Globalization of markets and production continues to increase; consequently the world economy often becomes the relevant corporate environment for multinational enterprises (MNEs). National sovereignty gives international business distinctive characteristics: these include diverse host factor endowments, multiple national political objectives and worldwide exchange rate variations as everyday facts of life. As individual nations seek industrial supremacy,[1] requirements for specific local content percentages can affect competitive issues in both domestic and international arenas.

The basic difficulty is the ambiguity surrounding local content statements. Various definitions reflect different objectives and do not necessarily beget transparent disclosure of the actual value added locally.[2] Substance differences occur when local content is modified because of a change in the amount of local inputs. The U.S. content of a Honda automobile changes when an imported engine is substituted for an engine produced in Ohio. On the other hand, a difference in form arises when alternate calculation methods result in divergent local content values (Taylor, 1993). The decision to increase or decrease the degree of local content in a particular product is one of those areas where a MNE's strategy can reinforce or undermine a government's national goals. Due to transfer prices, "in the boom year of 1987, 59 percent of non-U.S. companies reported no profit in the U.S. and paid no tax" (Barnet and Cavanagh, 1994, p. 344).

This chapter seeks to explain how globalization affects the MNE's value of local content through an investigation of the underlying reasons why differences occur, and discusses policy implications for both home and host governments. It is theorized that value creation in an international context is firm specific, and is affected by the political economy of the host country and by worldwide environmental dynamics. To present a systematic view of the local content phenomenon, the holistic approach to value creation developed by Lecraw and Morrison (1991) is utilized to create a model that embodies economics, management and dynamics variables.

Theoretical Background

A plethora of incentives motivate firms like Nestle, Ford, Toyota and Siemens to source raw materials and intermediate goods internationally and to locate value chain activities around the world. MNEs can create a competitive edge through selective procurement in host factor markets with cheap labor or cheap raw materials. Other MNEs may direct their marketing activities toward countries with large populations, sophisticated demands and higher per capita income levels. Economics scholars focus on the nature and distribution of resources in the environment, rather than on the leadership within the firm, as the primal driving force shaping the organizational structure and strategy.

Industrial organization[3] theory accepts a deterministic line of reasoning: the market structure of an industry[4] determines the conduct of management and resultant economic performance. Government policy decisions[5] such as the institution of local content requirements will force a change in the industry structure and force the actions of management. For example, in preparation for NAFTA's 62.5 percent local content requirements, Honda followed Nissan's lead and announced plans to spend $50 million to expand Guadalajara's production to 15,000 cars. Japanese suppliers of auto parts have followed. Matsushita Electric Industrial Company will spend $36 million to open a battery plant in Tijuana following Sanyo and Sony (Malkin and Neff 1994).

Management theorists and researchers stress that, although environmental conditions shape strategy through incentives, firms retain the critical role and choose which local environmental advantages to exploit (Child, 1972). Morrison and Roth (1992) present evidence that significant discretionary differences exist between firms within the same global industry. Despite common threats from the external environment, firms exercise considerable discretion in how to meet the basic requirements of the market served. When faced with uncertainty due to scarcity, firms may choose a niche strategy to reduce the scope of resource dependence. Backward vertical integration is an alternate solution to resource uncertainty (Buckley and Casson, 1988; Tallman and Shenkar, 1994). Modern day strategic alliances cloud the issue further (Doz and Phahalad, 1989). Japanese and Korean industrial groups often make boundaries ambiguous; power and influence are often invisible. Unique MNE responses exploit learned routines (Kogut and Zander, 1993) and experience in government relationships (Chandler, 1991) to create competitive advantage.

Focusing more narrowly on the local content causality question, classic economic theory suggests factor endowments determine the local content of a product. If this is true, firms in any given industry will have the same amount of local content. The trade balances in finished goods as well as raw materials suggest MNEs respond differentially and influence the invisible hand of the market.

Multi-Faceted Viewpoints

Eclectic Theory

Consideration of these issues has evolved over time. Dunning's (1988) eclectic theory of foreign direct investment (FDI) explains the internalization of production activity as a result of the interaction between three conditions that create the potential for success. These are:

1. MNE ownership advantages specific to the firm (defined as MOA);
2. Host country location-specific factor endowments (defined as HF);
3. Internalization efficiencies of hierarchical governance.[6]

MNEs locate their value-adding activities where firm-specific resources command the highest return. Management decisions are a function of weighted goals.[7] Host country factor endowments create comparative advantage attracting investment by MNEs and domestic firms. FDI occurs when unique MNE ownership advantages surpass those of local firms.

Internalization deals with the make or buy question. Boundary decisions safeguard necessary inputs. According to Hrebiniak and Joyce (1984), MNEs use loose coupling techniques to protect the core business from external shocks. James (1990) offers outsourcing as a way to increase in local content with less risk. For example, Japanese firms use extensive subcontracting, cultivating suppliers rather than engaging in vertical integration. The trading relationship moves within firm boundaries only when hierarchical governance is more efficient than market transactions. In a survey of foreign firms operating in the U.S.A., 80 percent of the executives reported U.S. local procurement expenditures in both the raw materials and component parts categories (Taylor and Chandran, 1996). Local content value includes value added through local production activity and local parts procurement.

Host Factor Endowments and the Competitive Advantage of Nations

Michael Porter (1990) identifies four facets of a nation's diamond which represent the location-specific or host country competitive advantages which attract MNE activity. Advanced or created assets (i.e. highly skilled workers), are even more important than classic natural factor endowments (i.e. low cost labor population). Because rivalry spurs improvement, rivalry among domestic firms and clusters of supporting industries enhance local competitiveness as does the size and sophistication of market demand. Porter considers government policy as an exogenous force exerting influence on the national diamond, hopefully as a catalyst for upgrading the four corners.

MNEs' Influence on National Competitiveness

Dunning (1993) adds to Porter's theory by including MNE business activity (MBA) as a significant influence on a country's diamond. MNEs are independent actors with many roles in the world economy; as producers, investors innovators and traders, they make decisions that change the competitive environment, determine the level and direction of trade and foreign direct investment. Individual national governments have strong incentives to attract FDI to enhance economic growth; these same governments also want to regulate corporate activities thereby curtailing the power of MNEs (Tyson, 1994). Incentive preferences and attractiveness depends on the MNE (Brewer, 1993; Rolfe, 1993).

The Lecraw-Morrison Model

In the management literature, the Lecraw and Morrison (1991) framework casts the multinational firm (MNE) and the host country government as organizations seeking value in a competitive world environment. The effects of strategic goals, political ideologies, and administrative mechanisms are acknowledged. Whether or not increased local content is desirable from an individual government point of view or from a MNE's strategic perspective can be examined using a cost-benefit[8] framework where desirability is conceptualized as value creation. The value of local content is in the eye of the beholder reflecting various priorities that may be time specific. The paradigm that follows provides a way to consider the interaction of many value determinants arising from government economic and social policy, transnational management strategy and dynamic global competition.

Local Content Value: National View

Recent events have shown that political platforms and social ideology have significant influence on the propensity of a government to impose and enforce the use of domestic inputs by public and private enterprises located within national boundaries. These constitute the host internal environment (HIE). Consider the current trade regulations imposed by China, the U.S.A., and Canada. Local content could be defined as a government policy variable and seen as a political construct. To slow the growth in imports with Chinese content, in 1996 the U.S. unilaterally changed the rules that determine where an imported piece of clothing or fabric originates. Facing re-election in November, 1996, 'President Clinton clearly wanted to cultivate the southern states which have a big textile industry' (Anon., 1996).

Lobbying efforts have been shown to influence local content decisions. Some firms lobby for domestic content legislation while others fight against it. Sectors faced with strong competition from imported goods often become vocal and visible when their quality of life is threatened (McCulloch,1985). According to Coughlin's (1985) analysis of votes on this issue, auto and steel workers' views were very influential in shaping voting patterns on U.S. local content legislation. MNEs mobilize domestic groups, such as foreign car dealers, to achieve their political goals (Lee, 1987). The host internal environment affects the value ascribed to local content and resulting regulations and policy. Luger (1988) found that MNEs have more power in recessionary cycles.

Location specific advantages or host factors (HF) include both the comparative advantage of natural factor endowments, and the created assets identified in Porter's national diamond. Host factors attract FDI which, in turn, creates economic expansion and jobs. BMW's classic economic reason for increased U.S. local content is that wages are expected to be $12 per hour versus the $28 it has to pay in Germany (Barnet and Cavanagh, 1994). To some extent, host factor endowments are available to both domestic and foreign firms; they define the opportunity sets and constraints for government policies to maximize domestic welfare. However, Johnson *et al.* (1989) provide evidence suggesting foreign and domestic firms are not treated equally in Japan.

Motivation or lack thereof depends on expected results. Sovereignty, defense, employment, income equity, deficits and re-election complicate the HIE and affect the government view of local content value. A host country must have the factor endowments that attract localization and economic policy makers must perceive value creation through increased local content. The EP value construct depends on both HF and HIE. This is one side of a crossover model.

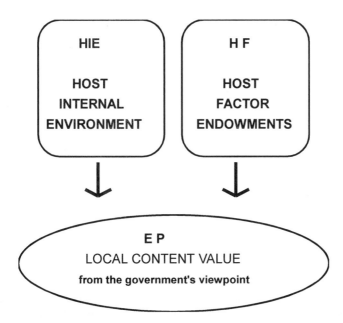

FIGURE 5.1 *Economic and Political Variables*

Local Content Value from an MNE View

Individual firms have many incentives to disperse and configure procurement and production along a value chain (Porter, 1991; Kogut, 1985a,b). Lower production costs, logistics, legal requirements, product differentiation, tax minimization and foreign exchange risk management influence profit potential—management's primary goal for both the short and long term. The determination of desired domestic content percentage is in fact a derivative decision of the localization-globalization strategy choice (Ghoshal, 1987). The MNE can also outsource intermediate goods or subcontract production.

Competitiveness relative to rivals is ultimately the result of implementation of a global strategy to coordinate dispersed production in dynamic environments. To accomplish this, MNEs must understand and accommodate national economic goals and objectives including domestic content requirements which coexist with and may directly and indirectly influence their own strategic goals.

The eclectic theory, in the FDI literature discussed earlier, asserts that MNEs need some firm-specific advantages to overcome the natural advantages of indigenous firms. A MNE's ownership advantage (MOA) is defined by its strengths, opportunities, constraints and competitive threats. This bundle of firm-specific resources is often referred to as the core competence or competitive advantage of the firm. The MNE's internal administration (MIE) also affects whether or not local content is perceived as creating value from the firm's viewpoint. Choices balance the complexity, stability and munificence elements in the industrial environment with the internal strategic decision-making power structure and network demands (Ghoshal and Bartlett. 1990). Middle level executives can "not only redirect a strategy, delay its implementation or reduce the quality of implementation but can totally sabotage its implementation" (Guth and MacMillan, 1986). This internal environmental variable includes the strategic direction and the organization's structural constraints. The local content value for transnational management (TM) is conceptualized as a function of both MOA and MIE. First, a firm must have some ownership advantage to exploit; then, management must perceive value in localization and prevail in implementation. There is an interactive aspect to value creation in the firm, just as there is in the economic political arena. Perceptions of LCV from an MNE perspective may not completely coincide with the host government viewpoint.

Crossover

Explanatory factors such as compatible resource bundles, the possibility of improved domestic welfare, and profit potential motivation combine

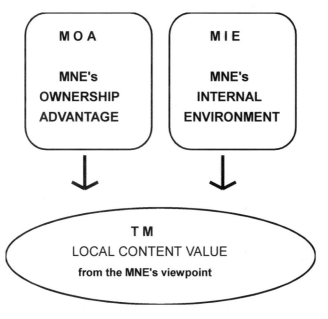

FIGURE 5.2 *MNE Variables*

with precipitating circumstances and the social decision process to create local content value. Governments try to maximize domestic welfare and MNEs strive to maximize profits. In the world environment MNEs and governments compete for shares of the value created by local content. Each sees the value of local content as the net of positive results of a cost-benefit analysis. Management seeks profit; economic policy seeks welfare maximization. Assuming "rational" self-interest guides decision making of both business and government, the value ascribed to local content arises from increased profitability or domestic welfare.

Environment Dynamics and Local Content Value

Commonalities do exist in industrial organization and strategic management theory. For example, there is a general belief that both government and business policy is shaped by constituent, external, political and economic pressures and that the relative causality is complicated by the endogenaity of relationships.

Benefit seeking interactions lead to a dynamic worldwide market-place. Between 1991 and 1993, for example, Siemens increased its local content as a percentage of sales from 73 to 82 percent (Langer and Hoser, 1995). Externalities changed; proximity fostered interaction

124   V. A. Taylor

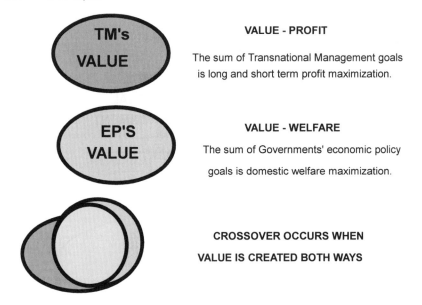

VALUE - PROFIT

The sum of Transnational Management goals is long and short term profit maximization.

VALUE - WELFARE

The sum of Governments' economic policy goals is domestic welfare maximization.

CROSSOVER OCCURS WHEN

VALUE IS CREATED BOTH WAYS

FIGURE 5.3 *Crossover of Value Creation*

between firms, suppliers and customers. As nation states strengthen their economic ties on a regional basis, local content regulations and rules of origin become important to ensure that outsiders cannot take advantage of negotiated tariff reductions (Jensen-Moran, 1996).

Morning after effects occur on both the management and economic policy sides. Environmental dynamics are inevitable and will influence the value of local content. Trade remediaries such as anti-dumping duties or more active enforcement of tariff, quota and anti-trust laws may encourage higher local content over time (Broeman, 1991; Root, 1994). China's government is now indicating that today's 40 percent local content requirement will not be sufficient for cars manufactured in the year 2000 (Engardio and Roberts, 1966). The establishment of local content, a value crossover between one government and a particular MNE, has global implications for the others. In a continually evolving environment, competitive interaction takes place between MNEs and nations and the best value for each is relative to the alternative choices available at the time.

As individual MNEs and governments try to create the best possible value, each from their own perspective, they affect the competitive environment. Therefore, the concept of crossover should always be viewed in the context of a dynamic world environment. Governments offer incentives and MNEs negotiate special deals. Tariff and tax rates affect profits. Environmental dynamics is not a new concept to

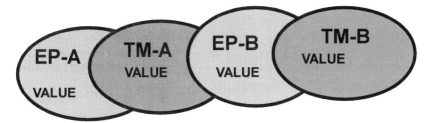

FIGURE 5.4 *Interactions Among MNEs and Governments*

management by any means. Restrictive rules on automobiles in the European Community (EC) inspired U.S. companies to modify their strategies. "The EC was the pioneer of using rules of origin as a trade policy to encourage EC content, EC sourcing and hence investment in EC manufacturing facilities" (Jensen-Moran, 1996, p. 247). Today China is forcing MNEs to provide research facilities and local parts factories in addition to joint venture assembly plants (Engardio and Roberts, 1966). Environmental dynamics can originate within or between MNE and host or emanate from the world environment. Factors such as compatible resource bundles, the possibility of improved domestic welfare, profit potential and the social decision process combine with precipitating circumstances to create them.

Implications for Governments

MNE activity has a significant influence on a country's national diamond of competitive advantage. Local content decisions can create positive economic effects for the host country which are multiplied if the host becomes an MNE export platform for worldwide or regional distribution. Imported technology and capital investment increase the productivity levels of indigenous workers and enable more effective use of factor endowments. For example, Siemens has invested $200 million in training and manufacturing facilities in the U.S.A. (Langer and Hoser, 1995).

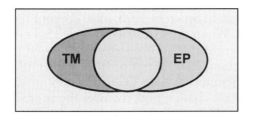

FIGURE 5.5 *Dynamics in the Worldwide Environment*

China's State Planning Commission in Beijing has identified five pillar industries—autos, electronics, petrochemicals, machinery, and building materials—for future development with FDI. FDI has spawned an economic growth cycle in the Pacific Rim where new job creation and enhanced worker skills have generated an emerging consumer class with seemingly insatiable market demand (Engardio and Roberts, 1996). To capitalize on the growth environment, companies like INCO invest in new Asian production facilities (Hand, 1995). FDI will have a favorable balance of payments (BOP) effect if it represents import substitution or production for export, but will have a negative effect if 'screwdriver plants' increase parts imports or if overpriced capital equipment mortgages drain funds to home office. Government action can be a catalyst for the expansion of local supplier bases to meet increased demand for intermediate goods. In the U.S.A. clusters of related industries have developed in North Carolina, which has become home to 185 foreign owned companies (Barnet and Cavanagh, 1994).

As a result of outward FDI, the home government in countries with long term employment contracts may experience either an upgrading of the domestic workforce to more productive use or overemployment with reduced productivity and competitiveness. On the other hand, heightened unemployment in response to less local labor demand may cause political turmoil, increased welfare expenditures, and may change the employment relationship to adversarial.

National defense requires an national industrial base which maintains minimum domestic capacity in key industries such as chemicals, metals, fabrication and motor vehicles in order to meet military surge demand (Gordon and Lees, 1986). Diminished intermediate goods supplier bases may curtail critical interaction between domestic firms and the country can experience hallowing out of a domestic industry. Both Boeing and McDonnell Douglas have shifted aerospace R&D and production to China causing U.S. layoffs (Engardio and Roberts, 1996) and possibly damaging future capacity in the U.S.A. for critical local content. Foreign exchange rate volatility and deterioration in BOP can result from lower tax revenues, fewer exports, and increased imports.

Newspapers and business periodicals are full of current examples of what happens when the rules change. When Ford opened a manufacturing operation in Spain in 1973, local content requirements were set at 60 percent. When these restrictions were lowered Ford was able to find cheaper worldwide sources which improved their bottom line (Kahalas and Suchon, 1992). Prior to 1989, semiconductors assembled in the EC were deemed to have EC origin and avoided a 14 percent tariff. A sudden rule change now requires the process of diffusion be local for EC origin. U.S. companies now have 40 fabrication facilities in Europe. Prior to the new rule most American firms performed this process in the U.S.A. (Jensen-Moran, 1996). There is clear evidence that the issue of local content via the placement of value added activity by MNEs is a vital component for competition among nations around the world. The model presented and the research it is based upon provide a framework to examine and monitor local content activity from multiple perspectives in a variety of circumstances.

References

ANON. (1996) Tussle over garments: America's new textile rules pose a daunting test to Asian exporters. *Asia Week*, 19 November.

BARNET, R. J. and CAVANAGH, J. (1994) *Global dreams: Imperial corporations and the new world order.* Simon and Schuster, New York.

BREWER, T. (1993) Government policies, market imperfections and foreign direct investment. *Journal of International Business Studies*, Vol. 24, 101–120.

BROEMAN, P. (ed.) (1991) *New Jersey: A basic legal guide for foreign businesses.* New Jersey State Bar Association, Section on International Law and Organizations.

BUCKLEY, P. and CASSON, M. (1988) A theory of cooperation in international business. *Management International Review*, Vol. 28, 19–38.

CHANDLER, A. (1991). The functions of the headquarters unit in the multibusiness firm. *Strategic Management Journal*, Vol. 12, 31–51.

CHILD, J. (1972) Organizational structure, environment and performance: The role of strategic choice. *Sociology*, Vol. 6, No. 1, 1–22.

COUGHLIN, C. (1985) Domestic content legislation: House voting and the theory of regulation. *Economic Inquiry*, Vol. 23, 437–448.

DOZ, V. and PRAHALAD, C. K. (1981) Headquarters influence and strategic control in MNCs. *Sloan Management Review*, Vol. 23, No. 1, 15–29.

DUNNING, J. (1988) The eclectic paradigm of international production: A restatement and some possible extensions. *Journal of International Business Studies*, Vol. 19, No. 3, 1–31.

EISENHARDT, K. (1989) Agency theory: An assessment and review. *Academy of Management Review*, Vol. 14, No. 1, 57–74.

ENGARDIO, P. and ROBERTS, D. (1996) Global tremors from an unruly giant. *Business Week*. 4 March.

GHOSHAL, S. (1987) Global strategy: An organizing framework. *Strategic Management Journal*, No. 8, 425–440.

GHOSHAL, S. and BARTLETT, C. (1990) The multinational corporation as an inter-organizational network. *Academy of Management Review*, Vol. 15, No. 4, 603–625.

GORDON, S. and LEES, F. (1986) *Foreign multinational investment in the United States: Struggle for industrial supremacy.* Quorum Books, New York.

GROSSMAN, G. (1991) *Imperfect competition and international trade.* MIT Press, Cambridge.

GUTH, W. and MACMILLA, I. (1986) Strategy implementation versus self interest. *Strategic Management Journal*, Vol. 5, 313–327.

HAND, S. (1995) Message to shareholders. *Annual Report.* INCO Limited, Toronto.

HREBINIAK, L. and JOYCE, W. (1984) *Implementing strategy.* Macmillan, New York.

JAMES, B. (1990) Reducing the risk of globalization. *Long Range Planning*, Vol. 23, No. 1, 80–94.

JENSEN-MORAN, J. (1996) The coming rules of origin debate. *The Washington Quarterly*, Vol. 19, No. 4, 239–253.

JOHNSON, C. with TYSON, L. and ZYSMAN, J. (1989) *Politics and productivity: The real story of why Japan works.* Ballinger Publishing Co., Cambridge.

KAHALAS, H. and SUCHON, K. (1992) Stepping up to global competition: Interview with Harold A. Poling, Chairman, CEO of Ford Motor Company. *The Academy of Management Executive*, May, 71–82.

KOBRIN, S. J. (1991) An empirical analysis of the determinants of global integration. *Strategic Management Journal*, Vol. 12 (special), 17–31.

KOGUT, B. (1985a) Designing global strategies: Comparative and competitive value added chains. *Sloan Management Review*, Vol. 26, No. 4, 15–28.

KOGUT, B. (1985b) Designing global strategies: Profiting from operational flexibility. *Sloan Management Review*, Vol. 27, No. 1, 27–37.

KOGUT, B. and ZANDER, U. (1993) Knowledge of the firm and the evolutionary theory of the multinational corporation. *Journal of International Business Studies*, Vol. 24, 625–645.

LANGER, H. and HOSER, A. (1995) Management letter. *A Review of Siemens Businesses in the USA.* Siemens Corporation, New York.

LECRAW, D. J. and MORRISON, A. J. (1991) Transnational corporation-host country relations: A framework for analysis. *Essays in International Business*, No. 9, September, CIBER, University of South Carolina.

LEE, C. H. (1987) Foreign Lobbying in American Politics. *Dissertation Abstracts International*, Vol. 48, 2443A.

LUGER, S. (1988) Private power, public policy and the United States Automobile Industry. *Dissertation Abstract International*, Vol. 50, 1423A.

MALKIN, E. and NEFF, R. (1994) The Japanese have a yen for Mexico again. *Business Week.* AOL. 28 November.

MC CULLOCH, R. (1985) Point of view: Trade deficits, industrial competitiveness and the Japanese. *California Management Review*, Vol. XXVII, 140–156.

MORRISON, A. J. and ROTH, K. (1992) A taxonomy of business level strategies in global industries. *Strategic Management Journal*, Vol. 13, 399–418.

PORTER, M. (1990) *The Competitive Advantage of Nations.* The Free Press, New York.

PORTER, M. (1991) Towards a dynamic theory of strategy. *Strategic Management Journal*, Vol. 12, 95–117.

ROLFE, R. J. *et al.* (1993) Determinants of FDI incentive preferences of MNEs. *Journal of International Business Studies*, Vol. 24, 335–355.

ROOT, F. R. (1994) *International trade and investment.* South-Western Publishing, Cincinnati, OH, 7th edn.

SCHERER, F. M. and ROSS, D. (1990) *Industrial market structure and economic performance.* Houghton-Miffen, Boston, MA, 3rd edn.

SIMON, H. (1961). *Administrative Behavior.* Macmillan, New York, 2nd edn.

TALLMAN, S. B. and SHENKAR, O. (1994) A managerial decision model of international cooperative venture formation. *Journal of International Business Studies*, Vol. 25, No. 1, 92–113.

TAYLOR, V. and CHANDRAN, R. (1996) Survey in V. TAYLOR (1997) Determinants of local content value. Unpublished dissertation, Temple University.

TAYLOR, V. (1993) Local content regulations in North American trade. Paper presented at the Academy of International Business, Northeast Region, Scranton, PA.

TYSON, L. D. (1995) Managed trade: Making the best of second best. In KING, P. (ed.), *International economics and international policy.* New York, McGraw-Hill, pp. 129–157.
WILLIAMSON, O. (1980) The economics of organizations: The transaction costs approach. *American Journal of Sociology,* Vol. 87, 548–577.

Notes

1. Gordon and Lees (1986) describe a worldwide battle for industrial supremacy which is a function of factor endowments, trade/FDI policy, efficient domestic economy, appropriate macro policies and economic power of size. They feel that the U.S. needs to reorient policy to deal effectively with unfair conditions and a worldwide playing field that is not level.
2. Taylor's (1993) paper investigates the distinction between measurement variation and changes in local product expenditures. NAFTA, generally accepted accounting principles (GAAP), the European community (EC) and the IRS all have their own rules with different motives. Different calculation rules lead to divergent values without a difference in the local value-added activity. Changing the transfer price of imported raw materials or components has similar results.
3. The public policy perspective of Shearer and Ross (1990) judges industry performance by five factors: how well the consumer is served, efficient resource allocation, technological progress, full stable employment, and equitable income distribution.
4. Porter's (1990) model of industry structure introduces five forces that define the nature of competition within an industry. Rivalry is at the center, surrounded by entry barriers, buyer power, supplier power, and the threat of new entrants.
5. Gene Grossman (1991) feels government policy motives include: shifting profits to domestic firms, increasing government revenues, gaining more favorable terms of trade by either increasing export prices or decreasing import prices, expansion of domestic industry, protecting or expanding employment, and maximizing consumer surplus.
6. Oliver Williamson argues that efficiency analysis properly encompasses governance costs as well as production cost. Williamson (1980) and Eisenhardt (1989) propose transaction cost analysis as a decision tool for choosing between outsourcing with market contracts and internalization of value chain activities.
7. Herbert Simon (1961) presents functional and divisional goals as constraints on the organizational goals for strategic management. There is no optimal solution but rather a set of optimizing solutions which may change to reflect the weight or relative importance ascribed to the various strategic objectives of the firm.
8. See Franklin Root (1994) for an application of cost-benefit analysis to the determination of the FDI desirability. The role of government policy in investment and trade is national welfare maximization via four criteria: impact on the balance of payments (BOP), national defense, American competitiveness, and the general economy. The benefits are the positive economic consequences associated with higher local content. Using this as a guide to the effects of local content legislation on domestic welfare, sources of change include, but are not limited to, sector specific employment, expansion (final and intermediate goods), competitiveness of national firms, industrial policy and defense, increased/decreased consumer surplus, trade distortion, externalities, and balance of payments issues.

6

Outward Direct Investment Orientation, Structural Adaptability and Economic Revival: A Case Study of New Zealand

SERGIO CASTELLO

This chapter explores the outward direct investment orientation and structural reforms of New Zealand and discusses the country's rising competitiveness thanks to the continued growth in exports and direct overseas investments. It is postulated that the 'Kiwi' economic success is due to the smallness-induced patterns of outward direct investment orientation and structural adaptability. New Zealand, a small open economy, has demonstrated the success of more than ten years of economic globalization and restructuring by generating a budget surplus and a growth rate of 5.3 percent in 1994.[1]

Introduction

New Zealand serves as a good case study for other small nations to examine the processes of outward direct investment and structural adaptability. The country's economic structure has strong similarities with both developed and less-developed nations. It is a small, open economy with a large export agricultural sector and a high income level. New Zealand's size, isolation, cultural heritage, historical ties, and New Zealanders' individualism and entrepreneurial spirit have encouraged and supported specific forms of economic and political organization over long periods of time. New Zealand followed a more import-substitution and generally interventionist economic strategy than other high-income nations until the early 1980s.

New Zealand was a leader in the development of the so-called 'welfare state' during the 1930s. Nationalization and state control of industry were important throughout most of the British settlement. Furthermore, the New Zealand government relied heavily on economic regulations, trade policy instruments, subsidies, and protection of industries at all levels. In short, government intervention played a major role in New Zealand's development until 1982 (Lattimore, 1987).

More recently, the country found itself on the verge of economic disaster. The crisis was prompted by massive overseas borrowing, increasing failures of national state enterprises, and loose monetary policy which created an inflationary surge hitting a peak of 17 percent in 1982. New Zealand's government opted for a radical change in economic policy towards a more open and free market system in 1984. In just a decade, the nation has become one of the most vibrant economies in the world with a modern and competitive economy.

New Zealand, despite its short history, offers a remarkable record of support for the principles of democracy inherited from the British tradition. Moreover, it cannot yet be considered a fully developed country, despite its 155 years of history since the first organized settlement arrived from Britain. But New Zealand is one of the world's largest exporters of primary commodities, and attained a standard of living measured in GNP per capita of $12,300, in 1994, much higher than some Western European countries like Greece and Portugal, similar to Ireland and Spain, and not far behind Britain (World Bank, 1994).

The economic success that this small open economy is experiencing in the 1990s can be attributed to two factors. First, the realization of the necessity of further outward FDI orientation and its importance in economic growth and development during the late 1960s when it became less dependent on Britain, its main trading partner at the time. And second, the role of government in the massive structural reform and economic liberalization of domestic markets beginning in the mid 1980s.

The 'Kiwi School of Economics' advocates that all a country needs to economically succeed is the right policies based on structural adaptability and foreign direct investment orientation. This observation supports the idea of the investment development path (IDP) set out in Dunning and Narula (1996).[2] This chapter endeavors to identify and explain the economic significance of nation size, FDI orientation, and structural adaptability, based on the case of New Zealand.

Outward Direct Investment Orientation

The Problem and Salient Characteristics

In the early 1970s, New Zealand was faced with chronic labor shortages and a huge welfare system as a result of which there were plenty of jobs for low-skilled labor with low wages in heavily protected industries, thus producing overpriced goods for consumers with very little or no choices. This arrangement was supported by more or less guaranteed access for its products to the British markets. Moreover, New Zealanders seemed complacent with their colonial British dependence and abysmal levels of productivity growth. The turning point for the New Zealand economy came in 1973 with the first oil shock and the entrance of Britain into the European Economic Community (EEC). The country's economic environment was suddenly rocked by external economic conditions.

New Zealand tried to ignore the harsh economic realities at the time. The government borrowed heavily from overseas, gave support to industries through subsidies (including the agricultural sector which was already competitive internationally), and engaged in careless macro-economic policies which led to double digit inflation becoming the norm instead of the exception. And finally, the funding of huge energy projects ended in total failure which cost taxpayers billions of dollars (Lattimore, 1987).

Table 6.1 shows the performance of the New Zealand economy, which had worsened compared with its neighbor Australia and other Asian nations, particularly in the 1970s. New Zealand's GDP growth rate was only 1.05 percent for the 1973–88 period, much lower than Australia's GDP growth rate of 2.9 percent for the same period. Most

TABLE 6.1 *Economic growth rates (% GDP)*

Nation	1960–1973	1973–1980	1980–1988
New Zealand	3.8	0.3	1.8
Australia	5.2	3.7	3.1
Hong Kong	9.6	8.8	7.6
South Korea	9.3	6.9	8.3
Malaysia	6.8	8.5	3.5
Philippines	5.5	6.0	1.9
Singapore	8.8	7.6	6.1
Taiwan	10.5	8.4	6.7

Source: The Penn World Table (Mark 5): An Expanded Set of International Comparisons, 1950–88 (Summers and Heston, 1988).

alarming was the increasing gap of its growth rates compared to the newly-industrializing economies of Asia.[3]

Akoorie (1996) points out a New Zealand economic survey prepared by the OECD in 1980. The survey highlighted problems such as the agricultural sector becoming even more vulnerable to outside shocks, the high cost structure in the manufacturing sector causing the nation to lose its competitiveness internationally, and the exchange rate becoming extremely overvalued and generating upward pressure on export prices, thus reducing the competitiveness of the exporting sector. Finally, when inflation hit a peak of almost 20 percent in 1982, the New Zealand government reacted by freezing all prices and wages. As the distortions continued over the next two years, the country suffered a major currency crisis.[4]

Since the 1984 economic reforms, it is well established that, compared to its larger counterparts, particularly Australia, the 'Kiwi' economy has become more: (1) export focused in manufacturing; (2) likely to specialize in differentiated manufactures; (3) actively involved with direct overseas businesses, particularly in FDI; (4) sensitive in strategically managing exchange rates; (5) actively involved in international trade through varying degrees of economic integration; and (6) structural adaptable.

In other words, New Zealand has become more outward oriented and structurally adaptable than its larger counterparts in exploiting the opportunities in the global economy and forging a flexible and good economic environment—thus achieving a higher degree of competitiveness in international business and trade.

Moreover, these salient characteristics can, in part, be credited to the movement of New Zealand's economy into the latter phases of Stage 3 of the IDP, thanks to the non-FDI induced changes reflected by government policy determining the way in which markets and resources can be better organized, and the FDI-induced changes in the strategies of MNEs which influence the nature of OLI in present and future periods (Akoorie, 1996).

As of 1984, New Zealand entered a new period of economic and structural reform. In the early 1990s, the 'Kiwi' economy begun to reap the benefits of its extensive reform process. The economy grew by 2.9 percent in 1992–93 and 5.3 percent in 1994. Inflation has remained below 2 percent since 1991. In addition, the 1993–94 budget was in surplus of 0.6 percent of GDP.[5] This economic performance rests on the favorable international and globalization context, particularly by an expansion in export earnings in non-commodity manufactures and the domestic market liberalization strategies. In what follows, the New Zealand's specific economic strategies will be explored.

Trade Focus

Trade has long been an engine of growth for New Zealand, especially in its early stages of development, thanks to primary exports such as agriculture and forestry. Moreover, its economic recovery is continuing to consolidate with export growth as a primary contributor to economic performance. In 1992, the trade ratio (exports + imports/GNP) was 46 percent, almost twice Australia's 26 percent. Thus, about 50 percent of New Zealand's economy depends on international linkages provided by international trade and FDI (World Bank, 1994).

Since the major economic and structural reforms of 1984, exports and imports have increased by 60.5 percent from 1984 to 1992, particularly with Australia due to the two nations' comprehensive agreement on closer economic relations (World Bank, 1994).[6] New Zealand has increasingly focused on developing new linkages with other trading partners and has diversified its export markets in recent times. In 1993, Britain accounted for just 6.5 percent of New Zealand's exports compared to almost 67 percent in 1950. Furthermore, New Zealand's main trading partners are Australia (19.3 percent), Japan (15.3 percent), Europe (13.5 percent), East Asia (12.3 percent), United States (12.2 percent), and others (24.4 percent)[7] (New Zealand Debt Management Office, 1994).

Once again, this observation accords with Krugman's new emphasis on the geographical factors in economics (Krugman, 1991). It is cheaper and more efficient to trade with neighboring Australia than with Britain (once being its main trading partner) because of lower transportation costs. In addition, it is important to note that, in 1993, almost 50 percent of New Zealand's exports and 47 percent of its imports were with East Asian economies (New Zealand Debt Management Office, 1994).

Specialization in Niche-Market Goods

New Zealand's firms are being confronted with a small domestic market with less than 3.5 million customers, thus having to pursue diversification in both markets and products. New Zealand's corporations are already pursuing market diversification by trading with as many as 20 different countries located all over the world. Furthermore, New Zealand companies have also undergone major re-structuring of industrial production systems jointly with labor, capital, and goods markets, to pursue product diversification focusing in global 'niche-market' goods. In 1992, the manufacturing trade ratio (manufacture exports/GNP) was close to 6 percent, almost twice Australia's ratio of 3.5 percent. Again, it indicates the importance of the specialization of differentiated products by small economies to capture 'niche-markets'.

Indeed, this market and product diversification is a complimentary relationship that agrees with the imperfect competition theory of trade (Krugman, 1990). New Zealand's main exports are agricultural and commodity products such as meat, wool, dairy products, fish, fruit, timber, and pulp paper products. Also, exports of non-food products have expanded rapidly over the last decade, particularly in plastics, aluminum frames, electrical fencing, electronics, telecom-munications, and computer software, thus opening new and promising markets for 'Kiwi' corporations. These goods, perhaps with the exception of electronics, telecommunications, and computer software, are not *yet* extremely differentiated products that appeal to consumers worldwide. As a result, New Zealand's exports are still in the early stages of specialization in order to reach specific 'niche-market' goods. This is another sign of New Zealand's rapid move toward the latter stages in the IDP, as long as domestic firms continue to increase outward FDI establishing a presence in foreign markets through strategic alliances or wholly owned subsidiaries. There are some encouraging signs, especially within the software industry. Mr Pyne, managing director of the Bank of New Zealand, writes:

> We are only a small player in the global market . . . but there are niches where we have excelled . . . A diverse customer base has forced software developers to create products offering a wider range of functions than those available internationally.
> (The New Zealand Investment Conference, 1992)[8]

Software products are exported to developed nations, with 65 percent of these exports serving Australia, the U.S., and Canada (Tradenz Report 1993–94).

Involvement in Direct Overseas Businesses

The focus of this section will be on FDI alone.[9] Small open economies such as New Zealand realize the importance of inward FDI as an engine of economic growth.[10] Thus the country became involved in direct international business operations earlier in its economic development. The presence of MNEs in New Zealand, especially from Britain, has been a regular phenomenon since its colonization 155 years ago.

The wide fluctuation levels of FDI since the massive re-structuring of the economy in recent years reflect the high degree of uncertainty about the commitment of the government within the international community to continue the structural reforms of the goods, labor, and capital markets, and the reform of the government and its monetary and fiscal policies. During the 1987–93 period, more than two-thirds of inward FDI came from Australia, Britain, the United States, and Canada alone. Moreover, New Zealand's inward FDI has increased by 181 percent from 1985 to 1992, reflecting the confidence of international investors to the commitment of the domestic government to continue economic as well as structural reforms (UNCTAD, 1994).

At the same time, there has been a tremendous growth in outward FDI. New Zealand's outward FDI increased from $809 million to $4323 million between 1985 and 1992 (UNCTAD, 1994). Companies with ownership-specific advantages in the forestry, pulp, and paper sectors have expanded operations, particularly in Canada. Likewise, firms have entered the South East Asian markets in the engineering and software industry, acquiring ownership-specific advantages through flexibility and small scale attention to specific problems (Akoorie, 1996).

Indeed, New Zealand has been proportionally more dependent on inward FDI in its early stages of development, but the country is becoming partially more oriented to outward FDI as it continues its globalization and structural reforms. The ratio of inward FDI to GNP has increased from 9.1 percent to 13.75 percent for the 1985–92 period, but the ratio of outward FDI to GNP has almost tripled from 3.6 percent to 10.6 percent for the same period (UNCTAD, 1994). Furthermore, Table 6.2 shows New Zealand's growth in inward and outward FDI from 1981 to 1992. The figures illustrate the growth in inward FDI as foreign investors continue to approve and gain confidence in New Zealand's economic reforms. The corresponding growth in outward FDI in this period supports New Zealand's move toward the later stages in the IDP. The net FDI to GDP has increased from 0.32 in the period 1981–83 to 1.54 in the 1990–92 period. In addition, inward and outward FDI to GDP have increased by more than 20 percent in the early 1990s. However, Akoorie (1996) writes

TABLE 6.2 *Inward and Outward FDI, New Zealand 1981–93*

Years	I/GDP	O/GDP	Net FDI/GDP
1981–83	3.15	2.83	0.32
1984–86	4.27	1.72	2.54
1987–89	3.96	6.45	–2.28
1990–92	21.90	20.36	1.54

Notes: GDP at constant 1982/83 prices.
Source: Akoorie (1996).

that outward FDI is increasing at a similar rate as inward FDI. This suggests that New Zealand is following the pattern of resource-rich nations, where inward FDI will tend to be higher than outward FDI. Again, the radical economic reforms that began in the 1980s have influenced the growth in the rate of both inward and outward FDI, accelerating the rate and progress of New Zealand's IDP.

Inward FDI. Table 6.3 shows the increase of net FDI inflows for the 1987–93 period from Australia, U.S./Canada, Britain, other EU countries, Japan, and Asia. Investments from Australia, U.S./Canada, Britain, and Asia all had an increase of 10 percent or more, while investments from Japan and other EU countries had modest increases. In terms of the number of ventures, Australia continues to be the most important source of investment for New Zealand.

The sectoral patterns of inward FDI in New Zealand can be divided into resource-based and non-resource-based investments. Between 1985 and 1991 resource-based investments have been concentrated in agricultural services, hunting, fishing, and particularly forestry. Foreign MNEs have taken large stakes in the forestry sector to obtain *location advantages* since the privatization of the New Zealand's exotic forests and wood surplus. The non-resource-based investments in New Zealand relate to the service sector, particularly in communications and banking. The privatization of New Zealand's telecommunications network, later accompanied by deregulation in the sector, has attracted foreign MNEs such as Bell Atlantic. The company's purchase of the telecommunications network in 1990 resulted in the upgrading of local networks. Telecom New Zealand has benefited from such purchases by upgrading its technology and know-how and being able to update telecommunication networks in nations further down the IDP, such as Indonesia. The removal of interest rate controls, relaxation

TABLE 6.3 *Inward FDI to New Zealand: 1987–1993 ($NZ million)*

Country	Inward FDI	Total(%)
Australia	4,745	35.1
Britain	2,260	16.7
USA/Canada	4,079	30.1
Japan	432	3.2
Other EU countries	364	2.7
Asia	1,504	11.1
Total	13,545	100.0

Source: Akoorie (1996)

of entry restrictions into banking, a review of the state-owned banking activities, and the removal of restrictions on foreign ownership has brought a wave of specialization and rationalization in the financial sector. Of the eight major banking groups operating in New Zealand, only one is still New Zealand owned, five are Australian owned, and two are owned by British banks.

Outward FDI. Outward FDI by New Zealand corporations did not begin until 1984. The main recipients of New Zealand's outward FDI in the early 1990s have been Britain, other EU countries, Japan, and particularly Australia. The economic liberalization of the 1980s promoted industrial rationalization and specialization, and encouraged New Zealand's firms to relocate manufacturing facilities to Australia. The investment flows to these countries were at record levels during 1990 and 1991. For example, Australia received $NZ 2,863 million, Britain $NZ 1,721 million, Japan $NZ 26 million, and other EU countries $NZ 398 million. But in 1993 outward FDI became negative in all these countries except other EU nations. These negative investment flows may be a reflection of the economic revival in New Zealand, as the government's economic and structural reforms of the 1980s helped yield high economic growth rates, low inflation, and a more liberalized economy. More recently, New Zealand's firms have favored reinvestment in their own economy to service the Australian market.

In addition, the resource sector has been very aggressive in outward FDI to secure market access or resource acquisition. For forestry, the stimulus was the uncertainty regarding access to future domestic sources of supply. The main motivation for the acquisition of manufacturing operations in Canada was to secure access to North American markets for pulp and paper.

New Zealand based companies have also invested in Australia, Britain, and the rest of Europe to acquire strategic assets in the banking and insurance sectors. Moreover, domestic engineering firms have gained ownership advantages through joint ventures and competitive advantages in adapting technology based solutions to indigenous activities like geothermal engineering in the 1980s. The companies' adaptability and aptitude for small-scale, solutions-based engineering have been key to entering new South East Asian 'niche-markets'. These high-tech firms are becoming important players in moving New Zealand towards the latter stages of the IDP.

Strategic Management of Exchange Rates and Price Stability

Exchange rates are the link between domestic and global prices. The more 'globally oriented' a nation is, the more sensitively and strategically it manages and uses the exchange rate mechanism. In other words, the exchange rate is a key policy variable for a small open economy, and New Zealand is no exception.[11]

Obviously, what really matters for international competitiveness is not the nominal but rather the real exchange rate (whether home currency is undervalued or overvalued), which directly affects the profitability of domestic producers of tradeable goods and services.

The exchange rate policy of the New Zealand government in the 1970s and early 1980s was characterized by radical modifications. During this period, New Zealand's exchange rate regime went from being fixed to the sterling, to being fixed to the U.S. dollar, to being fixed against a trade-weighted basket of currencies. However, it moved to a 'free exchange rate' only in 1985, after a massive devaluation of 20 percent of its currency in 1984, and, just over one year later, the launching of its massive economic and structural reforms[12] (Sherwin, 1991).

New Zealand is mainly a small commodity-exporting country; in consequence its exchange rate becomes even more vulnerable to external shocks and rising world commodity prices. For example, a strong demand from its trading partners with rising world commodity prices puts upward pressure on New Zealand's exchange rate and export prices to ensure equilibrium in the goods market. But the non-commodity sectors, such as electronics and computer software, have been greatly affected by the appreciation of the NZ dollar, and in the later 1980s lost competitiveness and market share (Blundell-Wignall and Gregory, 1990).

Hence, New Zealand has even a greater need to strategically manage its exchange rate due to wild swings in world commodity prices creating short-run and perhaps long-run currency volatility under a floating regime. But simply a sterilized intervention, even though it has little or no impact on fundamental exchange rate movements, can provide the market with more direction when market inefficiencies dominate.[13]

The New Zealand experience during the 1985–92 period supports the hypothesis that New Zealand manages economic variables in such a way as to make its currency not overvalued and perhaps undervalued. For example, the NZ dollar nominal exchange rate appreciated 3.17 percent against the U.S. dollar, but the real exchange rate depreciated by 18.94 percent. Compared to its larger counterpart the Australian dollar, the NZ dollar's nominal exchange rate appreciated 1.13 percent, and the real exchange rate only depreciated 7.80 percent. In addition, New Zealand's experience fo the adverse consequences of the 1987–88 terms-of-trade cycle was absorbed rather well when the NZ dollar depreciated about 10 percent against the U.S. dollar in nominal terms and almost 17 percent in real terms during the 1987–89 period.

The 'Kiwi' economy has been very effective in attaining price stability through the effective use of monetary policy and the strategic management of its currency. Table 6.4 shows New Zealand's inflation figures for the 1985–92 period. Inflation surpassed 15 percent in 1986, but it was around 2 percent in 1992. This turnaround can be attributed not only to sound monetary and exchange rate policy, but also to the 1984 national structural reforms avoiding excesses in wage policies, budget deficits, and protection of industries. New Zealand has enjoyed downward pressure on prices due to higher competition within the economy, as a result of massive deregulation of markets and the privatization of state monopolies, international competition thanks to enormous trade liberalization efforts, and a budget surplus. These factors have provided the proper economic environment for price stability.

International Economic Integration

Many economists ask the question of whether the problems of smallness can be overcome by economic integration. The European Union may perhaps be the most successful attempt at regional integration in recent history, but various other attempts to achieve the benefits of economic interdependence are flourishing around the globe. These include the Association of Southeast Asian Nations (ASEAN), the Asia Pacific Economic Cooperation (APEC), and the Australia New Zealand Closer Economic Relations Treaty (ANZCERT).

Since the 1930s, border protection has been very important to the New Zealand economy, thus allowing for the growth of a viable domestic industry at the time. But a less desirable result was the reduction in the range of goods available and higher prices in the

TABLE 6.4 *Inflation rate (%), New Zealand 1986–92*

Years	Inflation
1985	–
1986	18.23
1987	11.73
1988	8.30
1989	6.18
1990	2.96
1991	1.44
1992	2.16

Source: World Bank Tables (1994).

market place. The cost of this isolation became alarming by the early 1980s, and the first major change was the negotiation of ANZCERT signed in 1983, with the provision to join the two countries in a free trade area by 1995. New Zealand's market has expanded to more than five times its domestic size through its economic integration scheme with Australia, diminishing its size disadvantages by reaping the economic gains of product differentiation, scale economies, and increased competition.

The country has also benefited from a tremendous increase in exports as a consequence of new trade alliances with other nations around the world, and particularly with its closest trading partners. It is also a member of APEC with the main objective of developing regional trade and economic integration among its members and was a fervent supporter of the GATT agreement.

These trade linkages, accompanied with major economic liberalization reforms, have affected both the amount and quality of New Zealand's factors of production, due to technological advances and innovation. Moreover, it has assisted the New Zealanders in the differentiation of manufactured products and the penetration of East Asian 'niche-market' goods. New Zealand's value of export manufacturing growth experienced almost a 90 percent increase from 1983 to 1992, helping to launch its economy to the top ten most competitive nations in the world (World Economic Forum, 1994).[14]

Structural Adaptability, Flexibility, and Economic Liberalization

International competitiveness, to some degree, is a matter of structural adaptability and economic flexibility. It is known that competitiveness requires constant change, and the flexibility already exhibited by the New Zealand economy in 1984 found its best ally in the new government elected at that time.[15]

The main and most important characteristics of New Zealand's institutional system has been its flexibility and structural adaptability. The newly elected government of 1984 dramatically shifted gears from an interventionism and protectionism mode to a liberalization one. In the last decade, New Zealand has become the fourth most open and free economy in the world, only behind Hong Kong (1), Singapore (2), and Bahrain (3).[16]

This major transformation has occurred as a result of several factors. Among these are, first, years of procrastination leading to economic chaos providing a sense of urgency; second, a high degree of social and political stability rooted in British influence and tradition; third, the possession of skilled labor thanks to compulsory schooling years in the tertiary sector and the work place; fourth, a long established record of promoting a more even distribution of income through the generous welfare system (accounting for almost 25 percent of GDP in 1993), thus providing health, education, income support for low income families, and a range of other benefits; and finally, a clear and transparent economic plan put forward through a reformed government willing to undertake such imperative changes.[17]

New Zealand's Turnaround Policies

The kind of economic polices that the government of New Zealand has implemented in the last ten years have been *complementary* to the interests of private businesses and markets, instead of the previous substitutable strategies of market imperfections. These policies have supported an efficient economic environment, good infrastructure, and incentives for science and technology.

Hence, the new reformed government has placed greater emphasis on economic strategies to strengthen public and private ties. These new strategies have provided a more conducive environment in which to do business in the country. New Zealand's reforms have attracted foreign capital and entrepreneurship that have assisted, and will continue to assist, in the creation of dynamic comparative advantages through the development of innovative products and technologies, thus providing a new focus on the 'niche-markets' of New Zealand's trading economic space, as well as the creation of domestic-based MNEs.

Economic Liberalization Policies. The principal micro-economic, macro-economic, and macro-organizational reforms will be briefly specified below. Some major *micro-economic* reforms have been the removal of protection and industry assistance, a uniform rate of value added taxes (VAT), infrastructural reforms, and new competition-enhancing policies. These strategies have been the main contributors of greater efficiency, productivity, dynamism, and flexibility in the goods market (Prebble, 1994).

In addition, Akoorie (1996) makes reference to internal regulatory and economic reforms involving the deregulation in the finance and transport industries, the removal of entry licensing in manufacturing and other services, the abolition of price controls and the easing of controls over merger acquisition and trade practices, the elimination of subsidies in the agricultural sector, the revision of corporate and personal tax structures, and the passing of the State Owned Enterprises Act in 1986 signaling the government's intention to restructure state-owned enterprises by removing their monopoly power and opening the way for a new wave of privatization.

The most significant *macro-economic* changes have been the removal of interest and exchange rate controls, abolition of ratio requirements, independence of the Reserve Bank with agreed targets of inflation new monetary policy, and increased competition in the banking sector with the creation of new ones (Sherwin, 1991). The reforms in the trade sector have included the elimination of import licensing, the reduction of tariffs, and the signing of a free trade agreement with Australia. These policy objectives were intended to create a stable economy with low inflation rates which would be attractive to both domestic and foreign investors (Akoorie, 1996).

The most relevant *macro-organizational* reforms have been a flatter tax scale, tighter eligibility rules for welfare benefits, new apprenticeship and training programs, higher education affordability, new industrial relation laws dealing with voluntary unionism, enterprise bargaining, and fixed term contracts. The signing of the Employment Contracts Act in 1986 changed the practice of nationwide collective wage determination in favor of individual or site-wide agreements (Prebble, 1994). It has been difficult to assess the full impact of these new policies, but, overall, workers now operate in a tougher environment with a much greater pace of change. In addition, there are more opportunities for training and advancement available to all, not only the privileged.[18]

Akoorie (1996) also writes about the effects of the relaxation of inward and outward investment controls, thus increasing international business activities. Although approvals for overseas investment are still required from the Overseas Investment Commission, the minimum amount required for such approval has been raised to $NZ 10 million. Restrictions on overseas media ownership as well as farmland ownership have also been removed.

Finally, reforms in government management, such as corporatization and privatization of companies, restructuring of the accounting system, and public sector employment tied to performance, have increased the government's accountability and responsibility to its citizens (Prebble, 1994). New Zealand officials have put in place a clearer, more transparent, and more stable economic climate in which corporations are willing to invest and are beginning to thrive. For example, the Fiscal Responsibility Act forces the government to prepare proper budget accounts limiting the scope for fiscal maneuvering. Subsequent governments can widen inflation targets or loosen fiscal policy, but they will have to state *openly* their intentions, thus increasing the political costs of irresponsibility.

Infrastructura Policies. Infrastructure provides the basic facilities and raw materials with which companies can become more outward FDI oriented by gaining access to new markets, customers, and suppliers. New Zealand's isolation from the rest of the world makes the development of excellent infrastructural facilities in air transport, port access, and telecommunications absolutely imperative for the economic success of MNEs.[19] The World Competitiveness Report ranked New Zealand number one in the telecommunications sector in 1993. The country's largest telecommunications companies are already servicing over 40 markets worldwide and are establishing marketing offices around the world, but particularly in Asia (TRADENZ, 1993/94).

Incentives for Science and Technology. As stated above, New Zealand's government has implemented major reforms in the areas of education, training, and technical careers, but R&D has taken a back position.[20] New Zealand's real growth in total expenditure on R&D from 1983 to 1991 has been only 0.5 percent. In 1981, the nation spent about 1.4 percent of GDP in support of science and technology. It only spent 0.87 percent of GDP in 1991, less than any other developed nation except Spain, Portugal, and Greece. New Zealand had only 15,000 R&D scientists and engineers in industry, while Sweden had over 115,000 (World Economic Forum, 1994).

The New Zealand government has finally recognized the importance of innovation, science, and technology, through private as well as public investment. In connection with the allocation of public funds in R&D, there have been substantial changes in recent years to the structures and processes for science awareness and delivery. These changes include the creation of a small policy ministry of research, science, and technology, the creation of ten crown research institutes to conduct R&D, and the continuation of a small technology for business growth program for partnership projects with individual businesses (TRADENZ, 1993/94).

New Zealand's Economic Model and its Future

Overall, the process of change has been painful for many people, but a vibrant economy is emerging in the midst of greater uncertainty for many. The fact that New Zealanders are now less complacent about the future may be seen in itself as one of the successful consequences of the reform process.

The outcome of the 1996 elections almost certainly marks the end of radical reform in New Zealand. It will be much harder for the new coalition government to take tough decisions. Radical reforms under both Labor and National parties helped turn New Zealand from one of the most closed economies in the early 1980s into one of the most open in the 1990s. In particular, the country has one of the least distorting tax systems and perhaps the most deregulated and flexible labor market in the world. New Zealand's reforms were painful, and the gains took almost a decade to arrive. But since then, economic growth has averaged 4 percent a year and unemployment has decreased to about 6 percent.

The country also has one of the best monetary and fiscal policies in the world by making policies more transparent and clear, and politicians more accountable. Also, several measures on the statute books create incentives for policy makers to act responsibly. For example, New Zealand's Reserve Bank has full independence in setting monetary policy to achieve an inflation target, and the Fiscal Responsibility Act forces the government to prepare proper budget accounts. For the past three years, the government has run budget surplus and contained inflation below 2.5 percent.[21]

The recent fall in the country's unemployment demonstrates the benefit of labor market deregulation. If Western Europe had been as bold as New Zealand in reducing the burden on corporations, its jobless rate today would not be above 10 percent. The world is watching whether New Zealand's new government is about to reverse its reforms. None of the main parties plan a complete turnaround embracing the policies dismantled in the 1980s. Hopefully, the longer New Zealand's reforms are allowed to show such impressive economic results, the harder it will be for others to ignore New Zealand's message to the world; namely, that outward direct investment orientation and structural adaptability yields economic prosperity.

Summary and Conclusions

It is apparent that New Zealand's radical reforms have caused considerably disruption among specific sectors of the economy, and particularly among those that enjoyed monopolistic profits due to high levels of protectionism and isolation from domestic and foreign competition. In contrast, New Zealand has enjoyed economic growth rates between 2 and 3 percent since 1991, with an impressive growth rate of 5.3 percent in 1994. These numbers by no means represent an economic boom, but they are much more impressive compared to the growth rates of most other developed nations, which are just recovering from recessions or starting to grow slowly.

Outward direct investment and structural adaptability have been two main driving forces behind this expansion thanks to the globalization and liberalization strategies taken since 1984. Obviously, this is not the result of an improvement in agricultural commodity prices, but rather it represents New Zealand's real expansion in a wide range of created assets or differentiated products such as electronic devices, engineering services, and computer software with increased foreign subsidiaries and international sales in new markets like Australia, Japan, Taiwan, and South Korea.

The government's economic liberalization policies coupled with infrastructure improvements, particularly in telecommunications, and new incentives for science and technology have encouraged domestic and foreign-based MNEs to increasingly influence the direction of New Zealand's economy. Access to forestry, telecommunications, and banking have allowed MNEs to use their competitive advantages to upgrade indigenous resources. Also, they have led to a substantially increased in inward FDI and the emergence of some New Zealand based MNEs in the sectors of forestry, banking, telecommunication, and engineering.

New Zealand's strategies of outward direct investment orientation and structural adaptability are by no means over, but few new radical reforms are foreseen in the near future. Instead continued progress in its international linkages through more trade, specialization in 'niche-market' goods, inward and outward FDI, strategic management of the exchange rate, economic integration, and economic flexibility and adaptability, are likely to continue to play an important role to support New Zealand's economic success.

References

AKOORIE, M. (1996) New Zealand: the development of a resource-rich economy. In DUNNING, J. H. and NARULA, R. (eds) *Foreign Direct Investment and Governments: Catalysts for Economic Restructuring*, Routledge, London, pp. 174–206.

BLUNDELL-WIGNALL and GREGORY, R. G. (1990) Exchange rate policy in advanced commodity-exporting countries: Australia and New Zealand. In ARGY, V. and DE GRAUWE, P. (eds) *Choosing an Exchange Rate Regime: The Challenge for Smaller Developed Countries*, IMF, Washington, DC, pp. 224–271.

DUNNING, J. H. and NARULA, R. (1996) The investment development path revisited: some emerging issues. In DUNNING, J. H. and NARULA, R. (eds) *Foreign Direct Investment and Governments: Catalysts for Economic Restructuring*, Routledge, London, pp. 1–41.

DUNNING, J. H. (1992) The global economy, domestic governance, strategies, and transnational corporations: interactions and policy implications, *Transnational Corporations*, Vol. 1, No. 3 (December), 7–45.

DUNNING, J. H. (1981) Explaining the international direct investment position of countries: towards a dynamic or development approach, *Weltwirtschaftliches Archiv*, Vol. 11, No. 1, 30–64.

KRUGMAN, P. (1991) *Geography and Trade*, MIT Press, Cambridge, Mass.

KRUGMAN, P. (1990) *Rethinking International Trade*, MIT Press, Cambridge, Mass.

LATTIMORE, R. (1987) Economic adjustment in New Zealand: a developed country case study of policies and problems. In Holmes, Sir F. (ed.) *Economic Adjustment: Policies and Problems*, Washington, DC, IMF, 34–84.

New Zealand Debt Management Office (1994) *New Zealand: Economic and Financial Overview*, (February), The Treasury, Wellington.

Organization for Economic Cooperation and Development (1983–1989) *New Zealand Economic Survey*, OECD Publications, Paris.

Ozawa, T. (1992) Foreign direct investment and economic development, *Transnational Corporations*, Vol. 1, No. 1 (February), 27–54.

Prebble, M. (1994) *New Zealand: The Turnaround Economy*, London, IOD, The Director Publications Ltd.

Pyne, L. (1992) Opportunities in the market. In the collection of papers of the NZ Investment Conference, *An Investment in the Future*, Auckland, New Zealand, NZ Investment Conference Publication.

Sherwin, M. (1991) Capital market liberalization: the New Zealand experience. In Henke, S. and Walters, A. (eds) *Capital Markets and Development*, Institute for Contemporary Studies Press, San Francisco, pp. 209–240.

Summers, R. and Heston, A. (1988) The penn world tables (Mark 5): an expanded set of international comparisons, 1950–1988, *Quarterly Journal of Economics*, Vol. 105, No. 2, 327–368.

Tradenz (1993–94) *Stretching for Growth: Building an Export Strategy for New Zealand*, NZ Trade Development Board Publication, Wellington, New Zealand.

United Nations Conference on Trade and Development (UNCTAD) (1994) *World Investment Report: Transnational Corporations, Employment and the Work Place*, United Nations, New York.

World Bank (1994) *World Development Report*, Oxford University Press, Oxford.

World Economic Forum (1994) *World Competitiveness Report*, World Economic Forum and IMEPE, Geneva.

Notes

1. See article: 'New Zealand Success Story' in *The Economist*, (July 9th, 1994). The investment development path (IDP) suggests that countries go through various stages of development typified by the relationship between inward and outward FDI, with net outward FDI being associated with later stages of economic development.
2. The authors explain that there are two catalysts for change which will affect a country's FDI orientation. These are changes in government policy and strategies of multinational firms. See Akoorie (1996) for further detail.
3. The underlying causes of New Zealand's economic troubles were partly structural in nature. Government intervention, to compensate for market imperfections, prevented corporations from making the necessary structural adjustments to accommodate to the changing global economic environment.
4. Countries have frequently changed course during an economic crisis. New Zealand was no exception, but it was slow in reacting, almost to the point where economic disaster became imminent.
5. Data extracted from: 'New Zealand: Economic and Financial Overview,' (February 1994), 'New Zealand; Success Story,' (*The Economist*, July 9th, 1994), and 'The New Zealand Experiment,' (*The Wall Street Journal*, July 21st, 1994).

6. Trade across these two countries flourished since the Australia New Zealand Closer Economic Relations Trade Agreement (ANZCERT), signed in 1983.

7. New Zealand's geographic distribution of exports by countries include more than 20. These are in order of importance: Australia, Japan, United States, Britain, South Korea, Taiwan, Germany, Hong Kong, Malaysia, China, Canada, Singapore, and other European nations.

8. Currently, there are more than 600 companies developing software applications or systems for perhaps only one client at a time (TRADENZ Report, 1993–1994).

9. See Akoorie (1996) New Zealand's figures on inward and outward FDI.

10. See Ozawa (1992) on the importance of FDI as an engine of economic growth.

11. A small open economy like New Zealand, when compared to a larger counterpart such as Australia, is more likely to manage economic variables to make its currency undervalued, thus gaining competitiveness in its export related industries.

12. The behavior of the exchange rate under the floating system has been somewhat unpredictable with respect to the U.S.-NZ dollar exchange going from 49.8 cents in 1985, up to 65.5 in 1988, down to 57.5 in 1991, and back up to 63.5 cents in 1995. Even though the exchange rate has fluctuated widely in the last decade, it has probably not wavered unreasonably, given both extreme volatility of major currencies through this period and the massive structural domestic reforms (International Financial Statistics, 1992–94).

13. Moreover, monetary policy can be adjusted in response to fundamental pressures on the exchange rate.

14. New Zealand ranks tenth in the latest 1997 world rankings of competitiveness in front of Japan (11), Britain (12), and Germany (14). See article: 'Business this Week' in *The Economist*, (March 29th 1997).

15. New Zealand became a sovereign state with a democratic parliamentary government after the signing of the Treaty of Waitangi in 1840. The New Zealand Constitution Act of 1852 provided for the establishment of a parliament with an elected House of Representatives, and the New Constitution Act of 1986 updated and provided for a legislative body, an executive and administrative structure and specific protection for the judiciary body (New Zealand Debt Management Office, 1994).

16. See article: 'Freedom and Growth' in *The Wall Street Journal*, (December 16th, 1996).

17. The peculiar geographical arrangement of the nation with many small islands adjacent to the two main islands does not facilitate face-to-face contacts, thus creating a lack of communication and consensus among all parties. This may provide some answers to the slow response from both public and private sector to the economic difficulties that have troubled New Zealand since the early 1970s.

18. It should be pointed out that the combination of these changes in all markets have been complementary of each other. For example, the results and performance in the goods market depend in part on the success of the reforms in the financial and labor markets. These reforms have created a much more efficient economic environment in New Zealand.

19. Indeed, the telecommunications industry is of great importance to New Zealanders, not only domestically linking the two main islands and the numerous small islands

adjacent to them, but also internationally linking this small open economy to world events and information.

20. Pressures on the labor market have created shortages for technologically skilled workers.

21. See article: 'Kiwis Turn Sour' in *The Economist*, (October 19th, 1996).

Part II

Globalization and Developing Economies

7

Some Consequences of Globalization for Developing Countries[1]

ERICH GUNDLACH AND PETER NUNNENKAMP

Globalization improves the prospects for developing countries (DCs) to catch up economically with industrialized countries. Depending on economic policies with respect to openness and factor accumulation, globalization may increase capital and technology flows to DCs, thereby generating a higher rate of income growth than would be possible in a less integrated world economy. Nevertheless, many observers draw an overly pessimistic picture of the perspectives of DCs in the era of globalization, mainly for three reasons. First, DC membership in institutionalized regional integration schemes such as in Europe and North America is sometimes considered to be a necessary precondition for economic success. Second, a low level of inter-firm technological cooperation between rich and poor countries is feared to delink DCs from technological progress. Third, a relatively high concentration of foreign direct investment flows on a few advanced DC hosts is said to limit the development prospects for the majority of DCs. The chapter shows that such concerns are largely unfounded.

Introduction

Globalization means a closer international integration of production and markets. The increasing interdependence of national economies around the world is the result of growing trade and capital flows and rising inter-firm technological cooperation. These trends reflect the liberalization of trade initiated by successive GATT rounds and, especially in the 1980s, the worldwide deregulation of financial markets and other business services such as banking and insurance. All this has led to more competition in the world economy, and to new profit opportunities for international investors. Developing countries (DCs) have to adjust to the changing international environment, if they want to participate in the ongoing globalization of production and markets.

Globalization is by no means an entirely new phenomenon. What has changed in the world economy during the last decade or so is that, thanks to the micro-electronics revolution, new communication technologies have evolved that allow for the international diffusion of new production and organization technologies at low cost. Transportation costs per unit of production are declining, since new technologies lead to economies of scale in transportation, and tend to reduce the volume of international transport in raw materials necessary to produce one unit of final output.

The relatively new aspect that makes globalization different from previous advances in the international division of labor is the ability of producers to slice up the value chain (Krugman, 1995), i.e. the possibility of achieving a geographically dispersed fragmentation of production. If firms place their production around the world, sourcing this component from one country and that component from another, it may still be easy to say where certain products have been assembled, but it will become increasingly difficult to say where they actually have been made. Therefore, complementary to slicing up the value chain, another new aspect of globalization is the emergence of large exports of *manufactured* goods from low-wage DCs to high-wage industrialized countries, and the accompanying increase of foreign direct investment (FDI) flows to DCs.

The hypothesis raised in this chapter is that globalization improves the prospects for DCs to catch up economically with industrialized countries. By contrast, many observers draw an overly pessimistic picture of the perspectives of DCs in the era of globalization, mainly for three reasons. First, DC membership in, or association with institutionalized regional integration schemes such as in Europe and North America is sometimes considered to be a necessary precondition for economic success. Second, a low level of inter-firm technological cooperation between rich and poor countries is feared to delink DCs from technological progress. Third, a relatively high concentration of FDI flows on a few advanced DC hosts is said to limit the development prospects for the majority of DCs.

Such concerns are largely unfounded. It mainly depends on domestic economic policies whether DCs can successfully grasp the chances for catching up involved in globalization. Controlling for differences among DCs in the rates of physical and human capital accumulation, we find that open DCs may realize substantial increases in their GDP within a shorter period of time than may closed economies. Depending on DC economic policies with respect to openness and factor accumulation, globalization tends to increase capital and technology flows to DCs that can generate a higher rate of income growth than would be possible in a less integrated world economy. This is why globalization should be seen as an opportunity for DCs rather than a threat, notwithstanding the implied restrictions for DC economic policies.

Developing Countries in the Global Economy: Major Issues

Stylized Facts

Globalization shapes the world economy in different ways. Most obviously, international trade and capital flows are affected. Over the last 30 years or so, international trade has grown faster on average than production (GATT, various dates; see also Table 7.1). This implies a more integrated world economy. Closer integration brings about opportunities for specialization, and hence increases inter-dependencies. This is highlighted by recent changes in the structure of world trade.

First, world trade in manufactures has grown faster than total world trade (Table 7.1), which supports the notion that slicing up the value chain has become a new opportunity in the era of globalization. International sourcing (that is, the purchase of intermediate inputs from foreign sources) has grown faster than domestic sourcing, and now accounts for about half of all imports by major countries (OECD, 1994). Second, intra-industry trade has risen significantly in almost all OECD countries, which share fairly similar factor endowments. However, it has also increased between Japan and its Asian neighbors, even in physical and human capital intensive products, despite fairly different factor endowments (Nunnenkamp *et al.*, 1994). Hence, the pattern of world trade is changing, slowly but steadily, in favor of trade in manufactures. Trade in manufactures seems to be less dependent on *overall* relative factor endowments, but more on relative endowments with *immobile* factors of production. This is a consequence of the increased international mobility of capital, as indicated by the recent surge in FDI flows.

In contrast to relatively steady changes in the pattern of international trade, a dramatic increase in FDI flows has taken place during the last decade. FDI flows have grown even twice as fast as international trade since 1983 (Table 7.1). In addition to rising FDI flows, other forms of international cooperation between corporations such as licensing, joint ventures, offshore processing, minority participations, and so-called strategic alliances have become more important in recent

TABLE 7.1 *Stylized Facts of Globalization*

	World production*	World trade		World FDI§	Note:	
		Total†	Manufactures‡		DC trade share¶	DC FDI share**
1983	100	100	100	100	13.1	24.2
1984	103.8	105.8	102.8	116.1	12.7	20.8
1985	107.5	106.2	102.8	119.0	12.0	23.6
1986	111.3	117.4	125.7	192.5	13.1	14.7
1987	113.8	137.8	153.3	298.0	14.7	11.6
1988	118.8	157.0	176.6	367.4	15.6	15.7
1989	122.5	170.3	188.5	470.6	18.2	14.7
1990	125.0	192.3	216.4	493.0	17.9	14.8
1991	123.8	197.5	223.5	392.9	19.6	26.5
1992	125.0	213.1	244.4	396.9	20.8	30.1
1993	127.5	212.5	246.7	460.7	23.8	36.0
1994	131.3	237.7	..	468.1	..	39.3

*Real GDP index, 1983 = 100.
†Average of world merchandise exports and imports plus world exports and imports of commercial services; 1983 = 100.
‡World exports of manufactures (SITC 5 + 6 + 7 + 8 − 67 − 68); 1983 = 100.
§Average of direct investment abroad and in the reporting economy; 1983 = 100.
¶Developing countries' share in world exports of manufactures (percent).
**Developing countries' share in world inflows of foreign direct investment, excluding developing countries for which oil production is the dominant industry (percent).
Sources: GATT, International Trade, Trends and Statistics; IMF, Balance of Payments Statistics; UN, Monthly Bulletin of Statistics.

years. As a rough approximation, the number of international inter-firm cooperation agreements has doubled over the 1980s (OECD, 1994).

All three aspects of globalization—international trade, FDI, and cross-border inter-firm cooperation—are currently dominated by OECD countries. But the dynamic East and South East Asian economies are rapidly becoming involved, as are some countries in Latin America and in Central and Eastern Europe. Taken as a group, DCs strongly increased their share in world exports of manufactures between 1983 and 1993 (Table 7.1). Likewise, their share in recorded world FDI inflows rose steeply, especially since the mid 1980s.[2] While these simple statistics confirm that the ongoing globalization of production and markets is not only an issue concerning developed countries, it may be open to question whether the closer integration of the world economy is due to regionalization rather than globalization, whether technology flows to DCs are severely limited, and whether FDI flows to DCs are concentrated on just a few fairly advanced hosts. We briefly discuss each of these issues in the following.

Globalization versus Regionalization

Some authors claim that there is no general trend towards globalization involving DCs. They argue that a strong move towards regional production and sourcing networks will impair the chances of DCs to benefit from technology transfers and to make full use of their comparative cost advantages (Oman, 1994). This would imply that DCs face the risk of being delinked from the growth dynamics of globalization, if they were excluded from major regional groupings, notably the North American Free Trade Agreement (NAFTA) and the European Union (EU).

This idea deserves further thought. It is definitely true that not all DCs have participated in globalization so far.[3] At present, economic dynamism is regionally concentrated, namely in Asia. In that region, intra-regional trade flows have grown faster than extra-regional trade flows. The share of intra-Asian exports of manufactures has increased from 22 percent of total Asian exports in 1980 to 36 percent in 1993 (UN, 1994). But these observations alone do not support the claim that regionalization, rather than globalization, is the rule of the game in the world economy.

Regional linkages, whether institutionalized or not, are just one among many other factors that may determine whether a country will participate successfully in globalization. Depending on the motivations of international investors, factors such as macro-economic stability, a high rate of factor accumulation, a relatively undistorted trade regime and openness for international capital flows may be more important than any gains that could result from a privileged access to a large market. Privileged market access *per se* is unlikely to advance the international competitiveness of new suppliers. That is, close ties with major regional integration schemes seem to be neither necessary nor sufficient for joining the globalization club.

To assess the empirical relevance of this hypothesis, we first compare EU import shares of manufactures for different groups of DCs. The EU is a large and relatively open market for manufactures, notwithstanding differential treatment of its external trading partners. For example, DCs from the African, Caribbean and Pacific region (ACP) rank well ahead of other DCs in the pyramid of EU trade preferences (Hiemenz *et al.*, 1994). Therefore, one should expect that ACP countries display a better performance in EU markets than other DCs, if institutionalized linkages to regional integration schemes actually dominated the presumed trend towards globalization. Table 7.2 shows that this is not the case:

ACP countries did not emerge as new suppliers on EU markets, despite their favorable market access. The share of EU imports of manufactures from ACP countries actually decreased between 1980 and 1993. As it seems, this fall was mainly caused by a drastic reduction of EU imports of physical capital intensive chemicals from ACP countries, whereas the EU import shares of ACP countries in human

TABLE 7.2 *The Regional Structure of Extra-EU Imports of Manufactures, 1980 and 1993 (percent)*

		Total	Machinery, transport equipment	Chemicals	Clothing and textiles
Extra-EU	1980	37.2	35.8	28.8	45.0
imports*	1993	40.8	40.1	29.5	36.3
thereof:†					
DCs	1980	16.5	7.7	10.5	45.2
	1993	22.1	19.3	11.3	41.8
thereof:‡					
ACP	1980	5.8	3.1	39.3	2.0
	1993	4.1	3.3	7.7	2.5
Asian NIEs§	1980	47.9	59.1	4.5	46.3
	1993	41.5	56.8	21.3	14.3
ASEAN¶	1980	6.7	8.8	2.0	6.4
	1993	18.8	18.7	5.3	18.1
China	1980	5.6	0.5	14.7	6.8
	1993	24.7	12.6	21.6	19.2
South Asia**	1980	10.2	1.5	2.4	15.6
	1993	10.9	1.4	8.2	40.0
Latin America	1980	11.4	14.3	22.9	7.6
	1993	8.4	8.7	21.9	5.8

*In percent of total EU imports.
†In percent of extra-EU imports; DCs defined as Class 2 according to EU classification.
‡In percent of EU imports from DCs.
§Hong Kong, Singapore, South Korea, Taiwan.
¶Excluding Singapore and Brunei.
**Bangladesh, India, Nepal, Pakistan, Sri Lanka.
Source: EUROSTAT (various dates.).

capital intensive machinery and labor intensive textiles and clothing largely remained constant at a low level.

Asian DCs, especially China and ASEAN member countries, increased their EU import shares of manufactures considerably, despite missing trade privileges and geographical distance. Asian NIEs, which have almost achieved the status of industrialized countries, did not gain overall trade shares, but instead shifted their supply from labor intensive textiles and clothing to physical capital intensive chemicals. South Asia, which is more comparable to ACP countries in terms of per capita income, did not achieve much progress in overall trade shares. Nevertheless, South Asian countries report a strong increase in EU import shares of textiles and clothing, which obviously reflects their comparative advantage.

Latin American countries record a relatively strong decline in EU import shares of human capital intensive machinery and transport equipment, but otherwise fairly stable EU import shares.

Recent changes in EU import shares of manufactures from different DC groups seem to be unrelated to trade preferences granted by the EU. To say the least, privileged DC groups did not gain market shares, and non-favored DCs did not suffer losses. Institutionalized ties with regional integration schemes such as the EU seem to matter less than DC economic policies when it comes to explaining success and failure in globalization.

Second, we refer to the distribution of worldwide FDI flows, in order to tentatively assess whether regionalization has dominated over globalization. If so, the formation of regional blocs should have resulted in FDI diversion away from non-member DCs. The deepening of EU integration in the aftermath of the internal market program of 1985 may provide a case in point. The EU indeed attracted substantially higher FDI inflows in 1989–91 (annual average US\$89.3 billion) than in 1983–88 (US\$27.4 billion) (UNCTAD, 1995c). As a result, the EU's share in worldwide FDI flows increased from 30 to 47 percent. EU integration caused higher intra-EU FDI as European companies became more Eurocentric, and EU integration also induced higher FDI inflows from Japan and the United States.[4] However, this boom did not result in a proportional effect on EU FDI outflows to various regions; it mainly affected EU FDI outflows to the United States. EU investors neglected DCs only temporarily and largely because of home-made economic disturbances in Latin America. Likewise, European integration has not led US and Japanese investors to curtail their FDI in DCs. Hence, the boom of FDI flows to the EU during the process of completing the internal market does not appear to have resulted in significant FDI diversion at the expense of DCs. Moreover, it appears to have been a rather short-term phenomenon. In 1992–94, the EU's share in worldwide FDI flows went down to 37.6 percent. At the same time, all DCs taken together nearly doubled their share from 18.8 percent in 1989–91 to 34.9 percent in 1992–94 (UNCTAD, 1995c). All this suggests that the recent revival of regional integration must not be interpreted as the dominant feature of the international division of labor.

Technology Flows to DCs

Another concern that DCs may be delinked from global trends is related to the marginal role of DCs in the generation of technological knowledge. As a matter of fact, strategic technology alliances are largely confined to OECD-based enterprises (Table 7.3). Especially joint R&D activities are almost exclusively pursued within the Triad of the EU, Japan and the U.S. The dominance of the Triad is somewhat weaker with respect to joint ventures not exclusively devoted to R&D activities, but the participation of DC companies is below 10 percent even in this category.

In contrast to a widespread belief, this observation does not imply that DCs are excluded from technological progress. Not surprisingly, technology motivated inter-firm cooperation is largely a business between equally advanced partners operating at the forefront of technological progress. With few exceptions, DC companies do not provide the required match of partners in this field of inter-firm cooperation. Factor endowments typically prevailing in DCs prevent a stronger role in the *generation* of technological innovations. Put differently, strategic technology alliances are an inappropriate means to integrate DCs into corporate globalization strategies. Nevertheless, DCs can derive benefits from transfers of technology. It is the *application*

TABLE 7.3 *Distribution of Strategic Technology Alliances, 1980–89*

	Number	Share of (percent):		
		Industrialized economies	Triad/NIEs	Triad/other DCs
Total	4192	95.7	2.3	1.5
thereof:				
Joint R&D	1752	99.1	0.5	0.4
R&D contracts, etc.	532	96.6	2.6	0.2
Joint ventures	1224	90.9	4.9	3.4

Source: Freeman and Hagedoorn (1994).

of internationally available technologies which matters most for DCs. Other vehicles than strategic alliances, notably international trade in capital goods and FDI, are better suited for transferring technology to DCs.

The empirical evidence on trade and FDI supports the proposition of an enhanced integration of DCs into globalization strategies. Closer trade and investment linkages are observed for all DCs taken together: Their share in worldwide trade and FDI increased (see Table 7.1). Moreover, Table 7.4 shows that exports have grown faster than overall production in DCs (proxied by their GNP), and the growth of FDI flows to DCs still exceeded export growth.[5]

However, the average development for all DCs obscures remarkable differences between various country groups. Both indicators presented in Table 7.4 reveal that it is mainly East Asia which has become more integrated into the international division of labor.[6] By contrast, the export-to-GNP ratio of Sub-Saharan Africa has not changed significantly since the mid-1980s, and FDI inflows have remained at a low level in this region (as well as in South Asia). Obviously, Sub-Saharan Africa in particular has not benefited from the trend towards globalized production and marketing. Nevertheless, Table 7.4 contradicts the notion that only few DCs, notably Asian NIEs, are participating in globalization. The FDI-to-export ratio suggests that Latin America has restored its locational attractiveness after several countries in this region had implemented far-reaching economic reforms. At the same time, transition economies in Eastern Europe have emerged as new competitors for FDI.

Some observers fear that new manufacturing techniques will render it more difficult for DCs to attract foreign capital in the future, which would increase the risk of DCs falling further behind technologically advanced economies (Freeman and Hagedoorn, 1994). By contrast, we maintain that the attractiveness of DCs for foreign capital is not determined by their role in producing new technologies. Rather, their attractiveness depends on their capabilities in *applying* existing technologies. In this respect, many DCs made substantial progress recently, not least supported by FDI and imports of capital goods.

Another question is whether DCs receive technologies that fit their factor endowments. What can be expected in a globalizing economy is that NIEs should receive a higher share of sophisticated technologies than less advanced DCs (LDCs). Table 7.5 provides some empirical evidence derived from the MERIT data base (Freeman and Hagedoorn, 1994) with regard to the relative importance of so-called core technologies in international inter-firm technology partnering. It is widely accepted that information technology, biotechnology, and new materials are likely to constitute the heart of many future technological

TABLE 7.4 *The Integration of Selected DC Regions into the World Economy, 1980–95*

	Exports in percent of GNP					FDI inflows (net) in percent of exports				
	1980	1987	1990	1992	1995*	1980	1987	1990	1992	1995*
AllDCs	30.3	20.5	20.6	21.4	25.1	0.7	2.1	2.7	4.7	6.6
East Asia and Pacific	23.2	26.5	28.1	29.9	34.8	1.3	2.7	4.3	6.5	9.5
South Asia	10.8	9.9	10.7	12.6	15.8	0.8	1.3	1.1	1.4	3.0
Latin America and Caribbean	18.1	17.5	16.2	15.5	15.6	4.8	4.6	4.6	7.9	7.5
Middle East and North Africa	50.7	25.4	34.9	31.6	29.4	−1.5	1.0	1.7	1.4	1.3
Sub-Saharan Africa	33.6	29.7	31.4	29.6	27.5	0.0	2.2	1.0	1.8	2.6
East Europe and Central Asia	–†	–†	13.9	17.2	13.7‡	0.0	0.0	0.2	3.1	7.4‡

*Preliminary.

†Not reported because of unreliable GNP data.

‡1994.

Source: World Bank (various dates).

TABLE 7.5 *The Share of Core Technologies in International Inter-firm Technology Partnering, 1980–89 (percent)*

	Share of core technologies* in:	
	Strategic technological alliances	Technology transfer agreements
Developed countries	73.0	60.9
Triad	73.5	61.4
Triad-NIEs	53.6	52.4
Triad-LDCs	23.4	38.5

*Information technology, biotechnology, new materials.
Source: Freeman and Hagedoorn (1994).

developments affecting manufacturing, but also many services. Technology partnering among industrialized countries, and especially within the EU, Japan and U.S. Triad, is dominated by these three core technologies. The share of core technologies in Triad-DC inter-firm technology partnering is much lower. Core technologies only account for about half of all partnerships between Triad and NIE companies, while two thirds of all partnerships involving LDCs are in areas other than core technologies. This pattern supports the view that the focus of technological cooperation is related to factor endowments of partners. Hence, DCs appear to be best prepared to participate successfully in globalization and attract appropriate technologies, if they specialize according to their comparative advantages.

FDI Concentration

The participation of DCs in the increasing division of labor would be severely restricted if FDI flows—which constitute a major channel of international technology transfers—were concentrated on a few advanced DC hosts. If, for whatever reason, such a pattern of FDI flows to DCs does not change over time, the majority of DCs would probably receive less capital and technology than would be necessary to benefit from the globalization of production and markets. As a consequence, these DCs could be caught in a poverty trap. Globalization would only support some advanced DCs that have a command of the relevant technologies, but would not induce economic development in less advanced DCs. However, the assumption of a more or less constant pattern of FDI flows to selected DCs is not compatible with changes in the regional distribution of FDI flows since 1980 (Figure 7.1).

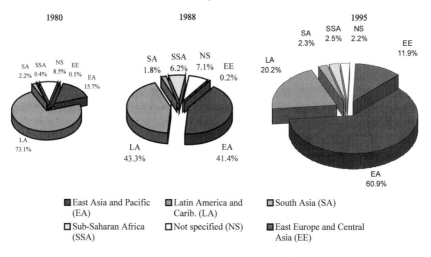

FIGURE 7.1 Regional Distribution of FDI Flows to DCs,[7] 1980–95 (*Source*: World Bank, various dates)

1. East Asia's share in world FDI flows has nearly quadrupled since 1980. This region did not maintain close institutionalized ties with either the EU or NAFTA. Moreover, increasing FDI among Asian DCs can only partly explain the rising share of East Asia in world FDI flows.[8] Hence, the dramatic shift of FDI to this region has to be attributed to globalization effects to a significant extent.

2. The rise in East Asia's FDI share is largely due to China's emerging participation in world capital markets. FDI in China soared from virtually zero in 1980 to US$33.8 billion in 1994 (World Bank, various dates). Asian NIEs have especially benefited from Chinese liberalization and have become major investors in this country (UNCTAD, 1995a). However, the rising attractiveness of China for foreign investors has not been at the expense of other East Asian recipients. FDI flows to East Asian DCs other than China increased sevenfold from 1980 to 1994.

3. Post-socialist countries in transition (notably those in Central Europe) represent the second group which increased its share in total FDI flows. This development is obviously related to the progress achieved in economic transformation, which is encouraging the integration of transition economies into the international division of labor.

4. Latin America, which traditionally was the preferred host region for FDI in the Third World, appears to be the main loser. However, the regional share in total FDI flows tends to obscure several factors relevant for assessing the position of Latin American economies

in the context of globalization. First of all, FDI flows to Latin America have recovered significantly since the late 1980s. The preliminary figure of US$17.8 billion for 1994 exceeded the inflows of 1988 by a factor of 2.2 (World Bank, various dates). Furthermore, several countries in this region (including Argentina, Chile, and Mexico) belonged to the best performers when average annual FDI inflows in 1993–94 are compared with 1983–88.[9] Particularly the favorable position of Argentina and Mexico indicates that an attractiveness for FDI may be regained in the aftermath of major economic crises, once consistent domestic policy reforms comprising macro-economic stabilization and structural adjustment are implemented.[10] The counterfactual situation is provided by Brazil, which was less reform-minded until recently. Brazil has lost its top position with regard to FDI inflows; FDI flows to Brazil in 1993 were only half the average figure for 1983–88, and recovered only in 1994 (UNCTAD 1995c, Annex Table 1).

The evidence on FDI in DCs is difficult to reconcile with the widespread belief that only few DCs may benefit from globalization. Underlying this belief is the observation that between two thirds and three quarters of total FDI flows to DCs have persistently been absorbed by the ten largest host economies (e.g. UNCTAD, 1995b). But the country composition of the group of best performers changes over time. The top ten of 1984 experienced a decline in their share in total FDI flows to DCs until 1994. This decline was rather modest (from 77 percent in 1984 to 73 percent in 1994), since China, which already belonged to the largest host countries in 1984, experienced a steep increase in its share (from 15 to 42 percent); excluding China, the share of the remaining nine top performers of 1984 was cut half to 31 percent in 1994 (World Bank, various dates).[11]

More importantly though, the notion of highly concentrated FDI flows to a few DCs is mistaken since the chances of newcomers of enhancing their locational attractiveness to foreign investors are determined by *per capita* FDI inflows. The frequently noted concentration is mainly because of a large country bias. In per capita terms, various small DCs proved more attractive for FDI than larger countries. FDI patterns in Latin America provide a case in point (Nunnenkamp, 1996). Within a sample of 18 Latin American host countries, the three smallest economies (in terms of population in 1992) were among the best performers in attracting foreign investors. For instance, per capita FDI inflows of Trinidad and Tobago in 1990–94 (US$216) were more than twice the figure for Argentina. In the same period, Costa Rica received higher per capita inflows (US$60) than Mexico (US$54), and Jamaica came very close to Mexico's per capita inflows.

Finally, the chances of newcomers to participate in globalization have further improved because some relatively advanced DCs have become involved in *outward* FDI. The contribution of DCs to worldwide FDI outflows is still fairly low. But their share increased from an average of 5.8 percent in 1983–88 to 14.8 percent in 1994 (UNCTAD 1995c, Annex Table 2). DC investors are playing a significant role in specific recipient countries. This applies especially to the Asian region, where NIEs have emerged as major foreign investors in ASEAN countries and China (UNCTAD, 1995a; Riedel, 1991). Taking all this evidence together, there is no empirical support for the claim that FDI flows are persistently concentrated on a small group of advanced DCs (see Chapter 13 of this book).

Policy Restrictions for DCs in the Era of Globalization

The previous sections have demonstrated that exogenous factors cannot account for the different degree to which various DCs are participating in the globalization of production and markets. Neither the recent move towards regional integration, nor the presumed delinking of many DCs from technology and FDI flows can explain why some DCs are catching up and why others are falling behind. This finding puts into perspective those DC economic policies that shape the international competitiveness of *immobile* factors of production. If they want to participate in globalization, DCs have to acknowledge that they are no longer free to pursue economic policies of their own liking. As it seems, there are no promising policy alternatives to striving for macro-economic stability, encouraging investment in physical and human capital, and ensuring openness with regard to international trade and capital flows.

Macro-economic Stability and Factor Accumulation

Macro-economic stability, namely the absence of high and volatile rates of inflation, is the first indicator of a sound business environment. High rates of inflation render it difficult for consumers and producers to identify relative price changes. The reduced informational content of observed price changes results in higher investment risks, and in a misallocation of resources. Inflation safe, though less productive investments will be preferred. Although unexpected inflation may have a positive output effect in the short run by reducing real wages, money illusion is unlikely to prevail for long. Future wage demands will take into account the *expected* rate of inflation. Eventually, this process may end up in hyperinflation, a decline in output, soaring unemployment, and political instability. Among DCs, Latin America performed most unfavorably in this respect until recently, followed by Sub-Saharan Africa.[12]

Persistent inflation is generally home-made, since budget deficits of the government are its main cause. This is most obvious when deficits are financed by printing money. Alternatively, the greater the budget deficit, the higher have to be the taxes that producers and consumers must pay. High business taxes impair the incentive to invest and, thereby, reduce productivity growth; high income taxes impair the incentive to work (except for work in the underground economy) and, thereby, further enforce the pressure to increase taxes. It follows that countries with large budget deficits and high rates of inflation are relatively unattractive locations for international investors, and cannot be expected to experience strong economic growth in the long run.

Macro-economic stability appears to be a necessary precondition for participating in globalization. In a stable macro-economic environment, investment can be expected to be higher because risks are reduced. More investment enlarges the stock of capital per worker, increases labor productivity, and produces higher incomes in the long run. With regard to physical capital accumulation, low-inflation East Asia displayed an outstanding performance among DCs.[13] Yet, the case of Central Europe indicates that high rates of investment do not guarantee successful economic development. In this region, centrally planned investment resulted in allocative distortions so that productivity growth remained sluggish until the regime shift. Moreover, physical capital accumulation is not all that matters. Human capital accumulation may be even more important as a driving force of economic growth. This is all the more so in the global economy, given that the diffusion of new technologies is advanced by declining information and transaction costs, and the application of such technologies depends on the availability of complementary local skills. Taking average years of schooling as proxy of the stock of human capital, this consideration is supported at least partly: among DCs, East Asia is again the best performing region (Gundlach and Nunnenkamp, 1996).

More systematic evidence for the hypothesis that factor accumulation in the form of investment in physical and human capital plays a leading role for an explanation of economic success comes from empirical cross-country studies (Barro, 1991; Mankiw, *et al.* 1992; Gundlach, 1995). These studies uniformly confirm that human capital formation is at least as important as physical capital formation for explaining the large differences in per capita income between industrialized countries and DCs. They also support theoretical models which predict that economic backwardness is not necessarily a permanent state of affairs. Low income countries have the chance to realize higher growth rates than rich countries, mainly because they can use existing technologies rather than having to invent them. Therefore, controlling for different rates of factor accumulation, one would expect a convergence of per capita income between poor and rich countries in the long run. But previous empirical studies concluded that the speed of convergence is fairly low, namely in the range of 2 percent per year or even less. Hence this "natural" catching-up process alone does not suffice to realize substantial improvements in the standard of living within reasonable periods of time. The East Asian example reveals, however, that there are ways to speed up convergence. Integration into the international division of labor appears to be crucially important in this respect.

Openness and Factor Accumulation

Openness in the form of largely unrestricted international trade and capital flows is of utmost importance for DCs to ease the necessary technology import, either through the import of investment goods or through FDI inflows and other forms of international investment cooperation. Openness promotes domestic competition and efficiency, and supports a closer integration into the world economy by shaping the production structure according to the respective comparative advantages of the economy. At the same time, a closer world market integration implies fewer degrees of freedom for domestic economic policies, unless one is prepared to run the danger of being delinked from world capital markets. Arguably, East Asian DCs have successfully attracted FDI and have become the economic powerhouse of the world economy just because their economic policies responded in a more appropriate way than those of other DC regions to the adjustment needs demanded from progressing worldwide economic integration.

Openness is likely to be more important for DCs than for industrialized countries. To see why this is so, consider a neoclassical growth model for the open economy. Barro *et al.* (1995) show that an open economy described by the production function:

$$Y_t = K_t^\alpha H_t^\beta \left(A_t L_t \right)^{1-\alpha-\beta} , \ 0 < \alpha + \beta < 1 ,$$

where Y_t is output at time t, K is the stock of physical capital, H is the stock of human capital, A is the level of technology, and L is labor, converges to its steady state at rate λ, which is given by

$$\lambda_{open} = \left(1 - \frac{\beta}{1-\alpha} \right)(n + g + \delta) ,$$

where α and β are the shares of physical and human capital in factor income, n is the rate of labor force growth, g is the rate of technological progress, and δ is the depreciation rate of human and physical capital.

The central assumption of this model is that physical capital is internationally mobile, but human capital is not. By contrast, the convergence rate for the closed economy with internationally immobile physical and human capital is given by Mankiw *et al.* (1992)

$$\lambda_{closed} = (1 - \alpha - \beta)(n + g + \delta) .$$

The standard parameterization for the rate of technological progress is 2 percent and for the depreciation rate 5 percent (Barro *et al.* 1995). For industrialized countries, n was about 1 percent in 1980–93 (World Bank, 1995). The share of physical capital in factor income is about 30 percent for industrialized countries (Maddison, 1987), and the share of human capital in factor income is about 50 percent.[14] That is, for industrialized countries (IC), the two rates of convergence to the steady state are predicted to be fairly similar in the range of 2 percent for open and closed economies:

$$\lambda_{open}^{IC} = \left(1 - \frac{0.5}{1 - 0.3}\right)(0.01 + 0.02 + 0.05) = 0.023,$$

and

$$\lambda_{closed}^{IC} = (1 - 0.3 - 0.5)(0.01 + 0.02 + 0.05) = 0.016.$$

The story is different for DCs. Labor force growth in DCs was about 2 percent in 1980–93 (World Bank, 1995). Moreover, the share of physical capital in factor income is much larger in DCs than 30 percent as in industrialized countries. For a sample of DCs that report detailed National Accounts Statistics to the UN, this share is about 60 percent on average, and the average share of human capital in factor income is about 20 percent (Gundlach, 1996). If so, openness seems to matter much more for DCs than for industrialized countries. The convergence rate for an open economy is now

$$\lambda_{open}^{DC} = \left(1 - \frac{0.2}{1 - 0.6}\right)(0.02 + 0.02 + 0.05) = 0.045,$$

and the convergence rate for a closed economy is

$$\lambda_{closed}^{DC} = (1 - 0.6 - 0.2)(0.02 + 0.02 + 0.05) = 0.018.$$

This difference is large. With a predicted convergence rate of 4.5 percent for the open economy, halfway to steady state is reached in about 16 years; with a predicted convergence rate of 1.8 percent for the closed economy, halfway to steady state is reached in about 39 years. Hence, the open economy DC is predicted to reach halfway to steady state almost one generation earlier than the closed economy.

If the model is correct, more open DCs should have experienced a better growth performance, i.e. a higher rate of convergence to the steady state. Whether a country is open or not can be measured by the degree of international capital mobility, as was first suggested by Feldstein and Horioka (1980). Montiel (1994) uses the Feldstein-Horioka approach in a time series context and finds a surprisingly high degree of capital mobility in his sample of DCs, although a large number of inconclusive cases remains. We select only those DCs from his sample which can be identified either as closed or open. Moreover, to control for data quality, we exclude DCs which do not report detailed National Accounts Statistics. Our resulting final sample consists of 13 open and nine closed DCs.[15] We use this sample to calculate the rates of convergence for open and closed DCs.

Mankiw *et al.* (1982) show that, based on the previously mentioned production function, the rate of convergence (λ) can be estimated by regressing the log difference of income per worker at time t and some initial date 0 on the determinants of the steady state and the initial level of income. Augmenting such an equation by a slope and an intercept dummy for openness, we get

$$
\begin{aligned}
\ln(Y/L)_t - \ln(Y/L)_0 &= CONSTANT + \left(1 - e^{-\lambda t}\right)\frac{\alpha}{1-\alpha-\beta}\ln(\Delta K/Y) \\
&+ \left(1 - e^{-\lambda t}\right)\frac{\beta}{1-\alpha-\beta}\ln(\Delta H/Y) - \left(1 - e^{-\lambda t}\right)\frac{\alpha+\beta}{1-\alpha-\beta}\ln(n+g+\delta) \\
&- \left(1 - e^{-\lambda t}\right)\ln(Y/L)_0 + OPEN - \gamma\, SLOPEN ,
\end{aligned}
$$

where $\Delta K/Y$ is the share of physical capital investment in output, and $\Delta H/Y$ is the share of human capital investment in output.[16] *OPEN* is an intercept dummy, which equals 1 for open DCs and 0 otherwise; *SLOPEN* is a slope dummy, which equals initial income for open DCs and 0 otherwise. All other variables and parameters are defined as before.

With only 22 observations at hand, a regression based on this convergence equation would result in a serious degrees of freedom problem. Therefore, we restrict the convergence equation according to the empirical results in Mankiw *et al.* (1992, Tab. VI, intermediate sample) as:

$$
\begin{aligned}
\ln(Y/L)_t &- \ln(Y/L)_0 - 0.506\left[\ln(\Delta K/Y) - \ln(n+g+\delta)\right] \\
&- 0.266\left[\ln(\Delta H/Y) - \ln(n+g+\delta)\right] \\
&= CONSTANT - \left(1 - e^{-\lambda t}\right)\ln(Y/L)_0 + OPEN - \gamma\, SLOPEN .
\end{aligned}
$$

That is, our regression equation uses the conditional growth rate as the new dependent variable. Thereby, we control for differences among DCs in the two rates of factor accumulation and in the rate of labor force growth, which together determine the steady state. Using this approach, we estimate the following regression coefficients and the implied rates of convergence (standard errors in parentheses):

Conditional growth rate =

$$2.53 + 3.62\ OPEN - 0.31\ \ln(Y/L)_0 - 0.41\ SLOPEN$$
$$(0.73)\quad (1.09)\qquad\quad (0.09)\qquad\qquad (0.13)$$

Number of observations: 22

$\overline{R}^2 = 0.76$ s.s.e. $= 0.22$

Implied λ_{open}^{DC} :   0.051

(0.013)

Implied λ_{closed}^{DC} : 0.015

(0.006)

Our empirical findings for the two rates of convergence roughly confirm the difference between open and closed economies predicted by the neoclassical model of economic growth, assuming that the share of physical capital in factor income is about 60 percent and the share of human capital is about 20 percent in DCs. Open DCs converge at a much higher rate to their steady state than closed DCs. Put differently, openness shortens considerably the time period until the steady state is reached, although it does not change the steady state itself. Taking the point estimates of the two convergence rates literally, the open economy would reach halfway to steady state about 33 years earlier than the closed economy. It follows that openness along with factor accumulation matters for economic growth, especially in DCs.

Conclusions

Our findings support the notion that globalization offers better chances for DCs to catch up economically with industrialized countries. Globalization is likely to ease the inflow of capital and technology, thus helping to increase the rate of factor accumulation beyond the level to be financed by domestic savings. But globalization also reduces the degrees of freedom of economic policy making in DCs. First of all, it requires openness on behalf of DCs. In addition, DCs characterized by pronounced macro-economic instability are unlikely to achieve a high rate of domestic (physical and human) capital accumulation, which is a precondition for economic success. Capital formation has largely to be financed by domestic savings. Hence, capital formation is impaired by high government deficits, which represent negative savings and are the main source of macro-economic instability. It will definitely prove difficult for many DCs to pursue economic policies that successfully combine macro-economic stabilization, a high rate of domestic savings, and a liberalization of external trade and capital flows. Yet there is no promising alternative in the era of globalization. Exogenous factors such as refused membership in major regional integration schemes and the lack of preferential trade agreements with such schemes, as well as the supposed concentration of FDI and international technology transfers on just a few DCs cannot be blamed for the failure of many DCs in the past to participate successfully in the international division of labor. Principal responsibility rests with DCs themselves.

References

AGARWAL, J. P., HIEMENZ, U. and NUNNENKAMP, P. (1995) *European Integration: A Threat to Foreign Investment in Developing Countries?* Kiel Institute of World Economics, Discussion Papers, 246, March.

BARRO, R. J. (1991) Economic Growth in a Cross Section of Countries. *Quarterly Journal of Economics*, Vol. 106, 407–443.

BARRO, R. J., MANKIW, N. G. and SALA-I- MARTIN, X. (1995) Capital Mobility in Neoclassical Models of Economic Growth. *American Economic Review*, Vol. 85, 103–115.

Eurostat (various dates) CTCI-5-Pays-Produits, SCE-2311, CD-ROM.

FELDSTEIN, M. and HORIOKA, C. (1980) Domestic Saving and International Capital Flows. *Economic Journal*, Vol. 90, 314–329.

FREEMAN, C. and HAGEDOORN, J. (1994) Catching Up or Falling Behind: Patterns in International Inter-firm Technology Partnering. *World Development*, Vol. 22, 771–780.

GATT (various issues) *International Trade, Trends and Statistics*. Geneva.

GUNDLACH, E. (1995) The Role of Human Capital in Economic Growth: New Results and Alternative Interpretations. *Weltwirtschaftliches Archiv*, Vol. 131, 383–402.

GUNDLACH, E. (1996) *Openness and Convergence in Developing Countries*. Kiel Institute of World Economics, Working Papers, 749, June.

GUNDLACH, E. and NUNNENKAMP, P. (1996) *Falling Behind or Catching Up? Developing Countries in the Era of Globalization*. Kiel Institute of World Economics, Discussion Papers, 263, January.

HIEMENZ, U., GUNDLACH, E., LANGHAMMER, R. J. and NUNNENKAMP, P. (1994) *Regional Integration in Europe and Its Effects on Developing Countries*. Kieler Studien, 260, Tübingen.

IMF (various issues) *Balance of Payments Statistics Yearbook*. Washington, DC.

KRUGMAN, P. (1995) Growing World Trade: Causes and Consequences. *Brookings Papers on Economic Activity*, Vol. 1, 327–362.

MADDISON, A. (1987) Growth and Slowdown in Advanced Capitalist Economies. *Journal of Economic Literature*, Vol. 25, 649–698.

MANKIW, N. G., ROMER, D. and WEIL, D. N. (1992) A Contribution to the Empirics of Economic Growth, *Quarterly Journal of Economics*, Vol. 107, 408–437.

MONTIEL, P. J. (1994) Capital Mobility in Developing Countries: Some Measurement Issues and Empirical Estimates. *World Bank Economic Review*, Vol. 8, 311–350.

NUNNENKAMP, P. (1996) *The Changing Pattern of Foreign Direct Investment in Latin America. Kiel Institute of World Economics,* Working Papers, 736, April.

NUNNENKAMP, P. and GUNDLACH, E. (1995) Regional Trends: Development Issues and Priorities. Background paper for UNIDO, Global Report 1996. Kiel, December (mimeo).

NUNNENKAMP, P., GUNDLACH, E. and AGARWAL, J. P. (1994) Globalisation of Production and Markets. Kieler Studien, 262, Tübingen.

OECD (1994) Globalization of Industrial Activities. Working Paper 2 (48). Paris.

OMAN, C. (1994) Globalisation and Regionalisation: The Challenge for Developing Countries. OECD Development Centre Studies. Paris.

PSACHAROPOULOS, G. (1993) Returns to Investment in Education. A Global Update. World Bank, Policy Research Working Papers, 1067, January.

RIEDEL, J. (1991) Intra-Asian Trade and Foreign Direct Investment. *Asian Development Review,* Vol. 9, 111–141.

SUMMERS, R. and HESTON, A. (1991) The Penn World Table (Mark 5): an expanded set of international comparisons, 1950–1988 *Quarterly Journal of Economics, 106* (2) 327–368.

UN (various dates) *Monthly Bulletin of Statistics.* May, New York.

United Nations Conference on Trade and Development (UNCTAD) (1995a) *Country and Regional Experiences in Attracting Foreign Direct Investment for Development: Foreign Direct Investment in Developing Countries.* TD/B/ITNC/3, February, Geneva.

United Nations Conference on Trade and Development (UNCTAD) (1995b) *Recent Developments in International Investment and Transnational Corporations: Trends in Foreign Direct Investment.* TD/B/ITNC/2, February, Geneva.

United Nations Conference on Trade and Development (UNCTAD) (1995c) *World Investment Report 1995: Transnational Corporations and Competitiveness.* New York and Geneva.

WALLRAF, W. (1996) Wirtschaftliche Integration im asiatischen-pazifischen Raum. *Wirtschaft und Kultur,* Vol. 59, 7–33.

World Bank (various dates) *World Debt Tables.* Washington, DC.

World Bank (1995) *World Development Report. World Development Indicators.* Oxford.

Notes

1. This chapter is based on a paper presented at the International Conference on Globalization sponsored by the School of Economics and Management of the University of Sao Paulo in May 1996 and organized by Professor Alvaro A. Zini Jr.

2. We are not aware of any systematic statistical information on the *change* of the share of DCs in international inter-firm cooperation agreements. However, casual evidence suggests that FDI and non-equity inter-firm cooperation agreements (NEC) are complements rather than substitutes (Gundlach and Nunnenkamp, 1996), which is why FDI figures can confidently be assumed to reflect NEC developments as well. For a detailed assessment of the relation between FDI and NEC, see also Nunnenkamp *et al.* (1994).

3. For a detailed assessment of the present state of globalization for various regional groups of DCs, see Nunnenkamp and Gundlach (1995).

4. For a more detailed analysis, see Agarwal *et al.* (1995) and Chapter 4 of this volume.

5. The temporary decline of the export-to-GNP ratio in the early 1980s is due to

the drastic fall in oil prices after their 1980 peak. In 1987, nominal exports of oil exporting countries were less than half the 1980 value.

6. The comparison of the export-to-GNP ratio across country groups is not meaningful because this ratio tends to be systematically lower for large economies. Hence, the interpretation of this indicator is restricted to its development over time.

7. Percentage share in FDI flows to DCs except Middle East and North Africa; this region is excluded because of negative (net) FDI flows in 1980. Data on Hong Kong, Singapore and Taiwan are not reported. Figures for 1995 are preliminary, and were estimated for East Europe and Central Asia.

8. According to Wallraf (1996), FDI flows within the group of Asian NIEs, ASEAN countries, China and Vietnam increased by US$19.8 billion in 1989–93. UNCTAD data (1995c) reveal that total FDI inflows to these countries increased by US$32.7 billion during the same period.

9. FDI flows to Mexico more than doubled, while FDI flows to Chile and Argentina rose by factors of 3.9 and 7.3 (UNCTAD, 1995c, Annex Table 1).

10. The peso-crisis of Mexico in December 1994 revealed, however, that remaining economic and political risks had been underestimated.

11. The share of the 25 best performers of 1984 in total FDI flows to all DCs declined from 92 to 78 percent if China is included, and from 77 to 36 percent if China is excluded.

12. For details, see Gundlach and Nunnenkamp (1996, Figure 7).

13. It should be noted that high investment rates usually reflect high domestic savings. This is so because the difference between investment and domestic savings equals the current account deficit, which rarely exceeds 5 percent of GDP over longer time periods.

14. The calculation of the share of human capital in factor income is somewhat tricky, because there is no National Accounts counterpart. One way to derive an estimate for the share of human capital in the *total wage bill* is to focus on the rate of return to education and average years of schooling, thereby assuming that investment in education is the same thing as an increase in the stock of human capital. For example, with a social rate of return to secondary education of about 13 percent and average school attendance of about 8 years, both figures representing worldwide averages (Psacharopoulos, 1993), it follows that investment in education raises income by a factor of three ($e^{0.08 \cdot 13} \approx 3$). Hence, income is predicted to be three times higher with human capital than without. Accordingly, the share of human capital in the total wage bill should be about two thirds. Multiplying this figure with the share of labor in factor income gives an overall share of human capital in income of about 50 percent.

15. According to the findings of Montiel (1995) for 1970–90, Benin, Cameroon, Chile, Colombia, Costa Rica, Ecuador, Malaysia, Mauritius, Mexico, Paraguay, Peru, Sierra Leone and Uruguay can be classified as open, while Honduras, Kenya, Malawi, Nepal, Niger, Nigeria, the Philippines, Venezuela and Zimbabwe can be classified as closed.

16. The share of human capital investment in output is measured as the percentage of the working age population in secondary schools, which is taken from Mankiw *et al.* (1992). All other variables are taken from Summers and Heston (1991). Time t is 1985, time 0 is 1960. For details, see Gundlach (1996).

8

Determinants of Outward Taiwanese Foreign Direct Investment, 1965–93

YINGSHING LIN AND MICHAEL SZENBERG

The purpose of the study is to empirically investigate the dynamic relationship between changes in macro-economic and micro-economic factors and changes in foreign direct investment (FDI) made by Taiwanese firms. The macro-economic determinants to be explored are domestic savings-investment surplus, capital-labor ratio, labor supply, exchange rate movement, and differentials in international interest rates and national economic growth rates. The firm-level determinants of Taiwanese foreign investment behavior is related to annual manufacturing growth and business export profitability. Multiple regression analysis is used to evaluate the effects of the explanatory factors on Taiwanese FDI. The empirical findings indicate that accumulation of capital, shortages of labor supply, establishment of a flexible foreign exchange system, export profits, market access to facilitate exports, and foreign economic growth rates all contributed to the growth of Taiwanese FDI.

Introduction

During the 1980s and 1990s, Taiwan's successful industrialization contributed to the growth of its FDI abroad. Between 1965 and 1993, Taiwan invested overseas more than U.S.$23 billion, which ranked it as the seventh largest source of direct investment capital in the world. This bulk of investment was concentrated in the late 1980s and early 1990s. In 1989 alone, the investment was U.S.$7 billion. Between 1988 and 1990, the total new investment amounted to U.S.$16 billion, which represented more than 70 percent of Taiwan's total outward direct investment. Since the early 1990s, Taiwanese FDI flows have been around the level of U.S.$2 billion annually, ten times those in the 1980s. The increase of FDI suggests that the country is moving rapidly toward becoming a developed, mature economy by the end of the twentieth century.

There are several factors that explain the emergence of Taiwan as a major source of global direct investment capital. First, the surge of outward Taiwanese direct investment capital has coincided with that of all FDI. Since the mid-1980s, world-wide flows of FDI have grown at unprecedented rates. Between 1987 and 1992, global FDI experienced an average nominal growth rate of 20 percent, compared with the world-wide growth rates of merchandise exports and Gross Domestic Product (GDP) of 13 percent and 12 percent, respectively. Taiwanese multinational firms were influenced by this trend and begun to participate actively by organizing their own corporate network around the world.

Rapid economic growth in the Asia-Pacific region has been the second factor contributing to the emergence of Taiwanese international direct investment capital. During the period of 1981–92, for example, the average GDP growth rate in the Asia-Pacific region was 7 percent, compared with a world average of 2.9 percent and 3.2 percent for all developing countries (UNCTC, 1992). Moreover, many countries in the Asia-Pacific region adopted open policies towards international trade and investment, which helped accelerate domestic economic growth and contributed to the growth of Taiwanese trade-related direct investment projects in the region.

Third, the emergence of Taiwanese world-wide investment was the direct result of the country's rapid industrialization and export-oriented development strategy. The success of Taiwan's industrialization strategy and outward looking trade policy resulted in a Gross National Product (GNP) of U.S.$233 billion in 1994, which translated into a per capita level of U.S.$12,000—the 24th highest in the world. In addition, Taiwan's commercial policies transformed the country into the 13th largest trader in the world, with international trade exceeding U.S.$170 billion and foreign exchange holdings surpassing U.S.$100 billion—the second largest in the world (only slightly less than that of Japan). At an industry level, Taiwan's rapid industrialization started with consumer-goods industries, such as textiles and shoes in the early stages, followed by the backward integration of petrochemical and steel industries, and finally shifted into high technology industries such as consumer electronics and computers. Taiwan's manufacturing strength has enabled its firms to invest overseas to take advantage of the ownership specific assets in the form of production facilities, marketing expertise, and innovated technologies.

Finally, shifts in Taiwan's international comparative advantage have played an important role in increasing the country's foreign economic presence. For Taiwanese firms, the search for new production locations abroad was triggered by the appreciation of domestic currency and the increase of real wage rates. In the face of rising domestic costs, the need to remain cost-competitive in the international market place caused Taiwanese industries to invest abroad.

Moreover, economic disparities among countries within the Asia-Pacific region have offered Taiwanese multinational firms an opportunity to exploit these differences by sharing productions and exports among their Asian affiliates according to their national comparative advantages. In summary, Taiwanese multinational firms have utilized their FDI to establish a corporate global network of exports and integrated international production.

The principal objective for studying Taiwanese FDI is to examine the dynamic relationship between changes in macro-economic factors and micro-economic variables, and the expansion in overseas direct investment. The macro-economic factors, which are external determinants, include domestic savings-investment surplus, capital-labor ratios, manufacturing growth rates, exchange rate movements, international interest rates, and national economic growth differentials. The micro-economic determinants which are internal factors influencing firms' foreign investment behaviors include business export profitability and other firm-level determinants.

This study focuses on the period between 1965 and 1993. The year 1965 is chosen as the starting point because in that year the United States government suspended capital aid to Taiwan, and there was only a small outward-bound direct investment at that time. Since 1965, Taiwan has primarily financed its domestic and overseas investments by domestically generated savings.

Taiwan's FDI figures have been obtained from three different sources: home government approval statistics, home government balance of payment statistics, and host government approval statistics.

Hypotheses

Two hypotheses are developed for empirical testing. These hypotheses are further divided into the macro-economic perspective and the micro-economic (business) perspective. The macro-economic hypothesis discusses the influence of changes in domestic macro-economic conditions on Taiwan's outward FDI. The micro-economic hypothesis discusses economic variables that affect Taiwanese businesses' FDI decisions. To test the hypotheses regarding the strength of the relationship between changes in economic determinants and variations of Taiwanese overseas FDI, the following four model specifications are examined using multiple regression analysis corrected for second order serial correlations: linear, semi-log (mixed), log linear (multiplicative), and inverse linear (reciprocal).

Macro-economic Perspective

The first hypothesis examined in this study postulates that the surge in Taiwan's overseas FDI was the result of a savings surplus. The excess of domestic savings over investment totaled more than 20 percent of GNP in the 1980s. The savings surplus was reflected in a trade surplus, as well as an accumulation of foreign exchange reserves, which provided an ample source for FDI abroad.

In general, when the domestic economy is in balance, savings closely follow investment. Early Taiwanese economic development was characterized by a contemporaneous increase in savings and investment due to the country's abundant labor supply, productivity improvements, and industrial expansion in the export sector. The initial balance between savings and investment for the Taiwanese economy was achieved by maintaining a domestic sector for local demand and an external sector for foreign demand. Rapid development of Taiwan's international trade improved the country's income per head and induced more savings. The accumulation of savings soon altered Taiwan's capital-labor ratio in favor of the development of capital-intensive industries and discriminated against the growth of labor-intensive industries. This restructuring process was accelerated by shortages of labor, particularly in the 15 to 64 working age group. Shrinking labor-intensive industries, particularly in the external sector, created a short-term disequilibrium in the savings-investment relationship due to low investment returns in the labor-intensive export sectors. The assumption of capital mobility is adopted to describe the possible outcome that surplus savings became the source of foreign investment due to limited domestic investment opportunities and low returns to capital.

This macro-economic hypothesis may be summarized as:

$$F = f\ (S, K, M, L);\ F_S > 0,\ F_K > 0,\ F_M > 0,\ F_L < 0 \tag{1}$$

where F is the foreign direct investment from Taiwan, S is the domestic surplus savings over investment, K is the capital-labor ratio, M is the average annual growth of the manufacturing sector, and L is the average annual growth of the labor force between the age of 15 and 64. The growth of Taiwanese outward FDI is assumed to be positively related to changes in the surplus of savings, the capital-labor ratio, and the average annual growth of the manufacturing sector; negatively related to the average annual growth of the labor force between the age of 15 and 64.

Micro-economic Perspective

The second hypothesis examined in this study postulates that Taiwan's overseas FDI has been driven by domestic wage increases, rapid currency appreciation, and its product pricing structure. Because of intense international competition, Taiwan's export industries have been 'price takers', with unit export values kept to a level that put pressure on producers to absorb increases in domestic costs. Under the pressures of tight profit margins, producers have resorted to overseas FDI to exploit international wage differentials by using international division of labor and specialization to reduce costs. The triple squeeze effect, resulting from appreciating exchange rates, rising domestic wages, and recognizing price constraints imposed by international competition, has forced Taiwan's export sector to establish offshore production facilities.

Finally, this study posits that international differentials in economic growth rates and interest rates have been instrumental in fostering Taiwan's direct investment abroad. Faster foreign economic growth and higher interest rates have generated higher returns, thereby attracting more foreign capital. Market potentials and rapid economic growth in South East Asia and China have offered fertile ground for Taiwanese industries, not only for their relatively cheap labor but also as an important source of raw materials. This micro-economic hypothesis may be summarized as:

$$F = g\ (R, \pi, G, I\ );\ F_R < 0,\ F_\pi < 0,\ F_G > 0,\ F_I > 0 \qquad (2)$$

where F is Taiwan's outward foreign direct investment, R is the Taiwanese dollar/U.S. dollar foreign-exchange rate, π is a composite profit index using unit export values divided by unit labor cost, G is the national economic growth rate differentials between Taiwan and major investment recipient countries, and I is the interest rate differentials between Taiwan and the rest of the world. From a business (micro-economic) perspective, Taiwan's outward FDI is assumed to be negatively related to the appreciation of the Taiwanese dollar and the shrinkage of export profits; positively related to differentials in national economic growth rates and international interest rates.

Model 1

To test the macro-economic hypothesis summarized in Equation 1, the following four model specifications are examined:

$$\text{FDI} = \beta_0 + \beta_1 \text{SSR} + \beta_2 \text{KLR} + \beta_3 \text{AMG} + \beta_4 \text{AGWP} + \beta_5 \text{D87} \tag{3}$$

$$ln\text{FDI} = \beta_0 + \beta_1 \text{SSR} + \beta_2 \text{KLR} + \beta_3 \text{AMG} + \beta_4 \text{AGWP} + \beta_5 \text{D87} \tag{4}$$

$$ln\text{FDI} = \beta_0 + \beta_1 \, ln\text{SSR} + \beta_2 \, ln\text{KLR} + \beta_3 \, ln\text{AMG} + \beta_4 \, ln\text{AGWP} + \beta_5 \text{D87} \tag{5}$$

$$(\text{FDI})^{-1} = \beta_0 + \beta_1 \text{SSR} + \beta_2 \text{KLR} + \beta_3 \text{AMG} + \beta_4 \text{AGWP} + \beta_5 \text{D87} \tag{6}$$

where ln represents natural logarithms, FDI is the outward FDI, SSR is the surplus savings ratio, KLR is the domestic capital-labor ratio, AMG is the annual manufacturing growth rate, AGWP is the annual growth rate of the working population aged between 15 and 64, and D87 is a dummy variable designed to capture the qualitative policy event of lifting of foreign-exchange (capital) controls in 1987.

Model 2

To test the micro-economic (business) hypothesis summarized in Equation 2, the following four specifications are examined:

$$\text{FDI} = \gamma_0 + \gamma_1 \text{FXR} + \gamma_2 \text{PROFIT} + \gamma_3 \text{DIFG} + \gamma_4 \text{DIFR} + \gamma_5 \text{D78} \tag{7}$$

$$ln\text{FDI} = \gamma_0 + \gamma_1 \text{FXR} + \gamma_2 \text{PROFIT} + \gamma_3 \text{DIFG} + \gamma_4 \text{DIFR} + \gamma_5 \text{D78} \tag{8}$$

$$ln\text{FDI} = \gamma_0 + \gamma_1 \, ln\text{FXR} + \gamma_2 \, ln\text{PROFIT} + \gamma_3 \, ln\text{DIFG} + \gamma_4 \, ln\text{DIFR} + \gamma_5 \text{D78} \tag{9}$$

$$(\text{FDI})^{-1} = \gamma_0 + \gamma_1 \text{FXR} + \gamma_2 \text{PROFIT} + \gamma_3 \text{DIFG} + \gamma_4 \text{DIFR} + \gamma_5 \text{D78} \tag{10}$$

where FDI is outward-bound FDI, FXR is the foreign-exchange rate, PROFIT is a profitability index, DIFG is economic growth rate differentials, DIFR is interest rate differentials, and D78 is a dummy variable designed to capture the qualitative policy event of adopting a floating foreign-exchange rate system for the Taiwanese dollar. Table 8.1 describes the variables.

Statistical Testing of Model 1

The statistical testings on Model 1 shows that the regression equation based on the double-log linear specification (5) yields the best statistical results among other specifications because all variables are significant and their coefficients of determination (R^2) are high. Regressions on two other Model 1 specifications (3 and 4) have a good power of explanation (high R^2 numbers), although not all variables are significant in these specifications. The reciprocal specification (6) has a low R^2 number because of a poor fit. The empirical results and other associated statistics (t-statistics in parentheses) with correction for second-order serial correlation are summarized in Table 8.2. The parameter estimates for specification (5) are correctly signed and

TABLE 8.1 *Definition of the Variables*

Dependent variables

FDI	The ratio of Taiwanese outward-bound FDI to the total gross domestic investment
LFDI	Natural log of FDIS
INVFDI	Inverse of FDIS

Independent variables

SSR	Surplus savings ratio
LSSR	Natural log of SSR
KLR	Capital-labor ratio
LKLR	Natural log of capital-labor ratio
AMG	Annual domestic manufacturing growth rates
LAMG	Natural log of AMG
AGWP	Annual growth rates of working population 15 to 64
LAGWP	Natural log of AGWP
D87	Dummy variable representing the lifting of exchange and capital control in the year 1987, i.e. D87 = 0 before 1987; D87 = 1 for 1987 and afterwards
FXR	Foreign-exchange rates (N.T.$/U.S.$)
LFXR	Natural log of FXR
PROFIT	A profit index defined in the ratio of unit export values to unit labor costs
LPROFIT	Natural log of PROFIT
DIFG	Differential ratios in national economic growth rates between major investment recipient countries and Taiwan
LDIFG	Natural log of DIFG
DIFR	Differential ratios of international interest rates between the Taiwan and Euro-dollar 90-day interbank offer rate
LDIFR	Natural log of DIFR
D78	Dummy variable representing the adoption of floating exchange rate system in the year 1978, i.e. D78 = 0 before 1978; D78 = 1 for 1978 and afterwards

statistically significant at traditional confidence levels of 0.05 and 0.10.[1] The estimated equation explains 87 percent of the variations in Taiwanese FDI in the gross domestic investment. The high F-statistic indicates that the complete set of explanatory variables is statistically significant. After correction for second-order serial correlations, the Durbin-Watson statistic is close to 2, which rules out the possibility of serial correlation.[2] Parameter estimates for this double-log linear specification suggest that variations in the FDI were elastic (2.86) with respect to changes in capital-labor ratio, inelastic (0.42) with respect to changes in annual manufacturing growth rate, and negatively elastic

TABLE 8.2 *Model-1 Parameter Estimation with Correction for Second Order Serial-Correlation*

Parameter	(3)	(4)	(5)	(6)
Constant	−0.072	−8.405	−11.752	25125.902
	(−4.50)	(−6.14)	(−3.82)	(3.08)
SSR	−	−	−	−
KLR	0.014	0.350	2.861	−1734.327
	(6.34)	(1.94)	(2.00)	(−2.13)
AMG	−	−	0.417	−531.362
			(2.34)	(-3.17)
AGWP	−	−0.250	-1.505	−
		(−1.65)	(-2.04)	
D87	−	1.877	1.936	−
		(1.69)	(2.03)	
ρ_1	1.209	0.817	0.797	0.408
	(9.63)	(4.07)	(4.04)	(2.18)
ρ_2	−0.910	−0.376	−0.402	−
	(−6.39)	(−1.73)	(−1.91)	
Total R^2	0.87	0.86	0.90	0.36
Adj. R^2	0.86	0.83	0.87	0.28
D-W	1.63	1.89	1.80	2.04
F-statistics	53.01	26.59	30.33	4.43
df	24	22	21	25
Chow test	10.42	4.11	3.55	0.73

Note: (−) represents that the variable is eliminated from the statistical analysis because of insignificant results.

(−1.51) with respect to changes in the labor supply. These results support the first hypothesis: changes of capital-labor ratio, manufacturing growth, labor supply, and lifting of exchange (capital) control contributed to the increase of Taiwanese FDI in the total domestic investment.

The coefficient (1.94) of the dummy variable (D87) suggests that the Taiwanese government's policy to abolish capital controls have caused the FDI amount to double. The significance of the dummy variable indicates that structural changes occurred in Taiwanese FDI after the foreign exchange and capital controls were lifted in 1987. The large intercept term (−11.752) suggests that other elements affecting Taiwanese FDI may be omitted from the model. To assess the effect of structural change and improve model specifications, Chow tests based on the year 1987 are performed on all four specifications of the Model 1.

Structural Change in Model 1

Chow-test statistics in three of the specifications (3, 4, and 5) indicate a high possibility of structural change in both equation slopes and intercepts after abolishing foreign exchange and capital controls in 1987. It is likely that the elimination of foreign exchange and capital controls completely changed the pattern of Taiwanese FDI. For example, prior to 1987, because of the government's rigid approval criteria, such as high financial requirements, only large enterprises were allowed to engage in outward investment.[3] The lifting of foreign exchange and capital controls in 1987 equalized Taiwanese firms' options to invest abroad without limitations on the size of firms. In addition, adverse domestic economic changes prompted many Taiwanese firms to invest abroad to stay competitive. The increase in FDI by Taiwan's small- and medium-sized firms caused a structural change in the composition of Taiwan's direct investment abroad. However, due to the small sample size (n = 29), separated regressions before and after 1987 failed to yield any meaningful results. Further research is needed as more data becomes available.

Economic Imbalance

Large surpluses in the external trade and the domestic savings accounts characterized Taiwan's economy in the 1980s. During the preceding two decades, the Taiwanese government had followed a conservative fiscal policy by controlling net government expenditures around 22 percent of the country's GNP and always maintained a small surplus in the government's budget. As a result, the surplus in the domestic savings account was fully reflected by the surplus in the external trade account.

In addition, declining investment rates from both public and private sectors contributed to the widening of the savings-investment surplus. Insufficient investments in Taiwan's public sector resulted from the government's conservative fiscal policies, which failed to provide adequate levels of public goods and services to support the dramatic economic growth.[4] Insufficient investments in Taiwan's private sector stemmed from structural changes in the domestic economy—the shrinkage of traditional labor-intensive manufacturing sector for exports. In summary, the disequilibrium in the external trade account reflected the surplus of domestic savings over domestic investment. The surpluses of domestic savings are hypothesized to be the sources of FDI capital in the late 1980s.

Capital-Labor Ratios

The empirical results in Table 8.2 indicate that the capital-labor ratio is statistically significant in explaining Taiwanese FDI. The capital-labor ratio was about 5 in the 1960s. The country's rapid growth in national income resulted in a sharp increase in domestic capital-labor ratios which reached over 14 in 1993.[5]

This high capital-labor ratio in Taiwan was caused by a decrease in population growth in the 1970s and a rapid capital accumulation that resulted from high savings rates. Taiwan's national savings as a percentage of GNP, for instance, averaged more than 30 percent annually in the 1970s and 1980s. The rapid accumulation of capital encouraged the development of capital-intensive industries, which competed with traditional labor-intensive industries in the use of productive resources by offering higher prices. The higher wage rates forced the traditional labor-intensive sector to contract their domestic operations, which caused Taiwan's industrial restructuring. The significance of capital-labor ratios in explaining FDI supports the Rybczynski theorem (1955). This theorem predicts that the disproportionate growth of production factors, as evidenced in a high capital-labor ratio, discourages the development of labor-intensive industries by making production factors more expensive. Thus, adverse domestic factor supplies caused Taiwanese labor-intensive industries to relocate overseas to continue business operation.

Annual Manufacturing Growth Rates

The statistical significance of annual manufacturing growth rates indicates the increasing importance of created intangible assets, such as manufacturing experience, technology innovations, and market connections, in explaining Taiwanese FDI. The development of manufacturing industries in the 1960s and 1970s was accompanied by an accumulation of many of these assets, which were difficult to patent but relatively easy to transfer to foreign production. In other words, these intangible assets were easier to internalize and transfer between parent and subsidiary than to sell to outsiders. Moreover, the transfer of existing firm-specific competitive advantages enabled Taiwanese subsidiaries in foreign countries to compete more effectively against indigenous firms. Thus, the statistical significance of manufacturing growth rates supports the internal hypothesis under the industrial organization approach, which indicates that the need to internalize intangible assets increases firms' incentive to invest abroad.

Labor Shortages

The annual growth rates of the labor force between the age of 15 and 64 are statistically significant in explaining Taiwanese FDI. The annual average growth rate of the labor supply exceeded 4 percent in the 1960s. Since the beginning of the 1970s, such growth rates have gradually declined following the slowdown in the population growth. Thus, Taiwan's declining population growth contributed to its labor shortages in the 1980s and 1990s, which became a limiting factor for its domestic industrial development.

The emergence of new industries in the 1980s and 1990s, on the other hand, significantly increased the industrial demand for labor. Insufficient labor supplies caused many industries to suffer from wage hikes in the 1980s, which discouraged Taiwanese firms' domestic investment and prompted their foreign expansion. Although the Taiwanese government promoted domestic investment in automation as a substitute for labor, and provided tax incentives for such investment, the high cost in replacing labor with machines hindered this policy. An industrial survey, for example, revealed that it was costly to invest in automation.[6] Taiwanese firms spent an average of U.S.$250,000 to replace one unit of labor, while the annual wage cost per worker was less than U.S.$10,000 in 1993. The prohibitive high cost limited the adoption of automated production methods to higher value-added industries and compelled many small and medium-sized firms in the traditional labor-intensive business to relocate their activities to low-wage countries.

Foreign Exchange Controls

The statistical significance of the dummy variable suggests that government's policy to abolish foreign exchange and capital controls in 1987 has created a structural effect in Taiwan's FDI. In the 1960s and 1970s, Taiwan maintained a fixed foreign-exchange-rate system with tight controls on foreign exchange holdings and capital movements. The Central Bank of Taiwan pegged the official exchange rate at the rate of US$1:NT$40 until 1978. Like most price controls, the fixed foreign-exchange-rate system failed to adjust according to market demand and supply for foreign exchanges, which was mainly derived from international trade activities. Following a currency appreciation in 1978, which changed the official exchange rate to 1:36, the Taiwanese Central Bank abandoned the fixed foreign-exchange-rate system and adopted a floating foreign-exchange-rate system.

In addition, Taiwan promulgated a variety of incentive programs to promote exports in the 1960s and 1970s. These export subsidies ranged from 2.5 to 12.5 percent of the total value of each export transaction. At the same time, the Taiwanese government implemented rigid controls to prohibit domestic firms and individuals from holding foreign exchange assets. Foreign currency proceeds derived from exports had to be redeemed at the Central Bank for domestic currency. Thus, without offsetting monetary policies, a significant trade surplus resulted in a corresponding increase in the domestic money supply.

During the process to curb inflationary pressures resulting from excessive trade surpluses, the government realized that capital outflows alleviated domestic financial pressures. Thus, the shifting of policies from prohibiting to permitting capital outflows sent a clear signal to domestic entrepreneurs and encouraged them to seek business opportunities abroad. This basic structural change is captured by the statistical significance of the dummy variable in our regression results.

Statistical Testing of Model 2

The results of the empirical analysis of four Model 2 specifications (7, 8, 9, and 10) are summarized in Table 8.3 (t-statistics in the parentheses). The regression equation based on the double-log linear specification (9) has a good power of explanation ($R^2 = 0.93$) and statistically significant parameters.[7]

The parameter estimates for model specification (9) have the correct signs and are statistically significant at traditional confidence levels. These results support the second hypothesis of this study, namely that the increase in Taiwanese FDI as a percentage of total domestic investment resulted from the following factors: domestic currency appreciation, shrinking export profits, rapid foreign economic growth rates, and high international interest rates. The statistics associated with the estimated regression equation show that 93 percent of variations of the Taiwanese FDI as a percentage of total domestic investment are explained by the variations in the complete set of explanatory variables. Tests on all four model specifications suggest that the rapid appreciation of the foreign-exchange rate was of greater statistical significance in explaining the surges in Taiwanese foreign investment than were other variables.

The high F-Statistics indicate the statistical significance of the model. Parameter estimates suggest that the variations in Taiwan's FDI are elastic relative to changes in foreign-exchange rates, export profits, and international interest rates, but inelastic relative to changes in national economic growth rates.

The elasticity measures show that a 1 percent increase in the foreign-exchange rates (depreciation of Taiwanese dollar) and business export

TABLE 8.3 *Model 2 Parameter Estimates with Correction for Second Order Serial-Correlation*

Parameter	(7)	(8)	(9)	(10)
Constant	0.296	2.443	16.595	3214.453
	(8.63)	(2.13)	(3.02)	(0.45)
FXR	−0.006	−0.157	−6.327	−383.412
	(−5.33)	(−4.76)	(−4.16)	(−1.91)
PROFIT	−0.046	−3.791	−4.023	11129.181
	(−2.23)	(−6.72)	(−5.52)	(3.05)
DIFG	−1.026	0.559	10137.420	
		(3.89)	(2.18)	(3.29)
DIFR	−	−	1.248	−
			(1.87)	
D78	−	1.727	1.129	-8526.805
		(5.98)	(2.47)	(−4.6)
ρ_1	0.897	0.561	0.432	−0.602
	(6.49)	(3.94)	(2.77)	(−2.89)
ρ_2	−0.852	−0.801	−0.738	−0.38
	(−5.37)	(−5.30)	(−4.76)	(−1.79)
Total R^2	0.86	0.93	0.93	0.48
Adj. R^2	0.84	0.91	0.90	0.33
D-W	2.08	2.01	2.56	2.18
F-statistics	34.98	46.61	33.71	3.12
df	23	21	20	21
Chow test	0.04	3.09	3.23	2.37

Note: (−) represents that the variable is eliminated from the statistical analysis because of insignificant results.

profits will reduce outward FDI as a percentage of total domestic investment by 6.33 percent and 4.02 percent, respectively. On the other hand, a 1 percent increase in relative national economic growth rates and international interest rates will bring about a 0.55 and a 1.24 percent increase in the relative percentage of Taiwanese FDI, respectively. These results suggest that foreign-exchange rates and export profits were major determinants for Taiwanese FDI.

The statistical significance of the dummy variable (D78) suggests the importance of policy changes in adopting a floating foreign-exchange rate system in 1978 to influence Taiwanese FDI by more than doubling its percentage in the total domestic investment. The statistical significance of the dummy variable also suggests the possibility of structural change.

Foreign Exchange Rate Apreciation

The parameter estimates for four specifications of Model 2 all indicate that the exchange rate appreciation strongly influenced Taiwanese outward FDI.

Taiwanese FDI during the period from 1986 to 1989 consisted of export-oriented business because trade goods were sensitive to relative changes in production costs as well as currency exchange rates. Since these export-oriented firms operated in an intensely competitive environment, a sharp increase in foreign exchange rates eroded their international competitiveness and drove production orders away, leaving these firms with significant idle assets in manufacturing, marketing, and management. Nimble Taiwanese firms quickly responded to this competitive pressure by transferring these idle assets abroad to build new production bases. In summary, the rise of domestic production costs forced Taiwanese firms to invest overseas to cope with the threat of losing international competitiveness.

The price structure of Taiwanese export products also played an important role in decisions of firms to invest abroad. If Taiwanese firms could raise export prices or improve productivity to offset the adverse impact of currency appreciation, they had less incentive to invest abroad. Nevertheless, keen international competition imposed a price ceiling on labor-intensive Taiwanese products and continuous domestic wage increases eroded productivity improvements. These two constrains reduced export profit margin and contracted domestic operations. Thus, shrinking export profits caused Taiwanese labor-intensive businesses to relocate abroad.

Export Profitability

The parameter estimates for all four specifications of Model 2 indicate the statistical significance of the index of business export profits in explaining Taiwan's FDI. Prior to 1986, Taiwanese firms' exports were profitable because their unit export values remained higher than their unit labor costs. After 1986, Taiwanese firms experienced a loss in their exports because unit labor costs increased faster than unit export values. This loss in export profits was an important factor which motivated Taiwanese firms to use international division of labor to reduce costs and regain sales.

On the other hand, domestic productivity improvements helped absorb the negative impact of exchange-rate appreciations and wage increases. In the case of Taiwan, productivity increases fell far behind increases of wage rates. From 1982 to 1992, rising wages and sagging productivity improvements caused the unit labor cost to increase by more than 40 percent. In spite of cost increases, between 1982 and 1992, unit export values (price) for Taiwanese goods dropped 12 percent, which suggests that Taiwanese manufacturers were 'price-takers' because of intensive international competition in traditional labor-intensive consumer products. Since Taiwan relied on exports to earn its income, shrinking exports associated with double cost and price squeeze pressured Taiwanese labor-intensive manufacturers to diversify abroad to avoid disruptions in export revenues.[8]

Foreign Economic Growth

The differential index of domestic and foreign economic growth rates are statistically significant in the regression analysis, although its effect on Taiwanese FDI is inelastic (0.559). Taiwan's rapid economic growth in prior decades decelerated in the 1990s.

On the other hand, other neighboring Asian countries, such as China, Indonesia, Malaysia, and Thailand, grew rapidly in the late 1980s and early 1990s. The growth rate differentials in national GDP narrowed between Taiwan and its Asian neighbors, which became a significant factor attracting Taiwanese FDI into these rapidly growing economies.

World Interest Rates

Another 'pull factor', the interest rate differentials between Taiwan and the rest of the world, is found to be statistically significant in explaining FDI. The 90-day Euro-Dollar rate was higher than Taiwan's interest rates during the 1980s. Higher international interest rates attracted more Taiwanese capital. This finding supports the prediction of the MacDougall-Kemp model, namely, that outflows of direct investment capital are absolutely correlated with favorable interest rates. Taiwan's investment flows seem likely to continue until domestic and international interest rate differentials converged.

Conclusions

At the Macro Level

Empirical analysis appears to confirm the first hypothesis of this study that the increase in outbound Taiwanese FDI resulted from rapid capital accumulation, which encouraged the development of capital-intensive industries and discouraged the development of labor-intensive industries. The accumulation of manufacturing intangible assets and labor shortages further stimulated the growth of Taiwanese FDI, while the policy to abolish capital controls provided a convenient overseas exit for domestic investment capital.

At the Micro Level

Empirical analysis also appears to confirm the second hypothesis of this study that foreign-exchange rates, export profits, foreign economic growth rates, and international interest rates were important determinants of Taiwanese overseas direct investment. The influence of the foreign-exchange rate changes was activated by the movement from a fixed to a floating exchange rate system. As changes in these economic variables have suggested, the Taiwanese economy experienced dynamic restructuring, particularly in the labor-intensive, export-oriented manufacturing sector. FDI was the result of domestic industrial restructuring in Taiwan's economy.

Economic factors have significantly influenced the FDI behavior of Taiwanese firms. This influence can be further divided into short-term and long-term effects. Foreign-exchange rate and interest rate fluctuations only have a short-term influence. Market disequilibrium theory predicts that once these differentials are eliminated, investment flows will cease. Nevertheless, Taiwanese enterprises began to invest abroad in the 1960s and 1970s when foreign exchange rates and interest rates were not favorable. Taiwanese firms continued to invest overseas in the 1990s even when the difference in these rates had been largely eliminated. Other long-term variables, such as capital-labor ratios, foreign economic growth rates, and manufacturing growth rates, played more important roles in affecting Taiwanese FDI. Specifically, Taiwanese manufacturing growth in previous decades helped develop the ownership specific advantages of Taiwanese firms, which enabled them to compete effectively against foreign firms and encouraged their investments abroad.

References

ABERBACH, J. D., DOLLAR, D. and SOKOLOFF, K. L. (eds) (1994) *The Role of The State in Taiwan's Development*, Armonk, New York, M. E. Sharpe, Inc.

ANDERSON, G. H. (1988) Three Common Misperceptions about Foreign Direct Investment, Federal Reserve Bank of Cleveland, July 25.

BHAGWATI, J., DINOPOULOS, E. and WONG, K. (1992) Quid Pro Quo Foreign Investment, *American Economic Review*, May.

BUCKLEY, P. J. (1990) Problems and Developments in the Core Theory of International Business, *Journal of International Business Studies*, 4th quarter, 658–659.

CHEN, E. K. Y. (1981) Hong Kong Multinationals in Asia: Characteristics and Objectives. In KUMAR, K. and McLEOD, M. G. (eds) *Multinationals from Developing Countries*, Lexington, Mass., D. C. Heath Inc.

CHEN, T. S. and SU, C. Y. (1992) *The Determinants of Taiwan's Direct Foreign Investment*, Chung Hua Economic Institute, Taipei, Taiwan.

CHUNG, C. (1994) *Taiwan's Direct Foreign Investment in Mainland China: Impact on the Domestic and Host Economy*, Chung Hua Economic Institute, Taipei, Taiwan.

DUNNING, J. H. (1977) Trade, Location of Economic Activity and the MNE: A Search for an Eclectic Approach. In OHLIN, B., HESSELBORN, P. O. and WIJKMAN, P. M. (eds) *The International Allocation of Economic Activity*, Holmes and Meier Pub. Inc., New York.

DUNNING, J. H. and NARULA, R. (eds) (1996) *Foreign Direct Investment and Governments*, Routledge, London.

FROOT, K. A. (ed.) (1993) *Foreign Direct Investment*, The University of Chicago Press, Chicago.

FROOT, K. A. and STEIN, J. C. (1991) Exchange Rates and Foreign Direct Investment: An Imperfect Capital Market Approach, *The Quarterly Journal of Economics*, November.

GALESON, W. (ed.) (1979) *Economic Growth and Structural Change in Taiwan*, Cornell University Press, Ithaca, N.Y.

GALESON, W. (1985) *Foreign Trade and Investment: Economic Growth in the Newly Industrializing Asian Countries*, The University of Wisconsin Press, Madison, Wisc.

GRAHAM, E. M. and KRUGMAN, P. R. (1991) *Foreign Direct Investment in the United States*, Institute for International Economics, Washington, DC.

GRUB, P. D. (1991) *Foreign Direct Investment in China*, Quorum Books, New York.

HARBERGER, A. C. (1980) Vignettes on the World Capital Market, *American Economic Review*, Vol. 70, 331–337.

HYMER, S. (1976) *The International Operations of National Firms: A Study of Direct Foreign Investment*, MIT Press, Cambridge, Mass.

JACOBY, N. H. (1966) *US Aid to Taiwan: A Study of Foreign Aid, Self-Help and Development*, Praeger Pub. Inc., New York.

KOJIMA, K. (1978) *Direct Foreign Investment: A Japanese Model of Multinational Business Operations*, Praeger Inc., New York.

KUO, S. W. Y. (1983) *Taiwan: Economy in Transition*, Westview Press, Boulder, Colo.

LI, K. T. (1988) *Economic Transformation of Taiwan (R.O.C.)*, Shepherard-Walwyn, London.

LIN, C. (1973) *Industrialization in Taiwan, 1946–1972*, Praeger Inc., New York.

MORAN, T. H. (1985) *Multinational Corporations: The Political Economy of Foreign Direct Investment*, Lexington Books, Lexington, Mass.

NEALE, B. and PASS, C. (1990) Foreign Direct Investment: Potential Costs and Benefits for Host and Source Countries, *Management Accounting*, February.

OBSTFELD, M. (1985) Capital Mobility in the World Economy: Theory and Measurement, *Carnegie-Rochester Conference Series in Public Policy*, Vol. 24, 55–104.

Organization for Economic Co-Operation and Development (OECD) (1993) *Foreign Direct Investment Relations Between the OECD and the Dynamic Asian Economies*, OECD, Paris.

SEKIGUCHI, S. (1979) *Japanese Direct Foreign Investment*, Allanheld & Publishers Co., New York.

SZENBERG, M. (1973) *The Economics of The Israeli Diamond Industry*, with an Introduction by Milton Friedman, Basic Books, Inc., New York.

SZENBERG, M., LOMBARDI, J. and LEE, E. Y. (1977) *The Welfare Effects of Trade Restrictions: a Case Study of the U.S. Footwear Industry*, Academic Press, New York.

TING, W. L., and SCHIVE, C. (1981) Direct Investment and Technology Transfer from

Taiwan. In Kumar, K. and McLeod, M. C. (eds) *Multinationals from Developing Countries,* Lexington Books, Lexington, Mass.

United Nations Center on Transnational Corporations (UNCTC) (1987) *Transnational Corporations in the Man-made Fiber, Textile, and Clothing Industries,* United Nations, New York.

United Nations Center on Transnational Corporations (UNCTC) (1988) *Foreign Direct Investment in the People's Republic of China,* United Nations, New York.

United Nations Center on Transnational Corporations (UNCTC) (1992) *World Investment Directory Volume I: Asia and The Pacific,* United Nations, New York.

United Nations Center on Transnational Corporations (UNCTC) (1992) *World Investment Report: Transnational Corporations as Engines of Growth,* United Nations, New York.

United Nations Centre on Transnational Corporations (UNCTC) (1993) *Small and Medium-sized Transnational Corporations: Role, Impact, and Policy Implications,* United Nations, New York.

United Nations Center on Transnational Corporations (UNCTC) (1993) *World Investment Report: Transnational Corporations and Integrated International Production,* United Nations, New York.

U.S. Congress, Office of Technology Assessment (1991) *Competing Economies: America, Europe, and The Pacific Rim,* OTA-ITE-498, October, U.S. Government Printing Office, Washington, DC.

U.S. Department of Commerce (DOC) (1993) *U.S. Foreign Trade Highlights,* DOC, Washington, DC.

U.S. Department of Commerce (DOC) (1992) *Foreign Direct Investment Transaction in the United States,* DOC, Washington, DC.

U.S. Department of Commerce (DOC) (1993) *Foreign Direct Investment in the United States: An Update,* June, DOC, Washington, DC.

Wells, L. T., Jr. (1978) Foreign Investment from the Third World: The Experience of Chinese Firms from Hong Kong, *Columbia Journal of World Business,* Spring.

Westphal, U. (1983) Comments on Domestic Savings and International Capital Flows in the Long Run and the Short Run, *European Economic Review,* Vol. 21, 157–159.

Whitmore, K. (1989) Foreign Direct Investment from the Newly Industrialized Economies, *Industry and Energy Department Working Paper Series No. 22,* The World Bank, Washington, DC.

Yoshihara, K. (1976) *Japanese Investment in Southeast Asia,* Kyoto University Press, Kyoto, Japan.

Notes

1. The equation summarizing final parameter estimates of the double-log specification (5) with standard errors and t-statistics in parentheses is shown here for reference.

$$lnFDIS= -11.752+2.861\ lnKLR+0.417\ lnAMG-1.505\,lnAGWP+1.936D87$$

$$(3.08)\quad\quad (1.43)\quad\quad (0.18)\quad\quad (0.74)\quad\quad (0.95)$$

$$t= (-3.82)\quad\quad (2.00)\quad\quad (2.34)\quad\quad (-2.04)\quad\quad (2.03)$$

Adjusted $R^2 = 0.87$; $F_{(4, 25)}= 30.33$; $DW = 1.80$; $n = 29$.

2. Serial correlation (autocorrelation) refers to correlation of residual terms in the regression analysis of a time-series data in which the standard errors and t statistics of parameter estimates are biased and needed to be corrected before interpreting final results.

3. Rigid financial requirements in the owner's equity, debt ratio, and profit ratio prohibited Taiwanese small and medium-sized businesses to invest abroad before the government abolished capital controls in 1987. See Taiwan Executive Yuan, *Regulations Governing the Screening and Handling of Outward Investment and Outward Technical Cooperations Projects,* June 12, 1964.

4. Insufficient public investment in the 1980s caused shortages of electricity, transportation facilities, and urban facilities, such as parks, libraries, and sewage systems, etc.

5. The DGBAS, *Multi-factor Productivity Statistics,* 1993 p. 29.

6. Figures were obtained from a survey conducted by the Task Force on Industrial Automation under Taiwan's Ministry of Economic Affairs in July 1992.

7. The equation summarizing the final parameter estimate results for this double-log model specification (9) with standard errors and t-statistics in parentheses is shown here for reference.

lnFDIS=16.595–6.327lnFXR4.032lnPROFIT+0.559lnDIFG+1.248lnDIFR+0.432D87

	(5.49)	(1.52)	(0.73)	(0.26)	(0.67)	(0.46)
t=	(3.02)	(–4.16)	(-5.52)	(2.18)	(1.87)	(2.47)

Adjusted R^2 = 0.93; F(5, 24)= 33.71; DW = 2.56; n = 29.

8. Inspectorate-General of Customs, Ministry of Finance, *Monthly Statistics of Exports and Imports, Taiwan Area,* March 1994.

9

Determinants of Inter-Asian Direct Investment Flows

MORDECHAI E. KREININ, THOMAS C. LOWINGER AND ANIL K. LAL

Introduction

During the 1980s and the early 1990s economic ties between East Asian countries have intensified, and their closer regional trade links have made an important contribution to the region's economic growth. Significantly, greater regional integration in East Asia has coincided with greater overall openness of their economies and an ongoing liberalization of their trade and investment regimes. Furthermore, the structures of East Asian countries' production have become increasingly based on their comparative advantage and their ability to absorb sophisticated foreign technology was enhanced by rapidly growing FDI flows. There appears to be a virtuous cycle at work in East Asia, with FDI contributing to export growth, which, in turn, is creating pressures for further trade and investment liberalization, and leading to an even greater volume of FDI flows. This chapter examines empirically the factors responsible for direct investment flows within East Asia.

East Asian Trade and Economic Interdependence

The rate of growth of East Asian trade in the 1980s and the early 1990s has been nothing short of spectacular. Between 1980 and 1993 East Asian exports quadrupled (from $124 billion to $505 billion) and the region's share of world exports more than doubled from 6.3 to 13.6 percent. Correspondingly, intra-area trade also increased dramatically.

To date, East Asian countries have not formed a formal trading bloc and there is no sign that Japan and the NIEs are interested in promoting or joining an East Asian FTA.[1] But 'private-sector integration' has proceeded apace through trade and investment. It has been argued that East Asia may constitute a 'natural' trading bloc, wherein a relatively high degree of integration can occur because of the existence of so called 'natural' of geographic proximities among East Asian countries.[2] Arguably, economic integration in East Asia could have proceeded spontaneously, without the benefits of a formal agreement or common institutions. Indeed, recent studies have shown that East Asia's intra-regional trade, as a share of total trade, has increased from about 33 percent in 1980 to 41 percent in 1990. Kreinin and Plummer (1994) define a 'natural' trading bloc as one that would preserve country's comparative advantage ranking should it choose to enter a regional trading bloc. Based on that definition, they conclude that a free trading area that includes Japan, Korea, and the East Asian developing countries would be economically efficient.[3]

Moreover, the greater intensity of East Asian direct investment flows (discussed in the following section), together with the persistence of their trade and overall market reforms, would be expected to act as a catalyst for greater economic integration in the region.

Recently, Frankel and Wei (1995) estimated a gravity model of trade and detected the existence of a powerful East Asian trade bias.[4] However, until the 1970s the relative importance of East Asian intra-regional trade had in fact been declining as the region forged ever closer ties with the U.S. and with other industrialized counties outside the region. But in the 1980s the rapid growth of the East Asian regional market began to outweigh the expansion of extra-regional markets, and intra-regional trade in East Asia was on the rise again. Significantly, greater regional integration in East Asia has coincided with a greater overall openness of their economies toward the rest of the world.

FDI Flows in East Asia

In recent years Asian countries have experienced a sharp upsurge in international capital flows. During 1990–93, the developing countries of Asia were the recipient of $150 billion in net capital inflows, more than double the amount they had received in the previous four years. The composition of capital flows into Asia has changed drastically in recent years. FDI, together with bond and equity financing, has largely replaced the formerly dominant form of capital flows into developing countries—commercial bank loans. In Asia a significant part of the increase in overall foreign capital inflow can be attributed to the rapid growth of FDI. FDI flows into several East Asian countries have risen in the 1986–89 period, and then have surged dramatically in the early 1990s.

During 1986–92, the sources of East Asian FDI flows have been primarily intra-regional: about one-half of all FDI flows in the region originated from other East Asian countries (predominantly in Hong Kong, Singapore, Korea, and Taiwan); less than a fifth originated from Japan and only one-tenth came from the U.S. and Western Europe (World Bank, 1994, p. 26). The sectoral composition of FDI has also been changing. In earlier years, direct investments from advanced industrial countries were channeled primarily into natural resource based industries and related sectors, while in more recent years the NIEs have been investing primarily in manufacturing, especially in electrical machinery, electronics, nonferrous metals and chemicals.

Starting in the mid-1980s, export oriented Japanese multinational enterprises (MNEs) began to shift their production base (and in some cases even their product development location) offshore, in search of lower production costs. The steep appreciation of the yen since the mid-1980s, together with visible protectionist sentiment in North America and Western Europe (directed primarily against Japanese exports), provided a powerful incentive for Japanese MNEs to globalize their operations. Japanese FDI in Asia has been increasingly channeled into export oriented activities. The relatively low cost of Asian labor, together with the relatively advanced level of production in the region, have induced Japanese MNEs to relocate certain parts of their operations—production, R&D, and sales—to East Asia.

Japanese and other foreign investors in Asia have become increasingly export oriented. In 1992, the ratio of exports to total sales of Japanese affiliates in manufacturing was 45 percent in Asia compared to only 23 percent in Latin America. Currently, parts and equipment imports of Japanese affiliates in Asia form Japan constitute a significant share of their total imports (about 38 percent of the total in 1992), and although local procurement already constitutes a large share (50 percent) of their total purchases, it is expected to rise even more in the future (MITI, 1994). The FDI-trade link in Asia has often been described in terms of the 'flying geese' metaphor, wherein Japan is the lead ('goose') country because of its advanced technology. The lead country's firms combine their technological advantage with the relatively lower factor (labor) costs in the host countries, which in turn make the follower countries' (initially the East Asian NIEs) production more competitive in world markets, which then allows exports from their Asian base to grow even more rapidly. Japan, the lead country in this scheme, is usually followed by the NIEs, which in turn are followed by Malaysia, Thailand, and later on China.[5]

The Pattern and Structure of FDI Flows in East Asia

In the span of a few decades, several East Asian countries (e.g. Japan, South Korea, Hong Kong, Singapore, and Taiwan) have transformed themselves from largely backward and poor countries, into relatively prosperous and technologically sophisticated economies. Initially, this group of countries, (except Japan) has been the recipient of most foreign direct investment flows into Asia. But, beginning in the late 1970s there has been a huge surge in foreign direct investment flows in other East Asian countries—China, Malaysia, Indonesia, Philippines, Thailand, and more recently Vietnam. The experience of East Asian countries suggests the existence of a strong connection between FDI and improved access to foreign markets. Initially, foreign-owned firms established subsidiaries in East Asia in order to exploit the local markets. However, more recent experience suggests that multinationals are adopting global strategies intended to link their subsidiaries in Asia through global assembly and marketing networks into 'borderless factories' (export-oriented FDI).

To analyze the reasons behind the increase in FDI flows in East Asia, we have classified the East Asian countries as follows: (1) Japan; (2) the Newly Industrialized Economies (NIEs)—Hong Kong, Korea, Singapore, Korea, and Taiwan; and (3) 'others'—China, Indonesia, Malaysia, Philippines, Thailand, and Vietnam. Japan has been the recipient of only small amounts of foreign capital inflows form other countries in East Asia, while it has been a major source of the foreign capital flowing into other countries in the region. For example, Japan has accounted for 52 percent of the FDI stock of Korea, 31 percent of Singapore's, 37 percent of Thailand's, and 27 percent of Taiwan's (Table 9.1). While the NIEs have become a significant source of foreign capital flows into 'other' East Asian countries, they have not been major recipients of foreign capital flows from 'other' East Asian countries. The NIEs were the source of 58 percent of the FDI stock of China (in 1987), 35 percent of Malaysia's (1987), and 20 percent of Thailand's (1988). Thus the direction of foreign investment flows in East Asia followed a stepwise pattern, meaning that there has been *unidirectional* investment flow from relatively advanced countries into the less developed countries of the region.

What factors are then responsible for the flow of foreign direct investment into the NIEs and 'other' East Asian economies? Using multiple regression analysis, we have to estimated the effects of relative market size, relative labor costs, exchange rates and the degree of openness, on foreign direct investment flows in East Asia.

In addition, we sought to test Findlay's (1978) theory that technological know-how among countries spreads much like a

TABLE 9.1 *Stock of FDI in East Asian Countries (percent of total)*

Host country (year)	EU	USA	Japan	Source NIEs	Others	Total
Japan (1990)	18.3	46.5	–	2.8	32.4	100.0
Hong Kong* (1989)	14.7	32.4	29.9	2.2	21.9	100.0
Korea (1988)	9.4	27.7	52.0	3.8	7.0	100.0
Singapore* (1989)	28.7	33.2	30.7	NA	NA	100.0
Taiwan (1988)	13.4	32.1	26.8	14.8	12.9	100.0
China (1987)	8.3	15.8	7.2	58.2	10.6	100.0
Indonesia (1988)	12.1	5.8	18.4	10.8	52.8	100.0
Malaysia (1987)	24.0	6.1	20.1	35.1	14.7	100.0
Philippines (1989)	11.2	55.7	14.5	9.5	9.2	100.0
Thailand (1988)	12.4	24.2	36.7	20.1	6.6	100.0
Vietnam (1989)	57.3	0.2	14.4	7.1	21.0	100.0

* refers to manufacturing only.
Source: United Nations (1992).

contagious disease, i.e. it disperses more rapidly and more extensively the greater the contact among people and businesses. As noted by Findlay (1978, p. 5), 'Contact with firms with a higher level of efficiency enables the relatively backward ones to improve not only by copying or imitating but also by inducing them to 'try harder'. In Findlay's model, international trade can be an important conduit through which people in one country come in contact with people in another, and through which they can learn about a foreign country's products and innovations. His model postulates that the rate of international technology transfer is higher, the greater is the technology gap between the advanced country (e.g. Japan) and a relatively backward country (such as a NIE). However a *minimum* level of technology in the host country is needed for the relatively backward country to be able to absorb the technology received from the more advanced country. Furthermore, the rate at which new technology can be transferred to a recipient country through FDI, may depend on a number of other factors (e.g. the educational level of the domestic labor force) that must be specified in the empirical estimation.

This study attempts to quantify the approximate causes of Japan's direct investment in eight East Asian countries, and to test whether the motivations behind Japanese direct investment were different for the NIE host countries that for the other East Asian host countries. Second, it attempts to quantify factors responsible for FDI flows from Japan and the NIEs into 'other' East Asian countries and to determine whether there is a difference between the Japanese and the NIEs' behavior as FDI source countries. Finally, we inquire whether the relative differences between the source and host countries, in terms of certain postulated economic characteristics, can explain the flow of investment into the countries. Accordingly, the following specification was estimated:

$$FDI(t) = f(PC(t), OPEN(t), ER(t), RWR(t), PEMP(t), POP(t), IGDP(t))\,1(1)$$

Where:

FDI(t) is the FDI flow from a source country into a host country, at time 't'.

PC(t) is the per capita GDP of the host country divided by that of the source country, at time 't'. (relative per-capita GDP)

GDP (t) is the GDP of the host country divided by that of the source country, at time 't'.

OPEN(t) is the overall degree of openness of the host country's economy (the proportion of total trade to GDP) relative to that of the source country, at time 't'.

ER(t) is the host country's exchange rate in domestic currency units, relative to that of the source country's currency at time 't'.

RWR(t) is the monthly industrial wage rate in the host country relative to that of the source country, at time 't'.

PEMP(t) is the proportion of host country population employed in its industrial sector, at time 't'.

POP(t) is the population of the host country relative to the population of the source country, at time 't'.

IGDP(t) is the proportion of total investment in GDP of the host country, relative to that of the source country, at time 't'.

Consistent data on FDI flows or stocks are difficult to obtain. In this study we have used United Nations (1992) data to examine FDI flows in East Asia. Since continuous time series data were not available for Thailand and Vietnam, those two countries were dropped from the analysis. The foreign investment data used for estimation purposed were obtained from the respective government agencies of East Asian countries. The data on explanatory economic variables were taken form the Penn World tables of the National Bureau of Economic Research (NBER) and have been updated whenever necessary. The data cover the period form 1984 to 1992, and the variables were expressed in current U.S. dollars, or have been converted to U.S. dollars using the current exchange rates.

Ordinary least squares were used to estimate the relationship given in Equation (1), and since all variables were expressed in log linear form, the estimated coefficients refer to the relevant elasticities. The

Durbin-Watson statistic was used to test for first order serial correlation, and the White test statistic was used to test for heteroscadasticity. The Chow test allowed us to test for structural breaks in the sample and adjustments were made to overcome the small sample problem. Table 9.2 reports the results of the first set of regressions, that tested the factors responsible for Japanese investment flows into eight East Asian countries—four NIEs and the four 'other' East Asian countries. The regression results suggest that the closer an East Asian country is to Japan in terms of its population, openness, and its relative wage rates in manufacturing, the larger is the investment flow from Japan in to that country. Also, the greater is the Japanese currency's appreciation relative to the currency of an East Asian country, the larger is the Japanese foreign investment flow into that country. This may have been the principal reason why Japanese investment flows into the NIEs have been significantly larger than that of other East Asian countries. We have also attempted to test whether the regressions explaining FDI in the NIEs differ from those destined into other East Asian countries. The Chow F test for structural break confirmed the null hypothesis that the regressions for these two sub-groups were not significantly different.

Finally, Table 9.3 reports the results of tests for FDI flows from Japan and the NIEs into 'other' East Asian countries. The Chow F test for structural break confirmed the null hypothesis that there is no

TABLE 9.2 *Estimated Equation for Japanese Foreign Investment in East Asian Countries (NIEs and Others)*

Variable	Coefficient
Intercept	−18.45
	{−4.86}
POP(t)	1.34
	{3.93}
OPEN(t)	2.94
	{8.24}
ER(t)	0.2
	{2.59}
RWR(t)	0.75
	{2.31}
R2	0.73
Adjusted R2	0.71
Durbin-Watson	1.86

Notes: The figures in parentheses indicate t-values.
The above coefficients are significant at 5% level of significance.

TABLE 9.3 *Estimated Equation for Japanese and NIEs Foreign Investment in Other East Asian Counties*

Variable	Coefficient
Intercept	−93.64
	{−4.02}
POP(t)	2.97
	{3.37}
GDP(t)	−3.39
	{−4.12}
OPEN(t)	2.64
	{3.30}
PEMP(t)	22.62
	{2.82}
RWR(t)	1.47
	{5.07}
R2	0.72
Adjusted R2	0.69
Durbin-Watson	1.78

Notes: The figures in parenthesis indicate t-values.
The above coefficients are significant at 5% level of significance.

significant difference in the regressions between the Japanese and the NIEs' FDI flows into 'other' East Asian countries. Once again, the smaller the difference between 'other' East Asian host countries and the East Asian source countries (Japan or the NIEs) in population, openness, and the wage rates, the greater are the FDI flows. On the other hand, the larger the difference in their GDPs, the greater is the foreign investment inflow into 'other' East Asian countries. Finally, the greater the ratio of employment in the industrial sector relative to the population of the host country, the larger is the inflow of foreign direct investment from the source countries. In general, these estimates accord with prior expectations and are generally consistent with received theory explaining direct investment flows.

Conclusions

This chapter has examined the pattern and structure of FDI flows in East Asia. FDI flows in the region have followed a consistent and unidirectional pattern, first flowing from Japan into the NIEs and subsequently flowing from Japan and the NIEs into 'other' less-developed East Asian economies. The regression results suggest that the closer an East Asian country is to Japan, in terms of its population, openness and the relative wages in its manufacturing sector, the greater will be the volume of investment flow from Japan into that East Asian country. Furthermore, an appreciation of the Yen relative to the host country's currency apparently resulted in greater flows of Japanese direct investment into East Asian countries. Similar results also hold for the NIE's direct investment flows into 'other' Asian countries.

References

BHAGWATI, J. (1992) Regionalism vs Multilateralsim, *The World Economy*, September, Vol. 15, No. 5, 535–556.

DAS, S. (1987) Externalities and Technological Transfer Through Multinational Corporations, *Journal of International Economics*, Vol. 22, 171–182.

FINDLAY, R. (1978) Relative Backwardness, Direct Foreign Investment, and the Transfer of Technology: A Simple Dynamic Model, *Quarterly Journal of Economics*, February, Vol. 62, No. 1, 1–16.

International Monetary Fund (1994) *International Trade Policies: The Uruguay Round and Beyond*, Vol II, Washington, DC.

FRANKEL, J. and WEI, S. (1995) The New Regionalism and Asia: Impact and Options. Paper presented at the Conference on the Emerging Global Trading Environment and Developing Asia, Asian Development Bank, Manila, May 29–31.

KREININ, M. E. and PLUMMER, M. G. (1994) Natural Economic Blocs: An Alternative Formulation, *The International Trade Journal*, Summer, Vol. 8, No. 2, 193–205.

KRUGMAN, P. (1993) Regionalism vs Multilateralism: Analytical Notes. In DE MELO, J. and PANAGARIYA, A. (eds) *New Dimensions in Regional Integration*, Cambridge University Press, New York.

MARTIN, W., PETRI, P. A. and YANAGISHIMA, K. (1994) Charting the Pacific: An Empirical Assessment of Integration Initiatives, *The International Trade Journal*, Winter, Vol. 8, No. 4, 447–482.

Ministry of International Trade and Finance (1994) *White Paper on International Trade*. Tokyo, Japan.

SUMMERS, L. (1991) Regionalism and the World Trading System, *Policy Implications of Trade and Currency Zones*, Federal Reserve Bank of Kansas City Symposium, Jackson Hole, Wyoming, August, 295–302.

United Nations Centre on Transnational Corporations (1992) *World Investment Directory 1992*, United Nations, New York.

World Bank (1994) Building on the Uruguay Round: East Asian Leadership in Liberalization. Discussion Paper, Office of the Vice President East Asia and the Pacific Region, Washington DC, April 22, 1–59.

Notes

1. Several countries in the region did form such a bloc. In particular, the Association of Southeast Asian Nations (ASEAN) was established in February 1977. It includes Indonesia, Malaysia, Philippines, Singapore, Thailand, and Brunei, with Vietnam

joining recently. In January, 1992, ASEAN member countries agreed to implement a common Effective Preferential Tariff Scheme (CEPT) with the aim of moving toward an ASEAN free trade area (AFTA). The stated objective of AFTA was to increase member countries' manufacturing competitiveness by attracting more FDI and thereby expanding their production base. See, IMF (1994, p. 125).

2. For arguments in support of the 'natural' trading bloc hypothesis see Krugman (1993) and Summers (1991). Among those that professed skepticism, see for example, Bhagwati (1992).

3. Despite the current relatively high share of intra-regional trade in East Asian total trade, East Asia has not regained the share of intra-regional in total trade that existed before World War II. Its trade share is significantly lower than those that prevail today in Western Europe. See, Martin, Petri and Yanagishima (1994, pp. 450–451).

4. The two most important factors that explain bilateral trade flows (exports plus imports) in the gravity model are: geographic distances between countries and their economic size (measured by their GDPs). By using an East-Asian regional 'dummy' variable in their panel regressions, Frankel and Wei (1995, p. 20) came to the startling conclusion that ' . . . two East Asian countries made 700% more than two random economies in the world.'

5. The computer industry offers an excellent case study of this process in East Asia. In the 1980s, U.S. and Japanese computer firms looked at the Asian NIEs as a low cost production base. Over time, growing technological sophistication in East Asia has increased the region's productive capability so that certain computer components are no longer imported. Singapore, for example, over the past 20 years has moved from making lower-end computer products to higher-end disk drives. Subsequently, lower technology disk drive production has switched to Malaysia and Thailand. This process has resulted in rapid growth and a greater regional integration that earlier industrial development strategies did not attain. Intra-regional trade in computers is growing much faster than external trade and it now accounts for 25 percent of the NIEs total trade in computers. East Asian exports consist primarily of PCs, disk drives, subassemblies, parts, and peripherals. See World Bank, 1994, pp. 30–32.

10

Trade and Production Networks of U.S. MNEs and Exports by their Asian Affiliates

ROBERT E. LIPSEY

Network connections within their own firms seem to raise export market shares for Asian affiliates of U.S. MNEs. In particular, Asian affiliates of U.S. MNEs export more to markets where their parent firms' exports to affiliates are larger, and less to markets where their parent firms export more to non-affiliates. However, the latter effect is much smaller per dollar of parent exports. Production in a market by a related affiliate usually appeared to reduce the Asian affiliate's exports to that market, but those effects are small and rarely statistically significant. These relationships are fairly consistent across industries and markets, across markets within two industries, across industries for two affiliate home countries, and across exporters and industries for individual markets.

Introduction

One of the benefits that host countries hope for from inward direct investment is that it gives firms producing within their borders, and therefore, indigenous factors of production, greater access to worldwide markets by linking them into the trading networks of the investing multinational enterprises (MNEs). The MNEs establish affiliates in countries with location bound advantages unlike those of the home countries to exploit their knowledge of production techniques and their experience in selling to particular markets accumulated through exporting and producing there. It is difficult to find empirical evidence for these propositions because few investing countries collect any data on the trade of their firms' foreign affiliates. The United States is the only country that collects fairly comprehensive data on the amount and direction of exports by affiliates of its MNEs.

In this chapter we use these data to ask whether exports to a market by Asian affiliates of U.S. MNEs are affected by the activity in that market of other members of their parents' MNE. That activity is defined broadly here to include both exports to the country by the parent of the Asian affiliate and production in that country by other affiliates of the same parent.

Gravity Model Explanations of Affiliate Exports

We begin by trying to explain exports by U.S.-owned Asian affiliates to particular destinations by the characteristics of the importing regions, ignoring the extent, if any, of related parent or affiliate activity. Ideally we would wish to have a detailed list of affiliate export destinations. Unfortunately, the BEA survey for 1989 that is the basis for our study lists as destinations only three specific countries other than the United States (Canada, the United Kingdom, and Japan) and six broad regions excluding the three countries (U.S. Department of Commerce, 1992). We have constructed, for these nine export destinations, measures of population, and nominal and real GDP, as would be done in a gravity model of trade, and the value of imports from all sources, classified by industry. The population and income data represent elements of total demand for goods. The values of imports, by industry, are intended to reflect both the composition of demand and the openness of each region to imports in general and to imports in each industry. We did not attempt to include distance measures because some of the destination regions were so broad.

The Asian exporters for which we have made these calculations include U.S. affiliates in Hong Kong, Singapore, South Korea, and Taiwan, and also Indonesia, Malaysia, and Thailand. The numbers of U.S. affiliates range from only seven in Indonesia to 175 in Singapore.

The dependent variable in these equations is the exports by an individual Asian manufacturing affiliate of a U.S. parent to a region of the world. Each affiliate is tagged with an industry according to its major activity, and the imports into the destination region that are the independent variable are the imports for each exporting affiliate's industry.

Of the 34 manufacturing industries in the BEA classification, 27 appear in these Asian countries, but the distribution across industries is very uneven. Of the 499 affiliates, 187 are in electrical and electronic machinery and equipment, mostly in electronic components and accessories, and 104 are in non-electrical machinery, mainly office and computing machinery.

A few equations along these lines are shown in Table 10.1. Coefficients for total imports into the region in the exporting affiliate's industry are always positive and significant, as are those for population and real GDP. Coefficients for nominal GDP and real GDP per capita are negative and the latter is significant.

Among these independent variables, population and nominal GDP are positively correlated. GDP per capita, which is GDP divided by population, is strongly and negatively correlated with population. Per capita GDP and population should not, therefore, be in the same equation.

Although there are significant positive coefficients for both population and industry imports, these equations do not explain much of the variation in affiliate exports. Industry imports alone account for most of the variance explained by any of these equations.

Related Firm Operations and Affiliate Exports

However, the main focus of this chapter is not in explanations of affiliate trade by size and openness, but in the extent and direction of any effects of same-firm operations in a host country on affiliate exports.

All Markets and Industries

The 'network' operations in a market that we consider consist of three parts. One is the MNE's production in that market, proxied by the net sales of the MNE's affiliates in that market, net sales being defined as total affiliate sales minus the affiliate's imports from the United States. The influence of related affiliate production could be both positive and negative. It could be positive to the extent that the producing affiliates import parts and components for their production from related Asian affiliates of their MNEs or that they open the local market to parts of their firms' product lines that they do not produce themselves. The effect on Asian affiliate exports could be negative to the extent that the destination region affiliate production substitutes for output that would otherwise be imported from the Asian affiliates.

The second MNE activity is exports by the U.S. parent to its affiliates in that market and the third is exports by the U.S. parent to unaffiliated purchasers in that market. Both types of parent exports could substitute for exports by the Asian affiliates of these firms. Parent exports to non-affiliates are presumably finished products and more likely to be substitutes for Asian affiliate exports. Parent exports of parts and

TABLE 10.1 *Equations Explaining Exports to a Region by a U.S.-Owned Asian Affiliate (AFFEX) by Region Characteristics*

Eq. No.	Independent variables						Constant Term	R^2
	POP(L)	NGDP (L)	CNDGP(L)	RGDP(L)	CRGDP(L)	IMP(KL)		
1–1	5.11	-2.83				4.79	2.02	.064
	(3.5)	(0.2)				(3.2)	(0.7)	
1–2	6.41		.178			4.51	-1.18	.065
	(2.97)		(0.7)			(3.6)	(0.3)	
1–3				2.75		3.32	-.51	.058
				(3.4)		(2.4)	(0.2)	
1–4					-.421	5.33	9.93	.054
					(2.6)	(3.9)	(3.9)	

No. of observations: 499.

t-statistics in parentheses.

AFFEX(IJKL) = Exports by Asian affiliate I of MNE(J) in affiliate industry K to market region L.

POP(L) = Population of market region L.

RGDP(L) = Real GDP in international prices in market region L.

CNGDP(L) = Nominal GDP per capita in market region L.

CRGDP(L) = Real GDP per capita in market region L.

IMP(KL) = Total imports of industry K products into market region L.

components could also substitute for similar exports by the Asian affiliates, but could also imply that the importing affiliates are not self-contained, are integrated into the MNE's trading network, and therefore represent a market for the Asian affiliates.

The results of fitting several equations to the data for the full set of Asian affiliates are given in Table 10.2.

Larger market region population or real GDP, and larger market region imports of the products of an affiliate's industry are always positive influences on affiliate exports. Parent exports to their own affiliates in a market are positively related to their Asian affiliates' exports to that market. Parent exports to non-affiliates in a market seem to compete with the Asian affiliate exports. However, the positive coefficient for parent exports to affiliates is far larger than the negative coefficient for arms-length exports. The effect of production in a market by affiliate siblings within an MNE network is not clear: the coefficients are negative, but never statistically significant.

Per capita nominal income in a market, included in Equation 2–1, has no significant effect on affiliate exports. If we drop that variable, as in Equation 2–2, the coefficients of the other variables are virtually unchanged. If we substitute a measure of real GDP in the market region for the population, as in Equation 2–3, the coefficient for aggregate imports into the region of the products of the affiliate's industry becomes insignificant, although it hardly changes in size.

If we omit all region characteristics other than MNE operations from the equation, we lose a little explanatory power but again find (Equation 2–4) that industry imports into and parent exports to a host region are positively and significantly related to Asian affiliate exports, parent exports to non-affiliates are negatively and significantly related to them, and the coefficient for related affiliate production is negative but not statistically significant.

Since the size of the market is taken into account in these equations, the sum of an MNE's affiliate net sales and parent exports to non-affiliates in a market represents the MNE's market share. That share may be supplied in many different ways. One is by local production (affiliate net sales). Another is by a combination of parent and affiliate exports to or through related affiliates in the market. And a third is by parent exports to non-affiliates. The larger the share of non-manufacturing, as compared to manufacturing, affiliate operations controlled by the MNE in a market, the more dependent that market share will be on exports to the market by the parent and by the MNE's affiliates elsewhere. A large manufacturing operation controlled by the MNE could conceivably substitute for exports by the parent and its affiliates, but does not seem to do so to any significant extent. A lack of non-manufacturing operations in a market, such as

TABLE 10.2 *Equations Explaining Exports to a Region by a U.S.-Owned Asian Affiliate by Region Characteristics and Related MNE Operations*

Eq. No.	Independent variables							Constant Term	R^2
	POP(L)	CNGDP(L)	RGDP(L)	IMP(KL)	NS(JL)	PEXAF(JL)	PEXUN(JL)		
2-1	4.53	.062		3.36	-3.51	75.0	-14.5	616	.162
	(2.2)	(0.3)		(2.7)	(1.2)	(7.6)	(2.4)	(0.1)	
2-2	4.11			3.39	-3.46	75.2	-14.4	345	.163
	(3.2)			(2.8)	(1.2)	(7.6)	(2.4)	(0.2)	
2-3			2.14	2.37	-3.73	76.2	-14.3	1,267	.158
			(2.8)	(1.8)	(1.3)	(7.7)	(2.4)	(0.5)	
2-4				4.04	-3.87	79.1	-13.9	3,275	.147
				(3.3)	(1.3)	(8.0)	(2.3)	(1.8)	

No. of observations: 499
t-statistics in parentheses
NS(JL) = Net sales (sales minus imports from the U.S.) of all affiliates of MNE(J) in market region L.
PEXAF(JL) = Exports by the U.S. parent company of MNE(J) to all MNEJ's affiliates in market region L.
PEXUN(JL) = Exports by the U.S. parent company of MNE(J) to all unaffiliated purchasers in market region L.

service or sales facilities, might reduce both parent exports to affiliates in that market and exports to that market by the MNE's affiliates in other countries.

Individual Industries

The role of affiliates, and in particular the way they fit into their MNE's allocation of production, could vary across industries, for example, because of differences in the tradeability of products. It would, therefore, be desirable to examine these relationships in individual industries. Our ability to do that is limited by the concentration of affiliates mentioned earlier, but we are able to perform similar calculations for two industries, electronic components and accessories (ECA), and office and computing machinery (OCM).

The equations (3–1 and 3–2) for electronic components and accessories in Table 10.3 explain a larger share of the variability of Asian affiliate exports in that industry than the equations for all industries, pooled, in Tables 10.1 and 10.2. The country's openness, or demand for this industry's products, as represented by the import variable, has no influence on Asian affiliate exports to the country, and almost all the explanation is provided by the parent export variable. If a parent's exports to a country are high, exports by that parent's Asian affiliates are also high.

For office and computing machinery, on the other hand, a country's general openness and demand for such machinery was the significant influence on exports to that country by Asian affiliates (Equations 3–3 and 3–4). A parent's exports to both affiliates and non-affiliates in the country are positively, but not significantly, related to exports by that parent's Asian affiliates, but production in the market by affiliates of the same MNE did appear to substitute in some degree for such exports.

Exports by Affiliates in Individual Countries

Just as there could be differences among industries in the way in which affiliates are fitted into the MNEs' networks of trade, affiliates in different countries may play roles in those arrangements that exploit the countries' locational advantages or comparative advantages in production. For two Asian host countries to U.S.-owned affiliates, Singapore and Taiwan, we have 100 affiliates or more reporting exports by region, and can calculate country equations across all industries, corresponding to those of Table 10.3 for individual industries across all countries.

The equations for exports by affiliates in the two individual countries

TABLE 10.3 *Equations Explaining Exports of Electronic Components and Accessories and Office and Computing Machinery to a Region By A U.S.-Owned Asian Affiliate*

Eq. No.	Independent variables						Constant Term	R^2
	POP(L)	RGDP(L)	IMP(KL)	NS(JL)	PEXAF(JL)	PEXUN(JL)		
Electronic components and accessories								
3-1			7.01 (1.6)	7.7 (0.8)	111.4 (5.4)	-20.8 (1.3)	-443 (0.1)	.247
3-2	11.7 (2.6)		-3.41 (0.6)	16.8 (1.7)	99.1 (4.8)	-21.3 (1.3)	203 (0.0)	.247
3-3		4.7 (1.0)	-3.45 (0.3)	10.1 (1.0)	106.8 (5.1)	-20.7 (1.3)	-3,814 (0.6)	.311
Office and computing machinery								
3-4			1.98 (3.7)	-65.4 (2.3)	70.4 (1.8)	283.8 (0.7)	727 (0.1)	.218
3-5	5.1 (0.8)		1.99 (3.7)	-56.9 (1.9)	60.8 (1.5)	239.9 (0.5)	4,577 (0.4)	.423
3-6		3.5 (1.0)	1.76 (3.0)	-59.0 (2.1)	63.5 (1.6)	220.8 (0.5)	-7,262 (0.6)	.321

No. of observations:
Electronic components and accessories: 150
Office and computing machinery: 60
t-statistics in parentheses

across industries do not fit as well as those across countries for individual industries, but there is, nevertheless, some consistency in the results (Table 10.4). Parent exports to affiliates are always a positive influence and parent exports to non-affiliates a negative influence, and the level of imports in the industry by a destination country is always a positive influence on Asian affiliate exports. Exports by affiliates in Singapore are accounted for mainly by the country size and openness measures and by parent exports to affiliates in that market. Exports by affiliates in Taiwan are largely determined by country imports in that industry. Other variables do not have significant coefficients, although the signs of the coefficients are the typical ones.

Exports to Individual Regions

Another possible source for differences in affiliate export behavior could be that related affiliate production and parent exports might play a different role in, for example, the U.K. or the EU countries from that in developing Asian countries. We attempt to test for that possibility, where we can, by separate regressions for those regions for which sufficient numbers of Asian affiliates report exports. If we set the lower limit at 60 observations, we eliminate six regions: Canada, the U.K., non-EU Europe, Latin America and other western hemisphere, Africa, and the Middle East. The equations of Table 10.5 are for the remaining regions, the European Union except the U.K., Japan, and Asia and Pacific except Japan.

These equations do not explain a large part of the variation in affiliate exports to specific markets, but there is one striking consistency among the equations. That is that the coefficient for parent exports to affiliates is positive and significant, and that it is always substantially larger than the negative coefficient for parent exports to non-affiliates. A strong position of parent firms in exports to their own affiliates in a market, perhaps reflecting a strong position of the affiliates in the market, means that Asian affiliates of the same parents will tend to export more to those markets. Large parent exports to non-affiliates in a market, however, may be competing to some extent with exports to that market by the parent's Asian affiliates, or they might reflect a weak position of the parent's affiliates in that market.

Conclusions

Various combinations or slices of the data on exports to individual regions by Asian affiliates of U.S. MNEs, offer a few fairly definite and some very tentative conclusions. Network or 'family' connections within an MNE improve export market entry and market share

TABLE 10.4 *Equations Explaining Exports to a Region by a U.S.-Owned Affiliate in Singapore or Taiwan*

Eq. No.	Independent variables						Constant Term	R^2
	POP(L)	RGDP(L)	IMP(KL)	NS(JL)	PEXAF(JL)	PEXUN(JL)		
Singapore								
4-1			39.9	1.44	60.9	-9.84	4,363	.090
			(1.9)	(0.4)	(3.6)	(1.1)	(1.2)	
4-2	8.21		30.1	1.01	57.6	-11.81	-328	.136
	(3.2)		(1.5)	(0.3)	(3.4)	(1.3)	(0.1)	
4-3		4.14	923	1.22	56.5	-11.20	-2,909	.120
		(2.6)	(0.4)	(0.3)	(3.3)	(1.2)	(0.6)	
Taiwan								
4-4			71.8	-5.93	10.91	-12.85	1,015	.143
			(4.1)	(1.5)	(0.8)	(1.0)	(0.4)	
4-5	-1.18		76.4	-6.22	10.98	-11.78	1,722	.140
	(0.8)		(4.2)	(1.6)	(0.8)	(0.9)	(0.7)	
4-6		-50.6	77.9	-6.00	10.94	-12.24	1,998	.136
		(0.5)	(3.7)	(1.5)	(0.8)	(0.9)	(0.7)	

No. of observations:
Singapore: 175
Taiwan: 101
t-statistics in parentheses

TABLE 10.5 *Equations Explaining Asian Affiliate Exports to Individual Regions of the World*

Eq. No.	Independent variables				Constant Term	R^2	No. of observations
	IMP(KL)	NS(JL)	PEXAF(JL)	PEXUN(JL)			
European Union, excluding U.K.							
5–1	2.91	–17.2	75.7	–20.8	6,793	.108	62
	(1.1)	(1.6)	(2.9)	(2.0)	(0.8)		
Japan							
5–2	–7.91	3.13	29.4	–7.1	4,184	.038	74
	(0.2)	(0.2)	(2.5)	(0.9)	(2.0)		
Asia and Pacific, excluding Japan							
5–3	2.09	1.06	113.2	–7.7	7,320	.149	158
	(0.5)	(0.2)	(5.3)	(0.5)	(0.6)		

t-statistics in parentheses

possibilities in individual markets for the MNE's affiliates located in Asian countries. The strongest and most consistent impact is that where parents export more to their affiliates, the Asian affiliates of these parents also export more to these markets. Higher parent exports to non-affiliates are associated with lower exports to the same markets by the parents' Asian affiliates, but that effect is much smaller per dollar of parent exports and not consistently significant. Production in a market by an affiliate of a parent is weakly, almost never significantly, associated with lower exports by the parent's Asian affiliates. One way of interpreting the opposite signs of the coefficients for parent exports to affiliates and non-affiliates is that higher parent exports to affiliates in a market reflect a strong position in that market for the MNE's affiliates located there, and that the strength of the affiliates in that market is helpful to other affiliates of that MNE, such as the Asian affiliates, in penetrating the market. Relatively high parent exports to non-affiliates in a market reflect a weak position for the MNEs affiliates in that market, and relatively poor conditions for the MNEs affiliates in other countries to export to that market.

The strongest relationships we found for Asian affiliate exports were within two individual industries, electronic components and accessories, and office and computing machinery. The equations for the latter industry were unusual in that the negative coefficients for affiliate production were statistically significant in a couple of cases and the coefficients for parent exports to non-affiliates were positive and large, although not statistically significant. Perhaps in this industry, in contrast to others, parent exports even to non-affiliates encouraged Asian affiliate exports to the same markets.

With data for only two separate industries, one can only speculate on the differences in MNE strategy that might explain the differences between them, and how these industries might differ from others. The electronic components and accessories industries appear to be dominated by a non-competitive relationship between parents and affiliates, and between affiliates inside and those outside a market. Perhaps they perform different segments of production or produce different types of products that are complementary in use, or gain from a common reputation. The office and computing machinery industry appears to be characterized by competition for markets between affiliates outside a market and those inside. The two sets of affiliates might produce similar products or there may be more protection of markets in this industry.

A broader issue is that the two industries, the two countries, and the Asian region as a whole may not be representative of other countries, regions and industries. Asian affiliates were far more export-oriented than those in other regions in the 1970s, although the differences were not as great in 1989, the year analyzed here. Asian affiliates are also much more concentrated in the machinery industries than those in other regions. It would be informative to compare the export behavior of these affiliates with that of affiliates in countries following more restrictive trade policies and encouraging import substituting, rather than export, activities.

Reference

U.S. Department of Commerce (1992) *U.S. Direct Investment Abroad, 1989 Benchmark Survey, Final Results*, Bureau of Economic Analysis, Washington, DC: U.S. Government Printing Office.

11

Foreign Direct Investment in Ghana's Emerging Market Economy

KOFI AFRIYIE

After years of economic decline and a near halt to multinational enterprise (MNE) activity, Ghana has experienced a dramatic increase in the flow of foreign direct investment (FDI) in recent years. This chapter aims to investigate the nature and extent of FDI in Ghana's emerging market economy. The focus here is to examine the country's performance in attracting FDI and to determine whether such investment is linked to external forces of globalization. The chapter explores sources of foreign investment in the context of national and regional origins of competitive advantages of investors and their preferences for entry modes and ownership arrangements. This study concludes with policy implications and future prospects of FDI in Ghana whose performance, along with other market-reforming economies, could mark the beginning of a regional market economy and core investment zone.

Introduction

This chapter addresses the following questions: What has been the nature of inward FDI in Ghana during the past several years? Does the flow of FDI into the Ghanaian economy suggest a pattern consistent with the forces of globalization that characterize international production elsewhere? What are the implications of Ghana's FDI performance for the emerging West African regional market? The chapter provides some insights into the possible motives of multinational enterprises (MNEs) and other investors, the sectoral destination as well as the national and regional origin of FDI in

Ghana. Within this context, the chapter explores potential forces of globalization that are at work in attracting FDI in Ghana and discusses the prospects for an investment zone within a region that has lagged behind others in generating inward and outward FDI.

The remainder of this chapter examines Ghana's FDI in the context of the eclectic paradigm and other theoretical constructs, and presents facts and figures on Ghana's FDI profile. This is followed by discussion of the basic findings, as portrayed in the profile and various data. Policy implications and future prospects of the country's FDI are then presented. The chapter concludes with highlights of Ghana's experience in attracting FDI.

Global Production and FDI in Africa

UNCTAD and other agencies as well as global researchers have for several years reported a global investment pattern identified in three regions known popularly today as the Triad: North America, East Asia and Western Europe. Estimates by UNCTAD show that, worldwide, some 80 percent of inbound and 81 percent of outbound FDI occur in the Triad.[1]

Largely absent from this international production system, except as supporting export platforms linking them to the Triad, are most African economies, as well as a number of Eastern European, Western Asian and Latin American countries. At $5 billion in 1995, Africa's inward FDI was among the lowest for any major region of the world.[2] According to UNCTAD (1997), Africa's share of global inward FDI actually declined from 2.4 percent in 1989 to 1.5 percent in 1995. Cantwell (1997, p. 155) suggests that Africa's share of global inward and outward FDI is likely to remain small for many years to come.

At the same time, the UNCTAD data suggest that several African economies have demonstrated an increasing capacity to attract FDI during the past few years (UNCTAD, 1997). For example, the increase in FDI flows going to Morocco, Tunisia, Ghana, Tanzania, Mozambique and Zimbabwe between the mid-1980s and the mid-1990s was greater than that of the global average. Ghana, in particular, appears to be on its way to becoming a popular destination for FDI in West Africa, besides Nigeria which is home to about half the population of West Africa and has led the region in inward FDI.[3] No systematic study exists, however, to determine the nature of recent inflow of FDI, including micro-level characteristics such as sectoral distribution of FDI projects, organizational modes of entry and potential linkages of investments to other national or regional economies. Would a non-Triad country in a region with a relatively small share of global

FDI show characteristics of international production similar to those observed in countries at the core of the FDI Triad?

Theoretical Constructs and Ghana's FDI

As an exploratory study, we are guided, in part, by the available data, as presented in the next section, and by a body of existing theoretical works. Together, data and concepts are used here to help explain a profile or an emerging pattern, where one exists, of inward FDI in Ghana.

Eclectic Paradigm and Ghana's Location-specific Advantages

The eclectic paradigm, as developed by Dunning (1981, 1988, 1995), provides a conceptual framework for explaining FDI in Ghana. The paradigm states that a country's propensity to attract inbound FDI is a function of three broad variables. First the existence of ownership-specific advantages as embodied in a firm's resources and capabilities; second, the host country's location-specific advantages comprising both natural as well as created resources, including physical and social infrastructure, intangible resources such as actions of governments that create an enabling business environment; third, the organizational forms by which firms combine their ownership advantages with location advantages of countries to maintain and improve their competitive position. Together, these advantages provide firms the motivation to expand overseas to capture internal benefits, or internationalization-specific advantages.

We assume the existence of ownership and internationalization advantages of firms that have expressed interest in investing in Ghana. Our attention focuses then on location-specific advantages that Ghana provides potential foreign investors and the ownership arrangements preferred by these investors in their quest to capture benefits of internationalization.

Ghana's Created and Natural Assets as Location-Specific Advantages

Ghana has for many years provided important created national assets in the West African region, in terms of human capital embodied in a relatively large educated workforce in urban centers, primarily in the Accra-Tema metropolitan area, as well as a transportation hub comprising airways, road networks and port facilities.[4] Additionally, since the 1960s, Ghana has been a major producer of low-priced hydroelectric power which it exports to the neighboring countries of Togo, Benin and Cote d'Ivoire.[5]

Ghana's most important natural assets include the following: a relatively large internal market of nearly 19 million people (the second largest in West Africa, after Nigeria with over 100 million people), substantial deposits of gold, industrial diamonds, bauxite and manganese and lumber. In addition, Ghana is a major world producer of cocoa and cultivates a variety of agricultural products for internal consumption and for exports. Together, extraction of natural resources provides a large portion of the country's foreign exchange earnings. Employing over 50 percent of the labor force, these natural assets form the basis of Ghana's comparative advantage in a resource-based, labor intensive economy.[6]

These important national assets, collectively, would seem to provide a 'pull factor' for inward FDI. Yet, for years, in the 1980s in particular, FDI in Ghana all but dried up. It seems, therefore, that, in the case of Ghana, these natural and created assets, by themselves, are not sufficient to determine the level or type of investments that will flow into the country in the first place.

The Role of Policy Environment as Intangible Location-specific Advantage A country's intangible, created assets may well be just as important as its natural and tangible created assets in a portfolio of location-bound assets, according to the eclectic paradigm (Dunning, 1995). Intangible assets include actions of governments that increase or decrease the cost of doing business in a country. The period of FDI examined in this study (from the early 1980s to the mid-1990s, with emphasis on recent years) spans the approximate period of a major policy shift in Ghana's political economy. Below, we outline the macro-economic aspects of this policy shift.

After years of economic decline that began in the 1970s, Ghana embarked on an economic recovery program (ERP) in 1983 that led to the full adoption of the World Bank/IMF prototype structural adjustment program (SAP). At its core, ERP-SAP was designed to liberalize the economy along the following key dimensions:

- An economic stabilization program
- A floating exchange rate
- Reduction in government deficit spending
- Reduction in and eventual elimination of import tariffs and other trade barriers
- Privatization of state-owned enterprises
- Elimination of barriers to FDI
- Upgrading of physical infrastructure and capacity building, among other initiatives.[7]

The extent to which government policy, designed initially to arrest economic decline, has also affected the flow of inward FDI has not been addressed. This study makes a preliminary attempt to explore the link, if any, between the market reform policies and the flow of FDI during the policy period. But it is not our goal in this study to evaluate the full social and economic impact of structural adjustment through ERP-SAP. That issue has attracted an extensive, and as yet unresolved, debate in policy and academic circles.[8]

FDI and Dynamic Comparative Advantage We examine a second theoretical construct to help explain an emerging pattern of FDI in Ghana. Ozawa (1992, pp. 36–40) has suggested that there is a link between a county's comparative advantage and the type of FDI it attracts as well as the nature of outward FDI the country's firms undertake in the rest of the world. Simply put, if we assume, as we do in this study, that Ghana's revealed comparative advantage lies in its natural assets combined with created physical and intangible assets, the country should attract, primarily, resource-seeking FDI. Likewise, the country's outward-bound FDI, if any, should comprise of the resource-seeking type. As a country progresses through the phases of economic development, changes in its inward and outward FDI will mirror changes in its factor endowment, with a shift from a resource-rich to a knowledge-based economy.

In general, the relevance of this theoretical model to Ghana's investment profile lies in the sectoral distribution of FDI at various stages of Ghana's economic and industrial development. However, Ozawa's notion of industrial upgrading through increasing factor incongruity, with its focus on both outbound FDI, while interesting, is only of partial relevance to this study, because of our focus on Ghana's *inward* FDI. Also, the required information and analysis on economic development and industrial upgrading lie outside the scope of this chapter.

Investment Development Path A third related theoretical framework to Ghana's FDI stems from Dunning's observation that a country's outward and inward FDI are related to the country's stage of industrial development. Specifically, the investment development path model (IDP) states that a country at the earlier stages of economic development will experience excess of inward over outbound FDI. As the country progresses through increased industrialization or industrial upgrading, its outward-inward ratio will be highest at full industrialization when the country also has a higher propensity to be a recipient of inward FDI (Dunning, 1988; Dunning and Narula, 1996).

Because Ghana's outward FDI is negligible, relative to its inward FDI, *prima facie*, the IDP seems to confirm the position of Ghana and many African countries at the early stages of industrial upgrading when their outward FDI is insignificant, relative to inward FDI. Nevertheless, there are strong indications that specific countries such as South Africa, Nigeria, Morocco, Zambia as well as Ghana itself, are at a threshold in steadily increasing their stock and flows of outward FDI (UNCTAD, 1997). Clearly, more research is needed to test the IDP model for Ghana and other African economies.

Facts and Figures: Ghana's FDI Profile

Sources of Data and Analytical Approach

This study utilizes data from a variety of sources. UNCTAD provides a database on FDI flows and stock as well as shares of FDI in total capital formation through its 1996 *World Investment Report* and the 1996 *World Investment Directory*, Volume V, the focus of which is on Africa.

A significant portion of this study is based on data gathered from Ghanaian sources, primarily from Ghana Investment Promotion Centre (GIPC), which screens and evaluates both domestic and foreign direct investments. GIPC's records on national origin and sectoral destination of FDI provide valuable insight into the overall investment activity in Ghana and the nature of FDI, in particular.

Although reliable data is problematic in most developing countries, substantial information and figures on FDI exist at specific periods of time in GIPC's database, which provide an opportunity for closer examination of FDI in Ghana. In addition to annual aggregate FDI data, we use project-level information to explore issues related to national and regional origins of foreign investors, ownership arrangements, sectors of operation and numbers of approved projects. Combining aggregate FDI data with information on specific projects in large numbers enables us to present a more dynamic and lively portrait of inbound investment in Ghana.

The GIPC classifies approved projects into two broad categories: (1) projects targeted at *production* in the three traditional sectors: primary, secondary and tertiary; and (2) projects targeted solely at the *wholesale* and *retail trade*, a growing sector of economic activity in Ghana today. While tertiary activities in the first category of projects may also involve some trading, such trading occurs only to support services in diverse areas such as hotel and restaurant management, engineering services and tourism. In the second category of projects, trading constitutes *the* primary activity in the wholesale and retail sector.

This study focuses on the first category consisting of 191 approved projects in the three traditional sectors emphasizing production, rather than trade, over a two-year period in 1993 and 1994. Not all approved projects materialize into actual inward FDI. The value of *actual* FDI as a percentage of the value of *approved* projects in 1993 was about 83 percent. A comparable figure for 1994 was about 78 percent.[9]

Thus, approved projects in the two-year sample provides a fair representation of the actual annual aggregate of inward FDI during the period. The basic data for this study from the above sources consist of the following:

1. Inward FDI flows and stock: 1980 to 1995, the most recent year of data
2. The ratio of FDI in total domestic capital formation
3. National and regional origin of inward FDI
4. Sectoral destination of inbound FDI
5. Ownership and entry mode of FDI

Together, these data sets provide one of the most comprehensive body of information available for a systematic study on FDI activity in an African country. Even so, some of the data is incomplete, with some pieces of information existing for only a few years at a time. The 1993 and 1994 two-year sample of approved project data coincided with the years in which aggregate inward FDI increased by over 440 percent and 86 percent respectively over previous years.

Analyses and Findings

Based on analyses of annual stock and flow data on FDI as well as analysis of project-level information, the basic findings are highlighted below.

(1) Increases in Inward FDI Flows and Stock in the 1990s After falling to a mere trickle in 1983 and 1984, Table 11.1 shows that Ghana's FDI inflow rose slowly to about $15 million in 1990, a level roughly equivalent to that of a decade earlier. Between 1991 and 1995, however, there has been a dramatic 12-fold increase in the inward FDI to $245 million in 1995, an unprecedented increase in Ghana's post-independence history. By contrast, the African region as a whole experienced less than 66 percent during the same period.

Likewise, the stock of FDI in Ghana has grown substantially, nearly three times between 1990 and 1995, compared to a growth in stock of less than one-and-a-half times for Africa as whole during the same period.

TABLE 11.1 *Annual Inward FDI and Selected Stock in Ghana, 1980–95 (US$ million)*

Year	FDI inflow	FDI stock
1980	15.6	288
1981	16.3	
1982	16.3	
1983	2.4	
1984	2.0	
1985	5.6	312
1986	4.3	
1987	4.7	
1988	5.0	
1989	15.0	
1990	15.0	375
1991	20.0	
1992	23.0	
1993	125.0	
1994	233.0	776
1995	245.0	1021

Source: UNCTAD (1996, 1997).

(2) Increasing Share of Inward FDI in Gross Fixed Capital Formation As is shown in Table 11.2, the share of FDI in gross fixed capital formation grew steadily between 1980 and 1993, below the average for the African continent. But in 1993, the share of FDI increased dramatically. Not only did Ghana's share exceeded the average share for Africa as a whole, but the domestic share of FDI in gross fixed capital formation rose to over 22 percent, higher than the share of GNP in gross fixed capital formation in previous years.[10]

(3) National and Regional Origin of Inward FDI: Traditional Investors and New Actors Traditionally, most FDI in Ghana, as in many African countries, have originated from Western Europe, as a result of many years of corporate ties that date back to the colonial period. In Ghana, the most important of these firms have been of British origin. Firms such as Unilever, Cadbury, British Petroleum (BP) and Barclays Bank have operated in Ghana for decades.

The development of Ghana's major hydroelectric power project in the 1960s marked the beginning of a gradual shift away from the near-monopoly of British firms in FDI to a more diversified base of foreign investors. The U.S.-based Kaiser Aluminium and Reynolds Metal have been the primary beneficiaries of a cheap source of electricity in Ghana through their joint investment in VALCO, the major producer of aluminum in Ghana.

TABLE 11.2 *Share of Inward FDI to Gross Fixed Capital Formation, 1980–95*

Year	Share of FDI Stock (%)	
	Ghana	Africa
1980	1.8	5.8
1985	4.9	8.0
1990	6.0	10.8
1994	12.8	14.6

Year	Share of inward FDI (%)	
	Ghana	Africa
1980	1.1	3.6
1985	1.9	2.7
1990	2.3	4.2
1993	2.5	4.4
1994	9.4	4.9
1995	22.6	7.5

Source: UNCTAD (1996).

Table 11.3 shows that the trend away from U.K.-based MNEs continues, with Ghana attracting new FDI projects from non-traditional sources in larger numbers and in sectors where British and other Western European firms had dominated in the past.

Based on national or country of origin, Table 11.3 shows that Indian investors emerge as the source of the largest number of FDI projects with 24 or 13 percent of all approved projects in the two-year sample, followed by Germany with 21 or 11 percent. China (including Hong Kong-based firms) tied with Lebanon for third place with 16 projects each, followed closely by the U.K. with 15 projects (or 7.5 percent). The U.S. tied in fifth place with Switzerland, each with 14 projects (7 percent). Nine projects of Israeli origin were approved and seven for France in the two-year sample.

However, a regional breakdown of approved projects in Table 11.3 reveals a substantial lead by Western European investors, as a group, in terms of number and share of projects, 74 projects (38.7 percent), followed by the Asian region with 44 projects or 23 percent, a significant second place share of all approved projects, given their new-comer status, relative to the Western Europeans, in selected sectors. The Middle East, with Lebanon and Israel being the primary source countries, contributed 26 projects or 13.6 percent to the total number

TABLE 11.3 *Number and Percent of Approved Projects by National and Regional Origin in all Sectors, 1993–94*

	Number	Percent
Country		
India	24	13
Germany	21	11
China	16	8
Lebanon	16	8
U.K.	15	8
Switzerland	14	7
U.S.A.	14	7
Israel	9	5
France	7	4
Other	55	29
Total	*191*	*100*
Region		
Africa	7	4
Asia/Pacific	44	23
Middle East	26	14
N. America	15	8
W. Europe	74	39
E. Europe	5	3
L. America	0	0
Multilateral	20	10
Total	*191*	*100*
Triad status		
Triad	133	70
Non-triad	58	30
Total	*191*	*100*

Source: Ghana Investment Center (1994).

of approved projects. North America trailed with 15 projects, 14 of them (7 percent) originating in the U.S. The African region as a whole contributed seven projects or 3.7 percent of the total approved.

A new category of investors, consisting of joint national origins, designated here as the *multilateral,* contributed 20 or 10.5 percent of the approved projects (Table 11.3). The multilaterals initiated projects collectively as foreign investor entities and then either formed equity joint ventures with Ghanaians (17 of the 20 joint nationalities), or presented their projects as wholly-owned foreign investments.

(4) Sectoral Distribution of Inward FDI: Shift Toward Secondary and Tertiary Sectors? The data on approved projects presented in Table 11.4 show clear sectoral destinations of projects: the most frequent destination is in the secondary sector, with 93 or 48 percent of all approved projects, followed closely by the tertiary sector with 82 projects or 42 percent and the primary sector trailing with just under 10 percent of approved projects in 1993 and 1994. This distribution reflects the increasing importance of manufacturing and assembly operations as well as a diverse array of projects in services, including building and construction, tourism and technical services.

Table 11.4 also shows the regional origin of projects by sector. Most of the Asian projects (61 percent) are located in the secondary sector, while 50 percent of all the approved projects of European origin are located in the tertiary sector. Slightly less than half of North American approved projects, primarily of U.S. origin, targeted the secondary sector. On the other hand 73 percent of all approved projects of Middle East origin went to the secondary sector, primarily in manufacturing, while the small number of projects of African origin were concentrated in the tertiary sector.

(5) Ownership and Entry Mode of FDI Projects As indicated in Table 11.5, by far the more preferred mode of entry or ownership arrangement was through the equity joint venture (EJV), consisting

TABLE 11.4 *Number of Approved FDI Projects by Sector and Regional Origin, 1993–94*

	Primary	Secondary	Tertiary	Total
Region				
Africa	1	1	5	7
Asia/Pacific	4	27	13	44
Middle East	0	19	7	26
N. America	3	7	5	15
W. Europe	9	28	37	74
E. Europe	0	4	1	5
L. America	0	0	0	0
Multilateral	1	6	13	20
Total	*18*	*92*	*81*	*191*
Triad status				
Triad origin	16	62	55	133
Non-triad	2	30	26	58
Total	*18*	*92*	*81*	*191*

Source: Ghana Investment Center (1994).

TABLE 11.5 *Number of Approved FDI Projects by Ownership Type and Region, 1993–1994*

	Wholly-owned	Equity JV	Total
Region			
Africa	1	6	7
Asia/Pacific	6	38	44
Middle East	1	25	26
N. America	2	13	15
W. Europe	9	65	74
E. Europe	1	4	5
L. America	0	0	0
Multilateral	3	17	20
Total	*23*	*168*	*191*
Triad status			
Triad origin	17	116	133
Non-triad	6	52	58
Total	*23*	*168*	*191*

Source: Ghana Investment Promotion Center (1994).

of 168 projects or 88 percent of all approved projects, compared to 23 projects (or 12 percent) through the medium of wholly-owned foreign ventures. Without exception, the joint venture entry mode was selected by significant majorities of approved projects in each of the regional sources of FDI. For example, all but one of the 26 Middle Eastern investors (96 percent) preferred the equity joint venture entry mode.

Discussion of Findings

Trends in FDI

The increasing trend in inward FDI coincides with the period of economic recovery program (ERP) initiated in 1983. The evidence points to several years of a slow steady increase, suggesting a period of transition from the mid-1980s to the mid-1990s, a period that appears to reflect caution on the part of foreign investors. During this period, Ghana experienced real growth in its GDP of between 4 percent and 5 percent annually, a sufficiently long period of substantial economic growth to boost investor confidence. This observation seems to confirm conclusions reached by the Multilateral Investment Guarantee Agency (MIGA) of the World Bank that a relatively long period of transition occurs between a country's initial adoption of wide-ranging economic reforms and the beginning of substantial FDI inflows.[11]

FDI Contribution to Domestic Capital Formation

Foreign direct investment has often been seen as a means of closing the investment gap experienced by many developing economies. Given the universal scarcity of domestic capital in developing countries, the reasoning goes, FDI should help bridge the much-needed capital shortfall.[12]

The data strongly suggest the growing importance of FDI to the Ghanaian economy and the increasing substitution of foreign capital for domestic investment. The risk for Ghana is whether the country can sustain the magnitude of FDI necessary to satisfy domestic demand for investment capital. But, it is not clear whether or how increased FDI activity has affected the role of domestic capital in Ghana's economic and industrial development. Presumably, what a developing country such as Ghana should strive for is mutual reinforcement and complementarity of contributions between domestic and foreign capital.[13]

Diversity of FDI Sources: Forces of Globalization and Potential Investment Links

The last section presented a fairly even distribution of approved FDI projects among geographically diverse national and regional backgrounds. This confirms that Ghana now presents a very competitive investment environment to potential investors, much more than it has done in the past. Additionally, by creating an investment-friendly environment, Ghana's experience also suggests that a developing country can unleash the forces of globalization, even in a region that has been operating only at the margins of international production.

Furthermore, the fact that most of Ghana's FDI projects in the two-year sample originated in the Triad countries signals, at the very least, growing linkages between value-added production in Ghana and the core countries of global investment in Asia, Western Europe and North America. However, more corroborative evidence is needed to make a case for Ghana's emergence as an important national link in global investment networks and to determine the nature of that link.

We note also the increasing role Asian and Middle East investors of Indian, Israeli and Lebanese origin are playing in Ghana. Indians and Lebanese investors are not new to Ghana. In the past, they forged a major presence in the wholesale and retail trade sector and largely ceded the manufacturing sector to European firms. Their over-whelming presence in the secondary sector in the period under study may be indicative of industrial upgrading in their own countries and regions, since many of them left Ghana in the late 1960s under new immigration laws that severely restricted their participation in the wholesale and retail business. Preliminary analysis suggests that many are returning to the retail sector as well, but this time in partnership with Ghanaian investors.

An important step in empirical research on Ghana's potential global production link is to determine the extent to which the recent surge in FDI activity is, in part, attributable to expansion strategies of existing MNEs responding to improved location-specific advantages or to greenfield upstarts of a diverse group of *global entrepreneurs* responding to the same location-specific advantages of Ghana. Preliminary data on the size of individual investment values during the period show that the average value of investment per approved FDI project among the nine largest investors (comprising 71 percent of all approved projects) shown in Table 11.3 was estimated at just over $1 million. Many projects range in value from as low as $40,000 to over $40 million (GIPC database).

These figures lead us to believe that a substantial number of the approved FDI projects consist of small-scale operations of individual commitments in upstart firms. Thus, there is some evidence to suggest that foreign entrepreneurial, as opposed to corporate, investment may be a significant element of FDI in Ghana. Also, to what extent are these entrepreneurs part of a growing number of Ghanaian expatriates, now citizens of other countries, investing in Ghana as foreign investors, a phenomenon that has been observed among Indian and East Asian expatriates elsewhere?

A conspicuous absence as a source country to approved FDI projects in the sample is Japan, a key contributor of outward FDI in major regions of the world and a core Triad country in East Asia. UNCTAD has noted the general paucity of Japanese investment in Africa and attributes Japan's marginal role to, among other things, weak links between Japanese overseas development assistance and the country's FDI, lack of experience in operating within African economies and psychological distance from Africa (UNCTAD, 1996, pp. 49–50).

Sectoral Destination of FDI Projects in Ghana

The strong growth of inward FDI in the secondary and tertiary sectors runs counter to the expectation that most of such FDI activity would occur in the primary sector by resource-seeking investors, given Ghana's natural assets and comparative advantage. It is, however, not clear whether increased activity in manufacturing and downstream production activities reflects the voluntary preferences of potential investors or subtle institutional steering of FDI to specific sectors of the Ghanaian economy. What is known is that Ghana, as part of its market reform policies, has eliminated most of the sector-of-operation limitations it imposed on foreign investors in earlier years (See, for example, Ghana's Investment Code, 1991, 1985).

By targeting more projects in the secondary and tertiary sectors, we can infer that market-seeking is a prime motive of most of the investors with approved FDI projects: to produce and sell manufactured products and services. The data do not, however, indicate whether FDI production is for the export or domestic market or both.

The Equity Joint Venture Rules

The overwhelming preference for the equity joint venture (EJV) is significant, because Ghana has eliminated the ownership require- ments for investing in most sectors that were prevalent in the 1970s and early 1980s. Unless there are subtle ways in which the GIPC is steering investors into EJVs, it may be that investors themselves have concluded that it is probably to their advantage to seek local partnership in order to succeed in Ghana. Such partnerships can provide the foreign investor several advantages, including political accommodation and country knowledge (Afriyie, 1988; Beamish, 1985).

Beyond the EJV, there is evidence of some interest in non-equity arrangements on the part of foreign direct investors. For example, in 23 percent the 168 cases of EJVs, loan financing of the FDI project was part of the joint-venture arrangements. Most of these financing arrangements were between Western European and Ghanaian EJV partners and such loans were made more frequently by the British partner than any other national investor.

Future Prospects of FDI in Ghana and Policy Implications

Factors in Sustaining Economic and Political Reforms

The annual flows and stocks of FDI and the share of FDI in the domestic fixed capital formation of Ghana are likely to increase, if, at the minimum, current market-based economic reforms are maintained. The unprecedented surge in inward FDI suggests growing confidence in the Ghanaian economy. Also, recent political reforms may be helping to create an even more enabling environment in the future. In December 1996, or example, Ghana had its first successful civilian transfer of power since independence, based on multi-party elections. This can only help create political stability in the country.

In general, Ghana has eliminated most of the critical micro-level risks associated with targeting investments in specific industries for regulation and ownership restrictions reminiscent of the late 1960s and 1970s, periods of military dictatorships and extreme bureaucratic policing of domestic and foreign investment.

Some progress has been made in recent years regarding infrastructure upgrading, particularly in telecommunication, and increased privatization of state-owned enterprises. These are actions that can only boost investor confidence.

Efforts at Regional Integration

Ghana is a founding member of Economic Community of West African States (ECOWAS), designed, originally, as a customs union, to integrate eventually over 200 million people in 16 West African countries into a regional common market. However, intra-regional trade has increased rather slowly and cross-border investment is patchy. For example, the data on approved FDI data recorded only seven projects of African origin, although in the wholesale and retail sector many Nigerian, Ivorian and other West African enterprises have been established in Ghana in recent years.[14]

There are several regional destabilizing factors that have not helped the forces of economic integration in West Africa. These include civil strife in Liberia and Sierra Leone and France's currency pact with French-speaking West African countries which creates an economic schism with others in the region. It is too early to determine whether Nigeria's leadership and Ghana's support in maintaining security in the region through military intervention and political mediation in war-torn countries will translate into closer economic co-operation in the region. If that happens, Ghana stands to be one of the major beneficiaries as a transportation and investment hub in West Africa.

Currency Depreciation Risks and Profit Remittances

One economic factor to watch is the effects of continuous depreciation of Ghana's currency, the cedi, against the U.S dollar and other major currencies. While depreciation may boost FDI- related and other exports from Ghana, it can also be costly to importers, domestic and foreign alike, and reduce hard currency values of remittances. That prospect can limit the flow of inward FDI, depending on investors' time horizon and how they perceive the overall risk of operating in Ghana.

In general, increases in inward FDI and stock would suggest eventual increases in profit remittances and royalties paid to foreign investors over time. World Bank (1996) data suggest that profit repatriation increased slowly during the 1980s and the 1990s, relative to the more dramatic increases in Ghana's FDI during the period.

While a slow increase in repatriation of profits, relative to the surge in inward FDI, may be attributed purely to a lag effect in the investment-return cycle, another explanation may center on the rapid depreciation of Ghana's currency, the cedi, vis-a-vis the US dollar and other major currencies. For example, from an exchange rate of about C326.00/US$1.00 in 1990, the cedi has depreciated by over 500 percent to about C2,000.00/US$1.00 during the second quarter of 1997.[15] Operating in such a weak currency environment, it is unlikely that firms would undertake any major repatriation, given the economic risks arising from asset exposure. Those investors who do are likely to cover themselves in some fashion against exchange losses, including tax write-offs in the case of U.S. firms. The potential risks remain, nevertheless.

A related explanation is that, realizing the potential losses inherent in converting the cedi to hard currencies, many foreign investors are simply plowing back their profits and other remittances, a process that, by definition, would actually be increasing the flow and stock figures of FDI. Clearly, opportunities exist here for further investigation into what foreign firms are actually doing as they operate in a weak currency environment.

Conclusion

We conclude by highlighting briefly important lessons from Ghana's performance on inward FDI. First, a country's natural and created assets may not be enough to sustain a good level of FDI, unless they are also accompanied by intangible, policy actions that create an enabling environment for FDI. Thus, a country's propensity to attract FDI is not bound by perceived or classical notions of comparative advantage, based on factor endowment. Determinants of FDI, in the case of Ghana, involve a complex play of natural, created, tangible and intangible assets. The implication for research into corporate behavior in an emerging market economy lies in the recognition that other factors, including domestic demand for specific goods and services which foreign producers can best provide, may play a far more important role than has been acknowledged thus far in studies on international production.

We note in passing, for example, that Ghana is a net importer of services and has maintained a merchandise trade deficit for several years now.[16] Increasing demand for these services, and imported manufactured goods which drive Ghana's trade deficits, more likely are providing foreign firms with growth opportunities in the secondary and tertiary sectors, relative to the primary sector. Thus, demand factors, as location-specific advantages, rather than factor endowments, may also be key determinants of FDI in Ghana and other emerging market economies.

A tentative conclusion from this study is that there may be a relatively long lagged effect of economic reforms on inward FDI. However, it seems that investor confidence can increase dramatically, once a threshold of economic and political reforms have been achieved.

Finally, Ghana's experience demonstrates that individual countries can perform well in attracting FDI, even in a region such as West Africa and other African subregions that are perceived to be in a state of economic marginalization, relative to other regions of the world.

Given global trends towards value-added, knowledge-based production and increasing sophistication of consumers in emerging markets, the capacity to sustain inward flow of FDI will most likely hinge on the pace of creating and strengthening national assets, including an attractive policy environment. In this regard, experience from East Asia and Ghana's own history suggest key roles for government. In creating enabling environment for FDI, government policy will have to emphasize continuous upgrading of social and physical infrastructure and promote aggressively the rapid development of human capital across all cycles of education and skill levels in the workforce.

References

AFRIYIE, K. (1988) Joint venture production and local manufacturing industries: Lessons from a developing economy, *Columbia Journal of World Business*, Vol. 23, No. 3, 51–62.

AFRIYIE, K. (1992) Enhancing FDI and value-added production in developing economies: Governments, MNEs, and development agencies, *The International Trade Journal*, Vol. 7, No. 1, 85–109, Fall.

BEAMISH, P. N. (1985) The characteristics of joint ventures in developed and developing countries, *Columbia Journal of World Business*, 13–19, Fall.

CANTWELL, J. A. (1997) Globalization and development in Africa. In DUNNING, J. H. and HAMDANI, K.A. (eds) *The New Globalism and Developing Countries*, 155–179, United Nations University Press, Tokyo.

DUNNING, J. H. (1981) Toward an eclectic theory of international production, *Journal of International Business Studies*, Vol. 11, 9–31, Spring/Summer.

DUNNING, J. H. (1988) *Explaining international production*, Unwin Hyman, London.

DUNNING, J. H. (1994) Re-evaluating the benefits of foreign direct investment, *Transnational Corporations*, Vol. 3, No. 1, 23–51, June.

DUNNING, J. H. (1995) Reappraising the eclectic paradigm in an age of alliance capitalism, *Journal of International Business Studies*, Vol. 26, No. 3, 461–491, Third quarter.

DUNNING, J. H. and NARULA, R. (1996) Foreign direct investment and governments, Routledge, London and New York.

Ghana Investment Code (1985 and 1991 editions) Government publication, Accra, Ghana.

Ghana Investment Promotion Center (1994) Database of approved investment projects. Accra, Ghana.

KAPUR, I., HADJIMICHAEL, M.T. *et. al.* (1991) *Ghana: Adjustment and growth, 1983–91*, Occasional Paper 86, International Monetary Fund, Washington, DC, September.

MOSLEY, P. and TOYE, J. (1988) The design of structural adjustment programmes, *Development Policy Review*, Vol. 6, 395–413

OZAWA, T. (1992) Foreign direct investment and economic development, *Transnational Corporations*, Vol. 1, No. 1, 27–54, February.

Statistical Service (1991) *Quarterly Digest of Statistics*, Vol. 9, No. 1, 102–109, March. pp. 475–478.

Statistical Service (1996) *Quarterly Digest of Statistics*, Various monthly editions.

STREETEN, P. (1987) Structural adjustment: A survey of the issues and options, *World Development*, Vol. 15, No. 12, 1469–1482.

TODARO, M.P. (1989) *Economic development in the third world*, Longman, New York.

United Nations Conference on Trade and Development (UNCTAD) (1997) *World investment directory 1996, Volume V: Africa*. United Nations, Geneva.

United Nations Conference on Trade and Development (UNCTAD) (1997) *World investment report 1996*, United Nations, Geneva.

United Nations Conference on Trade and Development (UNCTAD) (1996) *World investment report 1995*, United Nations, Geneva.

United Nations Conference on Trade and Development (UNCTAD) (1992) *World investment report 1991*, United Nations, Geneva.

West Africa (1997) May–June. Various editions.

World Bank (1984) *Ghana: Policies and program for adjustment.* World Bank, Washington, DC.

World Bank (1996) *World debt tables*, Oxford University Press, London.

Notes

1. See UNCTAD, *World Investment Report*, various editions since 1992.
2. UNCTAD (1997) provides detailed annual flows of FDI in African countries between 1981 and 1995.
3. UNCTAD (1996, 1997).
4. See *Quarterly Digest of Statistics* (Statistical Service, 1991), a publication on economic and social statistics of Ghana; see also UNDP, *Human Development Report* (1991) on national development indices.
5. *Quarterly Digest of Statistics* (Statistical Service, 1991).
6. *Quarterly Digest of Statistics*, (Statistical Service, 1991).
7. See World Bank (1984) and Kapur, Hadjimichael *et. al.* on specific content of Ghana's Economic Recovery Program and World Bank/IMF conditionalities.
8. For a comprehensive review of this debate, see Mosley and Toye (1988), Streeten

(1987) as well as numerous articles in *West Africa* (1989, 1990, 1991 editions), with essays on the theme, African Alternatives to Structural Adjustments, developed by the United Nations Economic Commission on Africa.

9. All project-level data used here were obtained from Ghana Investment Promotion Center (GIPC), Accra, Ghana. The GIPC is the principal government agency charged with screening and evaluating domestic and foreign investments in Ghana. Because a significant number of projects were approved in the second category whose primary activities are restricted to the wholesale and retail trade, we believe this category warrants a separate study.

10. For several measures and estimates of capital formation in Ghana, see *Quarterly Digest of Statistics* (1991), (op. cit.), p. 105.

11. See MIGA's in-house publication on a Round Table Conference on Foreign Investment Policy in Africa held in 1992, which featured participants from the private and public sectors in Africa and around the world.

12. Todaro (1989) provides an extensive review of various perspectives on the role of FDI as a vehicle for filling in gaps between domestic supply of savings and desired levels of investment necessary to achieve growth and development goals.

13. For a comprehensive survey of potential contributions of inward FDI to the improvement of a host country's competitive advantage, see Dunning (1994).

14. From information contained in the GIPC database.

15. For a weekly report on currency values and exchange rate movements in African countries, see, for example, May and June 1997 editions of *West Africa*.

16. See figures in Statistical Service's *Quarterly Digest of Statistics* (1996 and various editions).

12

Impact of Trade and Investment Policies on Economic Transformation in East Asia, the Middle East, and Latin America

M. RAQUIBUZ ZAMAN

This chapter examines the nature of economic transformation in selected countries in the Middle East, East Asia, and Latin America to ascertain the economic as well as non-economic factors that produced the divergent results. It assesses the linkage between foreign direct investments (FDIs) and economic development, and it asserts that until some fundamental changes occur in social policies, the countries in the Middle East and Latin America cannot expect to join the ranks of the newly industrialized countries (NICs) any time soon.

Introduction

One would expect that nations with relatively small populations but endowed with an abundance of marketable natural resources such as petroleum should have an easier task in transforming their economies than their counterparts with larger populations but very few national resources. When it comes to the oil exporting Middle Eastern countries, we find that billions of dollars of yearly export earnings has brought little economic transformation during the past twenty-five years.

As compared to the Middle East, the East Asian nations (including some of the South East Asian countries) emerged from the oil price shocks of the period with much stronger and broad-based economic foundations to produce the 'East Asian Miracle' (World Bank 1993).

Some of these countries have now been elevated to the ranks of the NICs. Unlike the East Asian nations—but to some extent, like the Middle East economies—the Latin American countries fared rather poorly in economic transformation during the 1975–94 period. Chile, from the Pinnochet period, and Argentina in recent years, are examples of some exceptions to the general pattern of the region.

The divergent rates of economic transformation is of particular interest to the students of economic development since many Third World countries, at one time or another, followed similar strategies of import substitutions and export promotions, along with an assortment of policies regarding tariffs, subsidies, and trade regulations.

The objective of this chapter is to assess the divergent patterns of economic transformation of selected Middle Eastern (because of the lack of credible data, only a few could be selected), East Asian, and Latin American countries over a twenty-five year period (1970–95) by examining changing data on economic structures, exports and imports, inward and outward FDIs, and other macro-economic as well as non-economic factors. The aim is to shed some lights on the future prospects of the lagging economies in view of the experience of the NICs. The analysis begins with a brief review of the literature on comparative economic performance of the three selected groups of countries.

Literature Review

Interest in the economics of development began to emerge with the end of the colonial rules in the mid-1950s. This is the period when the newly created multilateral agencies such as the World Bank and the International Monetary Fund (IMF) were called upon to assist the less developed countries (LDCs) in their economic development efforts. This period witnessed the works of Rostow (1952), Nurkse (1953), and Bauer and Yamey (1957) on the processes and factors of economic growth and those of Prebisch (1950) and Myrdal (1968) on the specific regional development problems with global ramifications. Myrdal emphasized that there are no exclusively economic problems, but simply problems, and that economic as well as non-economic factors must be considered as determinants of economic growth.[1] The apparent pursuit of similar economic policies by various nations with different results give credence to Myrdal's theory.

The development efforts by the LDCs in the 1950s and the 1960s were not, in general, very successful. A number of economists tried to explain what factors and policies might set the stage for 'take off' to sustained economic growth. Some of the noteworthy treatise of the time were Aggarwala and Singh (1963), Johnson (1967), Pearson Commission Report (1969), Meier (1967), and Helleiner (1972). The Pearson Commission Report nudged the developed countries to pursue more favorable economic policies towards the LDCs.

To a large extent, however, the pace and depth of economic transformation have been due to the initiatives taken by the LDCs themselves. Overall, economic conditions of many of the LDCs were similar in nature in the early 1960s. That is, most of them were poor in natural resources, had very low rates of capital formation, but often had sizeable human resources that could be harnessed with proper national polices on education and training. During the last three and a half decades, some of these nations (East Asians as well as Latin Americans) pursued similar strategies of import substitution and export promotion polices at various stages of their economic growth. This is also the period when views on the economic development process, especially concerning the relationship between trade and economic growth, underwent a major shift (Grabowski, 1994). Import substitution polices with facilitating fiscal and monetary polices to protect nascent domestic industries were followed, at one time or another, by Taiwan (Eckes, 1993; Chu, 1994; Birdsall *et al.*, 1995; Ranis, 1995), Korea (Alam, 1989; Aggarwal and Agmon, 1990; Dollar, 1990; Birdsall *et al.*, 1995; Ranis, 1995), Singapore, Malaysia, and the Latin American countries (Aggarwal and Agmon, 1990; Turner, 1992; Nelson, 1994). Subsequently, the East Asian nations switched to policies that promoted export-led growth. Krueger (1997) coins the term 'outer oriented trade regimes' that promoted production of export and import-competing goods through a fairly uniform system of incentives. As the evidence mounted about the superiority of these policies, other countries followed suit (Chen and Tang, 1987; Lomax 1988; Edward, 1989; Paus, 1989).

Unlike the East Asian and Latin American countries, the Middle Eastern nations have not drawn much attention from the academics interested in economic development. The interest in the region principally emanates from its vast oil resources and its proneness to political instability in the form of armed conflicts. Most of the states in the region failed to pursue any significant program in economic diversification or growth.[2]

Any discourse on economic transformation of the regions under review will be incomplete until due emphasis is placed on the roles of the FDIs and those of the multinational enterprises (MNEs) in shaping the nature of each economy. The linkage between outward and inward direct investments and economic transformation has been forcefully pointed out by John Dunning in his treatise, going as far back as 1979.[3] Since then he has developed and revised the concept of the investment development path (IDP) in a number of books and papers.[4] According to the latest version of the IDP (Dunning and Narula, 1996), countries tend to progress through five different stages of economic development in terms of their net outward investment (NOI) position, which is defined as the gross outward investment stock minus the gross inward investment stock. The propensity for each country to be inward or outward investors, in turn, depends on the relative competitive strengths of the domestic firms vis-a-vis MNEs in *o*wnership- and *l*ocation-specific advantages and their abilities to *i*nternalize cross-border market transactions. Dunning's use of the OLI configuration as an explanation of the movements of each country through the various NOI stages adds to the expositions of the development economists who are trying to establish the linkages between macro-economic policies and economic transformation of nations.

This chapter tries to synthesize the explanations about economic transformation by examining not only the role of FDIs, but also some of the traditional macro policy variables referred to in this brief review of literature.

Analysis of Data and Results

The data for this chapter were collected principally from the World Bank, the IMF, the U.S. Department of Commerce, and the United Nations. Data for the Middle East are often unavailable and, at times, unreliable. However, attempts have been made to procure as much data as possible for a comparative analysis of economic performance.

Tables 12.1 and 12.2 present data on FDI inflows and outflows, respectively, for the selected countries in the Middle East, East Asia, and Latin America. Data on FDI *flows* have been used as proxies for FDI *stocks*, used by Dunning and Narula (1996) in their analysis for two reasons. First, availability of data for a longer period, and second, *flows* seem to approximate *stocks* rather nicely for the selected countries. The FDI inflows for the oil exporting Middle East states have been essentially negligible for all countries except Egypt and Saudi Arabia. Jordan, a non-oil exporting country, which averaged approximately $37 million annual inflows during 1983–88, since then achieved that level only in 1990, 1991, and 1995.

Iran, despite its long struggle with Iraq and economic sanctions in recent years, appears to be a small exporter of FDIs. Kuwait's net FDI outflows possibly is more due to its lack of absorption capacity of capital than any fundamental domestic economic strength. Not much can be said about the rest of the economies in the list.

In terms of IDP and the stages of economic development, it is

TABLE 12.1 *FDI Inflows for Selected Countries, 1983–95 (U.S.$ millions)*

	1983–88 (ann. avg)	1989	1990	1991	1992	1993	1994	1995
Middle East								
Egypt	959	1,250	734	253	459	493	1,256	1,000
Iran	−72	−19	−362	23	−170	−50	−10	−30
Iraq	2	3	–	−3	−1	1	–	–
Jordan	37	−1	38	−12	41	−34	3	43
Kuwait	−1	4	−6	1	35	13	16	15
Libya	−70	125	159	160	150	160	80	90
Saudi Arabia	1,625	−654	1,864	160	−79	1,369	1,341	890
UAE	57	39	−116	26	130	183	113	110
East Asia								
China	1,823	3,393	3,487	4,366	11,156	27,515	33,787	37,500
Hong Kong	1,343	1,076	1,728	538	2,051	1,667	2,000	2,100
Indonesia	341	682	1,093	1,482	1,777	2,004	2,109	4,500
S. Korea	387	758	788	1,180	727	588	809	1,500
Malaysia	731	1,668	2,333	3,998	5,183	5,006	4,348	5,800
Philippines	249	563	530	544	228	1,025	1,457	1,500
Singapore	1,947	2,887	5,575	4,879	2,351	5,016	5,588	5,302
Taiwan	448	1,604	1,330	1,271	879	917	1,375	1,470
Thailand	439	1,775	2,444	2,014	2,116	1,726	640	2,300
Latin America								
Argentina	512	1,028	1,836	2,439	4,179	6,305	1,200	3,900
Brazil	1,503	1,267	989	1,103	2,061	1,292	3,072	4,859
Chile	439	1,289	590	523	699	841	2,518	3,021
Columbia	570	576	500	457	790	960	1,667	1,200
Mexico	2,272	3,174	2,549	4,742	4,393	4,389	7,978	6,984
Venezuela	50	213	451	1,916	629	372	764	245

Source: United Nations, *World Investment Report, 1995 and 1996*, Annex Table 1.

difficult to classify the countries in any of the five stages described by Dunning and Narula (1996) because of lack of consistency in their NOIs.[5] One is tempted to classify Egypt, Saudi Arabia, Libya and UAE as stage 2 countries, and consider Kuwait and Iran hovering towards stage 3! Iraq and Jordan may qualify for stage 1 classification.

The data for East Asia countries give a much clearer picture. China, Indonesia, Malaysia, Philippines, and Thailand appear to be stage 2 countries, while Singapore is in stage 3. Hong Kong, South Korea, and Taiwan appear to be in stage 4 of economic development.

The Latin American countries of Argentina, Brazil, Chile, Columbia,

TABLE 12.2 *FDI Outflows for Selected Countries, 1983–95 (U.S.$ millions)*

	1983–88 (ann. avg)	1989	1990	1991	1992	1993	1994	1995
Middle East								
Egypt	13	23	12	62	4	–	43	16
Iran	–	–	–	–	–	–	–	–
Iraq	–	–	–	–	–	–	–8	–3
Jordan	2	17	–32	14	–3	–53	–23	–32
Kuwait	282	841	239	–186	1,211	848	1,075	1,044
Libya	30	35	105	–	–	–	–	–
Saudi Arabia	255	611	–613	–198	5	–49	82	13
UAE	9	2	–13	1	17	8	–48	–8
East Asia								
China	467	780	830	913	4,000	4,400	2,000	3,467
Hong Kong	1,453	2,930	2,448	2,825	8,254	17,713	21,437	25,000
Indonesia	11	17	–11	13	52	–31	15	12
S. Korea	107	305	1,056	1,500	1,208	1,361	2,524	3,000
Malaysia	224	282	532	389	514	1,325	1,817	2,575
Philippines	4	6	–5	–26	5	–7	28	9
Singapore	147	882	2,034	1,024	1,317	1,784	2,177	2,799
Taiwan	843	6,951	5,243	1,854	1,869	2,451	2,460	3,822
Thailand	33	50	140	167	147	221	493	904
Latin America								
Argentina	18	79	50	–41	46	–26	36	19
Brazil	128	523	665	1,014	137	491	1,037	1,384
Chile	7	10	8	123	378	431	883	644
Columbia	39	29	16	24	50	240	152	147
Mexico	104	107	224	167	730	16	1,045	597
Venezuela	100	136	375	188	156	886	525	522

Source: United Nations, *World Investment Report, 1995 and 1996*, Annex Table 2.

and Mexico seem to belong to the stage 2 of economic development, while Venezuela exhibits the traits of petroleum exporting countries of the Middle East.

The relative situation of economic transformation, or lack of it, of the selected countries can be clearer as we proceed with the other relevant information presented as follows.

Table 12.3 presents data on the annual percentage change in real gross domestic product (GDP) of selected countries in the three regions under study during 1977–86 and from 1987–94. In the Middle East, the two non-members of the Organization of Petroleum Exporting

TABLE 12.3 *Annual Percentage Change in Real GDP of Selected Countries*

Country	1977–86	1987	1988	1989	1990	1991	1992	1993	1994*
Middle East									
Egypt	6.2	8.7	3.5	2.7	2.3	1.2	0.4	1.5	1.3
Iran	–0.8	–2.2	–9.7	4.5	11.2	10.7	6.1	2.3	1.6
Iraq	1.1	28.3	–10.2	12.0	–26.0	–61.3	–	–	1.0
Jordan	7.2	2.9	–1.9	–13.4	1.0	1.8	16.1	5.8	5.7
Kuwait	–2.2	8.1	–10.0	25.0	–25.7	–41.0	76.3	29.3	1.1
Libya	–2.6	–23.6	–10.2	7.2	5.6	3.6	–3.0	–6.1	–3.0
Saudi Arabia	2.5	–1.4	8.4	–0.2	8.9	9.7	3.1	–0.5	–0.1
UAE	–1.2	5.5	–2.6	13.3	17.5	0.2	2.8	–1.5	1.1
East Asia									
China	9.0	10.9	11.3	4.3	3.8	8.2	13.1	13.7	11.5
Hong Kong	8.3	13.0	8.0	2.6	3.4	5.1	6.0	5.8	5.7
Indonesia	5.6	4.9	5.8	7.5	7.2	6.9	6.5	6.5	7.3
S. Korea	7.8	11.5	11.3	6.4	9.5	9.1	5.1	5.3	8.4
Malaysia	5.8	5.4	8.9	9.2	9.7	8.7	7.8	8.3	8.7
Philippines	2.0	4.3	6.8	6.2	2.7	–0.2	0.3	2.1	4.3
Singapore	6.8	9.5	11.1	9.6	8.8	6.7	6.0	10.1	10.1
Taiwan	8.4	12.3	7.3	7.6	4.9	7.2	6.5	6.1	6.5
Thailand	6.2	9.5	13.3	12.2	11.6	8.4	7.9	8.2	8.5
Latin America									
Argentina	0.5	2.6	–1.9	–6.2	0.1	8.9	8.7	6.0	7.4
Brazil	3.8	3.6	0.3	3.3	–4.4	1.1	–0.9	4.3	5.7
Chile	3.7	6.6	7.3	9.9	3.3	7.3	11.0	6.3	4.2
Columbia	3.9	5.4	4.1	3.4	4.3	2.0	4.0	5.3	5.7
Mexico	3.8	1.9	1.2	3.3	4.4	3.6	2.8	0.6	3.5
Venezuela	1.0	3.6	5.8	–8.6	6.5	9.7	6.1	–0.4	–3.3

* = estimates
Source: International Monetary Fund, *World Economic Outlook*, October 1995, Table A6.

Countries (OPEC)—Jordan, a non-oil-producer, and Egypt, a net exporter of oil—had a better record of economic growth during 1977–86 than their neighboring OPEC countries. Both countries thrived on the remittance income from their citizens working in the Gulf states. Egypt also received significant amounts of aid, principally from the U.S. The OPEC members all experienced significant instabilities in their economies throughout the period of study. Downward shifts in oil prices,[6] along with regional conflicts and general mismanagement of economic resources, contributed to the malady. Saudi Arabia, for example, enjoyed a per capita GDP of over $12,000 in 1982, but could only command around $7,000 in 1995 (Reed and Rossant, 1995).

Unlike the Middle East, the selected East Asian nations, except the Philippines, achieved remarkable rates of growth in their real GDPs during the same period. Their economic transformation has been so spectacular that the World Bank coined the phrase 'East Asian miracle' to describe the phenomena.[7] The relatively poor performance of the Philippines was, to some extent, caused by political instability and the resultant lack of coherent economic policies. The trade and economic policies that ushered in the 'miracle' will be clearer as we examine the structural changes in their economies over the last two decades.

The Latin American countries faced relatively lower volatility in the growth of real GDPs than the hapless Middle Eastern nations. Venezuela, the lone member of OPEC in this group, seems to have fared as well as Saudi Arabia. Chile had the best record for the group. It is interesting to note that during 1977–86—a period that witnessed rapid increases in oil prices through 1980, and then continued decline and a crash in 1986—Brazil, Chile, Columbia, and Mexico (a major oil exporter) all enjoyed almost identical growth in their real GDPs; whereas the growth pattern since then has been anything but similar. Not only the domestic political climate, but also the fiscal and monetary policies as well as trade and debt management strategies, differed among the countries during the last seven or eight years.

Before we discuss the various policy variables that brought about the divergent rates of economic growth in these three regions, let us examine some of the other pertinent data that are presented in Tables 12.4 through 12.7.

Table 12.4 presents data on the average annual growth rate in production by sector. Precious little data are available for the Middle Eastern countries. What is striking is the negative growth in the industrial sector between 1980 and 1992 for Saudi Arabia and the United Arab Emirates (UAE). For Saudi Arabia, even the service sector shrank during the 1980–92 period. Argentina and the Philippines are the only other two countries in the three regions that experienced declines in industrial sectors. Political instability and regional as well as domestic conflicts were the common factors between the four countries. Argentina and the Philippines also witnessed much slower rates of growth in their basic manufacturing than the previous decade. A rather high rate of growth in Saudi agriculture during 1980–92 was due to the concerted efforts to achieve a measure of self-sufficiency in some staples, despite excessive costs of irrigation. Overall, the annual growth rates in sectoral production confirms the real GDP growth rates shown in Table 12.4.

The data set out in Table 12.5 on the percentage distribution of

TABLE 12.4 *Average Annual Growth Rate in Production by Sector*

Country	Agriculture		Industry		MFG*		Services	
	1970–80	1980–92	1970–80	1980–92	1970–80	1980–92	1970–80	1980–92
Middle East								
Egypt	2.8	2.4	9.4	3.9	–	–	17.5	5.8
Iran	–	4.5	–	4.4	–	5.8	–	0.4
Saudi Arabia	5.3	14.0	10.2	–2.9	6.4	8.1	10.3	–0.2
UAE	–	9.1	–	–1.8	–	3.3	–	4.1
East Asia								
China	–	5.4	–	11.1	–	–	–	11.0
Indonesia	4.1	3.1	9.6	6.1	14.0	12.0	7.7	6.8
S. Korea	2.7	1.9	15.2	11.6	17.0	11.9	9.6	9.3
Malaysia	–	3.6	–	8.0	–	10.0	–	5.1
Philippines	4.0	1.0	8.2	–0.2	6.1	0.7	5.1	2.8
Singapore	1.4	–6.6	8.6	6.0	9.7	7.1	8.3	7.3
Thailand	4.4	4.1	9.5	10.1	10.5	10.1	6.8	8.1
Latin America								
Argentina	2.5	1.2	1.9	–0.1	1.3	0.4	2.9	0.6
Brazil	4.2	2.6	9.4	1.4	9.0	1.0	8.0	3.4
Chile	3.1	5.6	0.2	4.2	–0.8	4.2	2.8	5.1
Columbia	4.6	3.2	5.1	4.7	5.8	3.5	5.9	3.1
Mexico	3.2	0.6	7.2	1.6	7.0	2.1	6.3	1.5
Venezuela	3.4	2.6	0.5	2.1	5.7	1.6	6.3	1.7

* = Manufacturing is a sub-set of Industry.
Source: The World Bank, *World Development Report 1994*, Table 2.

GDP need to be studied along with those in Table 12.4. The Middle Eastern economies exhibit very little progress in economic diversification between 1970 and 1992. Shares of basic manufacturing ranged from 7 to 14 percent in 1992 for the region as compared to 16 to 28 percent for East Asia, and 16 to 25 percent for Latin America. Venezuela's production structure remained basically static during the last two decades. Overall, the Latin American countries in general progressed very little in terms of economic diversification when we compare the shares of the sectors between 1970 and 1992. The only real diversification occurred in East Asia.

Perhaps growth in the merchandise trade as well as in 'terms of trade' are good indicators of how nations have used international trade as a vehicle of economic progress and transformation. Table

TABLE 12.5 *Percentage Distribution of GDP in 1970 and 1992*

Country	Agriculture		Industry		MFG*		Service	
	1970	1992	1970	1992	1970	1992	1970	1992
Middle East								
Egypt	29	18	28	30	–	12	42	52
Iran	–	23	–	28	–	14	–	48
Saudi Arabia	6	7	63	52	10	7	31	41
UAE	–	2	–	56	–	9	–	43
East Asia								
China	–	27	–	34	–	–	–	38
Indonesia	2	0	36	23	29	16	62	77
Korea	45	19	19	40	10	21	36	40
Malaysia	26	8	29	45	21	26	45	47
Philippines	29	–	25	–	12	–	46	–
Singapore	30	22	32	33	25	24	39	45
Thailand	2	0	30	38	20	28	68	62
	26	12	25	39	16	28	49	49
Latin America								
Argentina	10	6	44	31	32	22	47	63
Brazil	12	11	38	37	29	25	49	52
Chile	7	–	41	–	26	–	52	–
Columbia	25	16	28	35	21	20	47	49
Mexico	12	8	29	28	22	20	59	63
Venezuela	6	5	39	41	16	16	54	53

* = Manufacturing is a sub-set of Industry.
Source: The World Bank, *World Development Report*, Table 3.

12.6 presents the relevant data for the selected countries. Saudi Arabia is the only country whose average annual growth rate in export became negative during 1980–92. Among the countries that experienced very slow rates of growth in export were Venezuela, Mexico, and Argentina. Saudi Arabia, Argentina, and Venezuela are the three countries that witnessed negative growth in imports. South Korea, the Philippines, Brazil, and Chile are the only countries that enjoyed some improvements in their terms of trade between 1985 and 1992.

When we look at the Table 12.7, which presents data on the values of exports and imports of selected countries between 1979, 1986, and 1993, we can see a little more clearly how their economies expanded during the period. For example, Saudi Arabia's exports halved between 1979 and 1986 with consequent declines in imports. The other major

TABLE 12.6 *Growth of Merchandise Trade (Average Annual Growth Rate)*

Country	Exports		Imports		Terms of trade (1987 = 100)	
	1970–80	1980–92	1970–80	1980–92	1985	1992
Middle East						
Egypt	–2.6	3.1	7.8	–1.2	131	95
Iran	–6.8	14.5	11.0	8.6	160	92
Saudi Arabia	5.7	–2.4	35.9	–6.2	176	83
UAE	4.9	4.8	27.3	1.1	171	87
East Asia						
China	8.7	11.9	11.3	9.2	109	99
Hong Kong	9.7	5.0	7.8	12.6	97	98
Indonesia	7.2	5.6	13.0	4.0	134	92
S. Korea	23.5	11.9	11.6	11.2	103	106
Malaysia	4.8	11.3	3.7	7.9	117	94
Philippines	6.0	3.7	3.3	4.5	93	105
Singapore	4.2	9.9	5.0	8.3	99	97
Thailand	10.3	14.7	5.0	11.5	91	91
Latin America						
Argentina	7.1	2.2	2.3	–1.7	110	110
Brazil	8.5	5.0	4.0	1.5	92	108
Chile	10.4	5.5	2.2	3.5	102	118
Columbia	1.9	12.9	6.0	0.2	140	79
Mexico	13.5	1.6	5.5	3.8	133	120
Venezuela	–11.6	0.6	10.9	–0.6	174	157

Source: The World Bank, *World Development Report 1994*, Table 13.

oil importing countries also saw similar patterns. They somewhat recovered by 1993. By contrast, the most significant increases in trade were recorded by the East Asian nations. Their two-way trade multiplied between 1986 and 1993. Hong Kong, China, South Korea, Malaysia, Singapore, Thailand, and Taiwan saw spectacular rises in their total trade. Per capita GNP figures for the selected countries[8] show that the per capita income of such oil exporting countries as Saudi Arabia dropped from over $12,000 in 1983 to around $7,500 in 1992 (and to $7,000 by the end of 1995 (Reed and Rossant, 1995)), Hong Kong and Singapore saw their figures shoot up from $6,000 to over $15,000 during the same period. This pattern was repeated for most of the other East Asian economies. It seems all OPEC members witnessed shrinkages in their per capita incomes over the last two decades. The

TABLE 12.7 *Total Exports and Imports of Selected Countries (U.S.$ billions)*

Country	Exports			Imports		
	1979	1986	1993	1979	1986	1993
Middle East						
Egypt	1.8	2.2	2.2	3.8	8.7	8.2
Iran	13.4	13.3*	–	9.7	10.5	–
Saudi Arabia	63.4	20.2	30.2	24.5	19.1	28.2
UAE	13.7	12.4	24.8†	7.0	6.4	19.5
East Asia						
China	13.6	31.4	91.0	15.6	43.4	103.1
Hong Kong	15.1	35.4	135.2	17.1	35.4	138.7
Indonesia	15.6	16.1	36.8	7.2	10.7	28.1
S. Korea	15.1	34.7	82.2	20.3	31.6	83.8
Malaysia	11.1	13.8	47.1	7.8	10.8	45.7
Philippines	4.6	4.8	11.1	6.6	5.4	18.7
Singapore	14.2	22.5	74.0	17.6	25.5	85.2
Thailand	5.3	8.9	37.2	7.2	9.2	46.2
Taiwan	16.1	39.6	84.7	14.8	24.2	77.1
Latin America						
Argentina	7.8	6.9	13.1	6.7	4.7	16.8
Brazil	15.2	22.3	38.6	19.8	15.6	27.7
Chile	3.9	4.2	9.2	4.8	3.4	11.1
Columbia	3.4	5.1	7.1	3.4	3.9	9.8
Mexico	9.0	16.3	30.2	12.1	12.0	50.1
Venezuela	14.3	8.7	14.1	10.7	8.5	12.2

*for 1985
†for 1992
Source: International Monetary Fund, *International Financial Statistics Yearbook 1995*, pp. 124–131.

progress in economic transformation has been a lot slower for the Latin American countries, yet better than that achieved by the Middle East. It is instructive to examine the policy variables that have brought such divergent economic results in the three regions.

Middle East

In the 1970s and early 1980s, development experts kept themselves busy worrying about how the Middle East's OPEC members would be able to absorb their almost 'unlimited' surplus petrodollars without disrupting the global economy. Some even classified these countries into 'high absorbing' and 'low absorbing' countries (Amuzegar, 1983). Algeria, Indonesia, Iran, Iraq, Nigeria, and Venezuela were grouped under the first category, and Kuwait, Libya, Oman, Qatar, Saudi Arabia, and the UAE under the latter (Amuzegar, 1983, p. 45). Yet, a decade and a half later, a good many of these economies, especially the ones studied here, are worse off than in 1983. Let us look at some of the reasons why.

Saudi Arabia did embark on a large scale infrastructure development and the establishment of various petro-chemical complexes. It also made progress in the development of its agriculture in the late 1970s and early 1980s. However, many of these projects were ill conceived and resulted in sheer wastage of surplus petrodollars. Foreign workers were brought in to do all the manual and skilled work, while the natives busied themselves with counting money. The expatriate workers were made to feel unwelcome and, as such, they had no stake in their work. A whole generation of Saudis—and for that matter, the Kuwaitis and others in the Gulf—grew up in an atmosphere of sheer luxury and pleasure without developing any work ethic. In the early 1990s, Saudis represented only 4 percent of the workforce in the non-oil industrial sector and 12 percent in the service sector (Allen, 1995) in that country. In neighboring Kuwait, where foreign residents outnumbered Kuwaitis by 1.1 million to 695,000, the government employed 93 percent of the 166,000 Kuwaitis in the labor force (Reed, 1996). A similar situation exists in UAE. Iran is still trying to recover from the eight-year war with Iraq and the U.S. embargo. Iraq continues to regress to the pre-oil economy under economic embargo by the rest of the world. Jordan's economy is tied to the oil wealth of its neighbors and when they suffer, Jordan also does poorly.

Between 1980 and 1991, Saudi Arabia purchased $143 billion of arms, Iraq, $91 billion, and tiny Kuwait, $8 billion, according to the U.S. Department of Commerce estimates.[9] These estimates do not take into account the cost of Operation Desert Storm, which ran into hundreds of billions of dollars. Saudi Arabia alone had to dish out $55 billion to support the operation (Reed and Rossant, 1995).

Lack of coherent and serious economic policies along with the still-high inflows of oil revenues have made these nations complacent. Egypt has become dependent on foreign economic aid, including remittances from its citizens in the Gulf. Its economy is going nowhere in particular. As a matter of fact, excluding Israel, the entire Middle East and North Africa, with a population of 270 million, exports fewer manufactured goods than does Finland, a country with only 5 million people. Per capita income in the region has been falling at the rate of 2 percent per year since 1986 (Rossant, Albrecht and Sandler, 1995). The fact that the two-way trade and GNPs of these nations move up and down with oil price changes and demand, is a clear indication that the region's economic transformation has not yet begun in earnest. Investment as percentage of GDP for these nations have been significantly lower than those of East Asian nations in recent years.[10]

East Asia

From the late 1960s onwards, the East Asian nations, especially Taiwan and South Korea, embarked on economic development with dynamic programs for the growth of their agriculture sectors and then shifted to labor-based technologies to promote exports (Ranis, 1995). This strategy lowered inequalities in income and served as a significant stimulus to further economic growth (Birdsall, Ross and Sabot, 1995). From the start, these nations also adopted a strategy to improve literacy and education, beginning with primary education, followed by emphasis on vocational training and skills, and then graduate-level science and technology-oriented education (Ranis 1995).

Public policies in East Asian countries have been geared to adapting to the changing needs of time, and to weathering external economic shocks. Their governments have stood ready to provide fiscal, monetary, trade, and industrial policies that are conducive to accelerated investments and economic growth. Import substitutions, trade liberalization, and export promotion policies were pursued at appropriate times in their drive towards modernization (Krueger, 1997).

Hong Kong and Singapore are special cases, the former being a British colony at China's doorstep serving as a transhipment center for the Chinese Western trade; while the latter is a tiny city-state pursuing systematic policies of import substitution followed by export-based economic activities and attracting massive inflows of FDIs. Singapore's liberal trade policies made it a transhipment center for ship-to-ship transfers of legal as well as illegal products.

Trade liberalization policies by Malaysia, Thailand, and Indonesia in the mid- to late-1980s are bringing results in terms of rapid economic development induced by heavy inflows of FDIs. The Philippines, too, is now beginning to gear up to meet the standards set by its neighboring countries.

Latin America

Until recently, most Latin American countries followed inward-oriented trade policies that led to the production of poor quality import substitution manufactured goods. In the process, these nations amassed massive amounts of foreign debt that they found difficult to service (Sachs, 1990, v. 2). Lack of discipline in fiscal and monetary policies, along with over-regulation of trade and investment policies, not only slowed down the economies, but also brought unprecedented levels of inflation into the region. It is only in the last decade that the Latin Americans began to enact reforms in their economic policies. Argentina embarked on reforms beginning in July 1989 with the return of civilian rule (Solanet, 1994). Even though Brazil has been emphasizing export-led economic growth, it has crippled its economy with protective regulations of domestic industries. Its economy suffers from over capacity in every sector (Turner, 1992) and its products cannot compete in the global market.

Chile's economic growth began with the economic reforms that were introduced during the eighteen-year rule of General Pinnochet. With continuation of those policies, economic growth is still continuing. Columbia has drastically reduced import tariffs, from over 60 percent in 1980 to nearly 20 percent at present.[11] However, some of these countries have reimposed trade restrictions with the recent Mexican peso crisis. The Venezuelan economy still resembles the oil economies of the Middle East. Oil continues to account for around 90 percent of its exports and manufactured goods account for over 80 percent of its imports. The IMF expects some turnaround in its economy soon.[12]

Trade liberalization and privatization policies that are increasingly being instituted in Latin America may not be enough for bringing in the sustainable level of high economic growth which East Asia has already achieved. This is because Latin America still suffers from a high level of income inequalities. Until major reforms are undertaken to remove this hurdle, economic prosperity of the region may remain elusive.

Conclusion

Economic performance of the nations in the Middle East, East Asia, and Latin America has been varied, not because of differences in their indigenous resources and capabilities, but because of policies their governments chose to pursue. East Asia emphasized economic growth based on better human resource management and income equality; the Middle East emphasized filling the coffers of its selective citizens at the expense of expatriate workers; and the Latin Americans paid scant attention to its impoverished majority. The experience of East Asia shows that policies which promote economic prosperity for the majority are likely to bear lasting fruit.

The prospect for sustaining economic growth appears to be rather bleak for both the Middle East and Latin America; the former because the continued inflows of oil revenue will fail to inspire the government to develop appropriate measures which would instill a work ethic in its native workforce. From recent accounts, it appears that the Kuwaitis have gone back to the extravagance of the pre-Iraqi invasion period. Latin America will continue to have a hard time because, due to the lack of social reforms, it is unable to garner the support and enthusiasm of the masses that are needed to ensure successful economic transformation.

References

AGARWALA, A. N. and SINGH, S. P. (1963) *The Economics of Underdevelopment*, Oxford University Press, New York.

AGGARWAL, R. and AGMON, T. (1990) The International Success of Developing Country Firms: Role of Government Directed Comparative Advantage, *Management International Review*, Second Quarter Vol. 30, No. 2, 163–180.

ALAM, M. S. (1989) The South Korean 'Miracle': Examining the Mix of Government and Markets, *Journal of Developing Areas*, Vol. 23, No. 2, January, 233–257.

ALLEN, R. (1995) Privatization: Deep-rooted Difficulties, *The Financial Times Survey*, December 20, p. III.

AMUZEGAR, J. (1983) *Oil Exporters' Economic Development in an Interdependent World*, Washington, DC: The International Monetary Fund, April, Occasional paper 18.

BAUER, P. T. and YAMEY, B. S. (1957) *The Economics of Underdeveloped Countries*, University of Chicago Press, Chicago.

BIRDSALL, N., ROSS, D. and SABOT, R. (1995) Inequality and Growth Reconsidered: Lessons from East Asia, *World Bank Economic Review*, Vol. 9, No. 3, September, 477–508.

CHEN, T. J., and TANG, D. P. (1987) Comparing Technical Efficiency Between Import Substitution-Oriented and Export-Oriented Foreign Firms in a Developing Economy, *Journal of Development Economics*, Vol. 26, No. 2, August, 277–289.

CHU, W. W. (1994) Import Substitution and Export-Led Growth: A Study of Taiwan's Petrochemical Industry, *World Development*, May, Vol. 22, No. 5, 781–794.

DOLLAR, D. (1990) Patterns of Productivity Growth in South Korean Manufacturing Industries, 1963–1979, *Journal of Development Economics*, October, Vol. 33, No. 2, 309–327.

DUNNING, J. H. (1981) Explaining the International Direct Investment Position of Countries: Towards a Dynamic or Developmental Approach, *Weltwirtschaftliches Archiv*, No. 119, 30–64.

DUNNING, J. H. (1986) The Investment Development Cycle Revisited, *Weltwirtschaftliches Archiv*, No. 122, 67–77.

DUNNING, J. H. (1988) *Explaining International Production*, Unwin Hyman, London.

DUNNING, J. H. (1992) The Global Economy, Domestic Governance Strategies and Transnational Corporations: Interactions and Policy Recommendations, *Transnational Corporations*, Vol. 1, No. 3, December, 7–45.

DUNNING, J. H. (1993) *Multinational Enterprises and the Global Economy*, Addison-Wesley, Wokingham, England and Reading, MA.

DUNNING, J. H. (1994) Reevaluating the Benefits of Foreign Direct Investment, *Transnational Corporations*, Vol. 3, No. 1, February, 23–52.

DUNNING, J. H. (1995) Reappraising the Eclectic Paradigm in an Age of Alliance Capitalism, *Journal of International Business Studies*, Vol. 26, No. 3, 461–491.

DUNNING, J. H., and NARULA, R. (1994) Transpacific FDI and the Investment Development Path: The Record Assessed, *University of South Carolina Essays in International Business*, No. 10, May.

DUNNING, J. H. and NARULA, R. (1996) *Foreign Direct Investment and Governments: Catalysts for Economic Restructuring*, Routledge, London and New York.

ECKES, A. E. (1993) International Trade Paradox, *Vital Speeches*, September 15, Vol. 59, No. 23, 734–736.

EDWARD, S. (1989) Debt Crisis, Trade Liberalization, Structural Adjustment, and Growth: Some Policy Considerations, *Contemporary Policy Issues*, July, Vol. 7, No. 3, 30–41.

GRABOWSKI, R. (1994) Import Substitution, Export Promotion, and the State in Economic Development, *Journal of Developing Areas*, July, Vol. 28, No. 4, 535–553.

HELLEINER, G. K. (1972) *International Trade and Economic Development*, Penguin Books, New York.

International Monetary Fund (1995) *International Financial Statistics Yearbook 1995*, IMF, Washington, DC.

International Monetary Fund (various dates) *World Economic Outlook*, IMF, Washington, DC.

JOHNSON, H. G. (1967) *Economic Policies Towards Less Developed Countries*, Frederick A. Praeger Publishers, New York.

KRUEGER, A. O. (1997) Trade Policy and Economic Development: How We Learn, *The American Economic Review*, Vol. 87, No. 1, March, 1–22.

LOMAX, D. (1988) Follow the Tiger! *Banking World*, October, Vol. 6, No. 10, 3841.

MEIER, G. M. (1970) *Leading Issues in Economic Development*, 2nd edn, Oxford University Press, New York.

MYRDAL, G. (1968) *Asian Drama: An Enquiry into the Poverty of Nations*, Pantheon, New York.

NELSON, R. (1994) Ignore the Hot Air, *World Trade*, July, Vol. 7, No. 6, 18–20.

NURKSE, R. (1953) *Problems of Capital Formation in Underdeveloped Countries*, Oxford University Press, New York.

PAUS, E. (1989) The Political Economy of Manufactured Export Growth: Argentina and Brazil in the 1970s, *Journal of Developing Areas*, Vol. 23, No. 2, January, 173–199.

PEARSON, L. B. (1969) *Partners in Development: Report of the Commission on International Development*, Praeger Publishers, New York.

PREBISCH, R. (1950) *The Economic Development of Latin America and its Principal Problems*, United Nations Economic Commission for Latin America, Lake Success.

RANIS, G. (1995) Another Look at the East Asian Miracle, *World Bank Economic Review*, September, Vol. 9, No. 3, 509–534.

REED, S. and ROSSANT, J. (1995) A Dangerous Spark in the Oil Fields, *Business Week*, November 27, 54–55.

REED, S. (1996) Kuwait Looks at its Soul—and Isn't Happy, *Business Week*, January 29, 49–50.

ROSSANT, J., ALBRECHT, K. and SANDLER, N. (1995) Can the Mideast Find its Way Out of an Economic Desert? *Business Week*, November 6, 64.

ROSTOW, W. W. (1952) *The Process of Economic Growth*, W. W. Norton & Co., New York.

SACHS, J. D., (ed.) (1990) *Developing Country Debt and Economic Performance, Vol. 2*, The University of Chicago Press, Chicago.

SOLANET, M. A. (1994) Privatization: The Long Road to Success in Argentina, *Business Forum*, Winter/Spring, Vol. 19, No. 1, 2, 28–31.

TURNER, R. (1992) Brazil: Industry—An End to Protectionism, *Institutional Investor*, July, Vol. 26, No. 8, 516–517.

U.S. Department of Commerce (various dates) *Statistical Abstract of the United States*, U.S. Department of Commerce, Bureau of the Census, Washington, DC.

World Bank (1993) *The East Asian Miracle: Economic Growth and Public Policy*, Oxford University Press, New York.

World Bank (various dates) *World Development Report*, World Bank, Washington, DC.

Notes

1. See Myrdal (1968), Vol. 1, Ch. 1, p. 42.
2. See Amuzegar (1983) and the semi-yearly issues of the *World Economic Outlook*, prepared by the IMF, and the yearly issues of the *World Development Report*, prepared by the World Bank.
3. Conference paper referred to in Dunning and Narula (1996), Ch. 1, p. 1.
4. See Dunning 1981, 1986, 1988, 1993; Narula 1993, 1995; and Duning and Narula 1994 and 1996.
5. See Dunning and Narula (1996), Ch. 1. Stage 1 is a situation where the L (location) specific advantages of a country is weak to attract inward direct investment (IDI), except for the ones arising out of possession of natural resources. At Stage 2, IDI starts to rise (mostly in import-substitution industries), while outward direct investment (ODI) remains low or negligible. At Stage 3, the country experiences gradual decrease in the rate of growth of IDI and an increase in the rate of growth of ODI. At Stage 4, ODI stock exceeds or equals the IDI stock, and the rate of growth of ODI is faster than the rate for IDI. At Stage 5 the NOI position of a country first falls and later fluctuates around zero level.
6. See *International Financial Statistics Yearbook 1995*, p. 181.
7. See World Bank, *East Asian Miracle: Economic Growth and Public Policy* (1993).
8. See the *World Development Report*, various issues.
9. See *Statistical Abstract of the U.S.*, various issues.
10. See *International Financial Statistics Year Book 1995*, pp. 171–173.
11. See *World Economic Outlook*, October 1995, p. 46.
12. See *World Economic Outlook*, October 1995, p. 15.

13

Third World Multinationals Revisited: New Developments and Theoretical Implications[1]

JOHN H. DUNNING, ROGER VAN HOESEL AND RAJNEESH NARULA

This† chapter suggests, and presents evidence, that multinational enterprises (MNEs) from Third World countries are now augmenting their foreign investments in other developing countries, by locating their technology and/or knowledge intensive activities in the advanced industrial countries. The chapter explores the reasons for this and argues that the traditional explanation for Third World NME activity needs to be reassessed.

Introduction

Beginning with Lecraw (1977), the phenomena of outward FDI by Third World MNEs (TWMNEs) was the subject of considerable research in the late 1970s and early 1980s.[2] Much of this research sketched a description of a 'new' kind of MNE that—so it was argued—differed considerably from that of the 'conventional' industrialized country MNE, in terms of its competitive or ownership (O) advantages, motivation, geographical direction and mode of overseas activity. In the context of the current study we identify such MNEs as the 'first wave investors'. Concurrently with this initial evaluation of MNEs from developing countries, several attempts were made to accommodate their activities within the existing theory of MNE activity. Two strands are woven through the literature. The first, proposed by Lall (1983) and Wells (1983) offered an theoretical justification for the specific characteristics of TWMNEs. The second, and more general, explanation put forward by Dunning (1981, 1988) was the investment development path (IDP), which offered, *inter alia*, an explanation of which countries would engage in outward FDI, and how the level and nature of this activity might be related to, and change with, their economic development.

Over a decade has passed since these studies were conducted, and, while recent research has confirmed some of the earlier findings (e.g. Tolentino 1993) there is increasing evidence that there has been a fundamental shift in both the character and motivation of much outward FDI from certain developing countries, which we shall argue constitutes the 'second wave'. The first objective of this chapter is to evaluate the outward FDI activity of developing countries in order to determine whether any distinct differences have emerged among the primary outward investors. To what extent have the forces behind globalization led to a change in the propensity of developing countries to spawn MNEs that engage in outward FDI? We contend that the 'new' wave of outward FDI reflect changes in the structure of the world economy that are a result of globalization and regionalization of economic activity. These phenomena are associated with, *inter alia*, (a) dramatic technological advances within sectors, and (b) the liberalization of markets, as well as the establishment of regional trading blocks. It is suggested here that these changes have impacted countries to different extents, and that the existence of a second wave of TWMNEs may simply represent a subset of the first wave whose home economies have responded more successfully to globalization.

The second objective of this chapter is to evaluate the current version of the IDP as set out in Dunning and Narula (1994, 1996) and Narula (1996)[3] in light of the evidence reviewed here. In other words, to what extent can existing theory explain the second wave of outward FDI from developing countries? We hope to demonstrate that the second wave is complementary to the first wave, and is simply and intermediate stage of evolution of outward FDI activities as the home country moves along its IDP. Such outward FDI activity has been a result of government-assisted upgrading of location-specific advantages of the home country, which in turn has helped upgrade the competitive advantages of their firms. Moreover, while these ownership-specific advantages remain primarily country-of-origin specific, they are increasingly being supplemented by FDI intended to augment rather than exploit such advantages.

Changing Characteristics of FDI

In this section we shall examine whether, and to what extent, the significance and pattern of TWMNE activity has changed in both relative and absolute terms since the 1980s. One of the primary difficulties in examining the evolution of outward FDI from developing countries as a group arises from the quality and standards of data availability. While outward FDI data for developed countries are, by and large, the same regardless of source, that relating to developing countries are less reliable. For instance, Dunning (1993) and Narula (1996) utilized estimates based on the U.S. Department of Commerce which suggest that total outward FDI stock from developing countries in 1980 was $15.3 billion, while UNCTAD (1994) and Tolentino (1993) place the figure at a fifth of that level, or $3.4 billion. Even more curiously, discrepancies exist in publications by the same source; for example, the estimate for 1980 published in UNCTAD (1995) gives the same stock figure at $6.1 billion, twice that of UNCTAD (1994), one year previously. Nonetheless, although such inconsistencies makes the relative significance of developing country outward FDI vis-a-vis total outward FDI stock vary considerably according to the data source, the patterns of change over time at the more aggregate level are similar.

Table 13.1 gives details of the changing level of outward FDI stock[4] by major geographical regions and countries for 1980 and 1993, based on *adjusted* UNCTAD data[5] and classifications. Between 1980 and 1993, outward FDI from developing countries as a group grew from $4.8 billion to $108.4 billion. In terms of their significance of total outward FDI stock outstanding, these countries increased their share from 1.0 percent in 1980 to 5.1 percent in 1992. It is by now an often cited statistic that FDI activity has grown faster than GDP or trade on a world-wide basis (UNCTC, 1991). As might be expected of developing economies however, their ownership advantages are insufficient to engage in outward FDI at quite the same pace; in consequence, exports remain much more important to these economies than FDI activities. Table 13.1 indicates that outward FDI stock as a percentage of GDP rose from 0.2 percent in 1980 to 3.1 percent in 1993. In contrast, the share of exports in the GDP of developing countries was almost 17 percent in 1993.

These data would seem to imply that an increasing number of developing countries are engaging in FDI. To what extent is this true for all developing countries? Table 13.2 presents details of changes in the mean and standard deviation of GDP and outward FDI stock of several sub-groups of developing countries for two periods. The classifications are based on World Bank (1994) estimates, and roughly comply with the first three stages of the IDP. For the low income countries (Group 1), Table 13.2 suggests that there is a greater propensity for least developed countries to engage in outward FDI, with mean outward FDI having increased by a factor of 11, despite

TABLE 13.1 *Significance of Regions in World GDP and Outward FDI Stocks, 1980 and 1993*

	1980				1993			
	OFDI stock (U.S.$ millions)	FDI share in total (%)	GDP share in total (%)	FDI/GDP (%)	OFDI stock (U.S.$ millions)	FDI share in total (%)	GDP share in total (%)	FDI/GDP (%)
Developed*	503,327	99.0	79.1	6.54	2,017,100	94.9	82.50	10.99
Developing	4850	1.0	20.9	0.24	108,358	5.1	15.87	3.07
Latin America	2152	0.4	8.6	0.26	10,441	0.5	6.00	0.78
Africa	258	0.1	2.5	0.11	1095	0.1	1.03	0.48
Asia	1777	0.3	9.7	0.19	90,579	4.3	8.58	4.75
Total	508,177				2,125,460			
	As % of total developing				*As % of total developing*			
Developing countries excl. middle east	4220	87.0			107,530	99.2		
Asian NIEs	1039	21%			71,860	66%		

*Developed countries include all OECD except Mexico.
Source: UNCTAD (1995) (adjusted, see Note 5), World Bank (1995), Dunning and Narula (1995).

TABLE 13.2 *Evidence of Catch-up and Convergence among Developing Countries in Outward FDI and GDP Per Capita*

	1980			1992		
	Mean	SD	SD/Mean	Mean	SD	SD/Mean
Group 1 (low income; N = 25)						
GDP	439.1	365.6	0.83	458.6	714.9	1.56
Outward stock	0.1	0.266	2.98	1.11	2.87	2.59
Group 2 (low-middle; N = 24)						
GDP	1123.5	424.3	0.38	1471.6	651.7	0.44
Outward stock	1.3	1.9	1.46	8.2	15.7	1.91
Group 3 (upper-middle and high income; N = 12)						
GDP	3788.2	1536.7	0.41	7101.8	5359.8	0.75
Outward stock	28.5	81.1	2.84	914.2	2052	2.24
East Asian NIEs (N = 4)						
GDP	3659.6	1920.2	0.52	12,901	5718	0.44
Outward stock	70.2	134.3	1.91	2592.2	3131.5	1.21
Group 3 excluding NIEs (N = 8)						
GDP	3861.8	1440.4	0.37	4202.2	1517.5	0.36
Outward stock	4.7	10.9	2.32	75.3	79.5	1.06

Source: as Table 13.1.

the fact that mean GDP levels of this group have experienced almost no change. However, the high standard deviation would indicate that this is a phenomenon associated with a relatively few countries. The same would seem to be true for Group 2 countries. This data would suggest that while more countries are engaging in outward FDI at an earlier stage in their development, this appears to be relatively insignificant. Indeed, examining the mean and standard deviation for the two periods in Table 13.2, it seems that it is only for Group 3 countries and the Asian NIEs that outward FDI seems to have increased to any significant level and has done so uniformly across countries. In other words, outward FDI by developing countries is dominated by a selected number of countries in each group.

While it certainly appears that outward FDI, even by the least developed countries, has become the rule rather than the exception, such investments remain rather piecemeal and relatively insignificant. In fact, in several cases this increase in outward FDI may represent flight capital prior to economic liberalization and the easing of restrictions on capital flows, while in others, such as oil exporting economies, large portfolio investments are often recorded as direct investments. Selecting the countries with outward investment greater than $100 million in 1980 or $250 million but excluding oil-exporting economies, we are able to identify the major source developing countries: These are listed in Table 13.3. Comparing the data in this table to those in Table 13.2, it is interesting to observe that of the 25 countries in Group 1, China and India account for well over 90 percent of all outward FDI from this group in 1993. There is considerably less concentration in Group 2, where the leading two countries account for just over 50 percent of this group (Table 13.2). In Group 3 (excluding NIEs) there is relatively little variation between countries, which are almost all relatively large outward investors, as might be expected of countries in Stage 3 of the IDP.

It is particularly noteworthy, therefore, that the concentration of TWMNE activity has remained within the same few home countries over time. If one excludes oil-exporting Middle East economies, these 15 countries accounted for 93.6 percent of all such FDI in 1980, and 93.1 percent in 1993 (Table 13.3). Nonetheless, as Table 13.3 illustrates, there have been significant changes as to *which* countries are the primary outward investors. In 1980, the top four home countries in terms of outstanding stock were Argentina, Brazil, Singapore and Malaysia; these countries accounted for 37.4 percent of all TWMNE activity, whereas by 1993, the top four were Hong Kong, Taiwan, China and Singapore, which accounted for 66 percent of stock in that year. Table 13.3 is illustrative of at least three facts: (1) that a relatively small group of developing countries are responsible for most TWMNE

TABLE 13.3 *Outward FDI for 15 Most Significant Home Countries, 1980 and 1993**

	(U.S.\$, millions)		Share of total DC OFDI (%)	
	1980	1993	1980	1993
Group 1				
China	40	11,802	0.82	10.89
India	130	601	2.68	0.55
Group 2				
Brazil	652	4651	13.44	4.29
Colombia	137	476	2.82	0.44
Philippines	171	128	3.53	0.12
Thailand	13	933	0.27	0.86
Group 3				
Mexico	136	1039	2.80	0.96
Argentina	990	960	20.41	0.89
Chile	42	1144	0.87	1.06
Venezuela	185	1995	3.81	1.84
Hong Kong	148	41,215	3.05	38.04
Korea	142	5555	2.93	5.13
Malaysia	414	4516	8.54	4.17
Singapore	652	6236	13.44	5.75
Taiwan	97	18,854	2.00	17.40
Total	3949	100,105	81	92
As % of developing less Middle East (see Table 13.1)			93.6	93.1

*Data for each year represent estimates for closest years available.
Source: as Table 13.1.

activity; (2) that while this core group has not changed, third world outward FDI is much more concentrated in 1993 than it was in 1980; and (3) within this group there has been a considerable change in the countries which are responsible for the lion's share of outward activity. It is interesting to note that the dominant countries of the early 1980s, or the 'first wave' investors (primarily South American) seem to have lost ground relative to the dominant investors in the early 1990s, which tend to come from Asian NIEs and 'new' NIEs.

One of the features of TWMNE activity as charted in the first wave literature was the direction and motivation of FDI, compared with 'conventional' MNEs. Table 13.4 summarizes the most salient

TABLE 13.4 *Characteristics of Outward FDI at Different Stages of the IDP*

	'First wave' (Stage 2)	'Second wave' (Stage 3)	Conventional' MNEs (Stages 4 and 5)
Destination	Regional FDI: neighboring countries and other developing countries	Majority still regional, but expanding to a global basis	Global basis
Motivation	Resource seeking and market seeking in developing countries	*In developing countries:* resource and market seeking *In industrial countries:* asset-seeking and market seeking	Efficiency-seeking MNE motivation aimed at optimizing use of each country's comparative and competitive advantages
Type of outward FDI	*In developing countries:* natural-asset intensive, small scale production in light industries (Heksher-Ohlin, moving towards undifferentiated Smithian industries	*In developing countries:* natural asset intensive sectors as in first wave; *In industrialized countries:* (a) assembly-type, market-seeking FDI primarily in Smithian industries (b) asset-seeking investment in Schumpeterian industries	Capital- and knowledge-intensive (Schumpeterian) sectors capital/labor ratio dependent on natural/created assets of host.
Ownership advantages	**Primarily country-of-origin specific:** Fundamental Oa advantages, no Ot advantages	**Both firm- and country-specific**	**Mainly firm-specific:** Advanced Oa and Ot advantages
Examples of ownership advantages (adapted and modified version of Lall (1983) page 7)	1. Conglomerate group ownership 2. Technology (mostly adapted) 3. Management adapted to Third World conditions 4. Low-cost inputs (including managerial and technical personnel) 5. 'Ethnic' advantages	1. Conglomerate group ownership 2. Management adapted to third world conditions 3. Low cost inputs (including managerial and technical personnel) 4. 'Ethnic' advantages 5. Some product differentiation 6. Limited marketing skills 7. Vertical control over factor/product markets 8. Subsidized capital	1. Large size—economies of scale 2. Access to capital markets 3. Technology 4. product differentiation 5. Marketing know-how 6. Cross-country management skills 7. Globally efficient intra-firm activity 8. Vertical control over factor/product markets

characteristics of outward FDI by both groups of MNEs. Much of the empirical work indicated a strong and marked trend for TWMNEs to focus their investments in neighboring and other countries which were at a similar or an earlier stage of their development. This preference was a direct result of their lack of international experience. Furthermore, their O advantages were of a type most suited to these L advantages (and often *induced* by them), and were based on technologies at the end of their product life cycles. In other words, these MNEs had few transaction-type ownership (Ot) advantages, and only the most basic form of asset-type O advantages (Oa)—namely, those that derive from the efficient acquisition and adaptation of imported technologies[6] (see Table 13.4). These O advantages were enhanced by the prevalence of import-substituting, inward looking policy regimes amongst most developing countries which encouraged small scale production, typical of that suited to these TWMNEs. The O advantages of these firms were primarily country-specific, determined by the market distortions introduced by the home country policies, and only sustainable where similar L advantages existed in other countries.

Moreover, as Table 13.5 shows, with almost no exception, at the beginning of the 1980s, a majority of the outward FDI was directed towards other developing countries, most often neighbouring countries. While some asset-seeking investment in industrialized countries was undertaken,[7] it was relatively minor with many large investments representing flight capital, as entrepreneurs utilized overseas subsidiaries to circumvent home country restrictions on outbound international capital movements. In particular cases, a large proportion of what is statistically recorded as outward FDI flows represents investments by the affiliates of 'conventional' MNEs. The case of Hong Kong outward FDI to China is an example of this. The PRC accounted for over half of Hong Kong total outward FDI stock in 1995, and two thirds of total inward stock in China. Although more recent data are not available, Chen (1983) estimated that just over 50 percent of outward FDI from Hong Kong was by affiliates of conventional MNEs in 1981.[8] A similar situation also exists in the case of Malaysia and Singapore.

From Table 13.5 we observe that for most countries in the list, developed countries have become a much more important target. This increase in activity in developed countries can only have occurred if either the O advantages of investing firms had increased to the extent that they were now able to compete with conventional MNEs on their home turf, and/or these TWMNEs were engaging in a higher extent of asset-seeking FDI. However, this change has not occurred evenly across developing countries. Cross-referencing Tables 13.3 and

TABLE 13.5 *Geographical Distribution, Outward FDI Stock, Two Periods*

		Developing (%)	Developed (%)
India	1980	91.05	8.95
	1993	77.53	22.47
China	1981	35.00	65.00
	1992	31.57	68.43
Hong Kong	1980	91.65	8.35
	1990	82.08	17.80
Argentina	1980	13.23	86.77
	1990	21.46	78.44
Brazil	1980	25.92	74.08
	1990	45.93	54.07
Chile	1990	89.00	11.00
	1992	93.80	6.20
Colombia	1980	78.00	22.00
	1990	75.40	24.60
Mexico	1980	23.00	77.00
	1990	7.00	93.00
Korea	1978	75.90	24.10
	1994	49.00	51.00
Taiwan	1978	79.00	21.00
	1994	77.20	22.80

Source: As Table 13.1.

13.5, the only countries for which the level of their outward FDI in developed countries was significant and increasing in importance (*viz.* over 20 percent of their total outward FDI or greater than $100 million in 1993) were Hong Kong, Korea, Taiwan, China and Singapore.[9] These form the core of the group that comprise the 'second wave' investors. Prominent first-wave countries such as India, Philippines, Argentina and Colombia did not show any significant increase in either the level of the total outward FDI between the early 1980s and 1990s, nor a significant shift towards developed country hosts.

That these first-wave countries also experienced very low or negative economic growth rates, and the second wave countries experienced rapid growth over this time period is no coincidence. Indeed, in the next section we shall examine in greater detail how economic changes due to globalization and the liberalization of markets have directly affected the extent and nature of outward FDI activity. In other words, we will identify the underlying developments that have resulted in changes in the L advantages and the O advantages of the firms from these countries and the mechanisms that caused these changes.

Background of the Second Wave

To explain the second wave of TWMNE activity, let us first return to the IDP. According to the IDP, countries at Stage 2 are home to firms engaging in elementary outward FDI. As they acquire experience in their international operations (thereby improving their O advantages), and as the L advantages of the country improve over time, they engage in an increasing extent of outward FDI. The interaction between FDI activities and development that underpins the concept of the IDP is essentially idiosyncratic and unique to each individual country. Nonetheless, there is a general pattern that, as these countries develop, they enter and progress through Stage 3 of the IDP; namely, these MNEs gain further experience in international business activities and develop competitive advantages that can be increasingly exploited in overseas markets. Indeed, as we have seen from the evidence given in the previous section and elsewhere (see e.g. Hikino and Amsden, 1994), many of the first wave home countries have remained in Stage 2, and have experienced little or no economic growth or improvement in their L advantages. It comes as no surprise, therefore, that their competitive advantages of their MNEs have not evolved either. Conversely, the second-wave countries have recorded rapid economic growth.

This has been further enhanced by the fundamental (but gradual) change in the structure of the world economy, much of which is often generalized as being a direct result of globalization. These changes can be considered from the developing country perspective as being of two kinds. First, there are those that have been largely *exogenous* to these countries, but which have affected their economic structure both as members of the world economic order and as individual economies. Whereas industrialized countries have been experiencing economic, technological and structural convergence, the majority of developing countries, rather than converge with the lead countries, have tended to diverge (Dunning and Narula, 1997).[10] This simultaneous process of convergence and divergence has impacted on firms by creating broader and more competitive markets across countries due to similar consumption and production patterns . This has had two effects on the converging countries: (1) Firms in each country are presented with larger markets, and this has led to developing global technologies that have large economies of scale and high minimum efficient scale; and (2) technologies have also converged, such that firms in certain sectors are now competing not just with other firms in the same country, but with other firms in the same country but not necessarily in the same industry (Cantwell and Sanna Randaccio, 1990). In other words, firms need to have competitive advantages that are globally viable, rather than domestically or regionally so, and this has been further enhanced by the innovation of space-shrinking technologies (Dunning and Narula, 1997). Although the development of *de facto* and *de jure* economic blocs such as the EU and NAFTA has primarily acted to enhance the positive effects of these developments for their members, they also represent barriers to entry to non-members and to developing countries in particular.

Second, there have been structural changes within individual countries often in direct response to these changes, and as such may be considered as *endogenous* to developing countries. These endogenous changes are primarily associated with the actions and policies of governments. One of the most important of these changes over the past decade or so has been a fundamental shift in the policy orientation of developing countries from a import-substituting role to a export-oriented, outward looking one. The extent of liberalization varies between countries; in some cases it is associated with a more proactive and market facilitating role, while in others it is simply reactive or even laissez-faire. Nonetheless, despite this broad spectrum of policy options, it is safe to generalize that the extent of government intervention in the developing world embraces a much wider spectrum than was the case fifteen years ago, and this variation is equally diverse with regards policy orientation towards MNE activity (see UN, 1995).[11] This fundamental policy shift has led to a decline in the L advantages of developing countries and a subsequent reduction in the country-of-origin-specific O advantages of their firms. We address these issues in greater detail below, before turning to an illustration of two prominent second wave countries, under the heading 'Illustrating the Second Wave: FDI from Korea and Taiwan'.

Stagnation of the Outward FDI from First Wave Countries

As discussed above and in Table 13.4, the O advantages of first wave investors were primarily country- (rather than firm-) specific in nature and based on barriers to entry due to import-substituting regimes. Outward FDI from these countries benefited from similar market conditions in host countries and thus enjoyed similar L-specific competitive advantages overseas. At the same time, such competitive advantages were declining (both at home and abroad), *inter alia* because of the competitive pressures exerted by developed country MNEs which are able to exploit their superior Oa and Ot advantages on a global scale, and which already enjoyed economies of scale and scope. Indeed, this change in economic stance often occurred due to the economic decline of these countries which led to economic restructuring, of which the withdrawal and/or stagnation of their

MNEs from outward FDI activity was symptomatic. Such promising first-wave investors as India, the Philippines, Argentina, Mexico and Colombia are examples of countries which experienced very low or negative GDP growth rates for much of the 1980s.

At first sight, the increase in TWMNE activity directed towards developed countries across both the first-wave and the second-wave home countries (Table 135) despite a decline in competitive advantages of first wave MNEs would seem to be somewhat contradictory. However, the increase in north-south competition due to liberalization has created an imperative to undertake asset-seeking FDI: Firms from these countries must upgrade and augment their domestically based Oa advantages if they are to survive even in their home countries. Globalization, therefore, has shortened the product life cycle concept, and forced these countries to *actively* restructure their economies. O advantages based on obsolete technologies are no longer assets capable of providing economic rent, since firms in a liberalized world must successfully compete with all other firms regardless of location. This, perhaps more than any other fact, helps explain the relatively lower threshold at which developing countries engage in outward FDI, although it remains quite insignificant in absolute terms for Stage 1 countries.

Economic Transformation of the Second Wave Countries

Although the fact that a small subset of the first wave of TWMNEs form the second wave, it is as much the success of the second wave as it is the 'stumbling back' of the first wave that underlies their success. The evolution and growth of MNEs from the second wave countries is, then, not surprising, given their rapid economic restructuring and development.

This industrial reconfiguration has also led to an increasingly geographical spread of outward FDI activity beyond simple regional, comparative advantage-based relocation of production, and is indeed a central feature of the second wave (Table 13.4). This shift towards a more global attitude can be seen as occurring due to two main changes. First, high R&D costs in innovation-intensive sectors have forced MNEs of all nationalities to seek larger markets in order to cover these costs. As the second wave countries have moved along their IDP, and towards more assembly oriented or innovation-intensive sectors, they too have needed to be globally competitive in order to achieve economies of scale. With economic liberalization, this need has been further enhanced—it is no longer sufficient to be regionally competitive, but globally competitive. While it may still be more cost-effective to engage in exporting, there remain strategic benefits of locating some production activity in the major developed country markets, both to avoid protectionist policies as much as to more efficiently develop marketing and service operations.

The second reason is associated with the need of global firms to continually upgrade and augment their O advantages, as innovatory capacity throughout the world becomes more dispersed. The competitive advantages of TWMNEs lie primarily in their ability to co-ordinate activities across sectors (which are transaction-type O advantages), while their asset-type O advantages tend to be in the latter stages of their product life cycles. The technologies underlying these asset-type O advantages were in natural asset intensive and undifferentiated technologies (characteristic of Stage 2 countries), which were relatively easily available through arms-length or joint venture agreements. However, markets for knowledge intensive and cutting edge technologies do not have markets that are as well defined. Furthermore, even where markets do exist, the firms that have proprietary rights to these technologies have become wary of the potential for direct competition with leading second wave firms, and are quite reluctant to provide them (Contractor, 1993). As such TWMNEs are left with the choice of engaging in expensive (and highly uncertain) R&D, or they may seek to acquire innovating capabilities through FDI in developed countries. This theme is also explored in greater depth in the next section.

This dichotomy between the two types of TWMNE activity is not entirely new. In fact a similar debate was prompted by Japan's outward FDI activity particularly during the 1970s, whose outward FDI characteristics at the time were very similar to today's second wave countries (Table 13.4). During the period in question, Japan was in Stage 3 of the IDP (Dunning and Narula, 1994). Indeed, the similarity of Japanese outward FDI in the 1970s to those of Korea and Taiwan currently is not entirely coincidental. It is worth noting that as Japan has progressed to Stage 4 and 5, the differences between Japanese MNEs and the then- 'conventional' MNEs which were highlighted by Kojima (1978) have essentially disappeared. In other words, the evolution of developing country outward FDI and the 'unique' characteristics of the first and second wave outward FDI largely represent the natural evolution of MNE activity as their home countries and experience with overseas production increases. As Table 13.4 shows, the characteristics of the second wave could be regarded as an intermediate stage between 'conventional', industrialized country MNE activity and first wave outward FDI by TWMNEs.

Underlying these differences between the first and second wave is the role of governments in determining the rate and direction of the economic growth and restructuring, all of whom are regarded as East

Asian NIEs or 'new' NIEs. Much has been written about these 'East Asian miracles' (World Bank, 1993; Wade, 1990), most of which has emphasized the primary role of governments in fostering economic development and restructuring, and which was absent in those countries which have stagnated since the first wave. The exploits of second wave TWMNEs have been subsidized by governments with government policy interacting (often positively) with the strategy of firms. We illustrate this with evidence from Korea and Taiwan in the next section.

Illustrating the Second Wave: FDI from Korea And Taiwan

Geographical and Industrial Distribution

In this section, we set out the experience of two prominent second wave investors, Korea and Taiwan, as they have proceeded along their IDPs over the past two decades. Table 13.6 presents the geographical direction of Korean and Taiwanese outward FDI stock for a number of years. In the case of Korea, we observe that, at the end of 1978, when only a very modest US$71.6 million had been invested, more than half went to countries in the Asian region; however by the end of 1995 the share of those countries had fallen to about 44.7 percent. Within Asia, no less than 76.6 percent of Korean FDI has gone into manufacturing, followed by mining (7.2 percent) and trade (6.1 percent).[12] China received the bulk of Korean FDI invested in Asia, and accounted for 41.2 percent of FDI stock in Asia by 1995. This is

TABLE 13.6 *Distribution of Outward FDI Stock from Korea and Taiwan, Selected Years*

	1978		1988		1995	
	Korea	Taiwan	Korea	Taiwan	Korea	Taiwan
South East Asia (%)	52.5	70.8	25.7	30.1	44.7	25.6
PRC (%)		0.0		0.0		35.5
Europe (%)	2.8	0.3	3.8	2.8	15.1	3.5
North America (%)	18.7	16.5	43.4	60.1	30.8	17.4
Latin America (%)	1.8	7.4	2.7	4.1	3.3	17.0
Oceania (%)	2.6	4.2	7.8	2.0	2.4	0.4
Other (%)	21.6	0.8	16.7	0.9	3.6	0.6
Total amount (U.S.$ thousands)	71,576	49,896	1,130,108	593,319	10,224,678	1,589,886

Source: The Bank of Korea, Investment Commission/Ministry of Economic Affairs.

quite remarkable since FDI into China only gained momentum from 1992 onwards. By 1995 North America had become the second most popular region for Korean investors, hosting 30.8 percent of outstanding FDI. Table 13.7 indicates that investments made in North America have, unlike those in Asia, not been as concentrated in manufacturing: trading activities were more important (36.3 percent), whereas 42.5 percent was in manufacturing. Since 1988, the share of North America has gone down, while the presence of Korean firms in Europe has increased considerably to 15.1 percent of their global investments by the end of 1995. In Europe, manufacturing (54.6

TABLE 13.7 *Sectoral and Geographical Distribution of Outward FDI Stock for Korea and Taiwan, 1995, percentages*

	S.E. Asia	N. America	Europe	Other Areas	Total
Korea					
Mining	7.2	3.6	0.9	25.7	6.9
Forestry	0.7	0.0	0.0	5.0	0.8
Fishery	0.4	0.7	0.2	5.1	0.9
Manufacturing	76.6	42.5	54.6	34.3	58.8
Construction	1.6	2.6	0.3	5.4	2.1
Transportation	1.2	0.4	0.1	0.8	0.8
Trade	6.1	36.3	32.2	7.6	19.5
Others	6.4	13.9	11.6	16.0	10.4
Total	100.0	100.0	100.0	100.0	100.0

	S.E. Asia	China	N. America	Europe	Other Areas	Total
Taiwan						
Mining	0.1	0.2	0.0	0.0	0.1	0.0
Agriculture and forestry	0.4	0.4	0.0	0.0	0.0	0.0
Fishing and animal husbandry	0.0	0.4	0.0	0.0	0.2	0.0
Manufacturing	74.3	92.9	49.3	56.7	18.0	65.0
Construction	0.6	0.3	1.8	0.0	2.0	0.0
Transportation	1.3	0.7	0.7	0.0	5.0	1.0
Trade	10.5	2.6	9.3	15.2	10.7	7.0
Banking and insurance	7.4	0.0	23.0	14.1	63.4	17.0
Others	5.4	2.5	15.8	14.0	0.6	5.0
Total	100.0	100.0	100.0	100.0	100.0	100.0

Source: The Bank of Korea, Investment Commission/Ministry of Economic Affairs.

percent) and trade (32.2 percent) are by far the most important recipients of Korean FDI.

The situation is broadly similar in the case of Taiwan (Tables 13.6 and 13.7). At the end of 1978, firms had invested only on a very limited scale abroad (US$49.9 million).[13] A great majority (70.8 percent) at that time was directed to South East Asia, whereas 16.5 percent was invested in North America. Although officially approved 'indirect' FDI[14] into the PRC have been registered only since 1991, their influence on the regional distribution of Taiwanese investments abroad is substantial. By 1995, the PRC had become the single most important host country for Taiwanese firms, having received 35.5 percent of total approved outward FDI. A great majority (92.9 percent) of this investment has been directed to the manufacturing sector. The dominant position of Asia as a host region is further underscored by the position of the 'rest of Asia', which, by the end of 1995, had attracted another 25.6 percent of Taiwanese FDI. Also here, most FDI has flown into manufacturing (74.3 percent). As a result of the spectacular increase of FDI in the Asian region, the share of North America has fallen from 60.1 percent to 17.4 percent in the last seven years. In this region, 49.3 percent of Taiwanese capital has been invested in manufacturing and a remarkable 23.0 percent in the banking and insurance sector.[15] Although Europe's share has risen, it is still not a very popular destination for Taiwanese firms.

Transforming the Economy and Outward Investment

The explanations behind the second wave of Korean and Taiwanese FDI are almost all directly or indirectly related to shifts in the structure of the world economy and especially the transformation of their own economies. This transformation has implied a simultaneous upgrading of the domestic industrial structure and phasing out of 'incompatible' industries. In both economies the industrial structure has evolved from being primarily based on labor-intensive ('Heckscher-Ohlin') manufacturing (such as textiles, sundries and other light industry goods) as the leading export sector to 'undifferentiated Smithian' industries (based on scale economies such as heavy and chemical industries) and 'differentiated Smithian' industries (assembly based, subcontracting dependent) such as automobiles and electric/electronic goods.[16]

This process of industrial upgrading reflects important changes in the OLI configurations and subsequent shifts from Stage 1 of the IDP to Stages 2 and 3. However although there are some broad similarities, the IDP of both countries have been fundamentally different. Most prominently, their firms accumulated new O advantages through conspicuously different means. In the case of Korea, the government has primarily fostered a licensing strategy, avoiding FDI and wholly owned MNE affiliates as much as possible. With the exception of the electronics industry, inward FDI has not contributed greatly to Korea's technological capabilities. From the mid-1960s onwards, the authorities preferred joint ventures (with minority foreign ownership) to wholly foreign owned subsidiaries. From the mid-1970s licensing agreements became more important than FDI as a technology source (Ernst and O'Connor, 1989). In Taiwan, on the other hand, since the initiation of an export-oriented industrialization policy in the 1960s, inward FDI was encouraged and the authorities played an active role in maximizing the benefits MNEs can offer by matching domestic L and O advantages in an optimal manner (van Hoesel, 1996). For many companies in both Korea and Taiwan, OEM contracts with leading industrial companies (e.g. in electronics) have also contributed to their O advantages—primarily as far as the development of production capabilities is concerned (ESCAP, 1991).[17] In attempting to reduce the dependence on Japanese and U.S. sources, the Korean and Taiwanese governments have recently begun to boost indigenous R&D efforts on a larger scale.

As we have already indicated, changing L advantages have also meant the phasing out of industries for which comparative advantages is eroding—a process witnessed in other industrialized economies (notably Japan) in the past. According to Ozawa (1992, 1995), in the 'tandem industrialization' process, the advanced nation's superiority in industrial structure and technological progress is transmitted to lower-echelon nations. *Inter alia*, the upgrading from Heckscher-Ohlin type to Smithian industries leads to a discrepancy between the early L advantages of a country (such as cheap labor) and the O advantages needed in subsequent stages. This is accompanied by so-called 'Ricardian bottlenecks'. Shortage of low-skilled labor pushes wages up, a trend that is reinforced by democratization tendencies which gives more room for wage demands by labor unions.[18] These wage increases are not normally matched by productivity growth.

In the case of Taiwan, not only were these features well demonstrated in the late 1970s and 1980s, but the country's L advantages were further reduced as a result of its sizeable exchange reserves (one of the largest in the world) that put inflationary pressure on the domestic economy and led to high price levels in the non-tradable sector such as real estate and stock market (San Gee, 1992). These developments encouraged Taiwanese companies to shift their more labor intensive production activities to countries where labor is cheap and abundant. Most of these resource seeking FDI stayed in the region—going to new NIEs (mostly ASEAN) and 'new' new NIEs (such as the China)—

although investments are also increasingly made in relatively less advanced economies outside the region but in the vicinity of important Triad markets (North America, EU). As in the case of FDI in Asia, these 'satellite economies' in Eastern Europe or Latin America offer cheap resources and, in addition, often established favorable import regulations with target markets.

Upgrading the resources and the capabilities of the Taiwanese economy has also led to more intense direct competition with producers from major trading partners. As a response to their export success, the US authorities (for both the most strategically important market) forced local currencies to appreciate.[19] This clearly made exporting from the home economies less attractive, stimulating FDI in production facilities overseas.

As compared to the first wave, Korean and Taiwanese FDI has become less of a regional phenomena. Smithian industries require O advantages based on scale or scope economies, making the maintenance and expansion of markets overseas (especially for relatively small economies such as Korea and Taiwan) mandatory. Threats of protectionism further induced Korean firms in some industries (such as consumer electronics) to shift production to within the borders of major economic blocks such as the European Union and NAFTA. These market seeking/retaining investments have not been without problems, however. In their study on FDI by Korean firms in the electronics industry, Jun and Yoon (1995) concluded that investments in developed countries have been premature and were a 'life or death decision'. According to them, competitive advantages common to 'conventional' MNEs are not present; instead these firms are dependent on home country L advantages for their competitiveness in world markets. Precisely this insufficiency of transferable competitive advantages form another motivation of firms in medium and high technology intensive sectors to invest in economically advanced regions. Frontier technology is not easily available through arm's length transactions. Although strategic alliances have emerged as an increasingly important mode to generate new technologies, in contrast to 'conventional' MNEs only a limited number of Korean companies and only very few Taiwanese firms are technologically advanced enough to have something to offer vis-a-vis potential partners. Therefore, next to technological efforts carried out at home, the second wave contains an increasing number of strategic asset seeking investments by Korean and Taiwanese firms which are mainly directed to the Triad economies.

Another major reason for the expansion of value adding activities in the Triad by TWMNEs is the accumulation of firm-specific advantages related to marketing capabilities. This is one of the principal motivations for the increased M&A activities of firms from these countries.

Since many Korean and Taiwanese firms initially primarily sold their products through OEM arrangements, building up global brand names and distribution channels has often been neglected in the past. For instance, to expand its sales network, President Foods Inc.—the biggest Taiwanese food processing company—bought Wyndham Foods—the third largest biscuit manufacturer in the United Sates. The Taiwanese Acer Group acquired U.S.-based Counterpart Computers which gave Acer access to the minicomputer business. In its search for production know how for special steels, the Korean Sammi Group purchased the steel division of Atlas Corporation of Canada. More recently, Samsung took a substantial stake (almost 50 percent) in U.S. computer firm AST. This move made Samsung/AST the fifth largest PC maker in the world and was geared at strengthening Samsung's position in information systems resulting and an improvement in its brand name and distribution systems (Business Korea, 1995).

In addition to M&A activity, greenfield investments in industrialized countries have also offered the opportunity of TWMNEs to scan foreign business environments. Examples are the many Taiwanese computer firms that have affiliates in Silicon Valley to tap locally available technological know how, or LG Electronics' Design Centre in Ireland (Dublin) where products are designed that are tailored to European lifestyles.

Notwithstanding these efforts to create or augment the O-specific advantages needed to break into advanced economies through FDI, most Korean and Taiwanese MNEs have not yet reached the same technological and commercial level as their counterparts from industrialized economies. How then can their production presence in Europe and North America be explained? In most cases, the local content of these activities is relatively low, as a substantial share of intermediate products is still produced in Korea, Taiwan or elsewhere in Asia. This suggests that, for the most part, the O advantages of Korean and Taiwanese firms are still based on country- or region-of-origin specific O advantages. Moreover, leading Korean and Taiwanese companies have typically built up a strong presence in Third World countries and economies in transformation (e.g. Eastern Europe). In these environments, TWMNEs can still compete on the basis of their 'traditional' first wave strengths, such as knowledge of the local environment and small-sized production. Furthermore, in most cases, Korean consumer electronics companies and Taiwanese computer firms (both important outward investors) supply the *lower end* of their markets—thus avoiding direct competition with MNEs from industrialized economies.

At the same time, the rapid advance of Korea and Taiwan to Stage

3 of their IDPs would not have been possible without a major change in government policy with regard to outward investment (UNCTAD, 1995). During the first wave, government policies towards outward FDI in most developing countries were mainly directed to capital export restrictions (UNCTAD, 1995). Also in Korea and Taiwan outward FDI for a long time was severely restricted. This attitude changed in the second half of the 1980s when the Korean and Taiwanese authorities, confronted with eroding comparative advantages in traditional sectors, and with the growing needs of indigenous firms to seek new assets overseas, decided to drastically liberalize their policy with regard to capital outflows. Indeed, since 1992, Korean FDI policy hav become an integral part of the nation's industrial policy. Extensive support is now rendered to potential overseas investors, among others by means of financial support and tax incentives. Takeovers, as well greenfield ventures, are often partly financed by cheap government credits thus providing an additional competitive edge (Hikino and Amsden, 1994). Although less extensive than in the case of Korea, also in Taiwan financial and tax arrangements are available for outward investors. The support measure illustrate the holistic government policies pursued in Korea and Taiwan (where conventional and non-conventional) inward as well as outward investment as a integrated policy integrated in the general economic policy aimed at a continuous upgrading of the domestic economy.

A topic not dealt with here is the possible de-industrialization effects of outward FDI. Unlike conventional industrialized economies, Korea and Taiwan started to invest abroad when they had merely reached the semi-industrialized stage. Since the size of these investments has increased at a very high rate, the risk of de-industrialization seems particularly high. According to Chen and Chen (1995), who investigated the possible effects in the case of Taiwan, for this purpose it is important to distinguish FDI aimed at reducing production costs ('resource seeking') from FDI aimed at differentiating products ('market seeking'). Their hypothesis is that when defensive, resource seeking FDI is greater than market seeking FDI, an industry runs a higher risk of being de-industrialized. The reasoning is that market seeking FDI often reflects intra-firm and intersectoral restructuring while resource seeking FDI may imply a relocation of production activities without a beneficial transformation of the investing industry. Although a lack of information about the possible linkages between domestic and overseas production may blur the outcome of their analysis, the evidence collected for Taiwanese FDI seems to support this hypothesis.

Idiosyncratic FDI Patterns: the Dominant Firm Structure in Korea and Taiwan

According to the IDP, individual countries show their own subpatterns of (inward and) outward investment, whose shape is influenced by its natural resource structure, home market size, economic system and the role of governments and the way in which economic activities are organised (Narula, 1996). South Korea and Taiwan are both poorly endowed with natural resources and have relatively small home markets. These characteristics, *inter alia*, have influenced their economic system, which since the 1960s has been based on export oriented industrialization. Although even the period over which both Korean and Taiwanese MNEs emerged on the international scene, there are significant differences in the role of the government in the organization of economic activities in both economies. These have clearly influenced the nature of outward FDI from both countries and can be expected to do so in the future. In late industrialization economies, governments have played a very profound role in the formation of capital and enterprises thus strongly shaping the structure of companies and institutions as a whole (see for instance Hikino and Amsden, 1994; Fields, 1995). Recent insights rendered by 'New Institutionalists' have revealed important distinctive characteristics of the Korean and Taiwanese business systems (Whitley, 1992).[20]

The most apparent difference concerns the dominant firm structure in Korea and Taiwan. In investigating the actors behind Korea's economic successes, most attention usually goes to the big, highly diversified conglomerates ('chaebol') and their relationship with the government. This is not without reason: the chaebol have played a crucial role in the country's economic achievements. Although the energetic entrepreneurship of their leaders should not be downplayed, they are primarily the product of government policy (see for instance Chen, 1995; Lee, 1992). Most chaebol were founded at the end of the 1940s and the 1950s. Only three of the present top chaebol (namely, Samsung, Daelim and Kia) were established in the pre-war era; the Japanese rulers effectively limited the accumulation of indigenous capital.[21] Although most present-day chaebol gained important favors during the import substitution regime in the 1950s which stimulated a rapid take-off, it was only after president Park came into power in 1961 that these companies really started to build up their present dominant position.

Using 'sticks' (e.g. tax penalties, revoked import licenses, calling in of loans) and 'carrots' (e.g. preferential loans, access to foreign exchange, tax concessions), the authorities directed the chaebol to realize export goals and other policy goals, such as the development of new industries (Cho, 1987). A famous example is the selection of Hyundai, Kia and GM Korea (now Daewoo Motor Company) to develop a domestic car industry. To this end, the government not only offered export subsidies but also granted protection against foreign competition on the Korean market and restricted the entry of potential other local producers.

In the mid-1970s the Korean government introduced the so-called 'General Trading Companies' (GTCs) to further expand the country's exports by penetrating new markets and realizing scale advantages. The requirements that were set to be designated as a GTC underlined the aim of the authorities to select and support large-scale companies that would operate in a large number of countries and sell a diversified range of products. In practice, therefore, almost all GTCs are part of a chaebol. The government continuously pressured the GTCs to expand their exports by raising the export value requirements (Song, 1994). In return, the GTCs received various subsidies and incentives ranging from the right to import raw materials for own use and for resale to domestic producers to tax reductions on trade commissions (Cho, 1987). Although most of these subsidies were gradually also provided to other large-scale exporters, companies remained very eager to obtain the GTC status. It not only improved the company's credibility in and outside Korea, it also helped in winning government initiated projects. In addition, the high esteem attached to the GTC status enabled these companies to attract the best university graduates. Although perhaps not yet as advanced as their Japanese examples (the 'sogo soshas'), these trading companies have contributed significantly to the country's export performance. In addition, they have served as important instruments to accumulate experience in operating on foreign markets. It is therefore no surprise that the chaebol to which the most successful GTCs (e.g. Samsung, LG, Hyundai, Daewoo), belong are among the most important present-day outward investors.

Although such highly criticized instruments as preferential loans have been abolished, the attempts undertaken to curb the power of the chaebol have not been very successful. A high economic concentration can be found in Korea at all levels; chaebol dominate most industries in which they participate. In 1991, the five biggest chaebol realized combined sales of US$116 billion, which equals almost half of the country's GNP in that year. According to Fields (1995), the economic concentration in Korea has only increased in the years since.

Table 13.8 suggests that, when compared with Korea, the Taiwanese economy is dominated by small and medium sized enterprises (SMEs) that show little vertical integration and depend heavily on sub-contracting relations. Although large enterprises do exist in certain sectors, these are mostly not outward oriented. In fact, the larger

TABLE 13.8 *Characteristics of Ten Biggest Companies in Korea and Taiwan*

	Korea*	Taiwan†
Total sales (U.S.$ millions)	133,805	19,668
Total employees	515,438	76,308
Employees/firm	51,543	7631
Sales/firm (U.S.$ millions)	13,381	1997
Share total workforce (%)	2.7	0.9
Share GNP (%)	47.1	9.3

*1991 figures
†1992 figures (with the exception of Chinese Petroleum, 1991 data)
Source: Fortune 500 and Taiwan Top 500 (in Chinese).

enterprises are often important suppliers of inputs (e.g. petrochemicals, steel) to the exporting SMEs which dominate Taiwan's exports (Wade, 1990).[22] In addition, the larger firms serve as a source of trade and working capital credits for the SMEs. What explains this divergent firm structure? It is beyond doubt that the Taiwanese authorities have played a significant role in preventing (or even actively discouraging) the economic system from domination by a limited number of companies. Taiwanese banks, which are largely government-controlled, have always been very hesitant to lend large sums to private enterprises, thus erecting a major hurdle to their expansion. It is also generally acknowledged that this bias against the concentration of private capital has historical roots (Amsden, 1991; Fields, 1995).[23]

This unwillingness to actually support large-scale companies has also been a major reason why the initiative taken in Taiwan at the end of the 1970s to establish international trading companies has failed. The limited debt-capacity of the 'Large Trading Companies' (caused by the unwillingness of the financial system in Taiwan to support them and the fact that the trading companies were not allowed to be associated with established business groups) made it difficult to finance the needed working capital and the expansion of overseas marketing networks (Cho, 1987).[24]

Partly as a result of these differences in industry structure, distinct strategic orientations of companies can also be observed. The Korean 'chaebol' have been prepared to invest heavily in realising high volume production and gaining market share—even if unit costs exceed prevailing market prices (Kuo, 1993). Government support as well as the possibility of cross investment between the members of the chaebol have enabled them to take a long-term orientation with regard to investments abroad. This certainly also helps in the attempts of some chaebol to integrate more deeply into overseas economies, thereby advancing further toward becoming truly 'global' companies. In addition, the global marketing networks built up by the trading arms (the GTCs) have meant a valuable first step on the way to further internationalisation of the companies.

Because of the small size and more limited government support, Taiwanese companies, on the other hand, usually follow a so-called 'bootstrap' strategy. At the core is the continuous exploration of new niche markets for non-standardized products. This implies a more opportunistic approach emphasizing short pay-back periods on investments. This short term orientation has a clear restrictive effect on the possibilities of FDI, especially in advanced economies where substantial financial and organizational commitment are required. As a result, Taiwanese FDI in production facilities in advanced economies in most cases is limited to assembly type operations. The latter is also caused by the relative lack of vertical integration of most outward oriented companies. Also, the high R&D expenditures needed to improve a company's technology capabilities as well as the massive marketing costs required to build up own brand names are usually related to large sized firms. Attempts to improve such capabilities are therefore more frequently observed in Korea than in Taiwan.

Since the competitive advantages of firms related to technological and commercial capabilities are typically associated with companies from advanced economies, Korean chaebol invest on a larger scale in the regions than their Taiwanese counterparts. Another important determinant of the geographic distribution of outward FDI in the case of Taiwanese companies are the relations with other ethnic Chinese communities, especially in South East Asia and particularly the PRC. Extensive networks with Chinese entrepreneurs abroad tend to support operations in these countries. For many of these SMEs, which are increasingly confronted with rising domestic costs and a lack of international experience and foreign language capabilities (Kuo 1993), these contacts are of prime importance. In other words, ethnic links in many cases have not only influenced the direction of Taiwanese investments, but have meant the survival of many smaller sized firms. In the case of Korean firms, ethnic links abroad have been only of minor importance and have certainly not stimulated the decision to go abroad.

Conclusions

This chapter has confined itself to addressing two questions regarding the outward FDI of developing countries in light of globalization. The first question pertained to whether TWMNE activity had undergone a fundamental shift that might be considered as constituting a distinct second wave of outward FDI activity that was distinct from that described by the research conducted in the early- and mid-1980s (referred to as the first wave). The evidence suggests that this was indeed the case although the two waves are not separate and distinct. The second question was whether this 'new' wave could be usefully explained within the framework of the IDP (Dunning and Narula, 1994, 1996; Narula, 1996). The evidence presented here suggests that the evolution from the first wave to second wave is entirely consistent with the predictions of the IDP and the analysis of Ozawa (1992, 1995), since the waves are complementary to each other—each appropriate to the home country's extent and pattern of economic development.

Hot on the heels of the NIEs, are the new NIEs, and the 'new' new NIEs that have adopted or implemented variations of the policies utilized so successfully by the second wave countries. Already considerable interest has been generated by the activities of MNEs from China, Indonesia and Malaysia, to name but three. These countries are already beginning to exhibit similar patterns of outward FDI activity (see e.g. Lecraw, 1993; van den Bulcke and Zhang, 1996) as they move towards Stage 3.

The evidence presented here indicates that the second wave consists mainly of the East Asian NIEs. The second wave represents part of a continuum, and can be best characterized as an intermediate stage in the evolution of MNE activity, between the first wave TWMNEs and conventional MNEs (see Table 13.4). Such growth has been conditional on the sustained improvement of the O specific advantages of firms, resulting *inter alia* from a continuous upgrading of the L specific advantages of the home country. While improved L advantages are a natural consequence of economic development and restructuring as countries move from Stage 2 to Stage 3, this process can be accelerated by a market oriented and holistic government policy towards trade, industrial development, and innovation. In the case of many (but not all) Third World countries, this has not only helped upgrade their indigenous resources, but has encouraged their own firms to augment their competitve advantages by acquiring foreign resources. This active aspect of governments, which they have practised for three decades as part of an outward looking, export-oriented policy, is something that sets the second wave countries apart from their first wave counterparts; it is no coincidence that economic liberalization and abandonment of import-substituting orientation occurred more recently amongst the first wave countries that did not progress to the second wave.

Indeed, it is this last point that is as much behind the emergence of the second wave as their economic success. The 'stumbling back' (Hikino and Amsden, 1994) of a large number of developing countries makes the success of the second wave countries much more apparent. The decline in the L advantages of these countries, due to structural adjustment programs, has also led to the decline of the O advantages of the first wave TWMNEs. These O advantages were primarily country-specific, often a result of barriers to entry associated with import-substituting programs. Such firms tended to invest overseas only in countries which have similar L advantages. With economic liberalization, their has been a decline in these L advantages, and consequently, the O advantages of their MNEs.

Our discussion of the second wave TWMNEs using evidence from Korea and Taiwan suggests that broad classifications disguise, but do not obliterate, country-specific differences due to idiosyncratic differences due to natural and created asset endowments. While these two countries broadly resemble each other in terms of outward FDI activity, government policy in many ways could not have been more different. Taking a closer look at the resulting investment patterns reveals important differences between both economies. Whereas in the case of Korea the leading investing companies are moving towards similar O advantages as possessed by 'conventional' MNEs, such a pattern is less clear for Taiwan. Although there are some important exceptions (e.g. Acer computers), most Taiwanese investors in advanced economies still combine the L advantages of the Asian region with the local presence in target markets; the companies' technological advantages are often still based on their production capabilities and their limited size has prevented them from strengthening their commercial capabilities. The huge investment amounts flowing to Stage 1 and 2 countries mostly reflect cheap labor ('resource') seeking FDI by small, relatively labor intensive companies that in the past became successful under L advantages that have in recent years have vanished from the island. This is an area which warrants further study, especially as regards such issues as the implementation of government policy to improve indigenous resources and capabilities, the efficacy of manipulating market structure, and the extent to which inward MNE activity can improve the competitive advantages of domestic firms.

The second wave countries are, in fact, at Stage 3 of the IDP, and, as might be expected of countries that are currently industrializing, have evolved economically towards industrial sectors which are capital and knowledge intensive. Their firms engage in outward FDI in Stage 1 and 2 countries as a means of moving their natural-asset intensive activities to locations with appropriate comparative advantages, while, at the same time, they are engaging in both market and strategic asset-seeking FDI in the Stage 4 and 5 countries. In other words, they are increasingly becoming global, demonstrating features of 'conventional' MNEs. This 'hybrid' type of MNE activity is not entirely new—similar observations were made with regards Japanese MNEs two decades previously (see e.g. Ozawa, 1979; Kojima, 1978) when it was at Stage 3 of the IDP (Dunning and Narula, 1994). One of the primary differences between the second wave countries and Japan has been the much more active promotion of outward FDI activity in general and strategic asset-seeking investments. This may have something to do with the process of globalization where it is no longer simply desirable to be globally competitive, but essential to be so.

References

AMSDEN, A. H. (1991) Big business and urban congestion in Taiwan: the origins of small enterprise and regionally decentralized industry (respectively), *World Development*, Vol. 19, No. 9, 1121–1135.

Business Korea (1995) Challenging the Global PC Market, *Business Korea*, April, p. 25.

CANTWELL, J. and SANNA RANDACCIO, F. (1990) The growth of multinationals and the catching up effect, *Economic Notes*, Vol. 19, July, 1–23.

CHEN, E. (1983) Multinationals from Hong Kong. In LALL, S. (ed.) *The New Multinationals*, John Wiley, Chichester, pp. 88–136.

CHEN, M. (1995) *Asian Management Systems: Chinese, Japanese and Korean Styles of Business*, Routledge, London.

CHEN, T.-Y. and CHEN, Y.-P. (1995): Taiwanese foreign direct investment: the risks of de-industrialization, *Journal of Industry Studies*, Vol. 2, No. 1, 57–68.

CHO, D.-S. (1987) *The General Trading Company; Concept and Strategy*, Lexington Books, Lexington.

CONTRACTOR, F. (1993) Technology acquisition choices for newly industrialising countries: the case of Taiwan, *International Executive*, Vol. 35, 385–412.

DICKEN, P. (1992) *Global Shift*, Paul Chapman, London.

DOWRICK, S. (1992) Technological Catch Up and Diverging Incomes: Patterns of Economic Growth 1960–88 *Economic Journal*, Vol. 102, May, 600–610.

DUNNING, J. H. (1981) Explaining the international direct investment position of countries: towards a dynamic or developmental approach, *Weltwirtschaftliches Archiv*, Vol. 119, 30–64.

DUNNING, J. H. (1988) *Explaining International Production*, London, Unwin Hyman.

DUNNING, J. H. and NARULA, R. (1994) Transpacific direct investment and the investment development path: the record assessed, Columbia, South Carolina, University of South Carolina, College of Business Administration *Essays in International Business*, No. 10 May.

DUNNING, J. H. and NARULA, R. (1996) The investment development path revisited: some emerging issues. In DUNNING, J. and NARULA, R. (eds) *Foreign Direct Investment and Governments: Catalysts for Economic Restructuring*, Routledge, London.

DUNNING, J. H. and NARULA, R. (1997) Developing countries versus multinationals in a globalising world: the dangers of falling behind. In BUCKLEY, P. and GHAURI, P. (eds) *Multinational Enterprises and Emerging Markets*, London: Dryden Press, forthcoming.

ERNST, D. and O'CONNOR, D. (1989) *Technology and Global Competition—the Challenge for Newly Industrializing Economies*, OECD, Paris.

ESCAP (March 1991) *Industrial Restructuring in Asia and the Pacific*, United Nations, Bangkok.

FIELDS, K. J. (1995) *Enterprise and the State in Korea and Taiwan*, Cornell University Press, New York.

HAN, C. M. and BREWER, T. (1987): Foreign direct investments by Korean firms: an analysis with FDI theories, *Asia Pacific Journal of Management*, Vol. 4, No. 2, 90–102.

HARROLD, P. and LALL, R. (1993) *China Reform and Development in 1992–93*, World Bank Discussion Paper No. 215.

HIKINO, T. and AMSDEN, A. (1994) Staying behind, stumbling back, sneaking up, soaring ahead: late industrialization in historical perspective. In BAUMOL, W., NELSON, R. and WOLFF, E. (eds) *Convergence of Productivity: Cross Country Studies and Historical Evidence*, Oxford University Press, New York.

HOESEL, R. (1996) Taiwan: foreign direct investment and the transformation of the economy. In J. DUNNING and R. NARULA (eds) *Foreign Direct Investment and Governments: Catalysts for Economic Restructuring*, London, Routledge, pp. 280–315.

JUN, Y. and YOON, D. (1995) An exploratory explanation of the reverse direct investment: the case of the Korean electronics industry Seoul: Paper presented at Annual Conference of *Academy of International Business* November 1995.

KHAN, K. (ed) (1987) *Multinationals of the South*, Francis Pinter, London.

KOJIMA, K. (1978) *Direct Foreign Investment: A Japanese Model of Multinational Business Operations*, Croom Helm, London.

KUMAR, K and McLEOD, G, (eds) (1981) *Multinationals from Developing Countries*, Lexington Books, Lexington.

KUO, W.-J. (1993) *Internationalization of Taiwan Industry: Globalization of Taiwan's Small- and Medium-Sized Enterprises*, CIER Working Paper, Taipei.

LALL, S. (1983) *Third World Multinationals*, John Wiley, Chichester.

LECRAW, D. (1977) Direct investment by firms from less developed countries, *Oxford Economic Papers*, 442–457.

LECRAW, D. (1993) Outward direct investment by Indonesian firms: motivation and effects, *Journal of International Business Studies*, Vol. 24, No. 3, 589–600.

LEE, C. H. (1992) The government, financial system, and large private enterprises in the economic development of South Korea, *World Development*, Vol. 20, No. 2, 187–197.

LEE, J. (1992) Capital and labor mobility in Taiwan. In RANIS, G. (ed.) *Taiwan: from developing to mature economy*, Westview Press, Boulder.

Narula, R. (1996) *Multinational Investment and Economic Structure*, Routledge, London.

OZAWA, T. (1979) *Multinationalism, Japanese Style*, Princeton University Press, Princeton, NJ.

OZAWA, T. (1992) Theory of FDI as a dynamic paradigm of economic development, *Transnational Corporations*, Vol. 1, No. 1, February.

OZAWA, T. (1995) Structural upgrading and concatenated integration. In SIMON, D. (ed.) *Corporate Strategies in the Pacific Rim: Global versus Regional Trends*, Routledge, London, pp. 215–246.

PERKINS, D. (1994) There are at least three models of East Asian development, *World Development*, Vol. 22, No. 4, 655–61.

POWELL, W. W. and DiMAGGIO, P. J. (eds) (1991) *The New Institutionalism in Organizational Analysis*, (etc.), University of Chicago Press, Chicago.

SAN G. (1992) *Taiwanese Corporations in Globalization and Regionalization*, Paris: OECD. Technical Papers No. 61.

SONG, C. (1994) *The Dynamics of Korean Economic Development*, International for International Economics, Washington.

TOLENTINO, P. E. (1993) *Technological Innovation and Third World Multinationals*, Routledge, London.

United Nations (1993) *Transnational Corporations From Developing Countries: Impact on Home Countries*, United Nations, New York.

United Nations Conference on Trade and Development (UNCTAD) (1994) *World Investment Report 1994*, United Nations, Geneva.

United Nations Conference on Trade and Development (UNCTAD) (1995) *World Investment Report 1995*, United Nations, Geneva.

UNCTC (1991) *World Investment Report 1991*, United Nations, New York.

WADE, R. (1990) *Governing the Market: Economic Theory and the Role of Government in East Asian Industrialization*, Princeton University Press, Princeton, NJ.

WHITLEY, R. (1992) *Business Systems in East Asia: Firms, Markets, and Societies*, Sage, London.

WELLS L. T. (1983) Third World Multinationals, Cambridge MA: MIT Press.

World Bank (1994) *The East Asian Miracle*, Oxford University Press, Oxford.

World Bank (various dates) *The World Development Report*, Oxford University Press, Oxford.

ZHANG, H-Y. and VAN DEN BULCKE, D. (1996) China: Rapid changes in the investment development path. In DUNNING, J. and NARULA, R. (eds) *Foreign Direct Investment and Governments: Catalysts for Economic Restructuring*, Routledge, London, pp. 380–422.

Notes

1. An earlier version of this chapter was published in a special issue of the *International Business Review*, (in press).

   Although increasingly redundant, we use the terms 'developing countries' and 'Third World' interchangeably throughout this chapter. Likewise, we do the same for 'developed' and 'industrialized'. However, the use of alternative groupings such as 'OECD' and 'non-OECD' countries are equally counter intuitive.
2. See especially Wells (1983), Lall (1983), Kumar and McLeod (1981), Khan (1986).
3. Similar conclusions are drawn in the work of Ozawa (1992, 1995). Although Ozawa's work utilizes a different argument, the concept is essentially the same as the revised IDP.
4. It is generally accepted practice that the sales of MNEs are considered as a monotonic function of its stock (see Dunning 1993 for a review of the literature).
5. Data from Appendix tables, UN (1995) has been adjusted based on earlier UN reports (especially UN 1993 and the *World Investment Directory*) and government sources.
6. This is also the view propagated by Lall (1983)
7. There are nonetheless many examples of market-seeking investments. See Table 9.11 and Table 10.14 in Tolentino (1993) for a description of several such investments.

8. There is nothing to suggest that this has changed, although a large share of this re-investment may now be from Taiwan. The use of overseas subsidiaries as a means to channel foreign capital is not limited to conventional MNEs. Harrold and Lall (1993) point out that up to 25 percent of China's inflows represent re-investment of capital by Chinese MNEs based in Hong Kong (and are therefore recorded as outflows from Hong Kong).

9. Although Mexico meets this criteria, much of the outward FDI stock represents a few large investments in a neighbouring country (U.S.A.) with which it has significant economic ties due both to its physical proximity and within the framework of NAFTA.

10. See also Hikino and Amsden (1994), Dowrick (1992). See also Table 13.2.

11. It is to be noted that the second wave investors have in fact been outward-oriented, export-oriented for over three decades.

12. In the early 1970s, investments in timber projects and construction were more dominant (Han and Brewer, 1987).

13. Data on Taiwanese FDI are known to be notoriously unreliable. For a discussion on the caveats of Taiwanese data sources, see van Hoesel (1996).

14. Taiwanese firms were forbidden to invest in the PRC. Firms circumvented this ban by investing via shell companies registered in third countries (mainly Hong Kong).

15. FDI in banking and insurance can be considered a response to the worldwide liberalization of financial markets and the deregulation of financial markets in Taiwan (Lee, 1992).

16. The distinction between Heckscher-Ohlin, undifferentiated and differentiated Smithian industries was made by Ozawa (1992, 1995).

17. OEM agreements are contractual agreements by which a foreign firm orders in volume products which the OEM supplier agrees to make according to its precise specifications.

18. As a result, wages in industrial sectors for the three years between 1990 and 1992 increased by 20.2 percent, 16.9 percent and 16.9 percent in Korea. Corresponding figures for Taiwan are 13.5 percent, 11.0 percent and 10.3 percent respectively.

19. Between 1986 and 1990, for instance, the Korean Won appreciated with 16.8 percent against the U.S. dollar. The New Taiwan Dollar went up with no less than 33.5 percent against the US Dollar between 1986 and 1992.

20. Various other terms—such as 'New Institutionalism' (Powell and DiMaggio, 1991), 'New Economic Sociology' or 'New Political Economy' (Fields, 1995)—are used to indicate an analytical approach in which the role of the state is perceived as an independent variable and which takes factors beyond economic rationality into account, such as 'the dynamics of familial or peer approval, community status, political power, and implicit and explicit coercion' (Fields, 1995, p. 17).

21. In 1940 only 6 percent of total paid-in capital of companies with more than 1 million Yen of capital was invested by Koreans.

22. In 1990, for instance, firms with fewer than 300 employees accounted for 60 percent of total exports (Fields, 1995).

23. There are at least two main reasons attributed for this tendency. First, there are ideological reasons stemming from the philosophy of Sun Yat-sen, who feared the negative consequences of a concentration of capital, and which has influenced the economic policy of the Nationalists' Party. The hyper inflation that occurred

under Kuomintang rule in mainland China (and is often seen as an important reason for the Nationalists' defeat) is also beleived to have butressed ideological support for a strong control of private capital. The second important motivation appears to be the sub-ethnic division of labor in Taiwan, where the political power is still controlled by the Kuomintang and the private sector by the local, Taiwanese majority (Amsden, 1991). The authorities have always feared that the strong position that the ethnic Taiwanese have built up in the private sector may result in a demand for more political power.

24. In addition, until recently, the import of bulk commodities and the export of such profitable products as canned pineapples, soy beans and corn were almost monopolized by state-sanctioned institutions.

Author index*

*(n) after some page numbers refers to notes at the end of each chapter.

Subject index*

*(n) after some page numbers refers to notes at the end of each chapter.